W9-AXA-561

Advance Praise for *Standardized Childhood*

"Guaranteed to raise the hackles of some, while be applauded by others, *Standardized Childhood* is fascinating reading. Brilliantly argued, this is the definitive word on universal preschool."
—Susan B. Neuman, Former Assistant Secretary for Elementary and Secondary Education, U.S. Department of Education and Professor of Educational Studies, University of Michigan

"*Standardized Childhood* is a must-read book for everyone who cares about early education in America today. Bruce Fuller takes on the thorny issues in the field and addresses them head-on. Should pre-K programs be universal? Who should pay for them? And, finally, what will help equalize access to preschool? The result is a refreshing and penetrating look at the condition of preschool in this country."
—Jeanne Brooks-Gunn, Columbia University

"Based on the values of individual initiative, attention to cultural difference, and respect for organizational pluralism, Bruce Fuller's analysis calls into question the belief in 'a one best system of early education.' Written in a clear and uncompromising way that will both enlighten and infuriate policymakers and practitioners committed to universal pre-K, the book uncovers the complexity of the issues facing early care and education today."
—Samuel J. Meisels, President, Erikson Institute

"Vivid, clear, and provocative, full of first hand reporting from states and cities that are experimenting with universal preschool, this is the most complete and interesting treatment of this issue I have ever seen. It tells a story, rather than disgorging another load of academic jargon. Everyone who talks about pre-school is going to have to quote from Fuller's book."
—Jay Mathews, *Washington Post*

"A frank, provocative critique of the pre-K movement. The basic question is not whether we should have a national policy in regards to pre-kindergarten education, but what should that policy look like. No other question in education policy is as timely and has the potential for such a long lasting, transformative impact on public schooling today."
—Cynthia García Coll, Brown University

BRUCE FULLER

WITH MARGARET BRIDGES AND SEETA PAI

Standardized Childhood

The Political and Cultural Struggle over Early Education

STANFORD UNIVERSITY PRESS

STANFORD, CALIFORNIA

Stanford University Press
Stanford, California

Printed in the United States of America
on acid-free, archival-quality paper

Library of Congress Cataloging-in-Publication Data
Fuller, Bruce.
    Standardized childhood : the political and cultural struggle over early
education / Bruce Fuller with Margaret Bridges and Seeta Pai.
        p. cm.
    Includes bibliographical references and index.
    ISBN-13: 978-0-8047-5579-5 (cloth : alk. paper)
    ISBN-13: 978-0-8047-6102-4 (pbk : alk. paper)
    1. Education, Preschool—United States. 2. Early childhood education—
United States. I. Bridges, Margaret. II. Pai, Seeta. III. Title.
LB1140.23.F85 2007
372.21—dc22

                                                          2006032138

Typeset by Classic Typography in 10/14 Janson

Democratic means and the democratic ends are one and inseparable . . .
a living faith in our common human nature and in the power of voluntary
action based upon public collective intelligence.

—JOHN DEWEY, 1937

Liberal democracy has always relied on elites to save it from itself.
If authoritative leaders see what is necessary to turn . . . the promise of
liberal rights into their guarantee, then elitism is perfectly compatible
with liberal democracy.

—JENNIFER HOCHSCHILD, 1984

Contents

Preface
Who Defines Childhood?

Few human activities are more essential, more joyful, than the act of raising a child. Until quite recently, bringing up our offspring took place solely within the family's private sphere, aided by kin or paid caregivers. The art of rearing a child—often with the coaching of self-assured male psychologists and their glossy guidebooks—remains primarily in parents' hands.

Early in life children do brush up against formal institutions. Church leaders still baptize babies. Parents dutifully drag their three-year-olds to the neighborhood library. For excitement we may visit the corner fire station or peer through the outgoing-mail slot down at the post office. Yet beyond such glancing exposures to civic organizations young children, historically speaking, have spent little time inside rationalized organizations before entering school.

A dramatic shift in the daily lives of America's youngest children arrived in the 1970s, in the wake of radical changes in their mothers' lives. Rising numbers of young women had been graduating from college since the post-war spread of higher education. The onset of the feminist movement then jolted women's aspirations and notions of how to construct a fulfilling identity amidst competing social expectations.

These breaks from the past recast how mothers, and even their partners, weighed the benefits and costs of raising children and advancing a career. As millions of women decided to juggle both children and work, young children began to spend more and more hours in the care of other adults. The term *preschooler* even seeped into everyday language, signifying that once those diapers (miraculously) remained dry, a toddler could promptly enter a child care center. The nation's short-lived war on poverty spawned thousands of Head Start preschools, establishing a firm public interest in young children.

As our society entered the twenty-first century, over nine million children under the age of five, whether from rich or poor families, attended a formal organization dubbed a *child care center* or *preschool* for at least part of each day.[1]

By the 1990s, the swirl of forces intensified, and a fresh civic discourse emerged centering on the family's faltering strength and whether a range of caregivers and formal organizations should play a larger part in raising young children. This debate grew louder, fed by the media's fascination with colorful photos of infant brains electrified by pulsating synapses, by surging concerns about poor families and welfare reform, and by the government's determined efforts to make public schools more accountable. Researchers began to detail how, even as youngsters entered kindergarten, the achievement gap between rich and poor students was starkly apparent.[2]

There's no turning back to the days when child rearing in America was merely a private concern. Children's activists and a growing range of political leaders have advanced a broad public awareness of young children's developmental potential and the telling consequences of their immediate environments, including the home and child care settings. Even so, debate persists over the optimal balance—for toddlers and parents alike—between time youngsters spend at home and time spent in formal institutions, especially preschools.

Preschoolers hit the political big-time in 1988, when then-presidential candidate George H. W. Bush proposed a national child care program—a provocative pledge, coming from Ronald Reagan's vice president, on which he would deliver two years later. Between the senior Bush's program—which funds vouchers for parents who (theoretically) choose from a variety of child care providers—and the steady growth of Head Start preschools, Washington now spends over $18 billion a year on early care and education. States spend another $4 billion for pre-kindergarten efforts.[3] If the costs absorbed by parents are included, about $48 billion was spent on the nation's archipelago of caregivers and preschools in 2005.[4]

These historical currents and the gaping holes in America's ragged non-system of child care—marked by a scarcity of affordable high-quality options—have spurred a variety of early education reformers to up the ante. Many have converged in recent years on a bold, narrowly drawn remedy: Make free, state-run preschools available to all three- and four-year-olds. Yes, another acronym—UPK, for universal pre-kindergarten—began to circulate among a widening circle of activists, foundation officials, and policy leaders.

The UPK movement is gaining traction—and political friction—in a variety of states. We will visit Oklahoma, where in 1998 the legislature quietly agreed to fold preschool enrollments into the routine calculation of state aid to local schools, prompting the robust spread of pre-kindergarten classrooms. Fully 63 percent of Oklahoma's four-year-olds were enrolled by 2004. Georgia is the better-known preschool pioneer; there, then-governor Zell Miller advanced the idea in the early 1990s, creating a half-day program for all that was first targeted on communities with the scarcest resources. Over 55 percent of Georgia's four-year-olds now attend preschool.

In New Jersey, an ambitious court settlement, the so-called Abbott decision, aims to equalize educational opportunity and achievement. It mandates free preschool for all kids within the state's poorest school districts. Almost three-quarters of all four-year-olds now attend. In Florida, voters approved a 2002 ballot initiative by a 59 percent plurality directing Governor Jeb Bush to create "high quality pre-kindergarten learning opportunities" for all families. In fact, this young program offers low-cost, portable vouchers to parents while leaning heavily on preschools run by community-based organizations (CBOs), not just on school-based programs.[5]

Building a One-Best System of Childhood?

Since the late 1990s the question of UPK has risen higher in the stump speeches of governors and school leaders. This book introduces you to a new generation of advocates who are eager to form alliances with education lobbies, teacher unions, even business groups—for in this brave new world of childhood the aim is to raise youngsters' tests scores not long after they shed those diapers.

What are the advantages and risks of the state's specifying, perhaps regimenting, what very young children are to learn and how they are to be socialized? Put plainly, should government—whether it is cast as progressively closing early learning gaps or viewed as an imperial "nanny state"—hold the authority to define how young children are raised?

The earlier policy line goes like this: if employers won't create greater job flexibility for young families, then government's best role is to enrich child care *options*, flexible choices for America's diverse parents. In stark contrast, the new, more convergent pitch that is gaining steam aims at building a one-best system of preschooling, largely attached to the public schools. The avant-garde UPK advocates argue that they are advancing the interests of children, given that the new *telos* of public schooling is to boost test scores beginning in the first or second grade. And besides, we can't narrow the achievement gap without moving youngsters toward English fluency more aggressively and earlier in their young childhoods, many UPK advocates argue. Other early educators, however, hearing that their liberal-humanist traditions have become old hat, fear that chanting phonemes and working on dittoed worksheets will replace colorful activity centers and "learning through play."

These are the prickly questions which parents are debating over the back fence, and which are discussed increasingly inside the halls of state capitals. When the topic of universal preschool hit conservative talk radio, you knew that it had arrived as a new front in the culture wars.

Few parents or child development experts argue against the urgent need to improve affordable child care options, especially in poor and blue-collar neighborhoods, where scarcity is stark and waiting lists run long. It's the notion of a universal, one-size-fits-all institution regulated by government that fuels the push-back.

One way to create universal preschool is to extend public schooling downward, to carve out new grade levels below kindergarten. The new generation of advocates propose far more ambitious measures than just expansion of Head Start or child care vouchers for poor families, measures that smell of welfare and would fail to reach middle-class families. Instead, like leaders of the kindergarten movement a century ago, the new UPK advocates have set their sights high.

By allying themselves with the broader school-accountability movement, via the No Child Left Behind Act (NCLB), the new advocates have widened their political appeal. California schools chief Jack O'Connell recently led with UPK as he articulated his reform priorities for a new legislative session. "Universal preschool is an idea whose time has come," he said, claiming it would go a long way toward improving children's flagging test scores.[6] Free preschool has become seen as an education reform for the middle class, but does it yield miraculous benefits for all children, as the proponents allege? This book sorts out the evidence for these claims.

The disappointing history of the nation's kindergarten movement worries others. During a century-long campaign its advocates won legitimacy and resources by incorporating kinder programs, once run by community groups, into the public schools. But what was sold as a romantic and humanistic "garden of learning" threatens to become just another grade level, committed to narrow cognitive skills and didactic teaching. Little evidence suggests that kindergartens are closing achievement gaps, in part because the most qualified teachers migrate to better-off communities. The UPK movement now prompts an eerie feeling of déjà vu, along with the question of whether contemporary advocates have learned much from their predecessors.

The universal preschool story is reminiscent of New Englander Horace Mann's crusade in the mid-nineteenth century to build a state-run system of "common schools." We see the same trust in central rules, faith in well-credentialed experts, and belief that children's development can be better engineered inside classrooms. There's a similar yearning for a well-oiled institution, the kind that Mann grew to love while visiting Prussia. The contemporary preschool movement evokes the same Calvinist verve as Horace Mann's crusade. "Nap time needs to go away," announced school superintendent Andre J. Hornsby in 2004, testifying before a Maryland legislative committee looking at early education. "We need to get rid of all that baby school stuff they used to do." Hornsby vowed to purge those slick vinyl mats to which, you may remember, our sweaty cheeks and arms adhered after nodding off.[7]

The present-day advocates of universal preschool are often aligned rhetorically with the *liberal-humanist* frame that has characterized our understanding of children's early development over the past century. Oklahoma's and New Jersey's regulations, for example, mandate that classroom practices be "developmentally appropriate," drawing from the constructivist, Piagetian notion that motivated learning builds from the child's own curiosity and shared stages of cognitive development. These potentials are to naturally burst forth when nurtured and facilitated within that engaging garden of learning (which *this* time will be preserved by the state, claim some advocates). The socialization goal within middle-class America is to move this robust little creature toward greater self-direction, linguistic fluency, and the pursuit of intrinsically motivated passions. It's the individuated child with the chutzpah to reason through and voice his or her interests, along with the agility to work cooperatively, that old-line liberal-humanists are eager to protect and enhance.

But the new reformers, while perhaps adopting this child-rearing philosophy for their own children, now wonder how useful it is for other people's children who must become "ready for school." For sure, many youngsters from poor families move through elementary school unable to read, or become proficient in English at a snail's pace. So, it's specific *academic skills* defined as "basic" that now should be emphasized, say the new advocates. The state is to make sure that preschool teachers get with the program, focusing their more structured lessons, worksheets, didactics on elements of language, printed materials, and mathematical concepts. If preschool teachers are properly "aligned" to the state's curricular goals, test scores should rise once children enter real school, according to this tidy systems argument.

As one school official in Tulsa, Oklahoma, told me, "The principals are under such pressure (to raise test scores), they say the sooner we get started on this, the better." And UPK advocates find common cause with proponents of top-down school accountability. The leading pro-UPK lobby in Washington, originally dubbed the Trust for Early Education, was founded inside the Education Trust, dogged defenders of President Bush's NCLB initiative.

The new regimentation carries a socialization agenda as well, pressing to ensure that children become "better behaved in class" and able to sit at desks, focused on dittoed worksheets, as one advocacy group puts it.[8] When I asked one leading proponent of universal preschool if she saw any risks in shrinking the core aim of preschool to bumping up test scores, she said: "Yes, we've been pushing cognitive outcomes . . . learning to speak English. It's a risk to just push K-12 (accountability) down into preschools. But school readiness helps us get traction and resources. Then we'll move toward a more holistic approach."

The Push-back

From high above, as if peering down to earth from a jet liner, the push for universal preschool makes abundant sense. Framed as education reform, this suddenly robust movement seems so timely—an inevitable extension of government's decade-long drive to specify clear learning objectives for elementary schools, to align and intensify child testing, and to install curricular packages that channel teachers' everyday work.

But as we descend closer to earth, landing inside particular communities, we can see that support for UPK is far from universal. Indeed, elite movement leaders—backed largely by a pair of national foundations and their analysts, pollsters, and public relations specialists—exemplify how elites within civil society recurrently attempt to push a normative way of raising children, even a standard institution, into the lives of America's breathtakingly diverse array of families. The nation continues to grow more pluralistic, not simply in its demographic complexion but also in the range of local organizations that support working families, including a vast array of nonprofit organizations, churches, and paid caregivers that make up the political economy of child care. We are no longer in the late nineteenth century, when modern institution-building meant creating huge hospitals, expansive universities, or a network of post offices—that is, engineering mass organizations.

Since World War II, child care centers and individual caregivers have sprouted throughout the land, like weeds sustained by sporadic watering. They are situated in YWCAs, church basements, even in licensed homes where women take in small gaggles of children. At last count, over 113,000 nonprofit preschools operated across the nation, two-thirds supported by parent fees and many others, created during the community action movement of the 1960s, serving low-income families. This vast archipelago of decentralized nonprofits reflects both organizational diversity and uneven quality. These neighborhood firms also help to thicken civil society, providing a base for countless community leaders to advocate for families, from the inner city to leafy suburbs.

Some opponents of UPK, conservatives included, are sounding a lot like developmental psychologists, arguing that civil society might first attend to the quality of primary social relationships, such as those between parents and the child. "Earlier, child care advocates were in favor of options. It makes sense, given the different ways in which children develop," argues Darcy Olsen, director of the Goldwater Institute in Phoenix. She worries that advocates will push government to create disincentives for parents or kin who still want to raise their own children: "It's as if attachment theory just went out the window."

Olsen set her sights on a formidable foil during our interview: Arizona's Democratic governor, Janet Napolitano. Releasing a new "school readiness action plan" in 2004, Napolitano defined her end goal as "ensconcing early care and education as a lockstep component of public schooling."[9] In response, Olsen said: "Over time government would be requiring parents to send their four-year-old to preschool, and then their three-year-olds. It's like reading *Brave New World*, which is creepy, it doesn't bode well for our children."

The push-back comes from progressive activists as well, often leaders in nonprofit agencies worried about state control from above, the regimentation of preschool classrooms, and the trickle down of didactic instruction to ensure that all the curricular "standards" are covered. Patty Siegel, a mother of three in the early 1970s, when she helped to create a child care switchboard in San Francisco, rose to become California's most influential advocate in Sacramento for child care funding. "There's a history we are losing . . . all those original community-based centers in San Francisco, elsewhere. There must be a touch point with universality, otherwise it comes to be seen only as part of welfare. (But) don't families need to see their options?" As Libby Sholes, leader of the moderate California Council of Churches, put it, "We are moving so fast in the institutionalization of children. We're taking kids away from their parents. Government's deciding what's best for our kids."

Tensions are palpable in other states, pitting advocates of school-run programs against leaders of ethnic communities. One New Jersey scholar and activist described a major group that runs nonprofit preschools as a "banana republic," expressing worries over program quality and the organization's political tactics. Still, in New Jersey 72 percent of children enrolled attend a community preschool, not one located in a public school, while all programs must meet quality standards set by the state education department.

Nor are union leaders unified in their views of government moving toward one best system of preschooling. Both the American Federation of Teachers (AFT) and the National Education Association (NEA) have put preschool reform among their top three lobbying priorities.[10] Other labor groups have long been organizing child care workers. Michelle Cerecerez helped to unionize women who run licensed child care homes in Los Angeles for several years. A self-proclaimed "Head Start kid," Cerecerez attended preschool at East Los Angeles College. "I remember singing songs in French," she said with smiling delight. But Cerecerez is not convinced that preschool should be mandated for all kids: "It's kind of arrogant to say every kid should be in a center, an institution, at such a young age."

The push-back also comes from local activists and scholars who see children's development as being embedded within particular cultural contexts. After the liberal-humanist tradition and the new focus on academic skilling, the *cross-cultural* framing of children's socialization and their underlying cognitive structures also prompts worries over how a mass preschool system, run by state agencies that habitually narrow and standardize notions of learning, could be responsive to the diversity of families and children that characterizes American society.

This framework, advanced over the past half-century by cross-cultural psychologists and learning theorists, takes seriously the notion of scaffolding up from the daily activities, linguistic foundations, and behavioral norms that youngsters experience at home and within their immediate environs. The framework mitigates against universalist notions of how children grow, whether it's the liberal-humanist tenet that all children move through biologically determined stages on their way to individual autonomy or the notion that uniform academic skills advance the child's well-being over time.

This book also delves into how cultural forces cohere and are expressed at the *institutional* level. In trying to understand how universal preschool plays out differently (in quite non-universal) ways among states, I discovered that the character of preschool classrooms and their tolerance for different philosophies of child development, not to mention languages of instruction, is shaped in part by the *political culture* of the state or region in which UPK takes root and sprouts. In Oklahoma, for instance, few with any clout ever challenged the implicit assumption that UPK funding should flow through the public schools. In Los Angeles, that possibility never even surfaced as a credible path to take, given this city's pluralistic and community-rooted politics.

Down at the grassroots, conservatives well understand the preschool's utility in advancing a *particular* culture's bundle of norms and valued skills. David Brooks, the *New York Times* columnist, is enthusiastic about stronger government efforts when it comes to early education, starting with the expansion of Head Start: "Progressive conservatives understand that while culture matters most, government can alter culture. Government [is] now trying to design programs to encourage marriage. Early-intervention programs [in addition] were not a conservative idea, but they work."[11] Brooks nails the basic point with refreshing candor: how young children are nurtured and taught inside preschools is, unavoidably, a *cultural* act advanced by institutions.

This debate over the child's inner nature and how best to nurture children also bumps into a classic dilemma that has beset educators throughout the modern period: should child-rearing institutions seek to *transform* youngsters and their communities, making sure they become members of the nation-state, acquiring individualistic skills which allow them to fill jobs in a competitive economic system? Or, should schools be *conserving* institutions rooted in the knowledge, language, and cultural mores of particular groups, working as democratic organizations that build from the social foundations of family and community? The debate over universal preschool intersects similar contention around charter schools, small schools, and vouchers for private and religious schooling. At its core, the question is: can a bureaucratic state be trusted to build one best system of education for a feisty, pluralistic society? Who gets to decide what children should be learning, through what forms of social relations? And when the state gains authority to make these decisions, whose interests are being advanced?

My aim in this book is not to push a single philosophy of the child's in-born nature, nor to advance one uniform institution to advance children's development. Instead, I hope to spark and empirically inform this essential debate over how young children should be raised and taught within a pluralistic society, and who gets to decide on the goals and means of child rearing. Part of my point is that the new advocates are pushing a standard remedy with little understanding of historical context, of how they risk closing off options. We will see how proponents, obsessively focused on finding an effective political strategy, may inadvertently narrow the way parents come to see, and feel confident about, how they are supposed to raise their own children.

"All theories of learning are based on fundamental assumptions about the person, the world, and their relations," as theorists Jean Lave and Etienne Wenger emphasize.[12] I would add that these assumptions become tacitly embedded in the *social organizations* that human beings create to nurture and teach their young children. And while good liberals and stalwart conservatives both pitch universal futures for America's children, this book urges you to think about whether modern systems-building assumptions still fit the diversity of families and neighborhoods that increasingly make up America's vibrant society. Overall, as the new advocates and a resurgent state pitch a universal institution for young children—seeking to reorder this early period of human life—I seek to unravel this tangled ball of contested philosophical stances and widening array of empirical findings.

Organization of the Book

Chapter 1 begins with the obvious question. Why did the UPK movement suddenly gained such political traction? We examine Americans' perennial belief in the boundless potential of the young child, a postulate of Enlightenment thinking now held by the middle class. But policy elites have come to think about the young child's cognitive potential in a new way. "We have recently come to understand that (preschoolers) are eager to learn . . . to be learning about reading and numbers," the developmental psychologist Deborah Phillips said in an interview. "From developmental science, not just the brain research, we now know they are eager to be learning. We used to think we should wait until age five."[13] Most well-off parents agreed with Phillips some time ago: almost 85 percent of four-year-olds in affluent families, those in the top fifth of the nation's income distribution, now attend preschool.[14]

We next consider the question of how best to define the public interest in expanding the state's role, in making government the paramount collective actor in casting preschool. Should government advance free, universally accessible preschool as the *exclusive* remedy—the single sanctioned organization in which all young children should be raised?

Chapter 2 examines how the period of early childhood has long been a contested area in Western society—both in our understanding of the child's inner nature and in theories of how youngsters' social settings can be better engineered by grown ups. We then fast-forward to contemporary times to see how some of these same forces are shaping how states and metropolitan areas design early education options today, looking in particular at the on-going struggle of women to balance work and family, the fusion of school accountability reforms with the new push to standardize childhood, and the colorful, decentralized array of community programs that presently serve young children.

Chapter 3 invites you into the Rainbow Room to see how contested ideals of development and cultural diversity play out inside classrooms. In this chapter we place our feet squarely on the ground inside a region of the country that is strongly committed to universal preschool. Seeta Pai, my research team's ethnographic leader, spent a year in several classrooms, and what she discovered is eye-opening. The UPK system she looked at remains dedicated to liberal-humanist ideals in spades, centrally regulating what's progressively called *emergent curriculum*, a very constructivist classroom strategy. At the same time, kindergarten teachers in the public schools are pushing hard for their preschool colleagues to focus on narrower academic skills, urging parents to help get their kids ready for school. The contradictions in this colorful and diverse suburb are both hopeful and instructive for those who favor a well-oiled preschool system.

In Chapter 4 we visit the unlikely leader of the UPK movement—the state of Oklahoma. Here preschool enrollments have risen steadily, climbing to the highest rate in the nation. My account of the subdued revolution in Oklahoma delves into the actors, ideals, and political interests that have pushed the issue forward over the past two decades. The Oklahoma case is marked by a civil, even mellow, discourse among a small circle of early educators and community activists, including Head Start and the YWCA, a system loosely overseen by local school boards. Yet tensions exist beneath the surface, as Latino parents worry about their four-year-olds not wanting to speak Spanish at home and early educators wring their hands over getting what they had wished for. Pressures on preschool teachers are rising to conform to curricular guidelines, to specify daily activities, and to NCLB mandates that trickle down to preschool classrooms.

In vivid contrast, Chapter 5 moves to the context of Los Angeles. There, leaders in this expansive county have created a universal preschool system that is neither universal (it progressively targets poor communities) nor limited to preschool (it includes family child care homes). California's decentralized governance structure interacts with the ethnic, highly democratic politics of L.A.—leading to a contest over which school authorities and nonprofit agencies get to deliver the new UPK program. The L.A. story holds implications for who gets to hold the tail of the UPK tiger: whether the state tries to run and regulate it, or simply contracts out to a colorful variety of preschools that pursue the developmental aims put forth by these local organizations spread across diverse communities.

Chapter 6 turns to the bold claims advanced by UPK advocates, and Margaret Bridges and I review the empirical evidence for each. Eager to win middle-class political support, for example, UPK proponents have contended that preschools yield clear benefits to all children, and across various domains of development. But after five decades of empirical work, the evidence is not so tidy. Not all the assertions made by the new reformers can be settled with scientific investigation, since the aims of child development are rooted largely in culture and philosophy, not science. But evidence can be informative. We also examine what elements of preschool quality most consistently boost children's growth, and how preschool's benefits vary across differing facets of early development.

Chapter 7 moves to a nettlesome patch of philosophical and scientific questions related to how public efforts might advance the early development of Latino children. I documented well over a decade ago that Latino parents enroll their children in preschool at much lower rates than other groups do. This led to a series of studies, both quantitative and qualitative, to understand how cultural values, family structure, social support, and the local supply of preschools all contribute to family demand. In this chapter, we also arrive at the cultural revolution in learning theory that began early in the past century, but went unnoticed in mainstream child development studies until just a generation ago.

Chapter 8 concludes the volume by sketching a third pathway for moving forward—relying neither on the rough, unfair edges of child care markets nor on the homogenizing regulation of childhood that the rush to universal preschool risks. Placed on a broader canvas, the battle over universal preschool is one example of the growing disaffection with mass institutions and top-down policies that run against the grain of America's ongoing democratization of individual expression and social organizations.

You may realize partway through this volume that my own agenda is to delineate a clearer sociology of childhood, focusing largely on the interaction of state action, civil society, and local pluralism. Traditionally, developmentalists have been trained in psychology and socialized to focus on the individual child's motivation and growth. This is a crucial area of study, but it has historically eclipsed our understanding of the social ideals and institutional practices that, in the end, shape the everyday settings that the grown-ups create for their offspring.

Many developmental scientists like to claim that their work avoids the messiness of philosophy, ideology, and cultural variation. Like physicists, they are illuminating *universal* stages, psychological processes, or causal models of development. But when parents or scholars work to advance a desired outcome, they must necessarily work from within a child's social location that's bounded by social class, language, or cultural heritage. Certain individuals and organizations hold concentrated capital or power that allows them to advance their ideals about the young child, or their favored social organization for raising other people's children. But presuming to know how other parents want to raise their children and toward what ends is risky business.

I do worry that the push to universalize and standardize preschooling in America will disempower parents from the most essential human task of all: raising young children. In my travels and in countless interviews I never sensed that well-meaning advocates are ill intentioned or aiming to advance corrosive institutions. But as Foucault so powerfully argued, modern mechanisms of regulation and conformity to the demands of big organizations and the economy can be tacitly embedded even in benevolent institutions, like the state.

It doesn't have to be this way. Liberal-humanist thinkers have been working on ways to separate reflective youngsters from dominant structures and didactic forms of "official knowledge" over the past five centuries. More recently, cultural psychologists have emphasized how the child learns within the immediate community and the nurturing support it ideally offers. Obviously all children should acquire basic literacy and communication skills.

Still, much of the discourse around education reform once again centers on how the state can more tightly regulate human learning, ensuring that all children speak in one exclusive language, read identical textbooks, and recite officially sanctioned knowledge. At issue is whether eager institution builders are listening to this debate, a struggle which has long characterized and befuddled democratic societies.

STANDARDIZED CHILDHOOD

CHAPTER ONE

Why Universal Preschool Now?

Framing the Problem

Long before Mrs. William Thurston—her first name lost in the catacombs of Boston history—hatched her subversive plan in 1828, a faint rainbow of modern ideals about the nature of toddlers spanned enlightened corners of Europe and America. These notions stemmed from Rousseau's and Pestalozzi's claims that children "naturally" blossom at their own pace and that learning emerges from playful activities, mindfully facilitated by mothers or tutors. Locke's postulate, that children could be taught to reason and to become reflective agents of their own fate, meshed well with young America's democratic instincts. Liberal-humanism was maturing and beginning to eclipse the pre-modern assumption that children would simply reveal their inborn will and character early in life, or the Calvinist suspicion of play, which cut into precious time needed to recite Scripture.[1]

It was Robert Owen—the Welsh factory manager and renaissance man—who inspired Thurston and her co-conspirators, some ninety Congregationalist ladies, to create one of America's first networks of preschools, then called *infant schools*, which served young children from poor and better-off families. Owen was active in a network of industrial innovators and social utopians, and he worried that the offspring of his factory workers would face a limited future unless they were given a head start. He proposed that they learn with their peers apart from their families in a part-day infant school. He created a handful of such schools in Britain and exported the model to southern Indiana, when he founded New Harmony there in 1825.

Owen believed that "infants," that is, children through age five, should "not be annoyed by books." All forms of learning were to be "for their amusement." Blue-collar families, he claimed, were too preoccupied by the demands of work to fully attend to their children. His innovative classrooms were filled with hand-crafted manipulatives—precursors to the blocks, games, and wooden toys omnipresent in today's preschool classrooms (absent only Legos). His guidelines emphasized teaching youngsters how to clap to music, to dance, even to march in a tidy manner.[2]

Thurston and her associates were left breathless. Infant schools began to pop up in New York and Philadelphia, often financed by elite families for their own toddlers. The common school movement was taking off in the East and Midwest as well, spurred by fellow Massachusetts reformer Horace Mann. Amazingly, an estimated 40 percent of the commonwealth's *three-year-olds* attended a public school in 1839, according to historian Barbara Beatty.[3] Owen's allies were concerned that children under six lacked their own institution, more carefully tailored to their own needs. He recognized that the new common schools might want to host programs for infants, but wanted his organizations to be "diametrically opposed in nature and tendency to the public schools of the present day."

Thurston's group, incorporated as the Infant School Society of the City of Boston, had created five small schools by the late 1830s, mainly serving children of poor and working-class families. These institutions advanced Owen's pedagogical philosophy and nudged working-class parents to improve their behavior, from drinking less to attending church more. One mother's words were recorded in the society's annual report, praising the "vast advantages" of infant schools to "such parents (who) have to work, as many do, from twelve to sixteen hours a day for their support." The Infant School Society also advised well-off Boston families, who established eight additional schools to serve their own children.

But just as the movement was getting off the ground, it fell to earth, crashed, and burned. Several American intellectuals (typically men)—including the editor of the *American Journal of Education*, William Woodbridge— reminded parents that Rousseau had worried about the risks associated with rushing the young child's pace of learning. "Precocity" was even deemed a disease by some scholars, presaging David Elkind's best-selling book of the 1980s, *The Hurried Child*. Woodbridge's journal attacked infant schools for providing the "occasion for remissness in the discharge of parental duties, by devolving the care of infancy on teachers, instead of leaving with the mother the full weight and responsibility of her natural relations." A Connecticut physician, Amariah Brigham, emphasized in his popular 1832 book "the necessity of giving more attention to the health and growth of the body, and less to the cultivation of the mind, especially early in life."[4] Other critics drew from Pestalozzi's idealized renditions of home-based learning, harking back to the presumed earth-mothers of pre-industrial village life.

The backlash from the pro-motherhood forces proved overwhelming. Faced with competition from church leaders who sought more resources for their middle-class Sunday schools, not infant schools for the poor, Thurston and her colleagues approached the Boston Primary School Committee to take over their fledgling programs. This, too, proved to be a dead end. School officials, after surveying their elementary teachers, found that many complained that infant school graduates were "the cause of restlessness and disorder among the other children." The graduates were "troublesome . . . from want of constant excitement . . . their attention with difficulty fixed upon their studies." They apparently just weren't ready for school.

Mid-century demographic shifts also fed the backlash against infant schools. Among the rising middle class, wives of prospering artisans and merchants were bearing fewer babies and finding more time for mothering, as reported by historian Steven Mintz.[5] The first guides to middle-class parenting were appearing. Catherine Beecher's *Treatise on Domestic Economy*, published in 1841, preached the crucial importance of moral education and that infant schools were no substitute for parents in shaping the young child's character.[6]

Early education advocates—at least those preferring a bounded institution for young children—would have to wait several decades until kindergarten advocates began to gain traction. The rise and fall of infant schools had yielded telling lessons. First, taking on the public schools leads to competition for resources and public legitimacy. Second, aggravating the nagging worry that institutions subvert parents' own authority over child rearing is risky, especially during periods when women have discretionary time and parenting experts hammer on the mother's alleged first duty, in the home. And third, if early education is about character development and socialization, as opposed to narrower cognitive growth or skilling, other established institutions will lay claim to this territory, including churches.

What Problem Will Universal Preschool Solve?

Given the perils faced by would-be institution builders in the past, why have the new proponents for universal preschool suddenly gained such momentum today? This question motivates this chapter. I begin by sketching the surface symptoms of the problems that advocates and child development specialists commonly emphasize, present company included. But how these symptoms have been framed, then fused to the exclusive remedy of universal preschool offers the key to understanding why this new movement has picked up steam in recent years. The new generation of advocates tends to headline their institutional, systems-like remedy; then, working backwards, they seek to attach "problems" and supportive evidence that are logically consistent.

Family demand for preschool, for example, has grown dramatically since the 1950s, but disparities persist in terms of which children gain access to quality settings. So, one compelling way to frame "the problem" is to start by reiterating that Americans have come to see early education as a *public* issue, not one that can be remedied through private action alone. Many UPK advocates proceed to argue that public educators will not close achievement gaps or raise test scores sufficiently until inequities in early learning are closed.

Then, a leap of faith is attempted, especially among those whom I call *institutional liberals*. The best way to close disparities in early development, as the postulate goes, is to create a universal, state-run system of preschool. The pitch here is to incorporate the far-flung archipelago of existing child care providers and nonprofit preschools into a tidier, state-regulated *system*, just as the common school movement did a century and a half ago. It is also reminiscent of how early industrialists deemed that one-room school houses were inefficient, unequally financed, and ineffective in transmitting uniform knowledge and imparting the dominant social norms (and language) in schools with rising numbers of immigrant families. The answer, under this conception of the problem, is to build a one best system of early education.

Like other social movements—and like their predecessors in the kindergarten movement a century ago—the new preschool activists are first and foremost *institution builders*, in pursuit of political legitimacy and public dollars. They advance a discourse that is often dominated by strategy, polling, and arguments aimed at piecing together public credibility ("the current array of child care programs is disorganized"; "preschools will boost test scores"; "the new brain research shows that . . . "). This is not a movement that has bubbled up from the grassroots. It is one led by earnest elites who work from within foundation offices, state governments, and universities. This new vanguard spends far more time poring over polling results and screening public service announcements than talking with parents about what they really want when it comes to raising their kids.

It's also a movement newly greased financially by an aging set of progressive men, as my Berkeley colleague David Kirp emphasizes. And these men expect to get their way. They are fathers or grandfathers who suddenly got religion when it comes to the importance of early childhood, men like director Rob Reiner in Hollywood, billionaire Warren Buffett in Omaha, and Pete Churchwell, the former head of Oklahoma's biggest power company. They want to get the institutional fix in place, now. Who should run a state's preschool system, how are children to be raised and taught in classrooms, or what is the nature of the mixed market of preschool organizations that currently serves communities—these are details. All this talk simply slows down progress toward the political win.

All this talk—the discourse and strategy constructed by contemporary preschool advocates—is a major focus of this study. In part, it is their ability to reframe "the problem," to emphasize perennially attractive ideals about young children, and to selectively draw on empirical research that explains their early success in several states. Traveling from California to Oklahoma to New Jersey and Washington, D.C., I listened carefully to the core arguments, tacit assumptions, and selective empiricism invoked by key players—from policy-makers to school leaders to preschool teachers. Much of it is "policy talk," in political scientist Richard Elmore's phrase, chatter heard among advocates or in the hallways of state capitols, ideas tossed against the wall to see what sticks within a local political culture.[7]

Competing Claims—How Young Children Should Develop

The clamor of voices heard across public discourses—to use a word that is overused in academic and literary circles—attempts to frame conceptions of problems and attach sensible policy remedies. The utility of listening carefully to the words and logic of key players is emphasized by the French philosopher Michel Foucault, who emphasized that dominant "texts" and oral conversation take on authority and power over how children and parents should normatively behave. In recent years, these quite public conversations about the nature of young children and their daily settings have been vying for the hearts and minds of parents, early educators, and politicians.

Elite thinkers emerging from the Enlightenment, for example, altered Western societies' dominant assumptions about the infant's basic moral and biological nature, rejecting the notion that babies were born as willful, sinful creatures needing strict discipline, and instead advancing the view that "the child had to be gradually trusted with his own conduct," in Thomas Popkewitz's words. "The parental relation was to win respect and esteem of their children through reason, benevolence . . . and affection."[8] Piaget and contemporary psychologists came to emphasize universal stages of cognitive development, linked to the child's motivated eagerness to understand material tools and social interactions, moving toward individual autonomy and self-direction, building on *liberal-humanist* ideals.[9]

The contemporary discourse linked to the state's logic of accountability and testing of children contends, however, that the upbringing of young children should focus on imparting certain cognitive *skills* and plugging three- and four-year-olds into the classroom's social routines, getting them "ready for school." Not coincidentally, this discourse helps UPK advocates secure support from public school interest groups. The emphasis on mental development fits nicely with the human capital logic of neoclassical economics: schooling imparts discrete skills and pieces of knowledge that help propel the lone individual through school and make him or her a more productive and efficient worker.

A recent pro-preschool session at the Committee for Economic Development in New York featured University of Chicago economist James Heckman reviewing the usual litany of cost-benefit analyses of preschool experiments. The Brookings Institution's Isabel Sawhill even claimed that investing in universal preschool would increase the nation's gross domestic product by $988 billion within sixty years. *New York Times* writer Tamar Lewin summed things up: "For the conference organizers, the intent yesterday was to reframe the warm, fuzzy image of early childhood programs, transforming them into a hardheaded, quantifiable matter of economics and work force efficency."[10] The rally was organized by a major UPK backer, the Pew Charitable Trusts of Philadelphia.

A third discourse gaining steam alleges the importance of scaffolding up from the child's own cultural and linguistic settings. This framing of the problem stems from a half-century of work by cross-cultural psychologists and learning theorists. It has gained in relevance as early educators and policymakers realize that America's diverse population of children arrive at child care and the preschool setting with different languages, knowledge, and social norms. Their parents also hold varying conceptions of what preschool is all about. This *culturally situated* conception of child development is promoted by community groups who argue that a public school takeover of preschool is imperial and unwise—not only from a neighborhood power standpoint but also because distant, state-run preschools are less likely to work up from the knowledge and normative behaviors that are rooted in the child's own cultural community.

Both the skilling frame and the cross-cultural frame directly challenge the liberal-humanist pillars of the contemporary field of child development. While adherents of the skilling perspective show no reservations about seeing young children as either normally proficient or somehow delayed, cross-cultural proponents reject the assumption that there is one normal way of raising young children, divorced from a youngster's particular community. Liberal-humanists focus more on the child's natural blossoming and lightly structuring classroom tasks to nurture intrinsic motivation; skilling and cultural proponents emphasize the well-being of the collective, be it the wider modern economy or the child's immediate community. Add to this the new advocates' buoyant faith that government—mainly state capitals and education departments—can uniformly define what classroom practices best advance children's growth, and you can see how contentious these three discourses have become within America's pluralistic society.

We are back to Foucault's concern about the pluses and minuses of the ongoing state-driven rationalization of children's everyday lives, which is tacitly pursued by modern institutions without any conspiracy implied and is promoted with little reflection by eager political leaders. The social regulation of children's behavior and even the practices of parents—including the inculcation of sanctified knowledge and narrow cognitive skills rather than the pursuit of a youngster's intrinsic curiosity—may come to dominate.

California schools chief Jack O'Connell, a left-of-center Democrat, pushed legislation in 2005 to mandate that all preschools follow "learning standards" to encourage "instruction . . . in a purposeful and playful learning environment." The phrase, "and shall be developmentally appropriate," was amended into the bill as it moved through the state legislature. Yet the first several instructional aims pertained to pre-literacy and vocabulary knowledge. All three- and four-year-olds would even be required to learn about "citizenship" and "national symbols."[11] As Rob Reiner was revising his UPK ballot initiative for a second run in 2006, O'Connell's staff inserted language requiring that funded preschools must have a curriculum aligned with K-12 learning standards, and "ensure, based on research, that English-language learner (be) making progress towards learning the English language."[12] Somehow, inserting the word "research" legitimated this ideological stance.

As I sat with key actors—whether inside state capitals or in classrooms—I was struck by how this emerging discourse says little, and even expresses little curiosity, about how America's diverse parents want to raise and instruct their own children. There's not much interest among the new advocates in stimulating public, democratic debate over this essential human activity. Instead, earnest advocates and political leaders arrive at one institutional remedy, backed by a few benefactors. And it's attracting the support of strong education interest groups who foresee more school funding, higher test scores, and more union members. If only Mrs. Thurston and her co-conspirators in

Boston could have afforded a wise pollster and political strategist, or could have attracted a sugar-daddy, a century and a half ago.

Let's move to the differing ways in which "the problem" is defined, sometimes constructed with rhetoric, other times founded upon evidence. Listen carefully to the frames created around these discourses, to whose voice rises above the others, and to how new members join or are distanced from the party.

Child Care Is Just Too Messy

Rob Reiner fills a conference call much like he fills a conference room, with imposing verbosity and impatience. He was instantly infuriated as he jumped on the call in June 2002. "I'm tired of people acting out of fear and alarm. I'm hoping there's a little bit of trust, [but] I can't tell you how many people in the child care community were opposed to creating Prop 10." Three years earlier Reiner's tenacity led to successful passage of California's Proposition 10, which boosted tobacco taxes to fund child care and health programs for children age zero to five. Los Angeles County had been banking much of their revenues, more like a foundation than a government agency, and Reiner was consulting with local leaders and academics about creating a universal preschool system across the far-flung metropolis.

Reiner's initial proposal was to fund a series of "beacon centers" that would provide high quality instruction for three- and four-year-olds along with comprehensive health and parenting services. The pristine and impressive Hope Street Center, based in downtown L.A., was the model put forward. But Reiner and his political advisers were feeling a stiff push-back from important groups, rather than the gracious appreciation Reiner had expected. The vast network of community organizations running child care centers across the county, from Watts and East L.A. to the well-heeled suburbs on the west side, didn't want to compete with a uniform, high-cost model. Other key advocates believed the priority should be on early intervention, focusing on children age zero to three (Reiner's own stance in the 1990s, during the early-brain-research media boom). Key county supervisors wanted to earmark accumulating tobacco tax revenues to ensure that working-poor families could access health insurance.

CHAOS OR INSTITUTIONAL DIVERSITY?

Reiner's sketch of the public problem emphasized a child care community in disarray offering a mix of settings for young children, led by associations who could never agree on how to move forward. His worries were understandable, given recent policy history. Former Republican governor Pete Wilson had dramatically widened child care options for low-income families, boosting spending nearly fourfold, to almost $2.8 billion in the 1990s, but he did so mainly through parental vouchers as pushed under the senior Bush's federal program. This only added to the messiness, in Reiner's view. Instead, the state's disparate child care groups needed to pull together and rally around his more sharply defined remedy: free, state-run preschool accessible to the middle class.

Also on the call were Karen Hill-Scott, who would soon be asked to design the Los Angeles UPK effort, developmentalists Deborah Stipek and Marlene Zepeda, UCLA research pediatrician Neal Halfon, and myself. We all felt the need to clarify for Reiner the range of groups that already served three- and four-year-olds across Los Angeles, literally thousands of community-based organizations (CBOs), churches, licensed homes, and local schools. Some programs went back to the post-World War II era, and many others were created in the wake of the civil rights movement and Head Start. We agreed that this patchwork quilt of child care organizations would be difficult to move in any one direction. Yet advancing a single, high-fidelity model of preschool—ignoring the thousands of caregivers and feminist activists who were already in the trenches in the 1970s, while Reiner was playing Meat-head on *All in the Family*—would likely undercut his good intentions.

Reiner's representation of the problem overlapped the emerging discourse advanced by UPK proponents nationwide. Reiner's first claim is that preschool makes a substantial difference in the lives of *all* children whose parents are able to find affordable, high-quality programs. So, pre-k classrooms should be deemed a public good, similar to public education, and should be offered to all families at no private cost.

Second, Reiner's persisting worry was that the crazy-quilt of child care alternatives—centers, licensed homes, and individual caregivers—that America has stitched together manifests uneven cost and quality and remains politically ineffectual.[13] We will hear from leading advocates who now actually stigmatize and attempt to sever the panoply of child care options from the real thing: preschool. The fluid and disparate institutional field of child care has long struggled to arrive at "industry standards" when it comes to defining high quality programs. It's a downside of operating with a vastly decentralized field. The new development is manifest in Reiner's punctuated emphasis on cutting out any form of child care that doesn't look like a school classroom. The constructed problem is that organizational messiness makes it difficult to gain wider political support for "high-quality programs," now defined as fusing preschool classrooms tightly to the public schools.

THE "UNFINISHED PART OF SCHOOL REFORM"

Reiner's storyline resembles the plot now sketched by the major UPK proponents. This framing accents the importance of building a tidier system, one that incorporates the array of existing child care centers, then pushes to make their classrooms more uniform, with a socialization agenda "aligned" with the *curricular content* that first or second graders are expected to know. Like the common school movement, uniform indicators of quality, centralized regulation, more highly credentialed teachers are to ensure that *instruction*—rather than creating engaging activities for children to explore—will be delivered in more uniform ways. And the state signals to parents that this is now *the* appropriate way to raise one's three- or four-year-old. Modern child rearing is equated with systems building in the eyes of UPK advocates— and parents hear this discourse through upbeat articles in daily newspapers, public service announcement, and from school authorities.

Libby Doggett articulated this logic when we met in Washington, D.C. She heads the Washington-based group Preschool Now, a wholly owned subsidiary of the Pew Trusts, first founded within the unflagging lobby for NCLB, a group called the Education Trust. "I think we made a huge mistake in child care," Doggett said. "(With UPK) we shouldn't sacrifice quality. I would never target the poor. I would target it as school reform. Some say this is the last, unfinished part of school reform." At one point, eager to cast her movement as school reform, Doggett even approached the editorial board of a major newspaper to convince them that the term "pre-k" was preferable to "preschool."[14]

Doggett speaks confidently, with a warm, slight Texas drawl, complaining of how government support of child care, since the Great Society, has been tied to poor families and welfare. Instead, "if you have middle-class families fighting for it, it's not going away," Doggett said. "We have realtors pitching this (UPK) for us." Like Reiner, she aims to create a distinct identity for the new preschool institution, purging the messiness of the disparate child care programs currently supported by Washington and state governments (to the tune, remember, of over $18 billion in public funds at last count). But this strategy also requires incorporating into state systems the thousands of non-profits that serve middle-class and affluent families, equaling at least two-thirds of all children enrolled.

Unequal Access, Uneven Child Development

Other advocates and scholars worry less about the decentralization of the child care field and more about which children gain access to, and truly benefit from, high quality settings. Remarkable progress has been made by government in equalizing access to three kinds of child care providers—preschools, family child care homes (FCCHs) licensed by the state, and vouchers which support family members who care for young children. But disparities remain, especially in the distribution of quality across differing families. Government covers between one-quarter and one-third of the total cost of early care and education nationwide, according to different estimates. At least one-fourth of all preschools are operated as for-profit firms, concentrated in blue-collar and middle-class communities, and they often display lower quality than nonprofit and publicly supported programs.[15]

Many parents opt for informal caregivers, not formal organizations. Looking across the nation's 18.5 million children under age five, 63 percent were in a regular child care arrangement in 2002, according to the Census Bureau.[16] Under one-fifth were enrolled in a center-based program or preschool. Grandparents accounted for another 23 percent of all caregivers; about 14 percent of all youngsters were cared for by nonrelatives, which included 6 percent in licensed FCCHs. Preschool enrollment rates, of course, are higher for three- and four-year-olds, detailed below.

Given this persisting reliance on less formal caregivers, just 43 percent of all working mothers report paying out-of-pocket for care. The growth of public child care vouchers, tax credits, and preschool slots has effectively lowered private spending for many poor and blue-collar families. However, middle-class parents who paid for child care and earned over $54,000 annually (the median family income nationwide in 2000) spent about $5,300 per year, twice the spending level of the average poor family (after setting aside low-income families benefiting from subsidies).[17] So, while government has lightened the financial burden associated with child care among families, child care costs continue to absorb a sizable slice of the income of many young families.

Rising maternal employment rates, along with the climbing legitimacy of preschool, have spurred steady growth of these human-scale organizations. The federal Lanham Act supported 3,102 centers during World War II, many built by the Works Progress Administration in the Depression. State governments matched federal dollars to expand options for women contributing to the war effort.[18] By 1982 the number of preschool centers nationwide had grown to about 30,800, climbing to just over 113,500 preschools in 2001. An additional 306,000 state-regulated FCCHs were operating across the nation in 2001.[19]

The remarkable growth in organizations appears to have slowed in some states since the early 1990s, as federal support, aside from that for Head Start preschools, has shifted toward parental vouchers. This is a major bone of contention for UPK advocates, who argue that quality preschool is fundamentally better than disparate home-based care. Several recent studies have shown that the average preschool center does yield stronger cognitive and language (but not social-developmental) gains for young children, compared with home-based settings, we will see in Chapter 6.

A parallel worry is that parental vouchers, while perhaps a wise income-transfer strategy benefiting those who keep child care in the family, have done little to strengthen neighborhood organizations which serve young children. Shelly Waters Boots and I found that the growth of preschools barely kept up with child population growth in the four years following welfare reform in California, rising from 13 to just 14 enrollment slots for every 100 children under five.[20] Support of vouchers rose eightfold over the 1990s, but the lion's share of this new funding moved to family caregivers. Voucher proponents counter that about half of these portable payments nationwide end up going to preschools in which low-income parents enroll their children.

Public schools have been a key player in lending shape to the burgeoning early education sector over the past generation, although their market share varies dramatically among states. Just 16 percent of all preschool centers were nested in schools in 1990, when the federal government last conducted a national survey.[21] This share of the entire preschool sector represented slightly more than the fraction run by Head Start. School-based preschools are more common in urban states which more effectively target public dollars on lower-income communities. Just over 40 percent of children served by publicly funded preschools in California attend school-based programs, while the remaining three-fifths are in community-based programs. In New Jersey's so-called Abbott school districts, under court-mandated universal preschool, almost 70 percent of the children enrolled attend a CBO program, while the overall initiative is directed by the state education department.

The progressive targeting of public funds on lower-income families has successfully widened access to school-based programs since the 1960s. Public schools situated in poor communities are twice as likely to have a preschool program than schools in better-off neighborhoods (51 versus 25 percent, respectively). This finding holds long-term import for the political economy of the early education sector: nonprofit preschools tend to thrive in leafy, better-off suburbs that do not feel price competition from subsidized programs. But as public schools expand their free preschool offerings, nonprofits charging fees will be less competitive and may die off.[22]

WHICH PRESCHOOLERS ENTER PRESCHOOL?

Sharp disparities across social-class and ethnic groups characterize which young children, age three or four, enter a preschool center. This stark inequity understandably fuels support for universal preschool.

Only recently have data become available to carefully examine preschool enrollments nationwide and among the states. One federal survey of parents and early educators, dubbed the Early Childhood Longitudinal Study (ECLS), traces the trajectories of over 22,000 young children over time.[23] We now know that almost two-thirds of all children attend a preschool center at some point prior to entering kindergarten. The enrollment rate is slightly lower for four-year-olds who attend the year immediately before kindergarten entry. About 14 percent of the nation's four-year-olds are served by Head Start preschool at least part time, and another 57 percent are in other preschools (either CBO- or school-based). In short, exposure to some classroom experience, of varying duration and quality, is already widespread for the majority of America's preschool-age children.[24]

Growth in enrollment rates since 1970 has been phenomenal. Over one-fourth of all four-year-olds attended some kind of center-based program in 1970, and that grew to two-thirds by 2000. Figure 1.1 displays the growth rate for three- and four-year-old children.

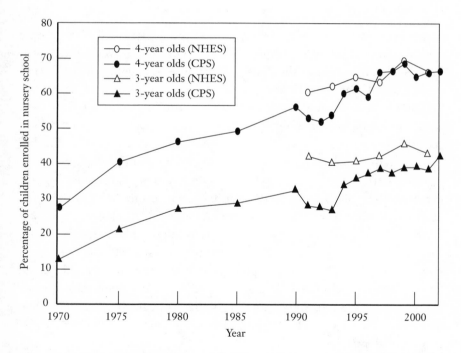

Figure 1.1   Preschool Enrollment Rates for U.S. Three- and Four-Year-Olds: 1970–2002. Enrollment rates estimated from the National Household Education Survey, conducted by the National Center for Educational Statistics, and from the Current Population Survey of the U.S. Census Bureau. All data compiled by Lynn Karoly and James Bigelow at the RAND Corporation.

The problem of unequal access for certain children is serious. But pro-UPK scholars have exaggerated the severity of the problem. The annual compendium of preschool statistics contains a wealth of useful state-level data. Its authors, led by Rutgers professor and UPK enthusiast W. Steven Barnett, claim that state-funded preschool programs (focused on low-income families) serve only 16 percent of all four-year-olds. But this finding does not include preschools funded by states and federal vouchers that don't strictly fall under the "state preschool" budget category, not to mention the more numerous preschools funded by parent fees.[25] The NIEER institute, like Doggett's Washington-based advocacy group, is sustained by the Pew Charitable Trusts.

INEQUALITY OR DIFFERING FAMILY PREFERENCES?

Enrollment rates do vary widely among states, social classes, and ethnic groups. But the answer to the question of which children are disadvantaged by these disparities is not always as predictable as you might expect. Recent studies reveal that many Latino and Asian American parents prefer less institutional forms of child care, and that two-fifths of all employed mothers work odd hours, weekends, or swing or graveyard shifts. We return in Chapter 2 to the question of whether preschool organizations can be flexible enough to match blue-collar parents' highly variable work schedules.

Some enrollment patterns, while troubling, are not surprising. Federal data from the mid-1990s reveal that nationwide almost four-fifths of children age three or four from upper-income families were enrolled in preschool, compared with just 45 percent of children from poor families.[26] The more recent ECLS data indicate that among the poorest fifth of families with young children in California, 23 percent of four-year-olds attended a Head Start preschool and another 26 percent were enrolled in state-subsidized or community-based preschools (totaling 49 percent). In contrast, more than 80 percent of four-year-olds from families in the top fifth of the income distribution attended preschool.[27]

It turns out that many blue-collar and lower middle-class families are feeling the most painful pinch when it comes to preschool access. They often earn too little to pay high fees for a private or nonprofit preschool but too much to qualify for publicly financed enrollment slots. Daphna Bassok at

Stanford and I split participating ECLS families into income deciles: from the poorest one-tenth to the richest one-tenth of all parents included in the national survey. In the poorest decile of *white families*, 65 percent of their four-year-olds had experienced some preschooling before entering kindergarten. This share *fell* to 58 percent among families in the third income decile, those earning about $36,000 yearly. Among families at the median income level (about $42,000), 69 percent of their four-year-olds had attended preschool, and there was 87 percent attendance for children in the richest decile of families.[28]

Disparities across ethnic groups remain stark overall, with unexpected patterns also discovered in recent years. A decade ago, colleagues Susan Holloway and Xiaoyan Liang and I found that African-American families with a working mother were the group most likely to select a preschool for their child, compared with all other ethnic groups; next were non-Latino white families. Comparable Latino families with an employed mother were 21 percent less likely to enroll their children in preschool.[29] The ECLS survey reveals that Latino access did not improve much during the 1990s. Again focusing on California, 59 and 58 percent of black and white four-year-olds attended preschool, compared with just 37 percent of Latino children, a gap that reflects national patterns.[30] A part of these differences stems from lower maternal employment among Latino women, varying education levels, and the availability of family members to provide child care.

Like Latinos, Asian American parents enroll their four-year-olds at comparatively low rates. Just over 34 percent of non-poor Asian families selected a preschool center for their four-year-old prior to kindergarten. Margaret Bridges analyzed Asian youngsters' cognitive proficiencies, assessed early in kindergarten and in English. They performed at high levels overall: their pre-reading skills, for instance, averaged 0.38 of a standard deviation above the average California five-year-old, approximating the increment of cognitive development observed over four months of kindergarten. Proficiency levels even for Asian children from low-income families—including letter and word recognition in English, oral reading comprehension, and knowledge of children's books—resembled levels observed for white children from middle-class families. This, despite Asian children's low preschool enrollment rates, illustrating the power of culturally situated forms of parenting and certain home environments.[31]

A related finding is that preschool organizations remain scarce in middle-class areas, even when compared with poor neighborhoods. This is especially true in states with long histories of targeting early education dollars on low-income families. The resulting pattern forms a U-shaped curve, with preschool supply higher in poor neighborhoods, declining in blue-collar communities, and then rising precipitously among wealthy families. This pattern again reflects the constrained purchasing power of many blue-collar families who remain just above the eligibility cut-offs for publicly financed preschool slots.

When Susanna Loeb, Annelie Strath, and I compiled census data from the 1990s, we discovered that 3.6 preschools operated for every 1,000 children under six years of age in zip codes with median household incomes under $20,000. This figure fell to 2.9 preschools per capita in zip codes with incomes averaging between $30,000 and $45,000, and then rose to 4.5 preschools per capita in affluent zip codes (with incomes over $75,000, all in 1990 dollars).[32] The scarcity of preschool opportunities, in turn, lowers the likelihood that mothers will enter the labor force and thus constrains family income.[33] One important argument made by UPK advocates is that universal access would close this disparity and de-link preschool from welfare programs that blue-collar families aim to avoid.

Organizational Diversity with Uneven Quality

Advocates claim that disparities in preschool quality, beyond basic supply, hit poor children especially hard. Within this framing, decentralized regulation is a principal culprit. The worry is that the state lacks authority to corral, then boost the quality of the wide range of preschools that have sprung up over the past two generations. The uneven quality of nonprofits corresponds to grossly unfair differences in the purchasing power of families, since preschool directors must peg fees, and thus teacher salaries and the quality of facilities, to what parents can afford to pay, a point that workforce expert Marcy Whitebook has long emphasized.

Community preschools serving affluent families can charge high fees in order to attract strong teachers with reasonable wages. But preschools in blue-collar and poor communities typically have lower teacher wages and more problematic working conditions. This pattern is quite clear with for-profit preschools, which typically serve middle-class families. Just 36 percent of this subsector's teachers report having attained more than a two-year college degree, compared with 87 percent of teachers in school-based preschool programs.[34] Sufficient wages and teacher quality can be supported for the one-fourth to one-third of all children who attend publicly subsidized preschool, depending on the state. But UPK advocates rightfully worry about static or falling per-child spending if the early education lobby within the state capital is politically weak.

Stark gaps in preschool quality occasionally make national headlines. Jack Grubman's struggle to win places for his twins in the coveted preschool at the 92nd Street Y in Manhattan led to his criminal indictment. A financial analyst, Grubman concocted a favorable stock rating that boosted the fortunes of his boss, Stanford Weill, at Citicorp. In return Weill made a one million dollar contribution to the Manhattan preschool, which was enough to reserve two slots. How else could Grubman ensure that his daughters would later enter a top kindergarten and elementary school?[35] The 92nd Street Y charges $14,000 for its full-time program—vividly contrasting the often ragged preschools I have visited, from Boston to Tallahassee to San Jose, that charge low fees to ensure a sufficient number of customers. The directors of these programs can only afford to hire 20-something high school graduates, who often merely corral their charges, display uneven social engagement, and offer few learning activities.

ON QUALITY — GOOD NEWS, BAD NEWS

Still, some governments and school districts have made long strides toward equalizing the quality of preschools, setting higher standards, and finding the financing to support competitive salaries. A pair of facts helps to frame the issue of uneven quality. First, the good news. We know that in carefully controlled, high-quality preschools, young children from *poor* families can make distinct gains in early learning and cognitive development. In addition, we are discovering that typical preschools operating in mixed markets–that is, not so controlled and larger in scale—also achieve significant cognitive benefits in some states. The bad news is that the initial beneficial effect of pre-schooling, seen by age five in kindergarten, tends to fade as the child moves into elementary school.

One encouraging finding from our five-year study with Sharon Lynn Kagan and Susanna Loeb, which followed a cohort of poor children from age two to age seven, was that the early boost these children received from steady exposure to preschool continued to give them a modest leg-up in elementary school, compared with youngsters who had never gone to preschool. Our results are consistent with earlier findings from the Chicago public schools: Arthur J. Reynolds found sustained gains among young children who had attended city-wide Child-Parent Centers, which offered preschooling of reasonable quality with strong parent participation, including home visits with mothers.[36]

The bad news is that preschools (given current quality levels) have been found to exert only modest benefits for children from *middle-class* homes. This disappointing finding comes from the National Institute of Child Health and Human Development's (NICHD) long-term study of child care. My own work with Bridges, Loeb, and Russ Rumberger has detailed much smaller cognitive benefits from preschool exposure for middle-class children than for poor children. Moreover, children of affluent families who spent long hours in preschool displayed markedly slower rates of social development than their counterparts who remained at home with a parent during part of each day. (This will be discussed further in Chapter 6.)

We don't know whether the preschool organization could exert more sustainable effects, and advance children's social development, if average quality levels climbed, nor do we know which specific ingredients of quality are most apt to elevate children's early learning. The emphasis has shifted in some policy circles away from unabated expansion to a more determined focus on quality improvement. As Senator Edward Kennedy's education adviser, Roberto Rodriguez, said in a Washington interview, "Now that we're up over 60 percent (of four-year-olds) enrolled, quality becomes *the* issue."

Once we frame the pressing problem in terms of uneven quality, additional questions come into focus: What's the overall level of preschool quality in America? To what extent are preschools of varying quality distributed unfairly across diverse communities? What investments would raise preschool quality most cost-effectively: mandating higher teacher credentials? lowering class size? structuring classroom activities in more invigorating ways?

HOW GOOD IS THE AVERAGE PRESCHOOL?

Parents' ever-present worries over child care spiked when the media widely covered a dismal finding from a 1995 study of preschool centers. The study was spread across four states and was headed by University of Colorado economist Suzanne Helburn. After observing classrooms in some four hundred programs nationwide, this research group concluded that about two-thirds were of poor to mediocre quality.[37] This inference stemmed largely from the use of one standard measurement tool, although the team also found the education levels of teachers and classroom aides to be uneven.

NICHD's longitudinal study did not reach such dire conclusions, however. Beyond the cognitive benefits of being exposed to preschool, it concluded that incremental gains in quality did not yield much of an additional punch, at least not for middle-class children. When my research group observed classrooms in 166 preschools serving low-income families in California, Connecticut, and Florida, we found wide variation in teacher training levels, in child-to-teacher ratios, and in how thoughtfully learning activities were structured in classrooms. Mean differences in quality also surfaced among states.[38] But we found that quality, on average, was not as dismally low as the Colorado study portrayed it. Still, the wide variations help to explain why preschool for middle-class children yields such disappointing benefits overall and tends to slow social development.

The extent to which preschool quality is maldistributed, favoring children in well-off neighborhoods, remains unclear. When it comes to local Head Start programs, the issue of quality continues to be hotly debated in Washington, D.C., given the disappointing results of evaluations in recent years. Democratic leaders like Kennedy and Senator Christopher Dodd have agreed that stronger regulation and quality assessment are required, prompting legislation that would require state education departments to set learning standards and test *all* preschoolers, not only those attending Head Start. "I've gone to some Head Starts called 'model programs,' and they just make me angry," said Grace Reef, Senator Dodd's top adviser. "They are just doing child care. You have people who are barely literate in front of the classroom. I don't mean moving to instruction with a No. 2 pencil. You can do learning through play, but the staff have to be taught how. I have seen writing centers in a dark corner (of the classroom) with a few pieces of paper and ragged books."

Reef also wanted to "give priority to programs that are performing well. If we raise the bar, they will have to meet higher standards." This approach lends support to the junior Bush administration's aggressive push to implement a national assessment system for children enrolled in Head Start, which would focus exclusively on oral vocabulary and letter recognition (preferably in English). I will return to this highly centralized specification of what young children should be learning. Another high-ranking aide on Capitol Hill complained that the early education lobbies "feel we're pushing kindergarten down onto three- and four-year-olds. . . . if it's not learning-through-play, it will stress them out." Indeed, liberal-humanist ideals are being challenged, even by liberal Democrats, when they advance this narrower emphasis on pre-literacy skills.

The new UPK advocates have gained little traction in Washington, however, in part because their preoccupation with subsidizing preschool for the middle class limits their interest in focusing resources on the poor. Washington over the past half-century has concentrated on the development of children from low-income families, and has viewed child care as a necessary foundation for encouraging mothers to work outside the home.

Congressional staffers do bemoan the lack of tidier preschool systems out in the states, and this takes us back to Reiner's original conception of the problem. Kennedy's adviser Roberto Rodriguez said: "Most states have a pretty evolved system for K-12. My boss believes that we need a similar system for all young children. A lot of people see the logic of No Child Left Behind moving into the (early education) realm." This view echoes Doggett's claim that UPK should be framed as the new cornerstone for NCLB-like accountability, helping to raise children's test scores. Democrats Dodd and Kennedy want to nudge states to require that preschool teachers obtain bachelor's degrees, as one way to professionalize state programs. When I asked Grace Reef if she thought this one feature of quality would boost children's growth curves, she said: "I think the evidence is mixed. (But) my boss believes that people self-select into community colleges versus four-year colleges." Rodriguez nodded when I asked the question: "I know, the evidence isn't consistent."

Weak State Involvement

A third conception of the problem, stemming from worries over unequal access to and uneven quality of preschools, is that the weakness of government involvement simply perpetuates these symptoms. But what organizational mechanisms would allow government—be it from Washington or from state capitals—to effectively advance supply and quality? More aggressive government involvement could mean stronger funding, higher quality standards and better regulation, or greater specification of what young children should be learning and how. Most of these remedies currently flow from a Weberian, NCLB-like conception of regulation from the center. Yet on the ground the preschool world remains highly decentralized and, some would argue, responsive to parents' and early educators' diverse preferences.

Some respected developmentalists today are promoting more standardized "learning guidelines" or formal curricular standards, along with regular testing of three- and four-year-olds. Deborah Phillips, chair of the psychology department at Georgetown University, said:

> I have been very sensitized by George Miller (Democratic congressman and coauthor of the No Child Left Behind Act). He has the Richmond (California) school district, and he tries to spend time in his schools. He comes away thinking that a lot of kids aren't being taught anything. To the extent this (accountability) language is code for children needing to be at grade level, I'm supportive of testing kids. Sure there are risks with formal curriculum. But I don't want to get back to where we were 10 years ago.[39]

Phillips later sought to clarify her position: "It's a moving train (the UPK movement) . . . let's get on it to be sure the testing is done right, (that) the curriculum isn't too narrow."

COMPETING NOTIONS OF STATE INVOLVEMENT

Many good liberals, impatient with the nation's mixed market of preschools, now bank on central government's capacity to regulate in ways that will advance children's development. But the theory of action specifying how centralized action would equalize availability and raise kids' growth curves remains hazy. These governance issues might begin with the question of *who* runs pre-school organizations on the ground—be it schools, CBOs, for-profit firms, or licensed homes? Then, what's the *state's* role in channeling dollars, up-grading the workforce, and providing local incentives for expansion with equity and for quality gains?

The role of the state differs among the initial handful of states implementing UPK schemes. New Jersey, for instance, promotes high educational credentials for teachers and plenty of in-service training. Georgia mandates that local programs pick from among several state-approved curricular packages, similar to how local public schools pick from among several state-approved textbooks.

The organizational pluralism that marks the early education sector—where a majority of preschools are run by nonprofits in most states—invites discussion of how to improve *decentralized* governance and local strategies for addressing the problems of access and quality. The sector originally grew from family welfare programs; in the early twentieth century, the original Children's Bureau within the federal government encouraged states to set regulatory standards for child care centers, both to ensure the basic safety of young children and to ration scarce public dollars for early care and education.

In the 1970s, children's advocates pushed the Congress to dictate quality standards for all centers and preschools, a position which even the Carter White House could not agree to. Still, concerns over quality have pushed Head Start administrators in Washington—under both Clinton and Bush II—to centrally specify what all young children should be learning. This is a tantalizing possibility for strong-state liberals as well, who seek the political will to advance heftier quality standards.

The debate between strong-state advocates and those favoring more decentralized strategies of organizational change mirrors the perennial contest over public school governance. The NCLB, in line with earlier state efforts at centralized accountability, has focused on specifying intended learning outcomes ("standards"), state-approved textbooks, more frequent testing, and the onset of "teacher-proof" curricular packages. On the other hand, scholars like Stanford's Anthony Bryk have argued that decentralizing who controls each local school—what he calls *democratic localism*—will help to drive community-based accountability and change.[40] In Chicago, for example, Bryk traced how a radical shift in school governance—allowing community members to elect local school councils, who then hire and fire principals—has led to pressure on educators to improve quality. This approach resembles direct *market accountability*, where parents can shop amongst a mix of public and private organizations, expressing demand for their preferred philosophy of child rearing and the forms of quality which they find most important.

GOVERNMENT'S SUCCESS IN RAISING QUALITY

The new advocates typically assume that to boost quality a more centralized system is required. Yet some states have raised and sustained high-quality preschools with strong standards and little micro-management. A study led by Phillips over a decade ago found moderate to high levels of quality inside preschools situated in poor communities, when compared with programs in middle-class areas, for so-called *structural* benchmarks such as the average number of youngsters per classroom, the ratio of children per adults, and the level of preservice training among teachers and aides. Yet in the responsiveness of classroom staff and quality of social interactions with children (*process* indicators), preschools in low-income communities did lag behind.[41]

Similarly, my research team's survey of 170 preschool directors in poor to middle-class areas of California found that those programs receiving higher public subsidies (as a share of their budget)—and thus subject to tighter quality regulations—tended to be better.[42] A second study with Kagan and Loeb found sizable differences in quality between programs located in California and those in Florida in terms of teacher education levels, the structuring of classroom tasks, and the character of child-teacher interaction. We also found high-quality programs in Santa Clara County, California—and steeper developmental trajectories for young children—even though they were located in poor communities. County agencies and local foundations had long invested in early education and had made efforts to improve quality.[43] I have called this *selective coupling*—where government regulates selectively to advance equity and quality while advancing diverse organizational forms responsive to local families.[44]

The proponents of UPK point out that for many middle-class families, preschool quality lags; this is often the case for small nonprofits or for-profit preschool franchises that charge low fees to retain their clientele. Their revenues are sufficient only to support less qualified teachers and larger classrooms. And state governments have often been ineffective in easing this situation, beyond improving the quality of preschools in poor communities. Susanna Loeb and I endeavored to explain the wide variation in teachers' education and wage levels nationally, and we found that the bulk of the variance stemmed from economic and demographic attributes of families who were from vastly different neighborhoods. Only a small slice of the variation in quality could be tied to differences in the states' quality regulation or spending levels. If state governments *were* effective in raising the average quality of preschools, most of the variation would be attributable to state-level factors, rather than local demographic and market forces.[45] The UPK advocates are right on one point: state governments have a long road to travel before their efforts effectively reduce disparities in access and quality.

The centralized regulation of life inside preschools carries worrisome risks, not unlike how the bureaucratic control of health care often serves to regiment the work of doctors and diminish the doctor-patient relationship. To attract families not well served by current programs, new preschools need to be inviting and responsive to local tastes. It's not clear how a highly centralized UPK system, run from a state capital or shaped by federal rules, would nourish the local roots of human-scale preschools. As historian Barbara Beatty points out, advocates have realized greater success when they advance public financing of preschools that are run flexibly by local organizations, rather than try to dictate what children must learn or what form of pedagogy must be followed.[46]

The discourse of school accountability permeates the Florida governance model for preschool. Governor Jeb Bush signed legislation to implement UPK stemming from a 2002 ballot initiative, which included centralized dictates that set low quality standards, in terms of teacher qualification, for example. One advocate told me: "They (Governor Bush's policy advisers) don't see child care as needing high quality." The legislation aimed at bringing local centers in line with the accountability demands of NCLB, as advanced by Jeb's brother in Washington. It also put an emphasis on developing pre-literacy and school readiness skills in preschool classrooms. The academic skills of participating children would be assessed in kindergarten, and preschools would share the responsibility of raising five-year-olds' test scores. If scores don't go up, the preschool would be sanctioned—a perverse incentive for programs to move away from serving poor families.

"It's a dangerous precedent, linking pre-k funding to kindergarten outcomes," said Mark Ginsberg, executive director of the National Association for the Education of Young Children. "It's pretty scary." A related fear is that better qualified teachers would flock from sanctioned preschools and into centers located in better-off suburbs.

Articulate UPK proponents like California's Hill-Scott promise that the movement will depart from the course taken by its predecessors, who pushed for universal kindergarten. They too argued for warm, human-scale institutions filled with engaging and developmentally appropriate tasks. The classrooms of real schools, however, are not like this. When Berkeley graduate student Alejandra Livas interviewed kindergarten teachers in Los Angeles, one told her: "They're having to sit and do so much paper and pencil stuff. We have these really rigorous pacing guides . . . they're all over us with a whip. At the beginning of the year . . . they're chewing their nails and they're crying, wetting pants . . . I mean just really stressed out. The stress level is so high with this academic focus."[47]

What progressive reformers have been slow to learn is that, once government gains broad authority and invokes its regulatory habits, it's tempting for advocates, governors, and legislators to intensify their Weberian ways, simplifying and standardizing what children are to learn and how social relations are to be regimented inside classrooms. And when public funds are scarce or declining, even progressives will push for stronger accountability and ever more frequent testing of a narrowing range of skills. The mechanics of government structure come to dominate what, and through what social relations, children are to learn, regardless of how virtuous policymakers' aims may be.

Framing the problems of early education as a lack of state regulation is surprising on a final score. The original ideals of preschooling stemmed from the likes of *local* reformers, like Mrs. Thurston in nineteenth-century Boston or later Dorothy Day, at the turn of the twentieth century in Chicago. Their disciples, such as Betty Cohen and Patty Siegel, gave birth to California's child care movement in their Berkeley living rooms, opening their doors in the 1970s as collective centers or firing up hotlines to advise other parents about child care options. The original Head Start summer programs began in the South, run by a network of community activists and funded by the Great Society's Office of Economic Opportunity. The explicit political strategy of its White House architects such as Richard Boone and Sargent Shriver was to create small-scale enterprises that would spark democratic participation and create jobs inside poor neighborhoods; they sought to minimize connections to a bureaucratic, homogenizing central government.[48]

Today's advocates of UPK see a political opening, however, if they can link their cause to the wider pressure for school accountability. Reiner assured a group of Silicon Valley business leaders that universal preschool is "the best way to fix the K-12 system, this is truly no child left behind."[49] By promising higher test scores, UPK advocates have brought governors into the chorus. The feminist ideals and child care movement that once challenged the bureaucratic forms and cultural hegemony of the central state—a critique of Big Government at times overstated—are being sucked into the formal political apparatus. Whether the benefits accruing to additional children from more accessible preschool will outweigh the costs—diminishing the involvement of neighborhood organizations and parents, and narrowing expectations for young children's development—is the question.

How to Create a Movement

This brings us to the advocates' problem of how to build the political will necessary to create a new institution for young children. Civic discourse alone—the public mulling over of the problems facing young children—does not remedy these pressing worries. Instead, institution building requires clear policy victories in the state's dominion. Doing so requires intense, well-focused political organizing. But it's also possible that how the problem is framed, and how the new role for schooling is expanded, is driven by political tactics, rather than from careful reflection over how parents and communities want to raise their children.

To understand why UPK has arisen with such force at this time, and why policymakers have veered toward academic skilling and centralized standardization, it's important to see how the key advocates have altered the conception of the problem, arriving at a crisply defined remedy. The problem, as national advocate Doggett sees it, is that preschool is "the unfinished part of school reform." Once education reformers embraced universal preschool—pushing grade school down one or two additional grades—the picture would be complete. Indeed, the very crispness of the remedy—and its growing appeal among public school interest groups—has come to shape how the problem is defined.

This straight-and-narrow party line stems partly from changes in the funding environment in which children's advocates have operated since the late 1990s. Major foundations—most notably the Pew Charitable Trusts and, in the San Francisco Bay Area, the Packard Foundation—made the strategic decision to shift their focus from improving child care options per se, and instead to put all their eggs in the UPK basket. The shift was motivated in part by shrinking endowments from losses in the stock market (including the collapse of Hewlett-Packard's stock). Foundation officials also believed that welfare reform had brought massive infusions of new child care funding, but had led to few gains in local infrastructure, thanks to the emphasis on vouchers. The rise of school accountability—ordained at the federal level with NCLB in 2002—meant that strong education constituencies could be more easily convinced of the utility of preschool in raising children's test scores.

Preschool enrollments had climbed dramatically in Georgia, Oklahoma, and North Carolina by the late 1990s, following legislation promising universal access. New York had rhetorically voiced support for UPK, and Los Angeles County's decision to set aside $600 million for universal preschool put California on the reform map. These developments buoyed UPK advocates, state policymakers, and scholars, who began to come together with the two influential foundations.

Earlier, Pew had funded policy efforts to help states move toward standards-based reform in public education. This effort had been led by Robert Schwartz, who had earlier shaped Governor Michael Dukakis's education accountability efforts in Massachusetts. Director Sue Urahn at Pew in Philadelphia convinced her board in 2001 to focus exclusively on universal preschool. I asked Urahn why Pew had suddenly shifted their portfolio into the UPK cause. "The board (of directors) had very little appetite to spend more on K-12 education," she said. "I was reading the research and findings that the impact was quite significant. We had a research base, an empirical reason to go in. We had public opinion polling data showing a rising comfort level, and state policymakers that were wanting to make a difference."[50]

Urahn artfully recast the nature of the problem, echoing the logic of advocate Doggett. "If you reframed it around an argument about education and not child care, you would be able to bring a whole new weight to it," she said, along "with the states' accountability agenda, it could be reframed as an education solution."

Pew began to pump funding into a variety of organizations, along with a handful of allied scholars who were eager to publish supportive evidence (striking in its empirical tidiness) and ready to appear at legislative hearings in targeted states. Urahn even funded two different associations of education reporters to talk up preschool issues and sniff out appealing story lines and hired polling firms to assess public support and strategize over ballot initiatives in Florida and California.

At the same time, Lois Salisbury, an unstoppable lawyer and children's advocate, joined the Packard Foundation in California. Her board had long backed advocacy and research on a variety of child care and family-support options. Salisbury convinced them instead to throw their lot behind the UPK cause, drawing a sharp line between (illegitimate) child care and (legitimate) preschool. She created Preschool for All, based in Oakland, which lobbies for UPK in Sacramento and has advanced two versions of Reiner's ballot initiatives. Throughout the state, Salisbury began to fund education and children's groups to get behind the party line. At one point Salisbury sent around a list of sixty-four organizations, from the National Council for La Raza to the California School Boards Association to my own research center—all funded to study dimensions of, or simply advocate for, universal preschool.[51]

The not-so-hidden message was to get with the program—"to mobilize a broad alliance of organizations and constituencies committed to ensuring preschool for all." Otherwise, don't expect support from the Packard Foundation. One advocate told me, off the record: "you know, Lois has created this fear in the community. We can't afford to raise questions about universal preschool." Another said to me: "Look, Bruce, you're a tenured professor, but my business may rely on my relationship with Lois." A foundation that once supported civic debate and research on a variety of child care options was now running a well-oiled, military-like campaign.

Only a small portion of these various education and children's lobbies have any members at the grassroots, with the notable exception of the teacher unions and the National Association for the Education of Young Children

(NAEYC), which casts a critical eye on UPK. Most of the groups that are being herded down the universal preschool path are small, left of center, and staffed by well-credentialed, sometimes well-placed policy analysts and lobbyists.[52] By mid-decade, these two foundations, at times backed by smaller benefactors, had pulled together the labor unions, local school boards, children's activists, sympathetic scholars, and media associations—all focused on the UPK policy remedy. Few public interest advocates talked any longer about older conceptions of the problem: a lack of child care options, few incentives for employers to help families balance work and child rearing, or the underlying issue of family poverty and income inequality across America. No one was funding this kind of thinking, this form of political action.

*   *   *

We will later visit two states—Oklahoma and California—to examine how the problem of young children is defined and how universal preschool is taking hold locally. But first we will dig deeper, examining how the contemporary debate flows from long-running historical currents. These broad and powerful forces, stretching back five centuries, more fully answer the question of why UPK now.

CHAPTER TWO

The Historical Contest over Early Education

The intensifying push for universal preschool stems not just from the contemporary problems that beset young children. Conflicting historical forces are at play as well. These deep-running currents are powered by both contested ideals and material interests. At the upstream source of today's debate over early education—akin to strident arguments that arose during the Enlightenment—are competing notions of young children's inner nature and potential, and how best to raise them.

This chapter examines four flows that have energized and challenged children's advocates, governments, and early educators over the past century. We first examine the long disagreement of Western philosophers and educators over whether *liberal-humanist* ideals truly capture the inner character of young children, how they "naturally" grow and learn, and whether state-crafted schooling is the best place for socializing them. Romantic developmentalists over the past five centuries—from Comenius and Locke to Froebel, Gesell, and Vygotsky—have viewed the young child as bursting with natural curiosity or multifaceted potential for engaging with her or his social environment. However, *institutional liberals*, from Horace Mann forward, have believed more in the power of universal organizations such as common schools to raise and instruct young children, to civilize our offspring for shared membership in the nation-state.

Today we can see the logic of specific academic *skilling*, didactic instruction, and testing seeping down into preschools. This fairly recent form is gaining popular legitimacy, promising to get children "ready for school." As counterpoint to the liberal-humanist and the skilling frames, others favor raising children with an eye toward their own *cultural and linguistic community* and in closer partnership with parents, rather than merely fitting youngsters into America's melting pot. We will examine the roots of each idealized view of child development.

The rise of preschooling is entangled with a second historical force: rising public concern over the *family's well-being* and a revolutionary change in *mothers' economic roles*. Women's ongoing struggle for a more fulfilling balance between career and child rearing has continued to shape both public and private investment in child care, and affected the spread of preschools. But does the sudden popularity of universal preschool widen or narrow how we think about the vitality of families, as opposed to the health of big public institutions?

A third historical force helps to explain why children's advocates are gaining traction, and considerable heat, over the UPK policy remedy. Unlike Head Start for the poor or child care vouchers for blue-collar parents, the idea of public schooling of three- and four-year-olds is proving attractive to politicians and educators as they try to make schools more accountable and as education interests search for new funding. This new formula—pieced together by UPK advocates since the late 1990s—advances *government's own legitimacy* by keeping policymakers in the middle of the wider debate over school reform.

These three forces—the competing ideals regarding young children, the family's economic dynamic and the aspirations of mothers, and the state's rising interest in early education—have fed a fourth, more recent, historical force. This involves the democratization of how early care and education are organized—at the neighborhood level—across the nation, including the over 113,000 preschool centers that operate nationwide, which are run by the kaleidoscopic array of community organizations introduced in Chapter 1. These little organizations make for a political economy of activists and institutions that remains as a highly decentralized counterweight to the incursion of public school interest groups in the contest over who raises young children.

Contested Ideals — Constructing the Nature of Young Children

The Educational Testing Service (ETS)—the people who bring you standardized tests in the public schools and the SAT for college-bound kids—recently published a report entitled *An Uneven Start: Indicators of Inequality in School Readiness*. It remains a useful piece, replete with data and details on how children from poor families are well behind as they enter kindergarten when it comes to early language and pre-reading skills. The ETS analysts defined "readiness" as the young child's ability to recognize letters and numbers and the phonemic utterances used by youngsters in sounding-out words, as well as reading alongside parents.[1]

The federal statistics office which has assessed thousands of kindergartners has sanctioned other measures for gauging school readiness, including attributes like "sits still and alert"; "tells needs and thoughts"; and "follows directions."[2] It's certainly reassuring to know that someone sitting in Washington has gleaned the one best way to socialize America's diverse toddlers. But I'm getting off track.

It's the philosophical roots of the ETS study that are most intriguing, departing sharply from the Enlightenment discourse over the inner nature of young children and how their environments might be enriched. ETS's brave new world sees children as members of a nation that suffers from low literacy: "we see a distribution of skills among 5-year-olds . . . that mirrors the distribution of skills in our adult population," writes an ETS vice president in the report's preface. Young children are no longer members of families or communities; they are creatures to be readied for the economy.

The report's author, Richard Coley, frames his research question by highlighting the Bush administration's recent focus on "increasing the academic content of early childhood programs such as Head Start." He continues: "The rationale for interest in school readiness lies in the evidence from various studies that greater school readiness is associated with subsequent school success." He then sets out to detail "indicators of precisely which students are at-risk with respect to school readiness." Alas, it's mainly poor children and their parents who display these "risk factors," as if afflicted by some terrible threat to public health on the outer shoals of civilized society.

Indeed, acquiring these skills is important. But remarkably, the philosophical starting point assumed by these analysts is that children bring to the preschool very little, and they obsess on but one slice of children's complex development. The likes of Friedrich Froebel—the father of the Euro-American kindergarten movement that began nearly two centuries ago—would be shocked to see the shriveled remains of his once-robust humanistic ideals for childhood and early learning.

THE PHILOSOPHICAL ROOTS OF CHILD DEVELOPMENT

Froebel (1782–1852) was a German naturalist and romantic who claimed that young children would blossom if raised under the right conditions. He followed in the footsteps of the liberal-humanists philosophers Jean-Jacques Rousseau and Johann Pestalozzi in his views on the child's developmental potential. These earlier thinkers had written to the budding European middle class during the two prior generations. Pestalozzi even named his first son Jean-Jacques and raised him according to Rousseau's admonition of letting natural developmental processes unfold. (At age eleven the boy still could neither read nor write.)

In turn, Froebel studied Pestalozzi's active-learning techniques with young children, at one point living with three pupils in isolation to experiment with naturalistic pedagogy. Froebel had earlier studied botany and horticulture and taken up geology at the Royal Museum of Berlin. Eventually he came to argue that in nature there is "one law of development," which he defined as unity.[3] This concept built on the Enlightenment ideal that the child emerges holistically across various domains of development.

He created his first early learning program for young children in Blankenburg in 1837, which he called "the institution for fostering small children"; later he arrived at the more evocative term "kindergarten." He wrote: "Growing plants are cultivated in accordance with Nature's laws, so here in our child garden, our kindergarten, shall be the noblest of all growing things. . . . " He advocated creating a distinct organization that would serve young children. He believed that all youngsters would blossom in rather uniform ways if nurtured at home and in kindergarten according to his pedagogical principles.

Froebel's *garden* metaphor is reflected in the belief of contemporary developmentalists that social environments should be formed that allow children's natural curiosity and potentials to come forth, aided by their hardwired biological stages of development and their intrinsic motivation to explore. The parallel term *culture*, which stems from ancient Latin, means a medium or process that optimizes the growth of crops or animals, as emphasized by the sociologist Raymond Williams.[4] "From the beginning, the core idea of culture as a process of helping things grow was combined with a general theory on how to promote growth," according to psychologist Michael Cole.[5] By the sixteenth century, the notion of culture was being applied to the nurturing of children; later it took on social-class connotations, as in describing a person as "cultured" or "cultivated." John Stuart Mill talked of the cultivated mind—seemingly detached from the person—as one that has been taught "to exercise its facilities . . . to which the fountains of knowledge have been opened up."[6]

Froebel was keenly interested in what today we call cognitive growth. Like Pestalozzi, Froebel postulated that nurturing young children's mental faculties and curiosity for learning was most essential, not imparting bits of knowledge. He created tasks for children based on twenty "gifts" and occupations, stemming from folk crafts and geometric concepts. To begin understanding the unity and symmetry that he believed characterized natural materials, the children became familiar with balls; by age four or five, they explored the properties of prisms, squares, cubes, and trapezoids. But these explorations were offered in the context of play, again building from Froebel's postulate that young children are naturally inquisitive. Other tasks for mothers and kindergarten teachers included sewing exercises, sketching geometric shapes on flat surfaces, even examining sticks and cubes of measured lengths and proportions.

Children were to spend lots of time outside, discovering how materials and shapes helped to form the natural world, and were characteristic of holistic ideals. Play was serious work for Froebel. He wrote: "Without rational conscious guidance, childish activity degenerates into aimless play, instead of preparing for those tasks of life to which (children are) destined to lead."[7] Countering the rise of specialists and the growing branches of scientific knowledge from the late eighteenth century forward, idealists like Kant and Fichte inspired German educators to focus on the unity and interdependent forces of the natural world, not the rationally engineered, commercializing world of west Europe. They, along with Hegel, argued that the human spirit, awakened by the unifying elements of nature, would advance society to more idealized states. Play must be structured for children, to activate their appreciation of the organic world. "Play is the purest, most spiritual activity of man at this stage . . . of the inner hidden natural life in man and all things," Froebel said. And play must be engaged in "thoroughly . . . with self-active determination, for the welfare of himself and others."[8]

Despite the rising social foment in Germany, in 1848 Froebel and his fellow educators opened forty-four new kindergartens. Froebel's more radical nephew, Karl, along with Karl's wife Johanna, led the charge in Hamburg through the Women's Education Society. But in 1851, partially in reaction to a failed revolution, the German government cracked down on the kindergarten movement, claiming its ideals to be subversive, even atheistic. Almost a generation had passed since the earlier Prussian regime had urged parents to enroll their children only in government-run schools.

KINDERGARTEN VERSUS RATIONALIZED SCHOOLING

The philosophers who preceded Froebel had expressed mixed feelings toward the idea of nurturing young children within formal organizations. In the early seventeenth century, the Moravian scholar and bishop Johann Comenius questioned how one teacher could thoughtfully attend to a classroom filled with children under six years of age. John Locke agreed, writing in 1693 that formal schools hosted "roughness and ill breeding." He believed that instead, virtue and strong character, "harder to be got than a knowledge of the world," should be advanced by parents inside the home. Locke opposed corporal punishment of young children, urging parents to reason with them, to build from their desire for "esteem" and their avoidance of "disgrace."[9]

Locke expressed optimism over what he saw as youngsters' natural curiosity and their desire to understand social norms, countering the deep-seated Calvinist pessimism toward the alleged dark side and in-born will of toddlers and even infants. Locke infused neoclassical liberal ideals into his assumption that children were born as innocent, well-intentioned creatures that would naturally blossom under the right conditions. He emphasized the child's capacity to reason, to articulate his or her own interests (perhaps an early version of "use your words").

Locke, Froebel, and later Arnold Gesell shared the view that how children emerged or were purposefully socialized was situated within a broader liberal conviction. They all believed that the individual learns how to become autonomous from adults yet with (some) institutional constraints, be they a doting mother, a religious doctrine, or "backward" village traditions. Indeed, Western notions of child development early on became a projective exercise for imagining how the individual is constructed and positioned relative to social collectives, large and small.

Founded on a belief in the individual's self-determined interests, modernizing polities were to help power free markets and democratic social relations. They required autonomous individuals who could think for themselves. "The development of individuals as well as nations progressed from the uncivilized to civilized, immature to mature, and undeveloped to developed," as the University of Wisconsin's Marianne Block puts it. "These discourses became embedded gradually within the reasoning of care and child-rearing, schooling for modern childhood."[10]

If you are skeptically thinking that this is all dusty history, listen to the contemporary liberal-humanist Constance Kamii: "Constructivist theory is embedded in a psychology of individualism. Independent thinking is valued over conformity and the acquisition of culturally transmitted knowledge . . . to envision new possibilities of understanding and acting."[11] As the classroom manual from the National Association for the Education of Young Children emphasizes, "An essential component of developmentally appropriate practice . . . (is) child-initiated, child-directed, teacher-supported play."[12] This perspective has deep roots in Western thought. "This emphasis on play carries a long tradition in early education, beginning with the ancient Greek, Aristotle, and progressing in modern times through Froebel," in the words of developmentalist Rheta DeVries.[13]

KINDERGARTEN COMES TO AMERICA

The ideas of German and Swiss romantics like Froebel quickly took root in the United States, not only in Boston but also in the Midwest. A Hamburg émigré, Margarethe Meyer, opened the first known kindergarten in Amer-

THE HISTORICAL CONTEST OVER EARLY EDUCATION 39

ica, located in Watertown, Wisconsin, in 1856. German was the language of instruction.

Elizabeth Peabody opened the first English-medium kindergarten in 1860, located in Boston; she emphasized that this human-scale institution would *not* resemble a school but was a very different kind of setting: here, the teacher "should always play with the children." Most early kindergartens served children from better-off families; not until the early twentieth century would town governments and public schools begin to finance wider expansion.[14] Peabody opposed the teaching of academic subjects in the second edition of her *Kindergarten Guide* in 1877. Teachers were to move from children's "spontaneous" and "natural" actions, "genially directing it to a more beautiful effect than it can attain when left to itself."[15] This approach presaged the notion of scaffolding-up from the child's in-born curiosity and desire to learn, to make sense of his or her environment.

The 1876 Centennial Exhibition in Philadelphia included a kindergarten exhibit, publicized by the companies that sold products to the fledgling kinder industry. About 7 percent of all five year-olds were attending kindergarten by 1900, rising to one-fifth in 1950. In 1970, only about 60 percent of the nation's five-year-olds were enrolled in kindergarten, but the enrollment rate rose to 94 percent by 2000. Just over half of all kindergartners attend a full-day program today, with rates ranging from 82 percent in the South to 31 percent in the western states.[16]

As the kindergarten was absorbed into the public schools, its liberal-humanist ideals and the creative practices devised by Froebel and his descendants began to fade. In the 1880s Peabody spoke out against public takeovers of "charity kindergartens," the community programs for five-year-olds in poor sections of industrializing cities. She expressed a "great dislike of institutional life" and argued that "the business character of superintendents had fallen below the philanthropic which should always preside over education." Peabody added that public schools had "deteriorated in spirit while improving in form."[17]

Peabody's fears proved to be well founded. Soon Massachusetts leaders were struggling with how to incorporate the complicated Froebelian kindergarten into a rationalizing public school system, with civic leaders and school administrators eager to follow the industrial model.[18] Kindergarten classes were sucked into streamlined school systems during the first half of the twentieth century, becoming yet another grade level, plugging into elementary school curricula and staffed by teachers adorned with higher credentials. Teachers' home visits and warm relationships with parents gave way to professionals encased in classrooms, just like *real* teachers.[19]

Still, since first-grade teachers in the early twentieth century complained that kindergarten graduates didn't know how to pay attention and be silent, and demanded more attention from the teacher, according to historian Larry Cuban, traditional classroom routines and curricula were pressed down into the kindergarten.[20] As the field of child study took hold in the academy, behavioral psychologists began to press the importance of children's forming "good habits" rather than character. IQ tests and readiness tests were introduced; tracking children by "ability" levels also percolated down into the new, lean and mean kindergarten.

Today, as Froebel spins in his grave, UPK advocates rejoice. The Washington-based lobby Preschool Now emails pithy quotes and news stories out to advocates and early educators around the country. One recent item, from a public relations specialist at Arizona's Washington School District, reads: "Kindergarten today is more like what first grade used to be. It used to be where kids came and got used to being in a classroom. Now, there are very stringent academic standards that children must master." When Berkeley graduate student Jennifer Russell traveled across California in 2003, asking kindergarten teachers whether they were feeling the school accountability movement, one teacher told her: "It has taken a lot of the fun out of the kindergarten experience, for the teachers and the parents and the children . . . not being able to teach the other subjects. Not having enough music, not having time to do as much art as we used to, [or] as much interaction, dramatic play, children playing together."[21]

THE LIBERAL-HUMANIST BOUNDS OF "CHILD STUDY"

Historian Steven Mintz reminds us that currents of social history don't always flow unabated in straight lines, down well-worn channels. At times unexpected forces divert these streams, even feeding countervailing rivulets. The formalization of kindergarten was emblematic of a modernizing society that was bent on rationalizing institutions run by professional experts and regulated by efficiency-minded officials. In a similar development, public health advocates in the late nineteenth century had spurred government to build huge hospitals. In the twentieth century, the Great Depression and Keynesian policies led to centralized management of the economy. And by the 1950s Clark Kerr and his fellow progressives would build gargantuan "multiversities." In Mintz's words, "new institutions were being created to ensure that children's upbringing took place in carefully calibrated steps corresponding to their developing capacities."[22]

Even so, unanticipated forces were pushing back on this formalization of economic and social life in America. The education levels of women had been rising steadily throughout the nineteenth century. One historical factoid remains startling: in 1700 just one-third of American women could sign their name; by 1900 this share had risen to two-thirds. As the middling commercial and artisan classes expanded and America's industrial transformation intensified in the late nineteenth century, birth rates were falling.

A growing class of mothers now had both time and literacy to read child-rearing guides published by the disciples of Froebel and Locke, the nation's premier generation of parenting experts, who favored careful engineering of early childhood. They included the likes of pediatrician L. Emmett Holt, who urged in an 1894 book that mothers establish feeding schedules for infants in order to inculcate regular habits; he even advised taping stiff splints on babies' elbows to discourage thumb sucking.[23] So, as education leaders began to back more regimented kindergartens, other experts promoted universal guidelines for child rearing to receptive middle-class mothers.

Another cross-current was a rising interest in how young children developed cognitive and social skills, which were now seen as more complex than earlier experts had assumed. The child study movement was fundamentally an offshoot of American psychology, replete with its affection for scientific assessment of the individual child's evolving proficiencies, diagnosis of maladies, and establishment of "normal" rates of maturation. It involved close observation of infants and toddlers in pristine laboratories, where all kinds of body movements, behaviors, and task performances were carefully recorded and categorized. The assumption that all children hold universal capacities and move through hardwired stages of biological development, a notion central to liberal-humanist thinking, was now awarded scientific legitimacy. And these experts saw many children as being in danger (at risk) of lagging behind normal rates of development.

America's new experts were quite comfortable with the philosophical principles of Froebel, Pestalozzi, Locke, and their ilk. "The most fundamental tenet of progressivism," as seen by contemporary philosopher Kieran Egan, "is that to educate children effectively it is vital to attend to children's nature, and particularly to their modes of learning and stages of development. The psychologist exposes the nature of students' learning . . . and the practitioner must make teaching methods and curricula in accord with what science has exposed."[24] The counterpoint, still popular at the close of the nineteenth century, emphasized the primitive appetites of infants and toddlers and how these creatures needed to acquire the habits and routines that well-adjusted adults displayed. The progressive, now scientific field of child study would bolster the fight against "the vicious system of rote learning," in the words of modernizer Herbert Spencer.[25]

One early, large-scale assessment of children was conducted by four kindergarten teachers in Boston working under the direction of the psychologist G. Stanley Hall of Johns Hopkins University in 1880. Hall was troubled to learn that of the four hundred participating youngsters who were entering the public schools, 65 percent couldn't locate their ankles and 93 percent didn't understand that leather came from the hides of animals. With Stanford University's Earl Barnes, Hall measured the children's height, weight, health, and knowledge, advancing age-specific averages; they established the first *norms* for average rates of development. Since the assumption was that young children followed universal stages of healthy development, then differences could be defined as delays or deficits.

After Hall became president of the newly founded Clark University, he mentored a bright student named Arnold Gesell, who gained his doctoral degree in genetic psychology there in 1906. Earlier, Gesell had also studied with Lewis Terman, a father of standardized testing. This training first pointed Gesell toward the examination of organic or biological determinants of maturation, not environmental causes. After attending medical school at Yale, Gesell started a clinical practice. He later joined the new education department at Yale, teaching there until his death in 1961. As Gesell's clinical research, based in New Haven kindergartens, got under way, he began to devise gauges for when a five- or six-year-old was ready to begin school. One indicator of school readiness, according to Gesell, was the emergence of the child's "sixth-year molar . . . (a) convenient punctuation point in the development of a human being."[26] The signs of normal development that were most scientific apparently stemmed from physiological processes.

Gesell, working with Frances Ilg and Louise Bates Ames at the Yale Child Study Center, recruited infants and toddlers into longitudinal observational studies, painstakingly recording basic physical movements or "motor skills." Gesell's team were the first to claim that around two and a half, young children temporarily became less flexible and adaptive—what parenting sages would come to call "the terrible twos."[27]

Yet Gessell also examined up close the manifestations of family poverty within industrialized regions of Connecticut and New York, and he argued that kindergartens were the neighborhood organization "strategically situated" to address the underlying causes of children's poor health and lagging rates of development. He advocated a "reconstructed kindergarten" that would help with "parental guidance and training," serve handicapped children, and ensure "hygienic regulation of school entrance." Gesell urged preventative strategies for aiding children in their community context: "conjoint and cooperative methods of attack must be evolved by both medical and educational agencies."[28]

Gesell's thinking came to fuse the philosophical and scientific aspects of child development in unprecedented ways. "We use the hyphenated term guidance-teacher to emphasize the fact that the workers in the field of early child development should think of the child in terms of guidance rather than of instruction or training," he wrote with Ilg in 1943, and spoke of "a science of child development as a cultural force," urging the field to focus on "the basic problem of environmental conditioning—the relationships between maturation and acculturation."[29] "The nursery school . . . is a cultural instrument for strengthening the normal functions of a normal home," he wrote. "The home, like the state, has its problems of government and must give controlled scope to the spirit of liberty which animates the growing child."[30]

CHILDREN MAKING MEANING

Jean Piaget (1896–1980), more than any other observer of young children (though he preferred to be called an epistemologist), shaped how early educators in America think about development. The connotations of the very term *development* in the minds of preschool teachers and research psychologists indeed stem from tenets set out by Piaget. These include such fundamental notions as the idea that cognitive capacities grow through fixed stages from infancy forward, as the child becomes able to understand more complex material properties, symbols and linguistic conventions, and social roles—and predictably hit recognized milestones. Piaget demonstrated that infants and toddlers can't understand why certain behavior is counter-normative, or why the volume of water remains the same when poured from a stout glass into a tall, thin one, until certain hardwired cognitive structures unfold and become more elaborate inside the young child's mind.

Administering a variety of tasks to young children in the 1920s, Piaget postulated that the minds of infants and toddlers move from grasping simple materials and social events to constructing the meaning of complex phenomena. "The problem of going from cognitive structures initially undifferentiated . . . to structures both differentiated and coordinated in a coherent way . . . dominates the whole mental development," Piaget said.[31] Young children progress, for example, from understanding concrete operations and the manipulation of objects to understanding symbolic representations of objects or the signs associated with the verbal utterances of caregivers. While such cognitive capacities unfold naturally, at predictable points in the child's young life, the physical and social environment contains a multitude of vivid and confusing stimuli to which the infant or toddler responds, seeking to understand, for instance, how blocks fit together to make a tower or what adults mean when they gesture toward the highchair or bath tub.

Piaget noticed that young children make all sorts of mistakes, misunderstanding that the number of objects stays the same when they are laid out in a different pattern, for instance, or that certain words or gestures have no sensible meaning when expressed in the wrong context. This allowed Piaget to depart from earlier philosophers like Rousseau, insisting that parents had not taught their children this misinformation and that children's brains were not naturally programmed with knowledge of the natural world. According to Piaget, developing infants and toddlers evolved various cognitive capacities to make meaning of objects, symbols, and people. As the child's cognitive apparatus becomes increasingly agile, the cultivators of the child's garden of learning—be they peers or grown-ups—could present increasingly challenging tasks. And these facilitators of learning should build upon the child's own cognitive and social scaffolds.

Piaget rejected the postulates of rival behaviorists who were gaining prominence in American psychology claiming that contextual rewards and sanctions were the true drivers of learning. He advocated "self education . . . what the child learns by himself, what none can teach him and what he must discover alone."[32] This closely resembled Pestalozzi's earlier view that the young child is naturally curious, eager to figure out how things work. Facilitating the child's intrinsically motivated pursuit of learning is more effective than didactic instruction, Piaget claimed.

In short, Piaget was an original *constructivist*, holding that, given the child's particular developmental stage, he or she constructs an understanding of the physical properties of a manipulated object or the meaning of specific forms of linguistic or social interaction. This view prompted early educators to pursue child-centered forms of preschool organization, such as creating "activity centers" in the classroom from which a child could choose intrinsically motivating tasks, guided by his or her sense of challenge and novelty. The position that so much cognitive blossoming was occurring early in children's lives bolstered public discourse around intervening into youngsters' daily settings, what a new generation of developmental psychologists would come to call *early intervention*.

The continuity between Piaget's framework, derived from years of child observation, and the insights of post-Enlightenment philosophy is remarkable. The Swiss epistemologist drew deductively from the work of Comenius, the seventeenth-century Moravian-Czech scholar. Writing from the Sorbonne in 1957, Piaget paraphrased Comenius' starting principles: "If the child is really a being in process of spontaneous development, then individual study, independent exercises, and the transformation of capacities with age are possible." Piaget juxtaposed this theory of how young children learn to the schools' didactic approach, that, as he put it, "all education can be reduced to external, verbal and mnemonic transmission of adult knowledge through the teacher's words to the pupil's mind."[33]

Piaget, directly quoting Comenius, stressed engaging the child in playful activities rather than having them passively listen to adults: "Craftsmen do not hold their apprentices down to theories; they put them to work without delay so that they may learn to forge metal by forging, to carve by carving . . . " Advancing the rudiments of developmental philosophy three centuries before Piaget lent them scientific respectability, Comenius had written: "Proceed by stages . . . violence is done to the intellect whenever the pupil is obliged to carry out a task which is beyond his age and capacities."[34] Comenius also presaged Piaget's emphasis on how young children learn from their peers perhaps more effectively than from adults: "Equal children by age, knowledge and courtesy, mutually sharpen the spirit . . . better than anyone."[35]

All but the most strident proponents of academic skilling or cultural differences recognize that learning tasks inside preschools are best pegged to children's levels of development. The phrase *developmentally appropriate* is commonly recited by early educators and advocates, who are eager to be seen as progressives, not evil-doers advancing "drill-and-kill" pedagogies. The National Association for the Education of Young Children (NAEYC) now publishes a 193-page manual for local educators, detailing classroom activities that are developmentally appropriate, stemming from contemporary interpretations of Piaget's basic framework.[36]

ENGINEERING EARLY INTERVENTION

If Piaget was right, then perhaps government could organize potent settings that would advance the child's cognitive apparatus. This hopeful theory was advanced by a new generation of discoveries in the 1950s, including those by psychologists Robert Hess and Dorothy Shipman at the University of Chicago. They began publishing results that detailed how parenting practices explained much of the variability in children's cognitive proficiencies long before they started school. And the most potent home practices, such as reading with one's toddler or conversing through complex language, were observed less frequently inside impoverished households.[37] Some parents apparently were more cultivated than others within their home-grown gardens of development.

This line stemmed from the earlier thinking of child study pioneers, such as Bird T. Baldwin at the University of Iowa, along with Kurt Lewin and Beth Wellman, who argued in the 1930s that intelligence was not a hereditary trait, fixed at birth. Instead, they thought IQ could be enhanced through environmental stimulation. This view was then amplified by other scholars, such as Yale psychologist Edward Zigler, just as the Kennedy Administration was casting about in search of remedies for family poverty and the low-quality, segregated schools in which many black children were trapped. The result was Project Head Start, included in the federal Civil Rights Act of 1964, which by the following summer had funded community action agencies in the South to open modest preschool classrooms.[38]

At the same time a group of young researchers in the Midwest was about to put Ypsilanti, Michigan on the map. David Weikart and colleagues had designed an enriched preschool program that put into operation what the liberal-humanists had long desired: learning tasks within classrooms that provided stimulating play and cognitively engaging activities such as puzzles, counting games, and pre-literacy exercises. The Perry Preschool—following the philosophical foundations of Pestalozzi, Froebel, and Piaget—rejected any notion of didactic instruction in phonics or vocabulary. All children served in this experiment, which began in 1962, came from poor or working-class black families. Most of the children attended the preschool for three hours a day, five days a week, over a two-year period. Notably, preschool staff visited mothers every week to teach them instructional techniques and enlightened ways of socializing young children.

Weikart introduced another pioneering idea: a control group, consisting of children who did not enter the preschool because their names were not drawn out of the proverbial hat. In 2004, Harvard professor David Ellwood said that the 123 participating families "may be the most influential group in the recent history of social science."[39] In a follow-up study at age forty, those who had gone through the Perry Preschool were significantly more likely to have completed high school than the control group (37 graduates in the treatment group versus 27 in the control group). The Perry graduates were also more likely to be employed (43 versus 35), and less likely to have been arrested more than five times (21 versus 31).[40] I offer a more careful analysis in Chapter 6 of what can be generalized from the Perry experiment. But it's the folklore around this early program that now matters most—these seemingly miraculous effects are taken as sacred truths by many early educators, advocates, and journalists across the country.

At first the Perry program allegedly saved seven dollars in public spending for every dollar spent and was linked to fewer special education placements and incarcerated teenagers; later figures rose to thirteen dollars back per dollar invested. However, officials at the Packard Foundation, a major funder of UPK advocates and (supportive) scholars, were disappointed to learn from the RAND Corporation that the economic return to quality pre-schooling had dropped to only $2.62 for every dollar invested. This statistic was based on the effect of size, realized by the Chicago Child-Parent Centers, which were more storefront and less boutique in character, serving poor black children in the 1980s.[41]

What has seeped into the UPK debate is the utilitarian logic. Sure, some advocates refer to the warm and invigorating garden for child development, just as kindergarten advocates did a century ago. But this human-scale raison d'être of preschools just isn't as tidy as—and is far less useful politically than— the macho persuasiveness of cost-benefit analysis. What's ironic is that the Perry Preschool and the Chicago centers never focused on a narrow skill-building agenda. Each program blended a Piagetian constructivist framework with holistic work with parents, attempting to enrich the home environment as well as the school.

Nationally some advocates remain loyal to five centuries of liberal-humanist thought, questioning the skilling or human capital approaches to early education. I asked the executive director of NAEYC, Mark Ginsberg, how Washington policymakers now think about the benefits of preschool. With an exasperated look, he responded: "(Analysts) at the federal reserve are advocating to withhold dollars to programs that aren't raising kindergarten scores [the approach adopted by Jeb Bush in the Florida UPK program]. Here you have a group of economists who think they are making lawn mowers, missing the human nature of child development."[42] Another Washington advocate complained to me that Amy Wilkins, of the pro-NCLB lobby Education Trust, "would like to see Head Start folded into Title I [of the federal Elementary and Secondary Education Act]. She likes the accountability mechanism, and now the opportunity to test every four year-old nationwide."

POLITICS OF THE BRAIN

Early in their California campaign, the UPK advocacy group Preschool for All distributed an eye-catching fact sheet, topped in bold blue print with the heading, "Ninety Percent of Brain Growth Occurs Before the Age of 5." Six lines below, in a slightly smaller font, it reads, "Yet, hundreds of thousands for California children start school each year without ever having been to preschool."[43] The postulate is that exposure to preschool will somehow boost brain growth, a claim that stems from the story of remarkable "new" research on infant brain development that captivated parents and the media during the second half of the 1990s. This episode continues to shape popular notions of child development.

How the brain research (old and new) has been appropriated by advocates, and then used to jump-start early education initiatives in several states, illustrates the recurring intrigue that surrounds children's *mental* development. The media boom over infant-brain research also attracted new, influential proponents to the field, like Hillary Clinton and Rob Reiner. These allegedly fresh discoveries in neuroscience sparked high-profile media coverage, despite the fact that the scientists didn't really say what the advocates inferred. Nor did it have much to do with the utility of preschooling.

Ron Kotulak's editor asked the basic question in early 1993: why do some children turn out bad and others don't? Was there anything happening in the brain-research field that could provide new answers and offer an appealing news hook? This question prompted Kotulak, a science writer at the *Chicago Tribune*, to craft a series of articles on what he claimed was new neurological research into the minds of young children. These fresh discoveries should, according to Kotulak, move parents and government to think anew about better ways to stimulate the learning of infants and toddlers.[44] What he advanced as newsworthy were allegedly unprecedented revelations regarding the early growth of babies' brains, not to mention neuroscientists' new-found ability to project the kaleidoscopic pulsating of tiny brains onto the big screen.

One oft-cited example of this "new" research was the important work of neuroscientist Harry Chugani and his colleagues. They were studying the brain metabolism of 29 epileptic children, ranging in age from five days to fifteen years of age. Chugani's team utilized brain-imaging technology that generated remarkable pictures of electrified sections of the brain, capturing the birth and death of synaptic tissue, which is necessary in sending messages throughout the neurological system. Not to be outdone by the *Tribune*, the *Los Angeles Times* soon ran its own series, featuring riveting photos of infant brains, teeming with what appeared to be biological blossoms unfolding before our very eyes. The color pictures produced by magnetic resonance imaging (MRI) proved irresistible to news editors.

Four months after the *Tribune* series ended, the Carnegie Corporation of New York released in April 1994 what became an influential report, titled *Starting Points: Meeting the Needs of Our Youngest Children*. The Carnegie task force had reviewed the empirical literature on early development, pinpointed major problems facing young children and put forward an action agenda—aimed not at preschoolers but at children age zero to three. The report's authors sketched a gap between research, which highlighted the importance of the first three years of life, and public initiatives aimed at improving the daily environs of infants and toddlers, which were scarce. New York writer Rima Shore, who drafted most of *Starting Points*, acknowledged that she did not thoroughly review the field of brain research, old or new. But the wide coverage received by *Starting Points*—in the *New York Times*, *Washington Post*, and other major dailies—stressed the apparent fact that "new discoveries" about the robust potential of infants' brains demanded major public initiatives.

Then the neuroscientists began reading *Starting Points*. Many were distressed by the inferences drawn by its authors or the embroidering of facts by eager reporters spinning out sexier news stories. One review appearing in the *Journal of the American Medical Association* praised the spirit of the Carnegie effort and underlined the obvious importance of the zero-to-three period, but added that " . . . the report's assertion of the permanence of early effects on later brain function is not well supported."[45] The Carnegie task force and the state and national advocates who then took up the charge—including early proponents of universal preschool by decade's end—blurred the empirical evidence when they made three pivotal claims, according to John Bruer, president of the James S. McDonnell Foundation in St. Louis, which funds research in neuroscience.

Researchers have long known that a baby's brain naturally produces trillions of synapses—the material that connects nerve cells and relays neurochemical messages for everything from feeling hungry to solving Piagetian tasks. After *Starting Points* appeared, many of the report's proponents claimed, first, that the more synapses produced, the better for enlarging the young child's cognitive capacity. Second, advocates argued that the first three years of life represented a "critical window" for development. "The first years last forever," as Reiner's website put it. In February 1996, *Newsweek* ran a cover story by Sharon Begley titled "Your Child's Brain," which averred: "Children who are not stimulated before kindergarten are never going to be what they could have been."

The third claim of the brain enthusiasts was that more stimulation would spark greater synaptic growth, leading to smarter infants and toddlers. The new research suggested to them that the baby's in-born mental apparatus would evolve more quickly, or somehow get bigger, when the infant's environs offered more intense stimulation. One of them, Georgia governor Zell Miller, who had recently created the first UPK program in the nation, urged legislators to fund the distribution of recorded classical music to expectant mothers. "No one doubts that listening to music, especially at a very early age, affects the spatial-temporal reasoning that underlies math, engineering, and chess," Miller said.[46]

What remains troubling is that the empirical work appropriated by journalists and advocates neither drew from new discoveries nor confirmed the claims that activists so eagerly advanced. Much of the research on synaptic growth, for example, had been performed during the mid-1990s on rats, monkeys, kittens—and even ducks. Few neuroscientists were dissecting human brains, figuratively speaking, and counting of billions of synapses remained an inexact science at best. William Greenough and colleagues at the University of Illinois, for instance, found that rats raised in enriched environments spawned more synapses in certain parts of their brains than rats growing up in bland conditions (assuming we can grasp what constitutes a boring life from the rat's perspective). In scholarly articles, Greenough clarified that this finding was not new and that it should not be generalized to apply to human brains. He denied that his work said anything about "critical windows" of neurodevelopment.

Neuroscientists Brian Cragg, Jennifer Lund, and others through the 1990s had documented an accelerating rate of synaptic growth during the first eight weeks of human life. But they emphasized the importance of "pruning"— that is, the process by which synaptic tissues die off. The key to cognitive processing may not be how many synapses the robust young brain grows, but how efficiently it prunes them to achieve more efficient messaging. Brain scientists don't yet know the answer to this important question.

The White House held a conference on Early Childhood Development and Learning in April 1997. In a review paper titled "Rethinking the Brain: What New Research on the Brain Tells Us About Our Youngest Children," Rima Shore wrote that "by about eight months (of age), the frontal cortex shows increased metabolic activity. This part of the brain is associated with the ability to regulate and express emotion . . . to think and to plan, and it becomes the site of frenetic activity at the moment that babies make dramatic leaps in self-regulation and strengthen their attachment to primary care givers."[47] This was a dramatic interpretation of Chugani's findings, but to cognitive scientist Bruer, her conclusion "[went] well beyond the evidence presented in the original scientific paper."[48]

Rob Reiner's reading of *Starting Points* galvanized his interest in early development. He and his wife, Michele Singer Reiner, were new parents and self-described "veterans of psychotherapy."[49] In 1996 he flew from Los Angeles to New York to ask Ellen Galinsky, director of the Work and Families Institute, to help manage a media blitz focused on the needs of infants and toddlers—what Reiner came to call the "I Am Your Child Campaign." He also convinced Teresa Heinz, president of the Heinz Foundation, to support the public relations campaign financially. Just before the 1996 presidential election, the Reiners met with President Clinton, reportedly for fifteen minutes. Clinton asked what he could do. His staffers were already planning a White House conference on children. The Reiners asked the president to make zero-to-three a domestic priority.

Joan Lombardi, Clinton's first director of the new federal Child Care Bureau, credits *Starting Points* and the Reiners as key forces that moved early childhood issues higher up the domestic agenda. The I Am Your Child Campaign led to an hour-long special, aired on ABC. *Time* magazine followed suit with their own cover story in February 1997; in the same week, Reiner and Carnegie president David Hamburg addressed the National Governors Association in Denver. The title of the session: "How a Child's Brain Develops and What It Means for Childcare and Welfare Reform." The media campaign "brought a message about the importance of early brain development to parents, child-care providers, and policy-makers across the country," according to Lombardi. "Although some questioned the interpretation of the new research, a higher level of awareness toward the early years was achieved, and another link was formed between education and high-quality child care."[50]

The Clintons would end up hosting two White House conferences on young children. The April 1997 session, ironically, included just one neuroscientist, UC Berkeley's Carla Shatz, who was allowed to speak for eight minutes. The strategists figured they had mobilized plenty of evidence, along with the public perception that science was on their side. But the earlier discourse around the crucial importance of zero-to-three was already fading. Neither Washington nor the states could find an institutional base from which to better serve infants and toddlers, and they assessed the voters' support for placing such young children in formal organizations as tepid at best.

Months later, in January 1998, President Clinton announced an unprecedented $21 billion initiative that emphasized child care options for America's families: it would offer tax credits to help middle-class families cover the cost of child and elder care, a new after-school program, a hefty expansion of Head Start preschools, and fresh dollars to improve high-quality care, mostly for preschool-age children. Several pieces of this package were approved by the Congress before Clinton left office in January 2001. His administration had successfully pushed to quadruple child care spending over his eight years in office. Most of these dollars moved to the states in the form of child care vouchers, building from the senior Bush's block-grant program, advancing options and supporting a mixed market of caregivers and child-care centers. Some UPK advocates would later claim that these huge policy steps, though they did expand child care, failed to advance the real thing—preschools linked to the public schools.

The nation's fascination with brain development largely sputtered out by decade's end, as state activists and foundation officials shifted their attention to the cause of universal preschool. The not-so-new brain research was invoked during the early days of UPK organizing. The Washington lobby Preschool Now still distributes a nifty PowerPoint package to local activists and early educators, the first slide of which shows an artist's rendition of a newborn's small brain, next to a much larger six-year-old's, sitting like two unequal cabbages in a vegetable stand. However, the mid-1990s focus on babies' brains again reverted back to the obscure world of neuroscientists. Reiner, the foundation leaders, and the governors pulled up stakes and moved on, leaving infants and toddlers behind.

Strengthening Families and Communities

The ascendance of UPK as a mainstream issue stems not only from contested ideals and scientific trends regarding the nature of young children. Mothers play a role as well—especially because of their widening aspirations and rising economic clout. The ideals that women have for their own lives, along with the persisting struggle over how best to balance work and family, sparked growing interest in child care options, going back to the 1960s as we saw in Chapter 1.

Then, flowing into this historical current is the perennial question of how government and employers can help to strengthen working families and neighborhood supports. Any sound, ecological theory of child development takes into account home and neighborhood environments. And feminist thinking continues to struggle with finding a balance across these differing worlds, which then drives the kinds of informal and institutionalized settings in which young children are raised.

FEMINIST THOUGHT, CHILD CARE OPTIONS

The founding conference of the National Organization for Women (NOW) convened in Washington on October 29, 1966. The fewer than three hundred attendees elected Betty Friedan as its first president and adopted a statement of purpose framed in the emancipatory language of the Civil Rights movement. NOW's thrust would eventually alter the everyday lives of middle-class families and their young children. Women "should not have to choose between family life and participation in industry or the professions," the charter read; nor should they be forced "to retire from jobs or professions for ten or fifteen years, to devote their full time to raising children, only to reenter the job market at a relatively minor level." The statement called for a national network of child care centers and "a true partnership between the sexes . . . an equitable sharing of the responsibilities of home and children and of the economic burden of their support."[51]

Senator Walter Mondale would lead the charge on one feminist front, moving a bill through Congress in 1971 that would have created a national child care program, first to serve low-income families. President Nixon vetoed the bill, saying it "would commit the vast moral authority of the National Government to the side of communal approaches to child rearing . . . against the family-centered approach."[52] It crystallized the widening split between conservatives, who sought to keep mothers and young children inside the home, and the feminists' imperative to create child care *options*.

Millions of women refused to wait for government action. Powered by rising education levels in the postwar period and galvanized by the liberating

spirit of NOW and other groups, women increased their labor force participation dramatically. The share of mothers with youngsters age zero to five
working outside the home rose from 15 percent to 58 percent between 1950
and 2001. Even among mothers *not* working in the labor force, the use of organized child care rose dramatically. In 1967 just 6 percent of children age
three to five with a nonemployed mother spent part of each week with a non-
parent caregiver. By 1997, slightly over half of this same cohort were in a
nonparental child care setting at least part-time.[53]

Economic incentives for educated women to work outside the home continue to be strong, beyond the force of widening aspirations. In 1967, married couples with a working mother earned just 13 percent more than one-
earner families. But three decades later, having a working mother boosted
family income by 39 percent in real (inflation-adjusted) dollars, compared
with the average income of families with just one wage earner.[54]

A steady growth of child care providers, whether individual sitters, nan-
nies, or fee-charging preschool centers, made these economic gains possible.
Having options was pivotal, since many women moved into low-wage or
service-sector jobs requiring them to work weekends or swing or rotating
shifts. Today, many mothers cannot predict how their work shifts will change
from week to week. For these women, conventional preschools that offer a
three-hour program or operate weekdays, 8:00 to 5:00, are not much help.
University of Maryland sociologist Harriett Presser details that about one-
third of all working mothers labor outside the hours of nine to five. Among
those who work regular day shifts, just under a third rely on a preschool as
their principal form of child care, and just 13 percent of children whose
mothers work late afternoons or night shifts rely on such programs.[55] This
helps to explain why enrollment rates have leveled off at or remain under
70 percent in Georgia, Oklahoma, and New Jersey, the states that are fur-
thest along in providing universal preschool.

Many women have taken on the infamous "second shift," a term coined
by Berkeley sociologist Arlie Hochchild, working for wages and then returning home to also manage the family. Contemporary fathers allocate just
slightly more time to household duties than fathers did in the 1960s.[56] Critical theorists even challenge the liberal-reform strategy of NOW and the
early feminists, arguing that they have simply freed up women's labor power,
offering employers a wide and deep new pool of lower-wage workers. State

expansion of cheap child care, in turn, brings a new set of productive laborers to the workforce.

Historian Sonya Michel points out that children's interests have long been interwoven with women's own economic interests.[57] But should the structure of work in America dictate how young children are raised, and by whom? Or should the economy serve to advance the family's vitality? Judith Warner, in her recent best-seller *Perfect Madness*, revisits the dilemmas around being ambitious and career minded, while cutting short the upbringing of children. She writes: "I read that 70 percent of American moms say they find motherhood today 'incredibly stressful.' Thirty percent of mothers of young children reportedly suffer from depression. Why do so many otherwise competent and self-aware women lose themselves when they become mothers?"[58] Agitating for a better balance between work and family, she argues not only for more child care options but also for more humane *work options*, from part-time work with livable wages to the ability to take leave and re-enter one's job without employer-imposed penalties, for which the feminist vanguard advocated three decades ago.

MATERNAL EMPLOYMENT AND CHILD DEVELOPMENT

Despite the dramatic rise in maternal employment rates, the amount of time working mothers spend with their children has remained constant over the past two generations, according to demographer Suzanne Bianchi of the University of Maryland. She finds that many mothers move to part-time work or exit the labor force entirely when their children are young, leading to sharp declines in family income. Yet mothers, and to a lesser extent fathers, are re-ordering priorities to ensure that the amount of time spent with their children does not fall.[59]

When mothers spend too much time at work, or young children spend long days in preschool, negative effects have been detected. Jane Waldfogel and her Columbia University colleagues discovered slowing rates of early cognitive development when mothers were employed full time during their children's first three years of life, based on a sample of 1,872 youngsters participating in the National Longitudinal Survey of Youth. These detrimental effects do not appear to be large, but they are significant, and are strongest for (non-Latino) white children.[60]

A similar finding is that older toddlers and preschoolers who spend long hours in preschool show slightly elevated levels of cranky and aggressive behavior. The long-running NICHD study of early child care first revealed this worrisome negative effect on children's social development for those spending long hours in preschool. This finding was replicated, and the effect found to be strongest for white children, in a study drawing on a nationally representative sample of five-year-olds that I conducted with Bridges and Stanford colleagues Susanna Loeb and Daphna Bassok. Our analysis for the Growing Up in Poverty Project similarly detected this negative effect: long hours inside centers aversely affected children's social skills as reported by teachers, as detailed in Chapter 6.

Nonetheless, a key fact is that parents—whether employed or not—continue to exert a far greater influence on their child's development than does any form of nonparental child care, including high-quality preschools. Perhaps it's no surprise, especially for most parents. But this fact is often lost in the narrowing policy debate over universal preschool. The NICHD team, following mainly middle-class families, found significant but short-lived benefits from preschool attendance, even after they took center quality into account. In sharp contrast, they found that mothers' sensitivity, education levels, and pre-literacy practices (such as reading together) powerfully advanced children's early growth.[61] Many studies, going back to Hess and Shipman's work with Chicago families in the 1950s, confirm that parents pack the biggest punch in shaping young children's learning. And parents who focus intently on developing their young child are much more likely to seek out and enroll their three- or four-year-old in a quality preschool.

CARING VERSUS SKILLING?

Feminist roots also nourish the persisting debate over the qualities that adults should express in raising young children—be they parents, paid caregivers, or preschool teachers. Many UPK advocates have arrived at the position that preschool teachers must acquire a four-year college degree to become a true professional. But should this facet of skilling—assuming that college programs effectively deliver discrete skills that graduates will exhibit in preschool classrooms—guide the development of young children and how we think about the competencies required of "expert caregivers"?

Some feminists think not, emphasizing that the rationalization of women's labor can purge the very qualities that are essential to nurturing a young child. It's not only women that should sustain and value these qualities; men need them, too. Yet the basic point is that simply requiring a higher credential discounts the importance of the affectionate, patient, and nurturing qualities that many caregivers possess and that bear on young children's robust growth and motivation.

Feminist writers like Carol Gilligan and Nel Noddings have contributed to this perspective. According to Noddings, men examine moral issues by entering "a different door" that stresses abstract principles such as justice or equity, whereas women emphasize "human caring and the memory of caring and being cared for." Feminist scholar Rosemarie Putnam Tong agrees: "women's emphasis on connections and relationships leads them to develop a style of moral reasoning . . . that stresses the wants, needs, and interests of particular people."[62] Essentializing the nature of women is risky. Still, the social history of caring does conflict with the contemporary, utilitarian focus on skilling.

UPK advocates respond that the current situation—in which many preschool teachers are paid less than burger flippers—is unjust and symptomatic of American society's distorted priorities. They rightfully focus on the quality of the teaching force, and argue that preschool teachers should attain the same status and wages as public school teachers. One way to sell UPK to the public is to raise the credentials of teachers—whether this costly policy move actually boosts children's learning curves or not. It's a matter of equity. But some feminists push back, arguing that child care, like other areas of public life, is becoming commodified, with even care by kin involving the exchange of money, sanctioned by government through vouchers—"cash in care," as Clare Ungerson has called it.[63] The wider quandary, these feminists argue, is how to raise the level of public investment in child care without purging the caring qualities and human-scale dynamics that benefit children's development.

STRENGTHENING COMMUNITIES FOR CHILD DEVELOPMENT

The feminist movement, of course, was one element of the broader push for civil rights forcefully renewed in the 1960s. Just as women were rethinking their own identities and how to best extract meaning (and fairer income) from daily life, so too were subordinated ethnic and cultural groups across the nation. The liberal-capitalist state, throughout the modern era, has been founded on the neoclassical notion of the autonomous *individual,* whose rights are to be protected in exchange for loyalty to the nation-state. But the modern period also has witnessed (so-called) public agencies that fail to protect these rights or lend support to particular *groups.*

With the rise of civil rights organizations, the pursuit of cultural or gender-based identity moved to the community level, leading to demands for public resources and a more decentralized governing authority. Central institutions and corporate firms were simply not responding to the aspirations or economic interests of women or ethnic minorities. Head Start preschools offer a case in point: originally funded from Washington through fledgling community action agencies that at times remain so, albeit with ample involvement from the public schools. Indeed, the architects of Head Start, public health clinics, and legal aid offices—the tools deployed by the Kennedy-Johnson administrations to lift up the black community—aimed to bypass and challenge segregationist local governments, unresponsive local school systems, and the bureaucratic state.[64]

Head Start was founded upon a theory of child development not unlike Gesell's framing at the Yale Child Study Center that emphasized that the local political economy sets the conditions in which many poor children are raised. Applying a treatment just to the individual child, though necessary, is insufficient to break down the process of family poverty passing down from one generation to the next. To this day, the program offers a comprehensive approach to development, including proper nutrition, health and mental health services, and home visits with parents. Head Start even created job ladders for women (without conventional credentials) to become classroom aides. Extensive community participation in preschool organizations appears to pay off under some conditions, as we saw in the Perry Preschool and Chicago Child-Parent Centers.

In the same period, the nonprofit sector has grown enormously in middle-class communities as well, with child care organizations representing one of the largest parts of it. The number of CBOs has tripled nationwide since 1967, exceeding one million organizations by 1999, according to Burton Weisbrod. They range from huge institutions like the American Red Cross to neighborhood health clinics and after-school programs. In total, nonprofits account for about 6 percent of national income and just under 10 percent of all jobs.[65]

At times, UPK advocates talk about CBOs as if they were part of the early education problem rather than part of the solution. Libby Doggett, head of Preschool Now, told me: "We want to build it (UPK) as part of the school system, to professionalize the field. Parents in some states are preferring school based (programs)." By implication, CBO-run preschools have less potential to become "professional" and legitimate.

SEGREGATED PRESCHOOLS

The decentralized, unplanned spread of preschools brought with it disparities along fissures of race and class. By targeting public dollars on low-income families, government has advanced the benefits of preschool, yet it has also created a layered system of preschooling. In it, young children experience quite different social relations inside classrooms, depending on the social-class character of their neighborhood and the kinds of teachers who work there.

This backdrop informs the contemporary question of whether greater control by the central state would remedy these local differences? And which of these differences are bad, leading to unequal rates of development, and which differences simply reflect the varying socialization preferences of parents?

The late University of Michigan sociologist Sally Lubeck tackled a portion of these questions. In the mid-1980s she spent a year inside one Head Start preschool in a poor community and another in a well-off suburb. She found that in the suburban preschool the ideals of learning through play—with children exploring in activity centers, dressing up and imagining scenarios, sitting in book corners, and teaming up to erect Lego structures—were alive and well. Teachers were attentive to the needs of each four-year-old. "Children were perceived as 'developing' . . . children according to age so that 'age appropriate' activities could be provided," Lubeck wrote. Piaget would have been delighted to read her field notes: "teachers were constantly making judgments about where a child was in terms of interest and ability."[66]

In sharp contrast, at the Head Start preschool, which served mainly low-income black families, the way teachers managed the children was more directive. "You are not here to play, you are here to learn something," she heard one teacher remark to a youngster. Roll was taken at the beginning of each morning, with three- and four-year-olds shouting out "Here!" reminiscent of a high school PE class. Children were taught how to recite their address, phone number, and birth date. This was not necessarily a bad idea in an unsafe community. A teacher gave a different reason, however: "If they don't know their name, address, and phone number, the kindergarten teacher will think they are stupid, and think that I didn't teach them anything." But certainly not all classrooms are so focused on drilling in specific bits of knowledge. In urban Tulsa, where many classrooms are racially integrated, I observed a wonderful cross-age exercise, lasting about thirty minutes, where third-graders worked cooperatively with four-year-olds to build bold and imaginative structures with index cards.

One major lesson from Lubeck's work and other ethnographic studies is that the political economy of early education in America has become organized along social-class lines, just as the quality of a public school can often be predicted by the demographics of its zip code. We earlier examined how some states have succeeded in equalizing the so-called structural indicators of quality: regulating the maximum number of children per classroom, the staffing ratio, and the training level of teachers. But a preschool situated in a well-off suburb can charge $12,000 a year for full-time preschooling, making bright, nurturing teachers and classrooms with colorful materials affordable. The decentralized character of the preschool world, and a market that is shaped mainly by the purchasing power of families, mitigates against the success of state policies aimed at reducing such disparities.

Advancing the State's Interests

Child care has been seen as a warm, upbeat topic in political circles ever since Bush I promised a new national effort in his 1988 campaign. Bill Clinton's lopsided support among female voters was tied in part to his support for school reform and increased aid for young families. Bush II promised to expand Head Start preschools in the 2000 campaign; his opponent, Vice President Al Gore, proposed a multi-billion dollar national preschool system for the middle class. A quarter-century earlier, in the wake of the Great Society, a majority of the states started preschool programs, focused on aiding poor families. The evolving interest of government in the daily care and well-being of young children—fired up by politicians trying to respond to parents' aspirations and economic pressures—represents the third major force that accounts for why UPK has become a national issue.

STAYING "ON MESSAGE"

Activists in liberal-democratic societies struggle with a first-order issue: convincing citizens and political leaders that their particular cause is in the broader public interest. The default is not collective action, given America's more individualistic political and cultural instincts. Libby Doggett and her colleague Amy Wilkins were engaged in this very struggle, sitting around the table one spring morning in 2004 in Washington, D.C.

Doggett and Wilkins, both at the Education Trust, had pulled together Washington's key education lobbies and children's activists to review a wealth of polling results. There was good news and bad news. On the one hand, "in the opinion of the pollsters, the high levels of public support they found make clear that pre-kindergarten has become a *public value* rather than a debatable policy issue," reads a briefing memo they drafted.[67] But after several years of flagging state budgets and two huge federal tax cuts, most voters around the country worried more about declining spending on schools and colleges than about the lack of money for preschool.

The public opinion experts, including Democratic pollster Peter D. Hart, detected warm feelings for preschools serving four-year-olds (which many respondents confused with kindergartens). Yet at least a third of those polled in the different state surveys were opposed, "because people believe the best place for our youngest children is at home with their parents." Based on their reading of the data, Doggett and Wilkens argued to the group that "this view of the locus of responsibility prevents a clear understanding of the benefits of pre-kindergarten for all socio-economic groups." The other problem, according to Hart's firm, was that "though no audience denies the value of the academic aspects of pre-K, they still consider children's social and emotional development to be of primary importance."[68]

The trick, according to Doggett, was to fine-tune the message, "framing pre-kindergarten as a necessary part of the strategy to boost K-12 achievement. The debate around the No Child Left Behind Act (has) raised the importance of student achievement for the public . . . (and) disruptions produced by under-prepared children in K-12 are recognized as a significant impediment to a productive classroom environment. Finding a way to capitalize on both these factors can lead to increased support for high quality prekindergarten."

Certain messages did resonate with the citizenry. Three-quarters of the respondents in one survey were "very" or "fairly convinced" that "90 percent of brain development occurred before age five." Seventy-one percent agreed that "kindergarten is school with an academic curriculum; kids need to be prepared for it." But 54 percent said that "school readiness is parents' responsibility, not government's."[69]

Crafting the message carefully had largely worked in Florida. Hart had urged, following his statewide poll in 2002, that the UPK ballot initiative be worded in particular ways: "participation is voluntary and choice is left up to parents"; access "would be universal and not only for low-income families"; and "high quality standards" would be established. The other message that rang true to voters was the notion of "paying now to save money later." Preschool could be sold as a preventive strategy. The Florida initiative passed easily, although whether the young program will deliver on these promises remains to be seen.

The other message that surfaced in polling: don't call it *universal* preschool. This adjective seemed to imply a mandatory program in the minds of voters, like compulsory schooling or universal health care. In democratic America, standard and uniform organizations apparently don't sell well. Within months, the leading advocacy groups and their funders (mainly the Packard Foundation and Pew Charitable Trusts) had shifted the entire name of the movement, at least within their coast-to-coast leadership circle. Now they were to pitch the initiative as *preschool for all*. When Reiner introduced his ballot initiative for a second time in 2005, the word universal was nowhere to be found.

These massaged messages were then beamed to a few eager journalists. In a *Sacramento Bee* column, Marjie Lundstrom summarized survey results: "There's still plenty of guilt—that fairy never shuts up—but the attitude about preschool in California is shifting dramatically . . . they (polling respondents) think it's important for kids to attend preschool before entering kindergarten." Reiner provided the color commentary: "Most educators view this as part of public education."[70] His state commission aired over $160 million of public service announcements featuring figures like Gloria Estefan and Maria Shriver, each talking up the importance of the early childhood period. Lundstrom claimed that among Latinos support had skyrocketed, from 30 to 76 percent in just two years (of course the polling question had changed).

FINDING THE POLITICAL CENTER —
PRESCHOOL TO BOOST TEST SCORES

We have seen how a small circle of well-meaning, yet elite, actors began to coalesce soon after Bill Clinton's departure in 2000, encouraged by the persisting glow of media attention to early childhood issues and key victories in small states. Frustrated with the far-flung, difficult-to-organize child care establishment, a new generation of early childhood activists and key benefactors settled on formal preschool as *the* policy remedy. We will see, when we look at Oklahoma and California, how the uniform framing and message spread from that D.C. conference table around the country, emanating from a core cadre of movement leaders.

But why would this ambitious set of advocates want to narrow the public discourse around work, family, and child rearing—putting forward such a narrowly defined policy remedy? And why are key government actors coming to see UPK as advancing both altruistic and instrumental political interests?

One explanation is that UPK advocates and their allies offer a cause that's emblematic of the popular political center within state capitals, appealing to a range of governors from moderate Republicans to liberal Democrats. This argument is reminiscent of Claus Offe's political sociology, which argues that the state—by mediating among competing political ideals and interests—advances its own institutional legitimacy at a time when the state's utility is under steady attack from conservatives.[71] This storyline has emerged repeatedly in the history of American education when it comes to faith in the (human capital) skilling of children, especially the importance of being able to read and write in English or to push your child's percentile score higher on ever-present standardized tests.

Within this pragmatic American context, selling preschool as a way of providing a crucial head start in school, with an eye toward raising test scores in the early grades, goes to the center of the moderate state's interest. When a conservative president such as Bush II signs into law the most centralized, micro-managed education proposal ever attempted by Washington—the No Child Left Behind Act—you know that improving schools and raising literacy is a priority first for voters, and second for politicians eager to take credit for it. State governments were at the center of the school accountability movement by the mid-1990s, long before the lightning rod of NCLB was approved in 2002. Test scores did rise in many states through the 1990s. If universal preschool could help states regain their momentum, and allow policymakers to brag about raising performance, it would be a political godsend.

Joe Eddins, the Oklahoma legislator who coauthored the bill sending regular school funding down to districts to serve four-year-olds, drove home the point during an interview. He was extremely proud of this accomplishment and was delighted when the Pew Charitable Trusts flew him to a National Press Club briefing. He added, "You'd like to be like Governor Hunt and make national headlines (with his support of the North Carolina *Smart Start* preschool effort), but I don't have what it takes to be governor." Eddins's quiet candor and self-effacing humor felt familiar when we talked. My mother grew up in Oklahoma; I spent many a summer chasing lizards across the parched prairie outside Ponca City.

What is clear is that politicians in democratic societies want to be in the middle of popular issues, in Eddins's case, leading the charge on pro-family reforms. Building a new institution and creating more teaching jobs is perennially attractive for many constituencies. It follows that preschool expansion slides comfortably to the center of school reform efforts in many states.

The problem is that government displays the Weberian habit of reducing complex strategies for organizational change down to simple, routinized solutions. Somehow the political imperative of clear benchmarks and the regulatory mentality of central government squeeze out human discretion on the ground. Bush II signed NCLB in January 2002, thus trumping the states' decade-long experiments with school accountability, finance reform, and efforts to upgrade teachers and improve their practices. And Washington has displayed little capacity to encourage innovative forms of teaching and learning as ways to better motivate students. Rather, the implementation of NCLB has been all about advancing "basic skills," even pressing for scripted curriculum packages. The federal government now requires standardized testing and sets the rules for how achievement "growth targets" are defined for every local school across the land, as well as deciding the sequence of escalating sanctions that are to be imposed if those benchmarks are not met. To conservatives and many moderates, the way to have accountability is to focus on raising basic literacy and mathematical skills.

The most stalwart defenders of NCLB in Washington are at Education Trust, headed by Kati Haycock. She has hung tight in support of the most highly regulated—and controversial—education reform ever attempted in U.S. history. And it was Haycock whom officials at the Pew Charitable Trust first approached to run the Trust for Early Education, which had been directed by Haycock's associate, Amy Wilkins, before the group split off in 2004 to become Preschool Now, run by Doggett.

The second Bush Administration moved to insert basic pre-literacy skills into federal Head Start and state-funded early childhood programs. Bush II proposed moving Head Start into the Department of Education from the Department of Health and Human Services (HHS). This was urged in a report by Chester Finn, Bruno Manno, and Diane Ravitch of the conservative Fordham Foundation in late 2000, prodding the administration to focus preschools on cognitive and pre-literacy skills while downplaying Head Start's holistic approach to child and community development.[72] Wade Horn, Bush's assistant secretary at HHS, moved in 2003 to put in place a cognitive skills test administered to three- and four-year-olds enrolled in Head Start preschools, backed by some congressional Democrats who remain worried about the effectiveness of many local programs.

Politicians also use the UPK cause to achieve broader ideological agendas, at times in contradictory ways, a pastiche of social or cultural signals that just don't fit together. When Jeb Bush reluctantly signed legislation in early 2005 to implement the voter-approved UPK program, he claimed it would provide "full parental choice," but took pains to say the effort would uniformly emphasize a "literacy based curriculum and accountability measures to continually increase the success of the program."[73] All this for only $2,500 per child, since he insisted on keeping down the price tag, with teachers having only about one year of college-level coursework.

Most telling for the UPK movement, the logic of school accountability has come to permeate the thinking of leading foundations and some academic think tanks. Aligning what is done in preschool classrooms to the standardized testing of first- or second-graders has become a key policy goal.

Kimber Bogard and Ruby Takanishi at the New York-based Foundation for Child Development suggest that government should engineer "an aligned and coordinated approach" for children age three to eight and add that "alignment implies a lining up of standards, curricula, and assessments for children in grades PK-3." And "alignment and coordination can be achieved through legislation on school organization . . . tools and practices, and through teacher education," they write.[74] It's strong-state NCLB logic applied to young children.

The risk is that universal preschool's credibility may drop with the declining popularity of NCLB. In a 2006 poll, one-third of Americans with knowledge of Bush's school reforms said they hurt the public schools. Another two-fifths said that NCLB had made no difference.[75]

Not all state leaders agree with this mechanical fusing of early education to public school accountability. The Oklahoma statute actually emphasizes "developmentally appropriate practices," for instance, as do officials overseeing UPK in New Jersey. Reiner's doomed ballot initiative in California didn't choose between these two positions: it would have mandated both. Thus, local preschools could have received new dollars by aligning their instructional program to elementary school tests and showing that activities are developmentally appropriate. But the dominating discourse in many school districts is about bringing preschool programs in line—to serve the political imperative of raising test scores. And, if they pull their weight, early educators will be more acceptable to the education interests and political leaders with whom many UPK advocates are allied.

RATIONALIZING CHILDHOOD—
BENEVOLENCE AND BUREAUCRACY

The education interests that are coalescing around UPK, of course, express benevolent motives as they attempt to standardize childhood. One manifestation of this motivation tacitly held by many progressives is what historian Michael Katz calls the desire to "improve poor people."[76] To advance equity, government must be at the center of reform efforts. But when does a top-down strategy become impositional rather than enabling for families?

This debate over the role played by public agencies in shaping family life goes back to the nineteenth century and Emile Durkheim's trust in strong central government to advance cultural hegemony. It's what sociologists John Boli and John W. Meyer have called "the great rationalization project . . . advancing state managed childhood at the institutional level."[77] It's a rather benevolent theory of governing, but one that relies on the bureaucratic machinery of government, exemplified by a rising eagerness in Washington and the states to specify what every three- and four-year-old should be learning, in what language, using what scripted curriculum, and in preparation for which specific test items. As government and UPK advocates identify a problem in social or economic life, their way of organizing a remedy is along bureaucratic and regulatory lines, as Max Weber and his disciples have seen so clearly.[78] In the eyes of many UPK advocates, not to impose more central control of funding, of conceptions of quality, and of specificity about how children should be raised would imply surrender to the rough edges of market-driven forces. This is the rub.

Institutional theorists from Durkheim to Weber to Meyer have emphasized that the ongoing rationalization of social life is not a partisan issue—it's an expression of the modern faith in systems and the reduction of complex public tasks into their component parts, elements that can be specified and regulated from above. Identify the outcomes that can be measured, then assemble the inputs, rules, and production processes that will efficiently deliver the outcome—whether it's running a post office, improving traffic flows, or organizing a preschool. The National Governors Association urged its member states in 2005 to "align early learning (preschool) and K-3 standards" as essential to school readiness efforts. "Children learn more from birth to age 3 than any other time in life," said Michigan's Democratic governor, Jennifer Granholm.[79] The policy imperative is now to rationalize what young children should be learning, even to specify through what pedagogical practices. We've come a long way from the post-Enlightenment ideals and developmental science of Pestalozzi, Piaget, and Froebel.

Historical Lessons

The forces reviewed in this chapter—contested ideals about the nature of young children, mothers' unsettled roles, and the state's rising interest in early education—will continue to power the UPK movement and shape the forms that the preschool institution takes. We will soon look at how activists and teachers are bringing to life these historical forces in a variety of local conditions. Any theoretical account of why school reforms arise and how policy comes to be crafted must take into account not only these broad currents but also local circumstances, along with the roles played by persuasive individuals.

Still, several lessons for policy activists and early educators stand out from this historical analysis. First, for all the talk of "developmental science" and "what the research shows," the key questions and dilemmas when it comes to raising young children are philosophical in nature. They can't be settled by evidence alone. What is the child's inborn potential to grow and learn? How should adults design social environments—inside the home or inside a preschool—to advance the attributes we value in our child? These questions continue to be informed by the ideals and philosophical claims considered by both parents and, increasingly, early educators.

The liberal-humanist conception of the child's potentials and the way that social environs nurture them have dominated (middle-class) discourse for the past century. But at the same time, parents understand that children must acquire the literacy skills and academic proficiencies to propel them through school. Our faith in public schooling as the great equalizer and engine of economic growth, even when the deeper structure of work and income remains so unfair, lends credibility to the notion that preschool should be part of the solution. The science of child development can neither arbitrate between these ideological stances, nor can it necessarily overcome the regulatory character of the bureaucratic state and the kinds of mass institutions that that state habitually builds and expands.

Second, the nature of work in America—especially the jobs held by millions of blue-collar and middle-class mothers—means that the need for child care *options* remains crucial for many, rather than the single remedy favored by UPK reformers. Up to two-fifths of women with young children are laboring when preschool centers are not open. In historical context, the current push to move all three- and four-year-olds into preschool, as the *optimal* setting, is a bold departure from the past. One elite group is now advancing not options, but a single normative place and social form in which all young children are to be raised.

The third lesson is that though the strategy of fusing the UPK movement to school accountability may be clever, it brings worrisome risks for young children. When advocates promise—setting logic aside—that universal pre-school will simultaneously raise all children's early school performance, narrow achievement gaps, and inculcate behavior appreciated by grade-school teachers, they do widen popular support. Teacher unions and early educators are enthusiastic about any reform that lessens the political pressure on them to raise test scores and attract new funding for public schools. But a century ago, the proponents of universal kindergarten made similar promises, and few would argue today that kindergarten—embedded in a school system beset by funding disparities and disappointing results in many urban areas—has narrowed early achievement gaps.

Fourth, a diverse range of child care organizations has arisen over the past half-century, situated in a variety of nonprofits, churches, for-profit firms, and local schools. UPK advocates have been slow to recognize the advantages of this mixed market of organizations, including the advantages for communities that accrue from this array of grassroots actors. The political economy of child care organizations remains driven largely by the purchasing power of parents, leading to uneven quality and stark inequities between middle-class and poorer areas. Still, some states taking the lead in widening access to preschool, especially Georgia and New Jersey, are actually strengthening the mixed market, rather than creating a public school monopoly.

Fifth, we must disentangle the high hopes and lofty ideals of well-meaning UPK advocates from what the evidence really says, or does not say. The tall tale about the "new" findings on early brain development is one case in point. Another is the myth that school-based preschools are more effective than those in CBOs, or that young children develop more quickly when their teacher holds a bachelor's degree (see Chapter 6). Playing fast and loose with research is not new in the wider field of school reform, and it will surely continue. But the popular backlash from failed education reforms has already proven costly politically.

Finally, history puts in sharper relief the wider battle over how a civil society maintains and enhances its educational institutions. Horace Mann's common schools made sense in an America where ideas like Protestant individualism and capitalist expansion were widely accepted and agreed upon. The village schools that common schools replaced were so far flung and unevenly financed that some centralization of funding and some quality control were warranted.

But fast-forward a century and a half to an America that is a rainbow of diversity, in both its people and its community organizations. The credibility of mass institutions that once signaled modern progress has slipped badly in recent decades. Communities have won the resources—from parents and government over the past century—to create a panoply of child care and preschool organizations. So, how should central government move to improve financing for early education, when the sector is so decentralized, populated by such a colorful range of local firms? This is the same dilemma faced by states that are eager to spawn charter schools, only to find that many are of low quality and that communities are unevenly served.

The push to define preschool as a *public good* is an important social movement. Yet this debate—stemming from the long-running push for public child care—lies at the cusp between public and private responsibility. The essential human task of raising young children remains a private responsibility. But private remedies alone are not sufficient: they favor better-off children and allow too many others to languish. So, it may take a village to raise young children, but in whose hut does child-rearing occur, and who gets to decide what, and how, children should be learning?

* * *

Next we move from these broad forces to see how early educators and activists are creating new preschools in their own images. Let's first visit the rainbow room, set in a preschool that serves a diverse and challenging range of children.

CHAPTER THREE

Welcome to the Rainbow Room

WITH SEETA PAI

It's circle time inside Gretchen Dodd's classroom. Grinning widely, with her hands in the air to punctuate the action and emotions of this morning's book, she resembles an orchestra conductor, leading her twenty-four charges in song, interweaving it with passages from the story. Around this particular circle, situated in a blue-collar suburb, sit an enthusiastic choir of four-year-olds, who together speak ten separate languages.[1] Gretchen points to the names of the author and illustrator on the book's cover. The final song, belted out by most in English, is titled, "There's a world of color outside my window." Gretchen asks that each child "think of some ideas of *different* things outside," and the gaggle then incorporates them into the refrain. She heaps praise on one little boy. "See, that's good. Aun San said a blue book. Now that's a different idea!"

Later Gretchen, herself the mother of a preschooler, said she disliked the idea of "preparing children" to fit classroom routines. Instead, she preferred to focus on the *process* of learning. She has resisted pressure to attend to letter recognition or school readiness via direct instruction. To her, this is "not something we need to push on them . . . it happens when it happens."

Bella couldn't disagree more. A few blocks away, in her preschool classroom at Rivera Elementary School—within the same region that's delivering on its promise of universal access to preschool—her circle time unfolds quite differently. Bella summons Natalia, a Latino girl, to the whiteboard, calls out a letter, then coaches and corrects Natalia as she arduously writes an uppercase K. Around the whiteboard is a poster displaying the alphabet, a chart of colors, each labeled in English and Spanish, and a panel displaying geometric shapes. The title of this visual pastiche reads: "We Are Getting Ready." Some children around Bella's circle comprehend only parts of her spoken English. When they drift into chatting with their neighbor, Bella shouts out, "Please stop talking. I don't like it." At one point, she rhetorically asks the four-year-olds in the circle: "Don't you want to get ready for kindergarten? When you go to kindergarten, and they ask you things, I want you to know all the answers. I don't want you to say you don't know."

This chapter invites you into what we metaphorically call the Rainbow Room, to peer into the daily lives of breathtakingly diverse children *and* teachers at two differing preschools. Each one operates within an area on the West Coast where local educators and community activists have joined forces to ensure universal access to quality preschool. This pair of preschools is located within corresponding elementary schools, yet run by a respected community organization, PreKare, that has long served this blue-collar suburb, which we call Midtown.

We will see in Midtown how the broad social forces that we sketched in Chapter 2 shape the character of daily life inside preschools. Here, the push to advance a uniform pedagogical approach that is rooted in liberal-humanist ideals runs headlong into the local school district's pressure to raise test scores. There is great variability in the parents' expectations, too, in this wildly diverse community (in which at least sixty-five languages are spoken, according to the 2000 Census).

We first describe the local setting and how Seeta Pai carried out the field work on which this chapter is based. Second, we record how PreKare managers articulated their own ideals about child development, aims that came into conflict with the skilling emphasis of school officials and kindergarten teachers. Third, we move inside classrooms to discover how preschool teachers, diverse in their own backgrounds, organize differing activities that result in differing kinds of cognitive demands and behavioral norms for youngsters. Fourth, the plot thickens as parents look in on their child or volunteer for the day. This section illustrates the range of cultural models that teachers and parents express when it comes to discipline practices, socialization goals, and how academic knowledge and skill-building may (or may not) be couched in social development.

By *cultural models* we simply mean a parent's or teacher's tacit understanding of how things should work—in our case, inside a preschool classroom. We borrow from the work of anthropologists and social psychologists with deep roots in phenomenology who have shed light on how members of groups come to believe in certain social facts and causal sequences that lend order to everyday life, including how adults should raise young children based on implicit conceptions of the nature of young children and notions about what adult practices lead children to be "properly" socialized. These cognitive models represent "common sense" within a particular community, both describing *and* prescribing their social life, their goals, and the ways to achieve them.[2] Our earlier work applied this framework to analyze how parents view their own role in nurturing or instructing young children, and how they perceive the utility and quality of child care options in their neighborhoods.[3]

Uniform Preschools in Colorful Suburbs

Old images of gritty urban scenes or bleak southern poverty still persist when advocates or policymakers talk about preschool. The historical hangover from Head Start, rooted in the South's civil rights movement, accounts in part for this, along with the fact that urban states have most heavily invested in child care programs, largely serving poor families. But the most vibrant growth in preschool organizations since the 1970s, with climbing rates of maternal employment, has happened in better-off suburbs, where parents can afford to pay thousands of dollars each year in fees. The families populating Midtown are somewhere in between.

Indeed a variety of new preschools have sprouted within the nation's new suburbs, once lily-white communities now transformed into demographic rainbows of second-generation families and blue-collar refugees of aging city cores. The count of families residing in areas of concentrated poverty nationwide has declined dramatically since the 1980s, due in part to the ability of families of modest means to find secure niches in blue-collar or strictly middle-class suburbs.[4]

The Midtown schools are situated in one such niche. Once an agricultural outpost, Midtown became a fledgling white suburb with humble cottages built in the postwar era. A regional economic boom in the 1990s spurred growth of elegant apartment buildings and condos, some nestled among tiny manicured lawns and hedges. Today a grid of wide avenues dominates this congested suburb, dotted with strip malls. There's little green space other than dusty, nondescript bushes struggling to survive within the concrete edges of the median strip leading to the nearby freeway. A keen eye can distinguish residential neighborhoods by the developer's version of pseudo-ranch exteriors or by the cookie-cutter floor plan inside. The city's demographic complexion has changed dramatically since the 1980s, with an influx of young Latino families, a rising number of middle-class South Asians, and a few blacks, who once worked in now-shuttered auto plants. Parents in Midtown share the hope of raising their children in a safe community, many commuting twenty-five minutes by freeway to jobs in light industry, construction, or the service sector.

The median income of families served by this pair of Midtown schools matched against two census tracts was $61,600 in 2000. Children served by PreKare come from lower-income families and benefit from these publicly financed preschools. In fact, the two preschools where Pai spent her year feed children into two corresponding elementary schools, Rivera and Norman, where the preschool classrooms are located. This organizational model—where preschool dollars move down through local school boards, which then contract out to CBOs, still providing classroom space inside local schools—is also common in other states.

In the 2003–04 school year, just under 56 percent of the children enrolled at Rivera Elementary were Latino, one-sixth were Asian (mainly South Asian), and just under 10 percent were African American. Almost half of them qualified for subsidized lunches, and school authorities classified 39 percent as English learners. The preschool's enrollment was even more heavily Latino: over 80 percent of the youngsters were of Latino origin, mostly native Spanish speakers. The Rivera neighborhood is largely blue-collar in character, with many parents qualifying for free preschool, meaning they earn under about $32,000 a year.

In contrast, the neighborhood served by Norman Elementary was less poor and included more middle-class families. Still, over one-third (37 percent) of the school's children met federal eligibility standards for subsidized lunches. The school's enrollment was 32 percent Filipino, 28 percent South Asian, and 15 percent Latino. Yet again, Norman's PreKare preschool enrollment is less middle-class than the elementary school it feeds, with most children qualifying for fully subsidized state preschool. A few of the preschool teachers that Pai came to know were South Asian.

The field work involved several months of participant observation inside each of the two preschool programs. Pai's research was based inside classrooms, tracking the day's rituals, learning activities, and events. She came to know seven members of the classroom staff well, including lead teachers, assistant teachers, and classroom aides. She also observed and talked extensively with parents who regularly volunteered in the classroom, most of whom were first-generation immigrants. After the first couple of weeks Pai blended into classroom routines, helping with meal time, arranging materials for activities, following the youngsters outside, and even joining staff meetings.

Additional time was spent interviewing parents (thirty in all) and PreKare managers, attending agency-wide meetings and professional development events, and observing at four other PreKare preschools in the same school district to better understand the nonprofit firm's policies and curricular preferences. PreKare had long operated state-funded preschool programs in the community before joining forces with the school superintendent to offer universal access for all families. Each preschool site—as designated by state quality standards—encourages parents to spend time in the classroom. On many field visits, one or two parents were present in the classroom.[5]

"Activity areas" comprised the key organizing dimension within each preschool classroom, including the block area, which typically sported a thick rug where circle time was held, a dramatic play area, a place for children's books enclosed by low shelves, table-and-chair arrangements to host play with "manipulatives" or art materials in true constructivist fashion. Each classroom included a small kitchen on one edge; an open-door restroom, with a pair of tiny toilets and a miniature sink; a teacher's corner with desk and computer; and, of course, cubbies where children stashed jackets and snacks.

PreKare has operated over forty publicly funded preschools and allied child care programs since the late 1970s. Its leaders joined with Midtown's school superintendent in 2001 to promise a free (or largely subsidized) preschool slot for every three- and four-year-old. PreKare's inventive chief devised a way to harmonize fragmented funding streams to deliver on their UPK promise. A fraction of families pay modest fees, which are pegged to their income under a sliding scale that's long been part of this area's preschool effort.

Old School Child Development

PreKare's top managers are enlightened romantics at heart. The nonprofit's founder and administrative disciples are devotees of the liberal-humanist or "developmental" conception of how young children best learn and thus how classrooms are to be organized. They aim to move from each child's natural curiosity and appraised level of development. PreKare abides by a teaching approach that one agency document describes as "developmentally appropriate, child-centered, and individualized to each child's needs."

Despite their philosophy, PreKare administrators and teacher trainers, as contractors to the schools, feel rising pressure from school authorities to address early language and pre-literacy skills—in English for this suburban rainbow of children. This rising pressure to attend to narrower academic skills is juxtaposed against what PreKare leaders call the *emergent curriculum*. This is a flexible pedagogical strategy that emphasizes how teachers should tend to the particular tasks that each child is motivated to engage in, given his or her level of competence and intrinsic interest (following Piaget's postulates). The curriculum is supposed to emerge in the context of exploration and peer interactions, and teachers' careful observation of what tasks and content are most inviting for the children. Only by tending to the child's social and emotional growth are the conditions set to address cognitive skills and academic knowledge, say PreKare's leaders. Their ideals come from Froebel's or Pestalozzi's playbook.

BUILDING FROM CURIOSITY AND CONFIDENCE

The PreKare philosophy is not just neoclassically liberal, centering on each child's growth and movement toward autonomy. It also manifests humanistic roots, making the romantic assumption that children's natural curiosity, when allowed to blossom, will energize early learning and build self-confidence. The organization's managers emphasize that "the most important thing is social-emotional development." As one PreKare manager told us, "Children who . . . focus too strongly on just the cognitive academic aspect of learning are gonna have a tough time if they can't get along with others, so getting along with others and developing a strong sense of their selves is really important."

To advance the liberal-humanist approach, PreKare managers and teacher trainers socialize their teachers and classroom aides through training sessions, bringing in consultants and guest speakers and introducing specific classroom practices aimed at enriching children's "joy for learning." Specific preschool programs are labeled as "model sites" where teachers have grasped the organization's philosophy and organize classrooms with a variety of "open-ended activities" that allow each child to take a task in a personal direction. "Problem sites," where teachers have taken a didactic course and veered toward an emphasis on pre-literacy skills, phonemes, and comportment, deeply worry the PreKare supervisors.

One PreKare manager, a child psychologist whom we will call Judy, spoke one afternoon to parents and teachers at the Norman preschool, a site serving a mix of families from Asian, Latino, and African American backgrounds. In her pitch she tried to combat a rising tide of concern over whether PreKare classrooms were skilling children in ways that would help them in kindergarten.

> One of the reasons we get worried about our young children is the media feeds us this idea that kids are going to grow up to be ax murderers if we don't involve them in learning and make them perform at an early age. There are increasing pressures on schools and teachers to meet performance objectives. The tests that we do may tell us what she or he knows about certain things, some facts, but . . . they cannot tell us how the child will do when she is in tenth grade.
>
> It's *not* letters, colors, numbers, or their name. That's not school readiness. The most important goal for children of this age is to learn to get along and participate in groups. It does not matter if they can't read. Children who do well in school are not academically prepared, they are the children . . . who have developed socio-emotionally.

Judy went on to emphasize how social-emotional factors, especially "a stable, nurturing, reasonable environment, both at home and school . . . an established routine," were key to children's development at this age. She reported that she was "not a proponent of *Hooked on Phonics*" or similar pre-prepared curricular packages. She reminded parents in the audience to volunteer in their child's classroom, since it's important that "you are available and interested." Elaborating on the liberal-humanist view, Judy relied on themes such as "curiosity," "confidence," "communication," and "self-control." "Allow them to solve their own problems . . . don't be afraid to let them *struggle* . . . support *their* interests, follow *their* lead . . . do things *they* are interested in . . . ask *them* questions . . . don't ever discourage your kids . . . allow *them* to express themselves," she added, crisply emphasizing each child-centered pronoun.

ACADEMIC SKILLING PRESSED FROM ABOVE

It was proving tough for PreKare managers to hold their ground, however, against the incursion of the narrower skilling approach. A couple of months later, just several blocks away, the Rivera preschool staff invited an elementary teacher to talk to the parents about the new rigors of kindergarten, what their children could look forward to after graduating from PreKare. The kindergarten teacher, Angela, shifted effortlessly between English and Spanish, indicating that she could "teach in another language" (unlike some PreKare teachers).

"I want to share my expectations as a kindergarten teacher," she confidently began. "As parents of preschool children who will be coming to kindergarten next school year, you need to know what we expect of them. The standards are very high these days; you will be surprised, compared to when you were in school. Back then, you only had to worry about playing. Nowadays, children are expected to write sentences, to know all their letters and sounds, and do this within 30 seconds," Angela said, as several parents glanced at each other, raising their eyebrows.

She then distributed a list of what five-year-olds would need to know, entitled "I Am Ready for Kindergarten," enumerating skills that departed radically from Judy's philosophy back at PreKare headquarters. Most of the list's seventeen items dealt with discrete skills, and the list was written in the first person: "I can draw circles and lines," "I can write some of my name," "I can count to five," "I can use a glue stick," "I know how to turn the page of a book." The seventeenth item in Angela's list was, "I like to have fun learning."

She then walked the parents through each item, rather didactically, elaborating on these "official" ways of getting ready for kindergarten: "When you teach your child to write his or her name, make sure you teach one capital letter and all other small. Some parents teach the child to write their name but in all capitals. They need to know one capital, other small. Your preschool is teaching them also, but you can work on them at home. We want all the children to start on the same footing."

Angela stressed that parents should clarify to their child his or her "official name," complaining that some children answer only to their nickname ("like Benito") but not to the name under which they are registered, "which is the only one we know." And she emphasized the need to sit still and listen. "When they first come, they need to sit quiet for 15 to 20 minutes, but by March we need them to sit quiet for 40 minutes. For first grade we have to prepare them. It's hard, but if you start now, they will be able to do it."

Some PreKare teachers responded in kind to this stress on skilling by kindergarten teachers, school administrators, and worried parents. The heavily Latino program at Rivera had received a "problem site" designation from PreKare managers because of the didactic practices adopted by Bella and some of her colleagues, but Bella remained popular among the parents who volunteered in her classroom. Even at the Norman preschool, where most staff members were either sold on, or simply accustomed to, the developmental model, Pai saw teachers quietly setting out dittos and exercises in which children were to trace the letters of the English alphabet. Indeed, several parents expressed concern that their children would lag behind same-age peers without this shift toward academic skills. "All the children may know the ABC song," said one parent, "but my (child) doesn't know what is A and what is B."

Teachers Construct Their Classroom Philosophy

As the skilling model was advancing in Midtown's elementary schools, the PreKare teachers were nudged to reflect on how they believe children are best nurtured and classroom practices best organized. PreKare managers have created lots of space for teachers to discuss how to organize activities and classroom materials through in-service training, attendance at professional meetings, and guest appearances by early educators. This internal discourse allows them to adopt a diversity of classroom approaches, and this recurrently troubles PreKare managers, who seek a more orchestrated, albeit emerging, pedagogical strategy.

THE EMERGENT CURRICULUM

Most PreKare teachers were trying in good faith to implement this new philosophy of classroom practice. For years PreKare had followed the general developmental principles of the High/Scope organization, the Ypsilanti, Michigan firm of Perry Preschool fame. When we began field work, PreKare teachers were beginning their first full year of implementation and managers felt that the variability we witnessed was indicative of the transitional phase. The phrase *emergent curriculum* stems from the North American disciples of Reggio Emilia preschools in Italy. PreKare's directives stress that the "ideal curriculum" involves warm and nurturing adults who foster in children "a positive self-concept, a joy for learning, and the ability to work and play with others." Hallmark practices include a project-based pedagogy, reminiscent of the constructivist principles of Froebel and Dewey, giving children an ample range of possible activities, rather than working from scripted lesson plans. The teacher structures learning activities in rising levels of challenge, depending on each youngster's "developmental readiness"; the children's progress is recorded and discussed with colleagues.

But as PreKare managers and staff trainers attempted to implement emergent curriculum with crisp fidelity, the teething process was painful. In one training session, teacher trainers passed around their extensive records of children's progress: splendid books resembling photo albums replete with children's drawings and writing samples, even digital pictures of activities selected by individual children. But as these artifacts and assessment packets circulated, some PreKare teachers whispered how it would double their load of paperwork. Dealing with state bureaucracies, and the state's own new child assessment, already required considerable time and effort.

Some teachers spoke of the dilemmas around "play versus work" or "open-ended versus structured" classroom activities, as they put it. The emergent curriculum approach required a complex and fluid arrangement of classroom activities, and steady attention to each child's motivation and proficiency level.

The challenge for teachers became even greater when monolingual English-speaking teachers could not communicate clearly with over half the children in some classrooms, who spoke Spanish, Tagalog, or Punjabi.

Gretchen highlighted the irony of PreKare management's promoting this constructivist philosophy in such a determined way. She appreciated the utility of the new practices: following the child's lead, keeping daily diaries, and challenging children with problem-solving questions. But, she added, "I think there's so many ways to do an emergent curriculum without having, having it so heavy. With kids we have for three hours a day, you know we can still follow their lead without . . . coming up with what our focus is going to be . . . (the organization) think(s) of something new and they go into it so heavy."

THE PRIMACY OF SOCIAL AND EMOTIONAL DEVELOPMENT

School officials' steady focus on test scores and skilling intensified debate inside PreKare over how best to organize classrooms. A subset of preschool teachers located at both Norman and Rivera were not necessarily opposed to introducing specific language skills into their daily routines, but they feared doing so would displace what they (and PreKare managers) saw as even more basic. "Expressing themselves has always been a big thing with me," Gretchen, the Norman preschool teacher, said. She encouraged children to become self-reliant, to be able to pursue their own interests, and to follow their own curiosity.

One morning Gretchen tried to ensure that Keisha, who had "trouble expressing what she wants," was "getting better at problem solving." After Keisha argued with another child over who was the rightful possessor of a toy baby bottle, Gretchen reassured the child that she "is not in trouble," then asked her to report "what happened," to "use her words." The child simply began to cry.

> G: Keisha, you're not in trouble. Was [the bottle] on the floor? Did you take it from the floor? If you use your words, I can figure out what happened here.
>
> K: It was on the floor (still crying).
>
> G: There's no need to cry, Keisha, I'm just talking about what happened. If you use your words, I can help you. You're not in trouble, if you talk to me I

can help you. I understand he might have been playing with it first, then he put it down and went away, and you picked it up. But I won't know this unless you tell me.

Meeting with Keisha's mother later that month, Gretchen described this episode as evidence that Keisha was "getting better at problem solving but . . . [is still having] trouble expressing what she wants."

Gretchen's focus on self-expression and autonomy was not just a theory of social behavior to her; it was a means towards nurturing the child's intrinsic motivation in learning. This emphasis on puzzling through ways of pursuing one's own interests, often in pro-social ways, is central to the Lockean tradition of socializing the child toward individual autonomy.

Gretchen kept coming back to her affection for circle time as the place for encouraging youngsters to express their own ideas and feelings, and to use language more inventively. Since she was monolingual in English, Gretchen realized that her complex learning agenda sometimes fell flat with children who were still acquiring English skills. "It's been a little difficult here (to read books and do felt-board stories), and I feel . . . it's important for children to keep their home language if they can." She remained opposed to any version of direct instruction in language skills. She encouraged all her charges to speak up, to "express their wants," to "use their words," and attempted to "have a conversation with them instead of just responding."

Gretchen was not alone among PreKare teachers. Several blocks away, newcomer Nadia was helping the staff of Rivera preschool shed its designation as a "problem site" by implementing fresh elements of the emergent curriculum inside her classroom. Her paramount developmental goal for the children: "Helping them to become interested in learning and enjoy learning as everyday activity, every minute of their life." Nadia continued: "I really like to encourage them to be curious and ask questions and find the solutions themselves, and become interested in books, reading books." After one staff workshop, Nadia came back even more enthusiastic and set up modest experiments with seedlings, enriched her activity centers with additional costumes, and lengthened circle time to squeeze in more oral book readings, singing, and rhyming exercises.

A MIDDLE GROUND?

The remaining five teachers or classroom aides that Pai came to know well at Norman and Rivera took a different tack, focusing more on children's language skills and academic knowledge, at the conservative edge of PreKare's developmental framework. One said, "They won't be able to just sit there and play with blocks all day." The teachers' belief in the importance of direct attention to pre-literacy skills originated in their own personal stories, since three were first-generation, variously acculturated, immigrants from South Asia who placed a high value on academic achievement. Two others were African Americans who felt that the three Rs were just as important as social development. As one of them put it, she worked "to get the child to have social skills. And then once you get to that point, then you can start teaching them some academic things."

The fact that the PreKare classrooms were located inside elementary schools brought teachers more into contact with public school teachers and administrators, as with the guest lecture by the Rivera kindergarten teacher. The effects of being embedded in the public school were evident from the comments of Bindu, one of the moderates in the skilling versus emergent-curriculum debate. "The kindergarten teacher tells us that they have to know these things: . . . they write their name, they know their home address . . . their phone numbers, and 1 to 20, and the alphabet. So we are doing this the whole year. And that's why I tell you we have to sit down with them [the children]. That's the way they'll learn these things. Only just reading the alphabet [is not enough] . . . we know we have to teach them these things."

Another moderate named Donna saw the contention as eroding PreKare's reputation among parents and the wider community. "There are certain things that they need to know, like recognizing their name, number ID, letter ID . . . all their shapes, know all their colors," she said.

> So that is why we focus on those things on the board, because we don't want our kids to not be able to go to kindergarten, because then what are we doing here? Then the school is going to be saying, "Man, their kids! All those kids from [PreKare] preschool were tested and none of them were ready to go to kindergarten." So that is why we focus on those things, but we do it in a fun way, where the kids like it and they enjoy it, and then they have activity time . . . make them do whatever they want to do.

Bella spoke to differing cognitive demands implied by time spent on skills versus time dedicated to open-ended activities: "Our job is to prepare the children for the next level, for kindergarten, so that's my goal, to have the kids be successful when they . . . move on." She was quite clear that four-year-olds have to learn what their job is, what work is required by classroom authorities. "They're gonna have to do it in kindergarten . . . they're gonna be asked to go to different areas of the classroom and to learn different things, and so when I tell them, 'okay, guys, we're getting ready for kindergarten, these are the things you're going to have to do,' I want them to get into the routine now, so they know what to expect when they get to the next classroom," Bella emphasized.

Some teachers at Norman were torn between their "developmental" instincts and the fact that several youngsters could say little in English. They interwove attention to discrete academic knowledge with more commonplace open-ended activities and play. One teacher said: "If it [were] my school, I would be teaching them at least to sit for 15 to 20 minutes, it's not going to kill them or hurt them, you know, or torture them. I think they should be doing at least something so that way they would be more ready for kindergarten. But PreKare doesn't want it, so I can't do it." Asked what the "it" was, this teacher replied, "sitting and writing"—having children practice writing and letter recognition. Other teachers echoed this sentiment. Occasionally these teachers "bent the rules" by offering these children time to work on dry-erase boards, a contemporary version of dittoed sheets, to allow time to trace and sound out letters or numbers.

The contention over developmental philosophy also affects social rules inside and outside the classroom, including teachers' classroom management or behavior management strategies. Struggling to herd her four-year-olds back into class after a period of "outdoor play" (once called "recess"), one teacher admonished her kids: "When you get to kindergarten, you have to be able to stand in line. You will have to stay in line." She later indicated that she disagreed with PreKare's "policy" that "children should not be made to wait" to begin or transition into activities, such as when they reenter the classroom. She saw it as a valuable "life skill . . . You know, you have to learn to be patient."

Parents Define Child Development

When parents volunteered in classrooms or filed in to evening meetings, frequently they voiced worries about a pair of issues. Many were concerned with the rate at which their child was acquiring oral and text-based proficiency in English. Though they saw lots of "play" unfolding in classrooms, they expected to see more "work."

ENGLISH LANGUAGE SKILLS

Just under 40 percent of youngsters enrolled at Rivera and Norman elementary schools were designated as having limited proficiency in English. In Norman and Rivera preschool classrooms, however, the share of four-year-olds with limited proficiency comprehending or speaking English exceeded 75 percent. The same children were entirely fluent in their home languages, which included Spanish, Cantonese, Farsi, Hindi, Punjabi, Tagalog, and Vietnamese.

One parent stood up at a Norman meeting and asked in halting English whether language tapes could be made available for her youngster, since no one spoke English at home. The PreKare psychologist responded: "I think you speak English well. I told you I'm not a fan of phonics and all that drill-and-practice. Kids will pick it up. Share with him, talk to him, you speak English just fine. And keep building his self-esteem." A parent at the Rivera parent-teacher meeting with the kindergarten teacher asked whether children needed to know how to write only their first name, or both first and last names. A father wanted to know whether his daughter should learn the entire English alphabet, or only vowels, or only the letters appearing in her name.

After the presentation at the Norman meeting, a small group of parents reacted to the lecture. Speaking quietly in Punjabi and Hindi, they questioned whether the model of "follow their (the child's) lead" made any sense within an extended family, where showering attention on one's child may be considered rude and unacceptable. "How to explain our family situation to these people? They don't understand," one mother said softly. "It's not just mother-father-child for us, how to explain the joint-family living situation? We can't just be talking and playing with the child in front of everyone."

Several Latino parents believed it was the preschool's responsibility to teach kids how to speak proper English, since PreKare classrooms were obviously nested within a public school and staffed by professional teachers. One mother, Pilar, expressed her concern about language skills versus time spent "playing" in the classroom. Speaking in Spanish she said, "Here they teach them to make little (arts and crafts) things. But I would like it if they would make them work more, in things like the alphabet, their name or how to write it, because almost all the time I see them, they have their activities that they do, or play, but they should have some time to study." A second mother amplified this theme: "They should write a little more and play less. They should have a little more pressure to learn the letters, like more pressure and less play."

Some parents clearly heard, in the visiting elementary school teacher's remarks, signs of the state's interest in back to basics, as relayed by Midtown school officials. One Latina parent volunteer said: "Right now it is all games, play, like right now they are outside. As a mother, I would like it if they taught more, such as the colors, to identify names, not only of their mother and father, more than that, because they are going to kinder. My son has been here a year, but I would like it if there was more . . . so they can go more prepared for kinder."

Another mother felt she was ill-equipped to instruct her child; she was worried that her own limited English would confuse her child, and that PreKare's official curriculum was somehow different than the curriculum back home.

> Since it's difficult for me . . . Well it wouldn't be hard for me to help him . . . but the learning system here is very different from the learning system over there (in Mexico). So for me, if it was the same, I would say okay, this is the way you begin to learn how to read or write, the numbers . . . and the ABCs. But I feel that I confuse my son too much, so I prefer not to do it myself.

Another immigrant mother, East Asian in origin, made a similar point, saying that she felt "so bad" because "when you don't have much education, you can't help kids that much in school homework and stuff." She was hoping that the PreKare program would get the children to "start writing" the alphabet because her child "was so ready to go . . . asking me for homework."

"CHILDREN LEARN BEST THROUGH PLAY"

This claim, so central to PreKare's ideals, sparks disagreement among parents and teachers alike. What's now defined as "basic" relates to phonemic awareness, vocabulary, math concepts, and how to find the title page in a kid's book. PreKare managers seemed not so concerned with the substance of this knowledge (nor its import), but rather with the didactic method implied by "basics" and what they saw as the failure of such teacher-directed practices to scaffold up from the child's own curiosity and autonomy.

In addition, a portion of these academic skills are viewed as crucial in the eyes of cultural groups who understandably want their children to succeed in elementary school. In a sense, the liberal-humanist tradition and its "developmentalist" disciples are now up against both the proponents of state-sanctioned knowledge *and* many parents who argue that self-expression and individual autonomy are not particularly relevant in their cultural settings.

Yet the PreKare romantics were hanging tough. For them, two ideals were intertwined: that the nature of the young child emerges through play, and that certain social settings are better at advancing growth than others. In the words of one thoughtful manager,

> Our philosophy is that children learn best through play . . . The academic part is [fulfilled] through learning through play. [W]e do want them also to be exposed to the alphabet, most of our children leave PreKare knowing how to spell their name, and this is without their being drilled . . . And in teaching them how to do that . . . teaching the child to love to learn is, again, very big.
>
> [If] you're focusing on the letter B, rather than drill the child on the letter B, upper case, lower case B, this is B, B, B, B, one of our programs, as a successful example, went on a field trip. First of all they stocked their classroom with exposure of the letter B, there [were] B stencils, there [were] books on items that began with the letter B, there was sponge painting, you know letter B, there was Blowing Bubbles, they are washing Babies in a Bath. [T]hen they went on a field trip and what they did is and again this is learning through play, they hopped on a Bus, and to think of how many children have been exposed to a bus and watching the doors that open, there's money that goes into a compartment. [I]t was promoting social development and language development, because

we're all sitting together having a good time and speaking about our experience.

This approach received mixed reviews from parents, including those who volunteered in the classroom. Middle-class parents most appreciated the organization's philosophy. One father said, "Preschool to me is more for socialization with other kids, . . . to interact with other kids, because his phonics, his reading, storytelling, you know, we do all that at home." Other parents, including one Latina mother, also endorsed the developmentalist approach. She felt that the present mix of play and structured academic work was fine, since "that way they won't get tired of just studying."

Other parents that Pai came to know in classrooms and through interviews held a counter-view, "more pressure and less play." One mother had seen the "commercials on television" conveying that preschool prepares children for kindergarten—brought to you by Rob Reiner's state children's commission—and she wanted to know how PreKare teachers were addressing school readiness. Other parents came from societies or local communities where the approach to early education was not focused on open-ended, playful activities as it was at PreKare. One Latina mother, comparing her child's preschool with a neighboring one, said, "(There) they work with objects and they make them learn . . . and here in PreKare they have everything, all the teaching materials, and they could work, but they don't force them."

After one community meeting at Rivera preschool, a parent asked a teacher to exhibit the Zoophonics worksheet mentioned by the lecturing kinder teacher. The worksheet was one element in a curricular package that involves interactive songs and chants, aiming to build awareness of English phonemes ("A, Allie Alligator, B-B-B-Bear") complete with diagrams and instructions for teachers on how to structure the activities. But at the parent meeting the teacher responded that she could not use these materials because it was against agency policy. As the parent continued to argue for the utility of such exercises, the teacher clarified that the issue should be raised with PreKare supervisors. She didn't have the authority to make curricular decisions.

Many teachers did value the developmental approach, including pieces of the emergent curriculum, to guide their practice and how they arranged classroom activities. But a significant subset felt that PreKare managers were too doctrinaire at times, attempting to stamp out new practices or time slots that focused on English language development and pre-literacy skills. Even Gretchen, the steadfast constructivist at Norman, sarcastically joked about PreKare management. "Oh no, you can't use that color on the bulletin board. You can't use blue, you have to use brown . . . The chair can't be here, it's gotta be there."

Another teacher said that she believed that "children learn best at the board," due to their desire to perform successfully in front of the teacher and the child's peers. "If they take [the writing practice] to the tables, one of them tears the paper, another starts coloring, another fights over the markers," she noted from her observations. Managers sent in new staff to prune back such practices, this teacher noted; she added that though she had been taught in didactic ways back home, she would follow the "new rule," even though she didn't agree with it.

The issue of *how* classroom activities should be organized was becoming entangled with *who* should make these pedagogical decisions. Even though PreKare is a nonprofit organization, operating quite close to the grass roots, it has created a layer of management and classroom oversight. As Gretchen put it, "I think [the organization is] getting too big . . . it turns out [to be] very cookie-cutterish . . . Because it's such a large organization."

Even Gretchen, the avid developmentalist, was cautioned against conducting a math activity that PreKare managers deemed as too didactic. "I was told it wasn't open-ended," she said. The violation occurred when Gretchen organized her four-year-olds into small groups, distributing equal numbers of colorful jelly beans to each. Hoping to advance the concept of estimating a count of objects, along with drawing a simple graph, she had each child stow their portion of jelly beans where they could no longer be seen. Then, working in their groups, each child reported their estimate of how many jelly beans were hidden away. This related to an earlier circle-time activity that she had organized in which each child indicated the mode of transport used to get to school and she charted the frequency of their responses on the easel.

However, PreKare supervisors discouraged this type of small group activity as being too convergent. Gretchen agreed that it is "like following a recipe, [but] you don't do an open-ended recipe . . . to see whose cupcake's gonna turn out right." She clarified that no child was forced to participate. "If the child sat there and ate the jelly beans, they ate the jelly beans."

Some teachers remained unaware of parents' recurring concerns about PreKare's developmental approach. "Most of the Spanish-speaking parents," one Rivera teacher said, "really respect what we do, and they are not challenging us . . . They just are very happy that their children come to school. They don't ask us any questions, they don't challenge."

Cultural Models of Raising Children

"I don't like it!" The phrase rang out one morning, annunciated in clear English by an otherwise Spanish-speaking child. It was followed by a peaceful return to imaginary play in a Rivera activity center. Most teachers were pleased to hear such sharp admonitions from the mouths of their babes and felt they were a healthy sign of emerging self-direction and autonomy. Faced with the possibility of physical harm or impending danger, teachers would quickly intervene. Otherwise, they advanced a hands-off method of discipline and conflict resolution.

Managers emphasized what is called "developmental guidance" in contemporary parlance, which involves teachers' modeling how best to "use your words." Bella demonstrated one morning in her Rivera classroom: "Well, sweetie, you need to let them know that you don't like when they do that." She continued to reason with the child. "If they're hitting you, you need to tell them. Did you tell them that you don't like that? Go tell them that you don't like that." The child then responded, "I don't like that." And then she heard the children translate in Spanish, "*No me gusta*." Bella reasoned that "[the perpetrator] won't do it anymore." Bella summarized, to be sure that the researcher understood: "That's how our culture is, you have to speak up for yourself, otherwise you get run over."

The PreKare model of encouraging children to reason and talk through social conflicts (the term "discipline" was rarely uttered) does not always match the cultural models of socialization expressed by parents, however. One Latina mother encapsulated the teachers' approach as the "I don't like it" method, and said it "sounded so white." She went on to compare it to the "Don't do that" method, which was more common in Latino households. Another mother talked of the *mano dura* (firm hand) approach to discipline at home. When one child refused to take part in circle time at Rivera, this mother asked the teacher why she took no action against what she saw as outright defiance. But, she continued, "the teachers say it's not a problem . . . that we can't make him sit down if he doesn't want to. In my country they don't let the children do that."

Two teachers expressed worry about parents or grandparents who said that "it was okay to hit the child" if he or she misbehaved. The more prevalent worry among parents, though, was whether having two approaches to discipline and socialization was good for the child. As one Spanish-speaking mother put it, "The way in which (teachers) treat the children is very free . . . they let the child be who they are, that they develop who they are by themselves. And at home sometimes we are . . . quick to call attention to what they are doing, if they are doing something wrong." Asked whether she agreed with the preschool's differing norms, the mother said: "Well, I don't know to what extent it is good that at school it's one thing and at home another, because it may even confuse the child. They may say if they let me do it at school, why can't I do it at home too."

SELF-ESTEEM, AUTONOMY, CHOICE

The notion of "developmental guidance" was deeply embedded in PreKare's wider aim of nurturing self-confidence, oral communication, and the ability to reason through social conflicts. Central to this model is the ideal of attending to each child's personality and "needs," rather than assuming that children are uniform vessels ready to be filled with standard information.

PreKare managers judge a teacher's quality by how well she can put this child-centered approach into operation. "Language development is huge," one manager told Pai; "being able to identify your own needs is really important, and being able to empathize with the needs of others is real key to getting along with others. But also be aware [of] developing a self-confidence and knowing what [children] want and respecting what it is that they want." Another PreKare manager said, "First of all we deal with self-esteem, the child needs to feel safe, needs to feel happy about himself or herself."

Developmentally appropriate guidance also means that the teacher should never become negative, remaining upbeat yet authoritative. The old method of time-outs for misbehavior is discouraged in this system, defined as too punitive and embarrassing to the child (undercutting self-esteem). Instead, praising correct behavior or subtly redirecting the child's attention indicates well-honed skills in the eyes of PreKare managers. Teachers are frequently heard encouraging children to reason through the consequences of their actions: "How do you think that makes him feel?" Or, "If you don't clean up the blocks today, I'll know you don't want to play with them tomorrow." Some teachers also avoid being seen as the ultimate authority, instead encouraging children to talk through their problems, feelings, and behavioral options, as in: "So, what are you going to do about that?"

We observed teachers who saw children's ability to choose their classroom activities as a natural right: "It's okay if you don't feel like playing with her right now." Much of this socialization strategy aims to have children take responsibility for their own actions and interests, rather than relying on the teacher to control behavior and define official forms of knowledge or more highly valued activities. This resembles a humanist conception of individualism that links self-interest and cooperative skills.

The liberal-humanist model is rooted so deeply in some American preschools that it tends to overwhelm novel curricular models grafted onto it. Take, for example, a debate between teachers at Norman about how to deal with Marcus, a large four-year-old who frequently imposed his greater physical strength on other children and teachers. One day Marcus—labeled by staff as "really aggressive"—simply moved from activity to activity, picking up materials and slamming them to the floor. At lunch he unabashedly helped himself to all the meatballs in the serving bowl, leaving none for his peers sitting around the table. During free play he asked for an object that was out of reach. When his playmate refused to get it, Marcus climbed up on the shelf to pursue the toy, knocking down several other items. When two teachers intervened, he began to hit and kick them along with nearby children. Staff members worried that if Marcus's social behavior wasn't remedied soon, kindergarten next year would surely be a place of conflict and failure.

This troubling case offered a new teacher, Bindu, the chance to practice the PreKare way of remedying the troubling behavior of a child, even though the strategy struck her as quite different than what adults in her native country would do in this situation. "Everybody brings their culture," the rookie teacher from South Asia said. "But we live in the United States, so we have to follow their philosophy. You know Marcus, he's very cranky, I have learned you have to observe, watch the children, see what he wants and how he's feeling. Even in [another preschool] I have seen there is another child . . . he has hit me many times. That is a cultural difference, I feel. They are doing something different, but you are a teacher . . . you have to observe them."

Providing options and encouraging children to choose according to their intrinsic curiosities further exemplifies PreKare's developmental philosophy. Managers think that high-quality classrooms are places where children can pursue lots of open-ended activities and use lots of materials, typically arranged around the learning centers. They encourage the children to choose activities to their liking during much of the part-day or full-day session. Children were served family style during mealtime, with bowls and platters placed at the center of the table, so children could help themselves to whatever food they preferred. For the most part, they were not told what to eat, nor that they should clean their plates, a familiar refrain for some of us in years past. Except for matters of hygiene (such as, "If you touch it, you have to take it") and the occasional signal to cooperate ("Make sure there's enough to share"), the youngsters were entirely "self-directed." At one lunchtime, while the teachers were distracted, two parent volunteers surreptitiously spoon-fed their own children to ensure they got enough to eat.

The children roam freely to activity centers to tackle their various toys, materials, books, blocks, or to the dress-up corner, and teachers rarely instruct them about how to use materials or toward what concrete end. If a child is repeatedly unsuccessful—say, if her Lego tower keeps toppling and the child is unhappy about this result—then a teacher may suggest alternative strategies, applying the best of scaffolding techniques, drawing on the ideals of Vygotsky or Piaget. Engaged teachers also hover nearby, posing questions or encouraging children to verbalize their strategies or new discoveries. According to the strategy, this process of self-directed engagement and exploration is what sparks new language and reasoning and gives rise to novel social interactions and reassuring routines.

These "developmentally appropriate" practices, right out of the textbook, so to speak, revealed themselves even more vividly when parent volunteers tried to inject their own approaches to teaching and learning. During one interaction between a Punjabi mother and her son, there was silence for almost the entire ten-minute episode, while she steadily guided his activities physically. The activity, created by Gretchen at the Norman program, was to glue beads onto craft paper. She had placed a big tub of beads in the center of the table and laid out individual bowls, paper, and glue tubes at each place around it.

While Gretchen had offered no verbal instructions, Ranjeet's mother sat next to him, picked a few beads, and placed them in the bowl. Then she carefully selected the ones he was to start with, placing them on the paper in front of Ranjeet. When he reached over to the bowl himself, she took hold of his hand and brought it to where the beads she already had collected for him were placed. She said (in Punjabi): "Use these first." As he began to pour the glue, she took the glue dispenser out of his hands as soon as a small drop had fallen. A few moments later he started to sing loudly, not any words in particular, but a sequence of lively sounds. Juan, who was sitting next to him, mimicked this "singing," and they cracked up, laughing hysterically. Ranjeet's mother clapped her hand over his mouth, and he instantly fell silent. She pointed to the paper, motioning for him to return to the assigned activity. This entire time, Ranjeet's mother had said just two words.

After Ranjeet was done, another (white) boy, Ben, came over to the table to attempt the same activity with his mother, Liz. In contrast to Ranjeet's mother, Liz talked almost constantly to her son. "Wow, Ben, that is so pretty. See here, you already have this big blob here, that will go to waste. Why don't you decorate that? Oh, you want these sparkles?" The verbal guidance continued: "You have to share, honey, give him the bowl," and so on. Liz offered a couple of direct utterances, urging Ben to cooperate with other children at the table. But much of the time she extended or elaborated on what her son said, asking him several questions along the way, inviting him to express himself and do his own reasoning about the task at hand.

GOING TO THE POTTY — AMIDST CULTURAL DIFFERENCES

People's tacit understandings of how things should or do work—what social scientists call *cultural models*—guide both the core work done by children and teachers and the tasks done on the organization's periphery. Such essential work on the edge as visiting the potty reveals differences in the normative models held by parents and teachers.

Each PreKare classroom has an open-door toilet area, making it easy for teachers to monitor who is where at all times, and to minimize the risk of legal liability. The restroom is a small square containing two sinks and two toilets, and sometimes a rather scaled-down urinal. When they were asked to go to the restroom before eating, the children trooped in together and some used the toilets. Girls and boys were not separated, all part of the focus on self-determination and freedom. A few parents and teachers readily spoke of their unease about this practice.

After an incident at Rivera when two girls "touched a boy's privates," Bella spoke with PreKare managers about implementing a "body curriculum" with her children. However, the child psychologist told her, "you don't want to over-react"; at age four it is "completely natural" for children to "touch themselves." Then one parent requested that separate potty times be designated for girls and boys, and asked that teachers install a curtain between the toilets so that the children, in her words, "can have some privacy."

PreKare managers set aside these requests, preferring that teachers have full visual access. Gretchen agreed, calling the parent's request "ridiculous" and arguing that youngsters should toilet together, so they learn about differences between the sexes. "I guess these are my beliefs, but there are personal and cultural differences about this. Some people may be uncomfortable with how we do it here. I think if there are closed doors, it's even worse, then we can't even keep an eye on the kids and won't be able to catch any inappropriate behavior."

Some of the PreKare teachers were put in the position of denying their own cultural models of what was appropriate, forced instead to carry out corporate policy. Bindu at Norman said, "Like the other day I saw in the bathroom, some boys were showing the girls their penis and everything (laughs). As a parent, I would tell my son that is a very bad thing to do, and our culture is different too. (But) I can't say (so) as a teacher." Another teacher, Devpreet, told of an incident in which a mother brought in a photo of herself giving birth, wanting to share it with the children. Devpreet was horrified and didn't know how to react. She said, "In our culture we are not so open. We would never do something like that."

LUCIA — HOW TO SOCIALIZE A "CHALLENGING" CHILD?

Lucia was a student at the Rivera preschool who defied her teachers and fought with classmates. One mother, in a quiet aside to Pai, said that if this "challenging child" were her daughter, she would "crack her butt," then "wash her mouth out with soap." Ellen, a mother who herself grew up nearby, frequently volunteered at Rivera and had tried to help tame Lucia. Lucia would shout at parent volunteers, "You're not the boss of me." She also would call them names, such as "fat" or "pregnant." She often hit other children, even those in her small circle of friends, and would strike teachers who attempted to restrain her.

"If a child is acting up and hitting a teacher, I believe they should have a time-out," Ellen said. "If they're hitting, they shouldn't even be at the school from my point of view." But she had attended a frustrating meeting with PreKare managers and staff trainers, who told parents that teachers "can't do time-outs." Ellen continued to feel that teachers needed more latitude to intervene with children like Lucia. According to her, children "need to learn that they're not going to get away with this. If [teachers] just let them go, they're going to keep getting away with it . . . and then when they get to kindergarten, they don't get away with it."

Bella displayed a range of strategies, often using her sense of humor and physical affection with Lucia and similarly "challenging" children. Bella could be firm; she told her, "Lucia, I am not going to fight with you today," when Lucia had (yet again) refused to join everyone else at circle time. She then added: "Do you want me to tell your mother about this? At this point you don't have a choice, you have to sit here in the book area until you are ready to be Lucia. When you are ready to be the Lucia I know, you can come to circle. Until then, you have to stay here and think about this."

When Lucia ignored these admonitions and continued to wander about the classroom, Bella went with her back-up strategy, pulling Lucia into a exchange that distracted her from the disruptive behavior and seemed genuinely affectionate. Bella asked, "Lucia, what are you doing?" The girl responded defiantly, "I'm gonna throw everything down!" Bella smiled slightly, and in a firm tone said, "No, you're not, 'cause I'm not gonna let you. I'm gonna throw you in the bathtub because you're a baby." Lucia came back at Bella, "I'm not your baby," and started to laugh. "I'm gonna throw you in the washing machine and wash you," Bella retorted. "Nuh-uh," responded Lucia. As the teacher recalled the story,

> We started doing the whole game, but she was totally calm and she was totally fine. You know, you just have to find . . . little ways to boost their self-esteem and let them get their anger and stuff out, but do it in a safe, calm

manner, instead of 'I'm gonna tell her mom.' You know, mom doesn't know, she's gonna freak out too, and parents get tired of you telling on their kids all day.

Another teacher, a recent arrival to the United States, didn't buy it. "Here teachers don't [punish children]. You can't do that. I think our way is correct. Because if a child does something wrong one day and the teacher punishes him, the next day he'll think before doing anything wrong, he will be afraid to do something wrong. Here children are not afraid of anything . . . there's a lot of freedom . . . the children themselves hit the teacher!"

Standardizing Liberal-Humanist Preschools?

We spoke with a prominent developmentalist a few years back who argued that cultural differences among families really don't matter all that much when it comes to improving the quality of preschools. "I don't see how it's relevant, I don't really see the point," were the paraphrased remarks I jotted down after returning to my hotel room. Advocates of universal preschool similarly duck the issue, struggling to avoid discussion of whether English immersion is a respectful or effective policy to advance, or whether developmentally appropriate practices would be eclipsed by the policy imperative of raising test scores.

As PreKare managers earnestly try to standardize their developmental approach, we see that cultural forces are pervasive. Actors on all sides hold tacit notions of how children "naturally" grow, what they should be learning, and through what kinds of activities and social relations. As more than one social anthropologist has said, fish are the last creatures you should ask to describe the nature of water. These implicit assumptions about young children and how they should be raised powerfully shape the way activities are organized in classrooms, and the way discourse unfolds in the home. At the same time, the learning-through-structured-play philosophy is no longer taken for granted: it has been directly challenged by school officials keen on pitching pre-literacy skills, as well as by parents who find the emergent curriculum rather strange and excessively liberal.

When PreKare's psychologist argues for nurturing children's own curiosities and autonomy to explore—from dressing up as Batman to building complicated Lego structures—she is advancing a particular model of child development. In the same manner, when the earnest kindergarten teacher, following the party line drawn by school officials, narrows in on phonemic awareness, insists on using a child's "official" name, or instructs a four-year-old to sit still for twenty minutes—she too is pressing a particular model of how children should develop.

What's so intriguing with the PreKare case is how meticulously the managers and trainers put into operation the developmental model, a coherent pastiche of practices set down by the likes of Dewey, Froebel, Locke, and Piaget. Children are to choose among a variety of open-ended activities; learning tasks are not intended to arrive at known information; the goal of building self-confidence trumps any kind of didactic instruction; and parents are not to worry if their child comprehends and speaks little English, because they have the wherewithal "to pick it up," as one teacher trainer put it.

PreKare teachers serve a diverse range of children and families; they face school officials who are under pressure from the state to raise still-mediocre test scores. Even so, PreKare managers stick to their guns, committed to a model that at present is losing ground in the early education field. The skilling model, in contrast, resonates with several parents, many first- or second-generation immigrants who rightfully associate English proficiency with hopes of upward mobility. Along with this model's emphasis on language skills and numeracy comes the notion that information is to be transmitted didactically from teacher to child. "Getting ready for school" also implies learning behaviors that encourage conformity, from standing in line to sitting still at a desk.

As if this bilateral skirmish between learning models is not enough, parents arrive to PreKare preschools with their own culturally specific models of child development. Not surprisingly, most middle-class and acculturated parents seem happy, applauding the organization's attention to their child's social and emotional growth, since, as one father said, "the phonics, his reading, storytelling, you know we do all that at home." But other parents want the preschool to look more like school, with more focus on cognitive growth and activities that resemble school *work*, not *play*. They do not feel that so much "free play" and facilitated exploration will result in better grades once their youngster enters school.

What's also striking about the PreKare case is that different models of development stem not only from the colorful backgrounds of parents. *Teachers* in transformed suburbs are diverse as well. Several teachers easily connected with parents who shared their ethnic or linguistic background, their common experience of being a first- or second-generation immigrant. In some ways, teachers have more in common culturally with parents than with the professionals who try to manage them from above.

One lesson in predicting (dare we say, theorizing about?) how universal preschool may unfold is tied to PreKare's attempts to standardize a liberal-humanist model, hoping to enforce routine ways for teachers to encourage autonomy and play. Gretchen captured the contradiction when she joked about a fictional memo coming down from PreKare headquarters mandating that only certain colors were allowable for bulletin boards. Builders of systems can't help but routinize and bureaucratize as an organization gets bigger and as the original vision, once human in scale, becomes stretched to apply to thousands of preschoolers.

This rationalizing habit, as Max Weber pointed out several decades ago, is itself a tacit model of how modern organizations are supposed to work. Rising political interest in early education leads the states and school systems to routinize the delivery of specified skills, meanwhile reducing the complexity of how the child's developmental potential is seen. But the bureaucratization of early childhood seems so modern: textbook companies can reduce learning into curricular units, governments can delineate measurable domains of development, and test scores rise, at least in the short run. Bureaucratized forms of learning are difficult to resist, even when the implementation of liberal-humanist ideals is the goal.

Don't misunderstand our point at this juncture. We are not arguing that the regularization of preschool systems is necessarily a negative development. PreKare managers, for instance, deeply believe that the child's social and emotional growth is fundamental. Raising the cognitive or linguistic demands on a child who lacks confidence, can't work or play well with peers, or dislikes learning is likely short sighted. The disruptive behavior of Lucia and Marcus, for example, bring this point to life. At a technical level, children with such significant social-behavioral problems are hard-put to realize cognitive gains. PreKare managers also exercised the authority to push back on school officials who were under pressure to raise test scores.

The PreKare case offers one final lesson for those eager to advance one particular model of development or to standardize classroom practice. The liberal-humanist model may work effectively for children who share the cultural heritage of the Enlightenment. Such youngsters understand the social behaviors expected, and they have acquired within the home the requisite pre-literacy skills demanded. But this model may be contested by parents and teachers with other developmental models that tacitly or quite explicitly guide child rearing in their own ethnic communities. As these models become less taken for granted and more contested, the stage is set for a debate over how to raise children within a pluralistic society. However, we are learning that system builders, confident that their developmental model can shape universally effective practices, are rarely eager for such a debate. They simply see it as slowing their efforts to standardize childhood, to build their one-best system of early education.

*   *   *

Next we move from Midtown to the Midwest, exploring how universal preschool is taking root on the plains of a rather unlikely frontier, Oklahoma. As we move from a local community's efforts to statewide efforts, poised to deliver UPK on a grand scale, we focus on the interest groups that often lead the charge.

CHAPTER FOUR

Oklahoma—The Brave New World

If you want to see Tomorrow Land, as sketched by the new preschool advocates, head for Tulsa. The future—well, one rendition of UPK nestled within public schools—has already taken root in Oklahoma. The state lays claim to the nation's highest enrollment rate, at 67 percent, having almost doubled children's access to free programs since the legislature made four-year-olds eligible for regular school funding in 1998.[1]

Much celebrated by proponents of universal preschool from afar, inside Oklahoma the revolution has been rather quiet and civil. "The difference between the movement in Oklahoma and the movement in other places is that there never was a movement in Oklahoma," said Steven Dow, director of the Community Action Program of Tulsa County, which contracts with the school district to run preschool centers.[2] Joe Eddins, the state legislator who co-authored the 1998 finance reform, punctuated the point. "Some states have made a big deal and the governor and the legislature say, 'let's do something big.' That's not the way we did it here in Oklahoma."[3]

So, how did they do it?

After I'd meandered around Oklahoma off and on for a year, Andy McKenzie revealed to me part of the answer. A phone call was transferred into his office as we talked, a modest but tidy room situated right off the entrance to the Mayo Demonstration School in Tulsa. Mayo is a beehive of activity, an open-space elementary school with a robust pre-k program. The lack of walls and easy flow of kids and teachers took me back to my own "school without walls" experience in the 1960s.

But that afternoon, a half-hour after parents and grandparents had swarmed into the cafeteria to pick up their kids, McKenzie's brow suddenly tightened, and a tone of concern entered his voice. No one had come to meet Trea, a slightly timid kindergartner, at his bus stop. McKenzie gave brief directions to his secretary. He returned to our conversation, still preoccupied.

The next morning, I tailed McKenzie, once the Tulsa Public Schools (TPS) administrator who helped create the district's original preschool initiative, who collared five-year-old Trea as he was merrily heading back from lunch. "Hey, what happened yesterday at the bus stop?" McKenzie probed. Confusion with his grandmother, he explained, since he only took the bus on Wednesdays to make his way home. Mystery solved, McKenzie continued weaving through the cafeteria, calling out names, hugging or joking with various children, occasionally cornered by a teacher with a pressing issue, big or small.

McKenzie's attentiveness to his kids, to human relationships, and the abundant trust inside the Mayo School are emblematic of the scale and warmth that marks much of public life in Tulsa. This is a rather small and quite civil society, at least among the circle of educators and civic activists who are trying to aid the city's mostly working-class families. Open conflict rarely surfaces in conversation; "political organizing" or ideological differences are pursued quietly or not at all. To fly in from either coast and start asking probing questions strikes some as odd; it's foreign to the tenor of the everyday culture.

Oklahoma is unabashedly conservative on many counts: George W. Bush won every county of the state in his 2004 reelection contest against John Kerry. Tulsa is the home to Oral Roberts University. It's the state where many believe Karen Silkwood was run off the highway, killed on her way to tell a *New York Times* reporter about leaky fuel rods at a plutonium plant south of

Crescent. UPK activists tread lightly here for fear of triggering accusations of backing a "nanny state" by right-wing activists (some flown in from Washington, D.C.) who stridently oppose any government involvement in the upbringing of children.

But a small gaggle of civic leaders and early educators in Tulsa—including the Republican head of the local power company, a Harvard-trained lawyer who resurrected the local Head Start agency, an unstoppable state education bureaucrat in spike heels, McKenzie, and his wife, Janet, who served on influential commissions while teaching preschool—pushed on allied fronts since the late 1970s. Their efforts have culminated in one of the nation's boldest experiments in early education. This small cast, with some supporting actors, was quietly irrepressible but always civil.

This chapter looks first at the creation story, as the key actors explain the forces that resulted in Oklahoma's pioneering move toward universal preschool in the late 1990s. Second, we examine how the resulting spread of preschooling has unfolded inside public schools, Head Start programs, and allied community-based organizations (CBOs). This discussion takes us into classrooms and the hearts and minds of preschool teachers. Third, we listen to parents and community activists who remain on the edge of mainstream society in Tulsa and outlying parts of Oklahoma. Tulsa is becoming more Latino in complexion, but despite some hand wringing, few sustained efforts are mounted to understand and serve this community. In eastern Oklahoma, the Cherokee Nation—frustrated by what its leaders see as an unresponsive public school system—has decided to go it alone, creating full immersion classrooms, in their native Cherokee.

Oklahoma offers an uplifting tale of how a small cadre of civic activists sparked a still-unfolding revolution in early education. At the same time, certain cultural groups—new and old—remain on the edge of civil society. Even in Oklahoma a one-best system of preschooling is feeling some growing pains.

A Revolution in Slow Motion

Just behind the warm hearts of Oklahoma's activists is a perennially cool economy, which has resulted in rising urban poverty, white flight from cities, and shrinking rural populations—forces that set the conditions in which extending school funding to include four-year-olds became very attractive.

When pollsters ask Oklahomans about their pressing worries, less than 2 percent say that poverty is a serious concern. Maybe that's because it's all around them. Sixty-one percent of the children attending the Tulsa schools in 2003 qualified for a free lunch under federal poverty guidelines, up from 36 percent in 1985. Among all families in the city with a child under five, 38 percent receive public health care via Medicaid.[4] Ever since the Great Depression, families have been escaping the depressed local economies of many rural areas, draining children from the public schools.[5]

Pete Churchwell, who claims to be retired, looks like a fit, confident urban cowboy. Sliding out of an equally muscular sports utility vehicle, he applied one of those Midwestern handshakes that leave your palm aching for several minutes. As the former president of the Public Service Company of Oklahoma, the state's main energy company, he's passionate about improving the lives of young children.

Churchwell spoke first of the conditions that made universal preschool so compelling. "We're a poor state, our population hasn't grown since the 1930s. We're the only state east of the Rockies to lose a member of the congressional delegation (from shrinking population)," Churchwell said. It seems to replay the stark scenes in the *Grapes of Wrath* when Henry Fonda's character, Tom Joad, returns home and finds that his family's been thrown off their failing farm. Everyone tells Joad that he should leave the state and head for greener pastures in California.[6] Today, "Oklahoma has high drop-out rates, the third highest female incarceration rate in the country," Churchwell told me. "The first thing any employer you are trying to attract is gonna look at is the education level of the workforce."[7]

A fellow corporate moderate, Bob Harbison, spoke of Tulsa's changing demographics. "Tulsa (city schools) effectively went from seventy or eighty thousand kids, down to forty-three thousand. You could really see the change in the city (in the 1980s) with white flight and young professionals moving to the city's edges." Harbison, former vice president of the Williams Company ("that big, big building downtown"), retired at fifty-one to volunteer for the Chamber of Commerce.

The Tulsa Chamber, then led by Martin Fate, Jr., head of the Public Service Company, had convened a task force on early childhood education.

Harbison was asked to devise a strategy. "I walked around and asked school principals, (and) to a one it was school readiness that was the biggest problem, the condition of the raw material (the impoverished mix of children entering the Tulsa schools) is how I'd describe it in business terms."[8]

Indeed Tulsa—a city with about 393,000 residents in 2000—represents a classic story of economic decline, rising numbers of poor black and Latino families, aggressive school busing into the 1980s, followed by white flight. Between 1970 and 2000, the share of families headed by a single parent doubled. Almost one-third of Tulsa's families earned under $30,000 annually in 1999.[9] Almost 40 percent of children under six in Tulsa County are now African American, Latino, or Native American. One in six births are now by Latino mothers. Median family income for blacks is half the average level earned by whites.

The advocates of UPK ironically owe a large debt to the decline of rural areas in Oklahoma. "A school superintendent called it to my attention . . . that four year-olds shouldn't be in kindergarten," legislator Eddins replied, when I asked how he first got hooked on the preschool issue. He continued: "Dr. Larry Burdick from Pryor. We each had a son who played basketball . . . Venita and Pryor played against each other every year." Eddins represents a slice of the northern prairie surrounding the village of Venita. Rural school districts by the early 1990s were steadily losing enrollments and administrators worried about excessive classroom capacity. In 1993, the legislature authorized districts to fill out a kindergarten with four-year-olds. "If you have a kindergarten classroom with say sixteen children, it's stupid to not fill those seats," as Eddins put it.

"For the first few years it wasn't costing so much . . . (just) making up for lost revenue because of enrollment decline," Eddins said. But the incentive to rural districts proved irresistible. "Boy, if we could go and recruit a number of four-year-old children, we could make a lot of money," was how rural superintendents saw it, according to Eddins. "You could go out and get these four-year-old children, and you get funding which is double for full day (two sessions of half-day kindergarten each day)." These initial four-year-old enrollments were supported through what capital insiders call *dilution*. "If we had another 1,000 (four-year-olds), every kid would get a little bit less," Eddins said. Without adding four-year-olds into the school finance formula, state spending on education would have declined. "And it's in rural Oklahoma, and nobody cares . . . what's happening in rural Oklahoma," Eddins said.

THE HISTORICAL ROOTS OF UPK

The prior conditions and the baby steps leading to a big reform are often forgotten: it's the big bang that's so vividly remembered. Oklahoma's history offers several lessons about the way local forces shape the timing and the variable design of early education reform—and bring to life the individuals and ideals that have moved the political apparatus over time.

To understand how Oklahoma's preschool revolution came about, movement leaders go back to the early 1980s, when a young legislator named Cleta Mitchell, elected to the Oklahoma House at age twenty-six, teamed up with an energetic junior bureaucrat in the state education department named Ramona Paul.

Head Start arrived to Oklahoma in the 1960s, fused to talk of a Great Society being designed in far-away Washington. These funds flowed through nascent community action agencies. A few urban school districts also began allocating federal Title I dollars from the Elementary and Secondary Education Act to "model preschools." The best-known example is the Bunche Early Childhood Development Center, on the predominantly black northern edge of Tulsa, created in 1973.

In 1981 the state school chief walked into the office of a young, idealistic bureaucrat and asked, "Ramona, what do you want for early childhood?" The equally youthful legislator, Cleta Mitchell, represented the Norman area, and she wanted to do something in the child care arena. A quarter-century later, I caught up with Mitchell in Washington. If you do a Web search for "find a Republican lawyer," her name pops up high on the list.

"I represented a suburban district that included the University of Oklahoma," Mitchell told me one winter morning in Washington; "the community revolved around educational institutions."[10] Mitchell and Paul together cooked up a $120,000 pilot program that would encourage schools and community organizations to create pre-k programs that would be open to middle-class families as well as the poor. "I would not support it if it were just another imitation of Head Start," Mitchell had told the state schools chief. "I beat up on the education establishment. In 1968 busing hit . . . All school districts were devastated by busing," Mitchell said with a discernible angst in her voice.

She also talked of how the old-boy leadership in Oklahoma had cared little about young children and the welfare of families at that time. In the 1960s,

Governor George Nigh had vetoed a bill to fund kindergarten. Mitchell paraphrased Nigh's position: "You know, 'I don't know if we need kindergarten.'" Mitchell had "read about the benefits of Head Start . . . I wanted to give all kids this." Mitchell and Paul moved quietly but effectively. "We stuck it through the back door. It was in a bill, and it was that thick," Mitchell said, grinning and holding her hands about a foot apart. Paul told me, back in Oklahoma City, that these became "model pilot programs for *all* children."

In 1992, the legislature passed a more ambitious preschool bill, successfully lobbied by Tulsa's early childhood activists and Ramona Paul. This legislation created an early childhood education (ECE) credential for preschool and kindergarten teachers, as required by the state's fledgling yet growing early education system. The bill provided about $1,100 for each child enrolled in a half-day preschool program situated in the public schools, according to Harbison, who was active on the issue at the Tulsa Chamber of Commerce. This funding was focused on children from low-income families, mainly those who met Head Start eligibility standards. The program was partially financed by "a sliding (fee) scale for children who were not Head Start eligible," Paul reported. This again revealed her sustained interest in serving a wider cross-section of families. The year before, 1991, the legislature also approved compulsory half-day kindergarten. Under House Bill 1017, each five-year-old enrolled, even for just half a day, would generate the same per-pupil apportionment from the state as a first-grader. Several school districts, especially those losing enrollments in rural areas, took note of these emerging incentives to enroll more young children.

A QUIET REVOLUTION IN SCHOOL FINANCE

In the spring of 1998, after considerable rancor behind closed doors and tempered Republican resistance, House member Eddins and state senator Penny Williams won approval to amend the school allocation formula to include four-year-olds as normal students enrolled in public schools.[11] In fact, school districts could weight four-year-olds more heavily in calculating their drawdown of state funds, a crucial incentive to which I return. Only a few people understood the implications of this statutory change. Urban school superintendents didn't pay much attention to it at first; rural superintendents, savvy to the smaller incentives legislated in the early 1990s, seized on this new revenue source more quickly. But how was this bloodless revolution won, and so quietly?

Bob Harbison had created the Tulsa Children's Coalition after diving into the children's issue. He credited Tulsa County's Kara Gaye Wilson for initially moving key business leaders. "She's not a little old lady superintendent, she's really pretty vivacious. She got it (the importance of early childhood) before it was part of the national dialogue." The Chamber of Commerce, on the eve of Harbison's arrival as chief strategist, organized a trip to Yale University with fifteen Tulsa educators and business leaders; there, he reported, we "stumbled on the school of the twenty-first century . . . we talked to Ed Zigler." Their delegation learned that "schools can be the center of the community."

Harbison tacitly situated the problem, along with the remedy, as inside the schools. The principals "felt it was getting worse . . . with all the demographic shifts in Tulsa. There was virtually no before or after-school care in Tulsa at the time (1994)." Harbison set about creating preschool and after-school programs, drawing on new child care funding coming from Washington, which flowed from senior Bush's new block-grant program, along with smaller flows of Title I and public school dollars.

"Joe Eddins had a predecessor . . . chair of the senate education committee (Ed Long), who took a couple runs to raise (family) income (eligibility) limits for the four-year-old program, but they failed," Harbison told me. The targeted state preschool program was growing, post-1991, but was restricted to low-income families. "The way politics work here . . . we tried to get it done quietly."

Eddins was elected to the legislature in 1995. "Joe called me, and we got acquainted. We were kindred spirits," Harbison said. Eddins also was approached by a local school superintendent from his district. Eddins recounted, with self-effacing humor, that "he (the local superintendent) couldn't get a strong legislator to carry the bill, so he needed an idiot first-timer to carry the bill." According to Harbison, "We shaped a bill the first year (of Eddins's term). At that point we were not thinking about universal." Preschool enrollments already had grown to 10,558 four-year-olds by 1997, prior to the 1998 enactment of the dramatic finance reform; that figure equals about one-fourth of the 2003 preschool enrollment level, due to the earlier legislative efforts.[12]

Child care centers, outside the public schools, also were growing in urban parts of Oklahoma. In Tulsa alone, another 4,638 enrollment slots—situated in 271 centers run by CBOs (excluding Head Start)—were operating by 1998 for children under five. In fact, Tulsa's child care movement goes back to the Friends of Day Care, a group of child care organizations and volunteers who organized in the churches, under the Tulsa Metropolitan Ministry, in the 1970s.[13] These programs were not immediately threatened by free preschool, since declining welfare rolls (in the wake of the 1996 federal reforms) allowed the county to redirect more dollars into child care. Oklahoma also had created a tiered reimbursement system, through which higher quality centers received more public funding. "This made (political) life a whole lot easier," Harbison said.

The strategic question for Eddins, Harbison, and their rural allies became how to move the preschool finance bill through a fiscally cautious legislature. The first two years, they got nowhere. But a constellation of forces began to align in early 1998. One star in that constellation was Ramona Paul.

I first met Paul late in the day at her Oklahoma City office, a stone's throw from the retired oil derrick that rises up above the capitol dome. She was running behind, attending to a brush fire of some kind. Paul zoomed into her office, answered the phone, then instantly rooted about in her desk to find the PowerPoint slide that would speak to my questions. Dressed in a snug leather jacket, she wore silver-loop earrings, with gold sparkles along the rims of her stylish eyeglasses. She showed no sign of tiring as the winter sun set, and harked back to first grade, when she and her classmates were instructed that boys and girls had to play separately, but added, "My mom said, 'that's not right,' and got involved to change the rule."

Paul proved to be as unstoppable as her mother. By the mid-1990s, "legislators were starting to say, 'well, I have a grandchild . . . who should get it (preschool) too.'" The other "big issue was school readiness once NCLB came into play (in 2002)." And, referring to the political effectiveness of Harbison and allied Tulsa activists, Paul said, "We had very strong leaders back in the 1990s. The Tulsa chamber made an economic decision" to back the preschool issue.

Paul pushed hard for two key provisions in the Eddins-Williams bill. First, she insisted that school districts be required to meet certain quality standards to receive their state apportionment. Preschool teachers would have to have a bachelor's degree with early childhood training. "It's that B.A. degree . . . the stamp that says you're smart," Paul said. Stringent staffing ratios that capped the number of four-year-olds per teacher and classroom aide also were included in the legislation.

Paul, Eddins, and Williams agreed to make CBOs eligible for preschool funding if they met the quality standards. As Eddins explained, "Oklahoma law, it doesn't say you have to have a classroom in a school building. So, I amended the law to (clarify that) you can have a program in a child care center . . . the teacher does all she'd do in a school building. The child gets the developmentally appropriate practices, and you don't have to build and heat a building." This amendment proved pivotal in allowing Head Start to create partnerships with the public schools, either to run preschool classrooms or to offer wrap-around programs for children attending a half-day pre-k class within an elementary school. And Head Start could also provide comprehensive services, such as health screening, mental health assistance, and outreach to parents that went beyond what school officials had typically attempted.

Steven Dow, the community agency director overseeing Head Start in parts of Tulsa, told me: "Joe and Penny and Ramona knew that those four-year-olds were in programs in the community. And they knew if they were to take the four-year-olds away, it would create opposition. It was a stroke of genius to permit schools to contract with existing providers." Eddins had known and respected Dow for many years. "His father-in-law and I were good friends," Eddins said. "He found a lot of oil, I mean *a lot* of oil."

By the spring of 1998, legislators Eddins and Williams had sharpened their arguments, and they went about trying to convince key Republican legislators that "simplifying" the state's support of four-year-olds made sense on fiscal and educational grounds. Rural and urban districts alike were taking advantage of their (entirely legal) ability to fill in kindergarten classrooms with four-year-olds. "With more four-year-olds . . . you have another couple kindergarten classrooms," Eddins said. Districts could score even more "weighted students" by offering a pair of half-day kinder programs morning and afternoon. "Republicans had a choice; they could kill the bill and stay with the program we had, or they could pass the bill, (make it) a little cheaper for the state and have a higher quality program," Eddins argued. By cheaper,

Eddins meant that per child reimbursements would go down. He shrewdly failed to mention that enrollments would likely shoot up.

Eddins and Williams won the necessary votes in the state House and Senate to pass the bill on to the governor. "Governor Frank Keating signed the bill . . . for the same reason," Eddins said; "I'm damned if I do, and I'm damned if I don't." Without the fix contained in Eddins's bill, districts could continue to exploit the fiscal bonus attached to four-year-olds and half-day kindergartners, while mixing the two in troubling fashion. Harbison picked up the phone the very next morning. A jubilant Joe Eddins was on the other end. "The governor's signed the thing," said Eddins. "What do we do now?" Without missing a beat, Harbison replied, "Well let's just sit back and watch enrollment grow."

Eddins didn't even try to get more money in the budget bill to cover additional four-year-olds, again relying on the principle of dilution. The first set of four-year-olds that school districts could now claim for state apportionments, numbering just over 13,000, was "offset by (enrollment decline in) the upper grades," according to Eddins. "So, if you appropriate the same amount of money this year as last year, then it's not a problem." According to some, many legislators didn't understand the finance complexities, but just didn't like "putting four-year-olds in kindergarten . . . as districts saw they could make money on it," said Dow.

Consolidating Political Support

Governor Keating had been present at this understated revolution, signing legislation that would come to inspire the fledgling UPK movement nationwide. But Republican Keating was beginning to hear from far-right conservatives dubbed the "nanny staters," in Pete Churchwell's words, on the airwaves and in the capitol. "To these libertarians . . . it was some commie plot to take over their children, to indoctrinate their kids," Churchwell said.

One local news columnist argued that Keating couldn't have it both ways, supporting ambitious preschool legislation, then bad-mouthing educators on the ground who were implementing pre-k programs. The governor also had tied the preschool effort to Democrats' backing of more school funding without tough accountability measures. "Usually in Oklahoma City, where it's fashionable to sneer at Tulsa, the governor has repeatedly ridiculed Tulsans and the Tulsa Chamber of Commerce for their belief that early childhood development is key to high performance in school and college and therefore in economic development," wrote *Tulsa World* journalist Ken Neal in early 2000.[14]

Governor Keating was coming over from Oklahoma City to speak at the Tulsa Press Club, and Phil Dessauer, head of a much-respected community agency, had an idea. He approached the legendary Robert LaFortune, the former four-term mayor of Tulsa (also a Republican), to press the governor on the early childhood issue. After Keating's speech, LaFortune rose from his chair and asked, "Governor, what are you doing for early childhood education?" We still talk about "the question," Janet McKenzie told me with a wry smile one night over dinner. Keating responded with agility, suggesting that maybe it was time to create a statewide task force that would consolidate the several initiatives which had been created in recent years.

Within five weeks the governor's office, working closely with Dessauer and Harbison, named a prestigious Task Force on Early Childhood Education, in recognition that "it is vital that every child arriving at school be prepared to learn . . . much can be done to equip children with the eagerness and ability to learn."[15] The governor's proclamation naming the task force emphasized children's broad motivation to learn—in liberal-humanist tones—rather than focusing exclusively on pre-literacy skills. Churchwell was appointed chair, and Tulsa's current mayor, Bob LaFortune, the former mayor's nephew, also joined. Andy McKenzie's sister, Camille, served as the LaFortune family's live-in nanny years before, helping to raise young Bob. Tulsa's civic circle often feels small and supportive.

The state's early childhood groups, led largely by the Tulsa coalition, had finally moved the Republican establishment—or so they thought. The task force reported its findings in March of 2001, urging creation of a new state office to oversee all early childhood programs.[16] As Harbison put it, "We had worked on some big things. One was the universal program for four-year-olds. But early childhood was nobody's job." The task force also urged funding for parent education efforts and a steady expansion of "high-quality child care" for all families.

Oklahoma's preschool movement had been "flying under the radar screen," as Harbison put it, but now UPK had put Oklahoma on the political map, and in the cross hairs of conservative groups. Darcy Olsen wrote a highly critical piece from her desk at the Cato Institute in Washington arguing that "the governor's Task Force on Early Childhood Education has produced nothing less than a blueprint for a state-run child care, health care, and education system . . . from the womb to age five."[17] Olsen continued: "Why on earth would anyone seriously propose helping children by taking millions of dollars from families so bureaucrats can run programs that few parents want or need?" The progressive likes of Harbison were stunned by the right-wing push-back. In the Oklahoma legislature, "we had a guy stand up saying, 'if you do all this, we'll have kids reading too early, it will hurt their eyesight,'" he said.

Next, the conservative Rutherford Institute ensured that Tulsa made national headlines by revealing that Head Start staff were conducting medical exams of children that included "a genital examination" without the knowledge or consent of parents. "The kids aren't lined up buck naked or anything like that," a Tulsa health official said to a reporter.[18] The Tenth Circuit of the U.S. Court of Appeals would eventually rule in Rutherford's favor.

Even so, legislative support to strengthen state initiatives remained strong. The Senate bill approving the inter-agency task force, dubbed the Oklahoma Partnership for School Readiness, passed 42 to 0; the House version was approved 73 to 23.[19] "That's when the nanny staters came off the wall," according to Churchwell.

Governor Keating had already vetoed a similar bill, back in 2000, prior to agreeing to the blue-ribbon task force. Now he faced the prospect of vetoing the ambitious agenda set by his own task force. Keating reached Churchwell, who was attending a meeting in New York City. "The task force had galvanized the support and the opposition," said Churchwell, and the governor was feeling the heat from conservatives. "He said, 'this is going to pass, but I want you to ask the legislature to withdraw it.'" Churchwell replied: "Frank, I personally can't do that. Let the bill run." The bill passed. Keating vetoed it for a second time.

This episode had a surprise ending, after Democrat Brad Henry was the upset winner of the 2002 gubernatorial race, unexpectedly beating congressman (and former University of Tulsa wide receiver) Steve Largent. Henry told Churchwell that the creation of the Oklahoma Partnership for School Readiness, largely funded with private dollars under the current bill, sounded like a good-government measure. "Gosh, this sounds like a Republican bill," Henry told Churchwell. The new governor endorsed the recommendations and signed the implementing legislation in early 2003.

After the Revolution—Life in Oklahoma Preschools

The preschool revolution seemed complete. Political support was firmly in place, and school districts around the state were drawing down the new dollars for pre-k classes. Strong quality standards were taking root, now shaping how Head Start and other CBO-based preschools were organizing their programs, hiring teachers with a bachelor's degree and paying competitive salaries. Both the 1998 finance legislation and the state-level early childhood partnership were advancing the best of liberal-humanist ideals, at least rhetorically urging a developmentalist approach inside pre-k classrooms.

Nevertheless, talk inside the Tulsa Public Schools was more and more about pre-literacy skills and basic academic knowledge. Tulsa's superintendent and his principals were feeling the heat to raise test scores, especially as fresh pressure from NCLB led to more specific curricular standards and tighter alignment with standardized tests. And the new crop of eager preschool teachers needed to be brought into line.

The story unfolding in Oklahoma is not simply about an unlikely set of bedfellows sparking a quiet revolution in school finance. It's also a tale about what happens with preschooling is firmly planted inside public schools.

THE MUTED BLOSSOMING OF PRESCHOOL

By fall 2004, the number of four-year-olds served had almost doubled, climbing to 31,712.[20] Fifty-nine percent of these children were enrolled in half-day programs and the rest attended full days. Of Oklahoma's 540 school districts, 509 were drawing down pre-k dollars from the state. This growth was spurred by incentives that would benefit school districts and, in turn, encourage them to contract out preschool efforts to Head Start and other CBOs.

In the state's largest school district, TPS, about 41,000 students were enrolled overall. In fall 2004, four-year-old enrollments numbered 2,498, or

6 percent of total enrollment. Enrollments had climbed from 1,615 four-year-olds in fall 1998, showing that Tulsa had already built a significant pre-k program. Another telling fact is that 36 percent of Tulsa's preschoolers were attending a Head Start preschool run by Steven Dow's community action agency or situated within Tulsa's YWCA or a handful of other CBOs.[21]

To understand how fiscal incentives work locally, I talked to Charles Stidham, the long-time treasurer of the Tulsa schools. Stocky in build and wonderfully candid, Stidham swung around to face his computer screen, his printer quickly spitting out answers to my many queries. "He acts as if every dollar comes out of his own pocket," one local staffer told me. But it is quickly apparent that he cares deeply about the new preschool effort.

Stidham also likes the fact that the state assigns a weight of 1.3 to four-year-olds attending a full-day pre-k classroom, explaining to me, "it's like economically disadvantaged kids who are weighted 1.25, or gifted kids at 1.05."[22] This weighting boosts district revenue beyond Oklahoma City's per pupil rate for regular students. The Tulsa schools received about $7.4 million dollars in state revenues to run their preschool program in 2004, equaling $1,856 for a child in a half-day program and $3,444 for a full-day enrollee, before fixed operating costs are included. When the cost of facilities and energy expenses are added in, the actual cost is just over $5,000 for one additional four-year-old in a full-day preschool classroom, according to Stidham.[23]

PARTNERSHIPS WITH COMMUNITY ORGANIZATIONS

In Tulsa County the community-based child care sector remains larger than the infrastructure operated by the public schools. County-wide, moving beyond the borders of TPS, the school districts served 4,193, or about 48 percent, of all four-year-olds in 2002. Head Start preschools, in comparison, enrolled 1,246 three- and four-year-olds, and independent centers enrolled just under 7,100 children from zero to five years of age.[24] Some double counting occurs, since a four-year-old may spend the morning in a school program and move to another center in the afternoon. But this organizational landscape creates the conditions for co-funded programs and occasionally competition. Stidham emphasized how TPS gains through its partnership with CBOs: "We have more four-year-olds on the rolls because of the outside groups."

The scarcity of facilities was a driving worry for Paul and local educators as preschool programs grew. She was eager to avoid competition with the well-established nonprofit sector, as Dow reported. "Part of the problem was that the child care people said, 'you'll take people from us.'" So, Paul responded proactively. "There's a church on every corner . . . (there are) children going into church spaces now. If I were a minister out there, I'd be recruiting those four-year-olds," Paul said. "Come along and work with us, but you have to play by our rules, meaning that you need a certified teacher."

David Sawyer, Tulsa's school superintendent, reported that "child care groups . . . see competition from our programs, and they are very adamant that their programs are not just play." Sawyer spoke of TPS's recent expansion of after-school programs: "The child care association isn't happy with that either. But we have an education objective . . . we're not just caring for kids. We can correlate it with the day-time program, getting ready for schooling or watching after homework." In this way the competitive pressure—with the public schools offering a program more narrowly aligned to the district's curricular objectives—may be altering the philosophy and practices of community-based preschools as well.

An ordained minister Steven Dow is not. His ultimate credential is from the Harvard Law School. But he is an evangelist of sorts. Fully one-quarter of four-year-olds claimed by TPS are enrolled in a Head Start preschool run by Dow's community group. Head Start enrollment ensures that children and parents receive comprehensive health and nutrition services, historically provided by Head Start but not by local schools. Dow has inventively blended the new UPK dollars with community block-grant funds and support from the George Kaiser Family Foundation to build impressive new facilities, at times located right behind a public school. TPS funds a portion of Dow's teaching staff in the four-year-old classrooms, freeing up federal dollars to improve health and family services or to expand enrollment slots for infants and toddlers.

Dow and his preschool teachers try to hold their ground when it comes to classroom activities and the TPS-imposed curriculum, resisting the narrowing skill-focused agenda. "It is absolutely essential that folks understand that when we're talking about kids . . . from low-income communities, that the challenges of educating them are more than just helping them get ready academically," Dow said. Superintendent Sawyer seems to grasp this point: "We're getting wiser in how to improve services . . . medical services, psychiatric services, you've got that under CAP (Dow's agency, the Community Action Program)." Returning to his classroom priorities, Sawyer added, however: "I expect them to use our curriculum, they are right in step with us."

Administrative fees, boring as they may sound, represent an attractive incentive for school districts to contract out preschool slots to CBOs. Treasurer Stidham, for instance, charged just over $390,000—15 percent of his total allocation to Dow's program from TPS—to keep the books and provide in-service training for Head Start staff in 2004. This is "unlike charter schools, where we're only allowed to hold back five percent," Stidham said. This practice doesn't bother Dow, who says it's a fair deal. But the practice is proving controversial in other parts of the state. Leslie Porter, who runs Head Start preschools in three rural counties in the Muskogee area, often in partnership with one of fourteen school districts, told me: "Sometimes they provide teachers. Sometimes they provide an aide. Sometimes they help teachers to meet the B.A. degree (requirement)." One of the collaborating districts draws down $4,063 (per child), according to Porter, "and we get half."[25] As the more supportive Stidham put it, there are "two ways to look at it: you can try to make some money or pass it through and run a quality program."

Melva Douglas and fellow Head Start directors expressed mixed feelings about their partnerships with schools, during a meeting on Tulsa's southwest side. They fear that superintendents could leave them to serve poor children while districts run new preschools in better-off communities. Charging Head Start higher administrative fees, they fear, has a Robin-Hood-in-reverse effect: superintendents hold back revenue from Head Start partnerships, which goes to subsidize middle-class programs. The claim is difficult to challenge, since the state keeps no data on the demographic features of children served by the UPK program, Head Start, or independent child care centers.

These CBO leaders also resist the schools' increasingly narrow focus on pre-literacy skills, echoing Dow's worry about a shriveling conception of child development in the face of testing and school accountability pressures. According to Douglas, at Tampa's Native American Coalition, "Although academics are important, there are lots of other things that we must focus on. We are concerned there will be a lot of performance standards (from school districts) . . . we're still concerned that low-income kids will lose the special services (traditionally provided by Head Start). The good programs were already teaching the alphabet. It's not what you do but *how* you do it," Douglas said.

CONTESTED MODELS OF CHILD DEVELOPMENT

A contradiction arises as one observes daily life inside Oklahoma's pre-k classrooms. School principals and district officials live under stiff pressure to raise test scores and to reduce the count of "failing schools" as defined by NCLB. Local newspapers in Tulsa and throughout the state now publish a list of flagging schools each year. Because of this, school authorities are, quite rationally, attempting to pull the new preschool teachers into line, synchronizing what four-year-olds are to learn with what's covered on standardized tests in first and second grade—this despite the liberal-humanist rhetoric and steady affection for developmentally appropriate practices endorsed by Paul and by old-school early educators.

The encroachment of the discourse around skilling and "school readiness" is celebrated when, for instance, Tulsa's Mayor Bob LaFortune talks up the virtues of preschool. He quotes from the now-dusty *Starting Points* report and an article from *Business Week* in which skilling is front and center: "Children form basic cognitive abilities in their earliest years, and those who don't get exposed to letters, numbers, and social skills at home quickly lag behind those who do."[26] These vying models of child development are not necessarily mutually exclusive. But let's examine the ideological conflicts they have sparked in Oklahoma.

School district officials have mobilized controls and tools for pressing the skilling philosophy, including specific learning standards and what some Tulsa educators call "canned curriculum packages." Central TPS staff have developed a "pacing calendar" for kindergarten teachers—somewhat reminiscent of a Parisian classroom, where the teacher knows precisely what skills are to be covered each day, as dictated by the French education minister. In Tulsa, the first curricular unit for pre-k teachers requires that the teacher "demonstrate the correct book orientation by holding the book correctly and indicating where to begin," and teach children to "recognize ending sounds in spoken words (e.g., the hard 't' in 'bat')."[27] Several teachers with whom I spoke said they appreciated the sequence of knowledge to be covered, which was often articulated in developmentally sensible ways. But others worried about an approach to child development that leads to greater regimentation, the didactic model of teaching that's implied, and the top-down press to teacher-proof the curriculum and limit the teacher's professional judgment.

Tulsa preschool teachers must complete a standardized "growth inventory" for each of their children. This four-page checklist begins with four "social-emotional" items like "separates from the caregiver" (when dropped off) and "displays adequate attention span." These items are followed by seventy-eight scales related to vocabulary, colors, phonemes, reading numbers, and counting.[28] This, at the very same time that state and district officials are arguing that they want to professionalize early education and preschool teaching.

Paul and others are rightfully proud of the 1998 policy requiring all preschool teachers to obtain a four-year degree in early childhood. But ironically, these eager graduates are entering school districts where discussion about how children develop or alternative ways of organizing preschool classrooms is ruled out. New pre-k teachers feel "torn between what they've been taught and then what they hit when they come into the classroom," one Tulsa coach for pre-k teachers told me. Janet McKenzie echoed this concern, saying they are "caught in the middle of what you know about Piaget and developmentally appropriate practices" and the skilling expectations of district officials.

Still, if anyone fears that liberal-humanist ideals are on the verge of extinction, she should go by Head Start's headquarters in Tulsa for a visit with Carol Rowland. Rowland's father attended a military school in San Antonio. "He wasn't a constructivist," she says, with a wide grin. "I had a grandfather who used to stuff him in trash cans in the 1950s."[29]

Rowland oversees teacher and curriculum development inside Dow's thirteen Head Start centers and works with staff spread across seventy-nine classrooms. Rowland, who is fifty-three, moves faster than most twenty-year-olds, dashing through the modest administrative office and darting into classrooms, her colorful boa trailing in the breeze. "We're early childhood focused and NAEYC focused. A child at three or four, you really need to work on social-emotional skills. If a child doesn't learn to sit still and play well with others and share . . . it's not a skill you teach but (one) you demonstrate with the child. Now they have to learn their letters, now they are drawing stupid calendars."

Rowland must accommodate not one, but two sets of learning objectives, since a rising share of her teachers are funded by the Tulsa schools under the state UPK program. In addition, there are fresh curricular mandates from Washington. Rowland still prefers the Head Start model, which remains attentive to multiple facets of child development and steady engagement with parents. "Public schools aren't really warm and inviting places for parents. They might ask you to come and see the science experiments . . . (but) parent involvement is huge for us."

Rowland has a supportive relationship with Pam Brooks, the TPS specialist in early education. In fact, Brooks is the only district-level staffer focusing on preschool and kinder programs. The district's early learning domains "mesh nicely (and) they haven't adopted a mandated, a canned curriculum." Still, Rowland's teaching staff have resisted the heavier weight awarded to pre-literacy skills as pushed by TPS officials. "A couple years ago when we came in with the literacy mentors they (the teachers) had trouble with the balance. We wanted to work on letter, word recognition. But we don't want to drill it. They are torn . . . (they are) under a lot of pressure from Head Start, the state, and the district." At the very same moment that Rowland's teachers were attending more training, becoming more "professional," the Bush Administration began to narrow what her three- and four-year-olds should be learning. "We have intelligent teachers," Rowland protested, "but now it's 'ba, ba, ba, bee, bee, bee. . . . '"

One teacher in a predominately Latino TPS elementary school, with a freshly minted bachelor's degree, told me, "We have to meet our standards and benchmarks. But it's done in an appropriate way. We don't have our kids doing worksheets, pushing pencils." As McKenzie pointed out, "We would be doing a disservice for our entire population if we didn't focus on vocabulary." The pursuit of balance between skilling and nurturing children's own curiosity preoccupies many early educators in Tulsa. And this struggle plays out with many four-year-olds who are, for the first time, operating in an English-speaking environment. "There are lots of times we call over to a child and say, 'tell him to do this,'" the rookie teacher said. This school's only bilingual aide had recently been promoted to work in the front office.

School officials themselves swerve between the focus on liberal-humanist ideals of child development and the competing emphasis on academic skills. Andy McKenzie began as a kindergarten teacher in 1976. "As an early childhood person we know that social-emotional piece, we need to maintain it . . . addressing the whole kid," he said. "(But) with the NCLB emphasis, the focus has shifted . . . (It's) how you are doing on reading and math tests, not how you are doing at school. The pressure is on them (the children) to perform, and sometimes it's not subtle."

DESKS ARRANGED IN ROWS

"The principals are under such pressure," Pam Brooks told me. "Those on the schools-for-improvement list say, 'the sooner we get started on this' . . . So they are putting in place programs that are developmentally inappropriate."[30] Brooks bemoans—although she must implement—the *Language for Learning* package marketed by McGraw Hill, which is "strictly phonics based, highly scripted," in her view. She added: "Kids don't need drill and kill . . . we have different brains coming to us. A lot of new teachers, after four years of developmentally appropriate practices (in their degree program) . . . just don't like the (district's) philosophy. They are really questioning their own careers."

Brooks kept circling back to school principals. "Leadership makes a tremendous difference. If the principal has an early childhood philosophy or has been an early education teacher . . . (then staff can) teach to the whole child, (and) this is how all kids learn." She has developed a quick diagnostic routine to sense each teacher's philosophy and practices as she makes her rounds to pre-k classrooms. "When I walk in and see how tables are arranged, name tags on their desks, I know they are doing the same thing at the same time." The district had recently capped at one hour per day the time that children would be allowed to explore classroom learning centers—building towers with blocks, dressing up while letting their imaginations wander, hanging out in the reading corner. As one long-term insider said, "It boils down to administrators who don't know much about early childhood."

A ONE BEST MODEL OF CHILD DEVELOPMENT

Another lesson for early educators pertains to what happens when government advances a single view of what all four-year-olds should be learning. Head Start's managers in Washington sent down an "information memorandum" in June 2003 to its preschool directors; it explained the new National Reporting System (NRS), "designed on the basis of President Bush's Good Start, Grow Smart Early Childhood Initiative and provisions of the Head Start Act . . . to create a new national data base on the progress . . . of children along specific child outcomes." It pressed Head Start teachers to use five "learning indicators": "using language to communicate," "using . . . complex and varied vocabulary," "acquisition of the English language," "identifying at least 10 letters of the alphabet," and "numeracy awareness." For anyone who might doubt that Washington lacked the authority to implement this new testing system, the riveting communiqué referred readers to "Sections 641A.(a)(1)(B), 641A.(b)(4), 641A.(c)(2)(D), 648.(c)(1)(B), 649.(b)(4)" of the federal code.[31]

This narrowing of learning objectives began during the Clinton Administration, as concern about the uneven quality of Head Start centers mounted and disappointing evidence of modest benefits of modest magnitude emerged.[32] Few questioned whether Head Start should be the object of rigorous evaluation. But the issue of how to meaningfully assess the program's effects, and what developmental benchmarks to use, struck at the heart of Head Start's ideals.

A more enlightened memo had come down from Washington in the summer of 2000, Clinton's last year in office, mandating eight domains that Head Start preschools should address.[33] It covered a balanced set of four pre-literacy and numeracy domains and four other domains including creative arts, social and emotional development, and physical health development. "I was very cool with the (eight) domains," Rowland said.

The Bush Administration's version spoke exclusively to pre-literacy skills and bits of academic knowledge. "What are they thinking?" Rowland said. "When I went down to get trained (in the NRS testing procedure) I was actually appalled." Psychologist Wade Horn, Bush II's chief on children's issues, had rushed to get the assessment in place by 2003, and worries about validity were largely set aside. One vocabulary item asks four-year-olds in Tulsa to point out a *swamp*. "Maybe if you live in Arkansas," was Rowland's comment. Another word that children were to connect with the right picture was *farm*, not especially a useful word for preschoolers who rarely left the inner city.

STARTING WITH FAMILIES

A third set of ideals—postulates regarding how best to advance child development—has sprouted in Tulsa. This alternative starts with parents, rather than only skilling four-year-olds. The philosophy is brought to life by the Tulsa schools' Even Start program.

The Kendall-Whittier school houses one Even Start program, set among dilapidated homes, just ten minutes from Tulsa's equally spent downtown. As I approached the school one winter morning, I passed a soiled brown house with a drooping front porch, weighed down by a weathered couch bursting at the seams. A pick-up truck rested on the dead lawn of a neighboring house. Kendall-Whittier, which once served poor white and black families, now enrolls over 1,100 predominantly Latino children. The school has ten kindergarten classes, and about half the area's four-year-olds attend a pre-k classroom. I ducked into a spelling bee being held in Kendall-Whittier's spotless gymnasium one morning. The bleachers were filled with exuberant parents.

Parents with infants and toddlers can sign up to win a slot in the Even Start program, which is run by Cindy Lance. Describing Even Start's approach, Lance said: "Children learn about their membership and identity . . . mostly outside of school." One key is "to break the cycle of illiteracy of families."[34] The program could afford to serve only thirty-four families in 2005, including twenty-six mothers with infants. Parents spend time at the school with their young children, and staff go out to homes once a month. "Parents love it . . . our parents feel they belong to the school . . . Word has gotten out that we are a community school," Lance said. One program staffer, Mariela Ortiz, reflected on her own childhood in Mexico, "We always respected teachers as the only ones who are going to teach us. We wouldn't use to read, we grew up hearing our grandparents telling stories." The average Even Start family reports earnings of $15,601, and has lived in the United States for about four years.[35]

The Even Start teachers and outreach staff talked of "teaching parents to be the first teacher of their child." One staffer said, "they don't get down on their floor, or flow with their kids." Another said, "it's amazing how much more language they (the mothers) are getting out of their children . . . they're (now presenting) more challenging tasks."

From time to time, Lance's staff paused to learn from the parents. The mother of one toddler, Michele, didn't want her doing any water play, a sacred element of early childhood programs. It turned out that Michele had contracted pneumonia three times prior to her third birthday. Ortiz said, "it goes back to beliefs, where we thought that you get wet, you're gonna get sick." By seeing development as rooted in home practices, not simply tied to the pre-k classroom, the Even Start team came to better understand such culturally situated child-rearing and mothers' early-learning practices and beliefs.

Tulsa as Movement Icon

"It's no exaggeration to say that the eyes of the nation are upon you," said Professor William Gormley, Jr., speaking to over a hundred civic leaders in Tulsa,[36] when Steven Dow opened the Reed Head Start center in late 2004. Gormley, a political scientist at Georgetown University, was asked to detail the early learning gains that he and Deborah Phillips had discovered as they tracked children moving through Tulsa's preschool program. Amidst the simmering contention over how children should be socialized and taught inside preschool classrooms, Gormley's team focused on cognitive skills, including letter recognition, word pronunciation, and mathematical concepts. Dow commented to me that he was "disappointed that Bill's study doesn't look at anything other than traditional cognitive outcomes, like social-emotional (and) health outcomes that are important for us."

The Georgetown evaluation continues to find sizable gains in cognitive skills among youngsters who spend a year in the Tulsa program. The findings are encouraging for early educators and useful politically. Paul told me that there's been "a huge, rapid change (in political support) since the Georgetown study." National UPK advocates and benefactors—the evaluation is funded by the Pew Charitable Trusts—broadcast these upbeat results widely. Gormley argues that "the advantages of pre-k programs are that if you can demonstrate big cognitive gains—which studies of child care and family child care haven't shown—then this will be attractive to Democrats and Republicans alike."[37] Again, we see a dark line being drawn between "questionable" child care and the more "legitimate" organizational form, preschool.

Tulsa has much to brag about. Gormley's first-round analysis, released in 2003, did include a teacher assessment of children's social skills and emotional development, drawing from the district's own assessment items, but revealed no discernible effects in these domains (as with the results of national studies). So, the Georgetown team narrowed in on cognitive skills, where they found notable benefits for children from poor families.[38]

Gormley's team undertook a second round of data collection, building from a more rigorous evaluation design.[39] In the fall of 2003, they trained teachers how to administer three subscales of the Woodcock-Johnson Achievement Test: letter and word identification, simple elements of writing letters and words, and simple math problems and reasoning. This nationally normed test avoided the ceiling effect—in which many white and middle-class children scored close to the top scale, making it difficult to detect preschool effects—seen with the district's own assessment tool in the first study.

Almost two-thirds of the children participating in the second analysis were African American, Latino, or Native American; the same proportion qualified for subsidized lunches. Teachers administered the subscales to 1,567 four-year-olds as they entered preschool and to 3,149 kindergarten children, 54 percent of whom had not attended a TPS preschool classroom in the prior year. The non-attendees became the comparison group, put up against the children who had attended. Gormley's team took into account some demographic features of the families and kids in order to control prior factors that might determine which children entered preschool.

To further address the possibility of selection bias, Gormley employed what's called a regression-discontinuity technique, essentially seeing if the association between child age and achievement (the regression slope) shifts upward for children who have spent a year in preschool. This was done by restricting the analysis to youngsters who were near the cut-off date for entering the preschool program. When this rigorous way of comparing the performance of children who did, or did not, experience preschool was employed, strong benefits were found on the cognitive development scales. The difference for scores on letter-word recognition equaled 0.64 of a standard deviation (SD), equivalent to what the average child learns over a six-month period in kindergarten. The difference on applied problem solving between pre-k and non-pre-k attendees equaled 0.38 SD. These are encouraging effects of notable magnitude.

The Gormley team linked these gains to the quality of teachers, attributing the benefits to the mandated bachelor's degree. But the team did not directly observe teacher practices or correlate training levels to child outcomes.

One alternative hypothesis is that Tulsa's more specific curricular aims and regimented instructional practices may boost children's cognitive scores independent of teachers' credential levels. The magnitude of children's gains equals the medium term rise in math scores displayed by the nation's fourth-graders in recent years, stemming from state-led accountability measures, independent of teachers' preservice training levels. Still, these promising findings do invite a closer look at which classroom-level mechanisms actually explain the sizable boost provided by Tulsa's preschool program.

Moving from his findings, Gormley vocally supports universal access to preschool. In his initial paper with Phillips, Gormley claimed that "it is possible that some of the classroom benefits that accrue to disadvantaged children are attributable in part to the presence of more advantaged children in the same classroom."[40] His team has yet to publish any pertinent results to substantiate this claim, however. In Georgia, an intriguing study by Gary Henry suggests that children from poorer backgrounds do benefit significantly from attending preschool with middle-class youngsters.[41] Gormley has also argued—betraying his political science training—that "universal programs are more likely to receive strong, sustained support from public officials and the general public, thus helping to ensure high quality."[42] This begs the question of whether all children experience lasting benefits from preschool, just like Tulsa's blue-collar youngsters.

Outside the Civic Circle—Color and Culture

As should be clear by now, the remarkable rise of universal preschool in Tulsa has stemmed from the work of a small civic circle deeply committed to young children's early growth. The likes of Pam Brooks, Andy and Janet MacKenzie, and superintendent David Sawyer labored inside the school system; respected business leaders like Pete Churchwell and Bob Harbison advanced the same cause with broader constituencies; and activists like Steven Dow and Carol Rowland, with deep roots in poor neighborhoods, have enlivened the ideological debate over how children best grow and learn. These typically modest and understated civic activists have accomplished much.

It's equally important to recognize, however, that this small civic circle, while certainly to the political left of the average Oklahoman, is far less diverse in class and cultural background than the wider society. The quieter voices of Tulsa parents are less frequently heard.

GAINING A PRESCHOOL, LOSING A LANGUAGE

Alma Calderon broke into tears at a round-table discussion with three other Latino parents.[43] "It's hard for him, I feel it's really hard," referring to her four-year-old son, who had entered a Tulsa preschool two months earlier unable to speak or comprehend English. I asked whether any of the teachers or classroom aides spoke Spanish; the Latina mothers shook their heads in unison.

One of them, Josefa Izquierdo, who was frustrated with this situation, said she "taught a Spanish class for the preschool kids in the afternoon." But to her, this felt insufficient without support from the principal. "I wanted to teach my daughter (age four) Spanish . . . but when I speak to her, she just ignores me. She says, 'But here everyone speaks English,'" Izquierdo told the group. "It's a nightmare." A third mother, Eva Livas, interjected: "My son took a (Spanish) class outside the preschool program, but he gets frustrated, he can't get through to his grandparents, who would rather speak Spanish."

Overall these parents were quite happy with their preschool options. They believed their young children should learn English while "starting school at four," as Livas put it. But they also saw their children slipping away from them culturally and linguistically. "It's really important to become bilingual," to Calderon, who hoped to get her daughter into the Spanish immersion kindergarten at Eisenhower International School, a TPS "school of choice."

These parents talked of differing social norms as well. "Everyone's so open here (within the preschool program), but I don't want her going up to strangers." Another said: "My daughter's just not used to being asked questions all the time." Still, their agitation centered on language, and the lack of a linguistic bridge between home and preschool, the first formal institution in which their four-year-olds were immersed.

When the question of Latino families is raised in Tulsa, the civic activists express generous benevolence and warmth toward these parents and children. But in a sense Latinos are viewed as the *objects* of early education reform. The actual voices of Latino parents are rarely heard in public conversations. Andy McKenzie got to talking about Tulsa's demographic shifts one evening over a hamburger downtown, and spoke with characteristic candor: "Hispanics are enjoyable to work with. Their families are tight, and they want their best for their kids . . . (but) we're not very good at communicating with these parents. We're a big old public school system, so we just say, 'tough.'" One morning, walking down the hallway in an elementary school, I asked a teacher whether any preschool or kindergarten programs adopted a bilingual approach; she shook her head and said, "Well, the civil rights people say, 'put the word *structured* in structured English immersion.'"

Within the coming decade almost one in five children to enter a Tulsa preschool classroom will be Latino. I asked Kendall-Whittier principal Judy Feary about their pedagogical approach when it comes to language acquisition. "It's just full immersion," she replied.[44] "The district was not prepared (for Latino growth). We had one ESL specialist, who now runs the Newcomer School." That's Tucky Rogers, an enthusiastic principal long committed to helping immigrant communities. The school, which started in 1981, was created to serve Cambodian, Hmong, and Vietnamese refugees who were relocating in Tulsa. Now most of its families are Latino. Rogers struggled to recruit a single bilingual classroom aide, who assists three kindergarten teachers.

Maria Carlota Palacios, at the Community Service Council, was equally candid when I asked how school officials were responding to the growing count of Latino children: "They know nothing about the families. TPS has really not reacted (how) they should have years ago," she said. "Now they are making some gestures . . . Just because they think (parents) have a brochure, they think they are successful."[45] She also worried that Latino organizing was still in its infancy. "We (Latino women) are not individualists . . . we are team players," Palacios said, "But we don't know how the process works, and when you don't look at the big picture, you don't know where you are going."

Tulsa educators also expressed heartfelt affection for, but sometimes stereotypical views of, Latino families. One principal told me: "Most Hispanic parents defer to the school, look to our guidance. If they don't come (to school events), we go get them." A teacher mentor told me: "Kids are coming with deficits because parents don't understand . . . we need to keep training parents, developing the parents' awareness of nurturing these little brains." At one Tulsa school, none of the preschool staff spoke Spanish, even though well over half the children were Latino. One teacher told me: "We don't get a lot of parent involvement. It's hard because most are Spanish speaking." Another principal said: "What you would give to have a bilingual staff person in the office." Out of desperation, Rogers, at Newcomer School, has taken to hiring skilled parents, and recently put a Peruvian mother on the payroll to run the after-school program. Andy McKenzie said: "We have teachers sitting back, saying 'this kid shouldn't be in my classroom, he doesn't speak English.'"

Harriet Patterson, who followed in Andy McKenzie's footsteps at the TPS district office overseeing pre-k programs, told me: "There's a pretty critical shortage of bilingual teachers to connect with parents . . . We're competing with Texas, who pays better."[46] She also talked of how the rise in credential requirements further limits the pool of bilingual teachers. "We lost a teacher from Guatemala because she hadn't taken American social studies," due to NCLB-inspired requirements. Classroom aides have to complete the equivalent of a two-year college degree under NCLB as well. Patterson mentioned political opposition within TPS to efforts to extend transportation allowances to more families who want to participate in the district's school choice program. "Then we would need more bilingual staff," she said.[47]

Rogers, at the Newcomer School, is thankful to have an English as a second language (ESL) coach. But, "with all the pressure from the district to raise test scores, the focus is on grades 3, 4, and 5," and the specialist is rarely available to coach preschool teachers. Rogers also expressed regret about a Spanish-speaking couple who had worked as classroom aides, "until No Child Left Behind . . . They couldn't meet the qualified teacher piece [of the requirement]."

Partnerships between TPS and community organizations, including Head Start, do help to relieve pressure on school officials to take Latino families more seriously. The CBO community has longer and deeper experience with this rising population, not to mention with African American and Native American families.

Several community leaders, such as Dixie Reppe, expressed a healthy skepticism about the capacity of big systems to respond to non-mainstream families. Reppe, the executive director of the Tulsa YWCA, told me: "We actually know more about the education of four-year-olds than the school district. They tend to see it as getting ready for kindergarten. We've learned that a preschool is not just a school for little ones. The same rules don't ap-

ply."[48] The YWCA has been able to expand preschool programs at three facilities around the county, due to Reppe's contract with TPS and private backing from the wealthy oilman George Kaiser. A recent convert to the early
childhood cause, he also endowed an infant-toddler center at the University
of Tulsa.

Reppe is closely tracking the growth of Tulsa's Latino communities. "It's
a fairly recent phenomenon that Hispanics are using child care centers. They
hold onto their kids. But it's really changing, because they want their kids to
do well in school." Reppe believes that CBOs, like her own, are better
equipped to serve this new group. "The principals say, 'the language barriers, cultural barriers are so great, we don't have enough time.'" Reppe's preschool team has pushed back against the district's laser-beam emphasis on
academic skills: to her, "the less it looks like school, the more kids can learn,
it just seems fun." And one supportive TPS official told me: "Head Start is
moving more aggressively on diversifying teachers."

A COUNTER CULTURE — CHEROKEE PRESCHOOLS

Assimilation is the unspoken notion that guides much of early education in
Oklahoma, not unlike other states. There has been little objection to it in a
political culture marked by consensus and typically polite civic discourse. But
drive a couple hours east of Tulsa and one discovers a quite different view of
how young children should be raised and how pre-k classrooms should be
created. Here, I learned from Harry Oosahwee how the Cherokee Nation
decided to break from the assimilationist ideology of child development.

After driving across the eastern plains, a flat expanse of brown during this
winter visit, I turned north to Tahlequah, the capital of "The Nation," as it's
called, where the trail of tears ended for the Cherokee people. During the
harsh winter of 1838, seventeen thousand Cherokees were forced to march
from their north Georgia homelands to the Tahlequah area. Four thousand
of them died. Today, the signs of cultural and economic integration are more
salient. Just south of Tahlequah I passed the brand-new Cherokee Casino, a
triple-wide trailer surrounded by forty or fifty pick-up trucks and late model
sedans.

Oosahwee acknowledges his boundless optimism. Tall, imposing, and quietly articulate, he's half cultural evangelist, half counter-culture theorist from

the early 1970s. Oosahwee's tee-shirt read: "Let it be." But the Beatles' adage doesn't exactly characterize his work. Here he has created a Cherokee immersion elementary school, which begins with preschoolers at age three. He described it to me: "It's more than just language learning . . . it's a spiritual trip, a cultural trip, it encompasses a way of life. Language *is* culture. The teachers are committed to this, to recover a way of life . . . to seeing the life of the Cherokee world view and how it's different than the English world, the Western view."[49]

Oosahwee grew up in a Cherokee-speaking home. "I can remember talks with my aunts and uncles, about life as a Cherokee person." His grandfather, a Baptist minister, wrote his sermons in the Cherokee syllabary from the 1890s forward. Oosahwee won a stint at the Monterey Language Institute in northern California while serving in the military. There, he rediscovered the cultural tenets of language, differing ways of seeing the world. He got a shot at putting into practice his desire to bolster the Cherokee language after the nation's demographers analyzed data from the 2000 census. They discovered that younger parents were giving up their home language; few could read and write in Cherokee. The Cultural Resource Center decided to experiment with a Cherokee immersion school—to counter the English immersion philosophy pressed on the Cherokee children by the surrounding public schools. And with the money flowing in from expanding casino operations throughout eastern Oklahoma, the nation had fresh resources to invest in early education.[50]

Oosahwee's three pre-k classrooms are situated in a spanking-new school just down the hill from the town's water tower—a landmark of sorts for the surrounding farms, strip malls, and small cottages that make up Tahlequah. Here, three- and four-year-olds eagerly speaking Cherokee were surrounded by a rich array of manipulables and literacy-related materials. Oosahwee and his teachers designed the original printed materials—colorful pictures of cows, cars, farms, people in various occupations, all with the corresponding Cherokee word below. Perhaps twenty binders of text-based language materials fill the shelf in one classroom; vocabulary and ideas get progressively more challenging for the forty-five children attending the preschool program.

While breaking from the dominant society, Oosahwee has drawn heavily from the liberal-humanist ideas of Pestalozzi and Dewey. With perhaps inadvertent irony, he speaks of a "Renaissance in language." The preschool is staffed by five teachers and classroom aides, all fluent in Cherokee, and advances a progressive pedagogy of sorts. Oosahwee told me: "Our approach is to make it fun with lots of activities. When they go out on the playground they're speaking Cherokee." He worries about his own kind of teacher shortage, however. "It's only older women who know Cherokee well." At the end of my afternoon visit, one of the teachers in her late fifties looked thoroughly worn out as her charges, still full of energy, greeted their parents during the pick-up period.

Oosahwee has explored becoming a charter school to win public funding. But, he adds, "if we go into state schools, the teachers have to be certified." He also would lose classroom aides who lack the two-year college degree required under NCLB. He has been working with Northeastern State University to create a preparation program for Cherokee-speaking teachers.

"I guess I'm a little selfish," Oosahwee told me. "Wouldn't it be wonderful if they could see the Cherokee world? It's really up to us to give that gift of language back to them. It's going to give (them) a much more colorful world for them to see."

Lessons—An Early Education in Oklahoma

As a UPK movement icon, Oklahoma is rightfully cited by advocates as a success story. The story is remarkable, especially in a state so conservative on many other issues. However, for anyone who believes that early educators should be reflective practitioners or for those who feel that families should help shape how institutions socialize their own children, the lessons from Oklahoma are more complicated and sometimes troubling.

The Oklahoma case illuminates how the timing and organizational form of UPK have been adapted to local conditions. Local politics do matter, as institutional and economic constraints open or close down policy and funding opportunities. By the mid-1990s, the circle of activists and early educators in Tulsa and within the state capital came to express a common set of *ideals* and *institutional assumptions*. The new generation of UPK advocates working at the national level really coalesced after Oklahoma's preschool finance revolution had occurred in 1998. As UPK's philosophical frame and legitimating evidence took clearer form, starting with the media blitz over the new brain research, they served to award political status to, and wider support of, state legislators like Joe Eddins and Penny Williams. These policymakers tied early childhood closely to raising test scores and promising a more able workforce. The older liberal-humanist themes grew faint.

Early UPK proponents such as Harbison and Paul believed that with child care and preschooling there was a public responsibility to support all families. They worked to define the problem and the institutional remedy as operating inside the schools. By rhetoric that separated child care from preschool, these civic activists came to define their movement as an educational reform. No strategy sessions were held to make this decision; it was almost inadvertent. Given the distorted incentives that existed for local districts to create mixed-age classrooms with young children, the opportunity arose to advance UPK in a bill aimed at fixing this *a priori* problem.

Neoinstitutional theorists, including Stanford's W. Richard Scott and John W. Meyer, emphasize how activists in a young sector predictably reach into a neighboring sector, such as the public schools, to build from an established logic of action and symbols of what a legitimate organization should look like.[51] Still, few could anticipate how the rising pressure for school accountability, higher test scores, and the crescendo of NCLB's enactment in 2002, together, would advance the skilling ideology and the unquestioned attachment of preschool to real school. The CBO-contracting provision acted as a pressure valve, to release any political opposition that was building to the preschool finance bill, and created a fiscal incentive for school districts to work with the nonprofit sector.

Outside the early education arena, *economic forces* continue to play a decisive role. Central Tulsa's economic decline, white flight in the wake of school busing, and the arrival of new ethnic groups altered the city's character in the space of two generations. These changes also created an opportunity for progressive activists, educators, and moderate Republicans to work together to aid low-income families. The decline of many rural communities and the out-migration of families created a political opening to backstop imminent losses in school funding—by simply adding four-year-olds to the school finance formula.

Middle-class women flocked into Tulsa County's wider labor force beginning in the 1970s, spurring popular demand for child care options. Even in this conservative heartland, feminist ideals were interwoven with mothers' aspirations and professional work. UPK powerhouses like Ramona Paul talk of preschool expansion as "a women's issue." The flip side of Dixie Reppe's business card, the veteran YWCA executive director, reads: "Empowering Women, Ending Racism."

The *state's own interests* continue to power Oklahoma's preschool revolution as well. State legislators Eddins and Williams, quite tangibly, came to the rescue of rural school districts to protect their school funding. Capital insiders told me that former Governor Keating raised significant campaign funds from conservatives who saw UPK as a new front in the culture wars. Keating also was able to step onto the national stage, when conservative Washington players like the Cato Institute joined the fray. When the Oklahoma initiative came to be defined as education reform for the middle class— not simply child care for the poor—various elements of the public sector benefited, from local school boards to teacher colleges to the teacher unions, which gained new members. And political leaders, promising to raise school test scores, promised that preschool would be a big part of the fix.

Political actors are not motivated only by self-interest. Effective players inside the civic circle like Eddins, Paul, and Dow continue to operate from their ideals about how to improve young children's daily lives and learning. They intend to sustain the same liberal-humanist ideals that were put forward by Froebel and Piaget. On this front, the twenty-first century has yet to overtake the eighteenth, to play on E. M. Forster's phrase.[52] However, these Oklahoma humanists operate in a political context in which the discourse of cognitive skilling and school readiness—and the political promise of raising test scores—appears to have broadened support for building more pre-k classrooms. It's not clear that corporate leaders such as Churchwell, Harbison, and Kaiser would have become so invested in the cause if it had been promoted as learning more through (developmentally appropriate) play.

Indeed, a key lesson for UPK enthusiasts is that the sales pitch can become the reality. Staying on message can result in dumbing-down how we come to see child development. School principals in Tulsa felt pressure to raise test scores, as Pam Brooks reported. So, they pushed expedient forms of instruction, drilling on phonemes, vocabulary, and counting. Only the Head Start and pre-k teachers working in CBOs still enjoy some distance from this narrowing of pedagogical philosophy. In Oklahoma hitching the UPK cart to the school-accountability horse has bolstered institution building. But some preschool teachers are now paying the motivational price for pacing schedules and reduced professional discretion. Those fresh young teachers with bachelor's degrees have been taught to be discriminating, sensitive professionals, only to enter a workplace that at times resembles an auto assembly line.

Die-hard developmentalists like Pam Brooks, Carol Rowland and the McKenzies continue to push for a balance between the rising emphasis on narrow academic skills and the liberal-humanist trust in the child's inquisitive nature. They don't deny the importance of advancing young children's early language and cognitive growth. As caring educators, they hope that test scores will climb in the elementary grades. But achieving a balance in the classroom between nurturing children's social skills and self-confidence and training them in more complex cognitive proficiencies is what the Tulsa progressives are trying to achieve. "(It's) challenging to balance . . . if you have true values of what child development is supposed to look like," Rowland remarked. "We talk about circle time, not (as) learning letters, shapes but (as) a time to ask open-ended questions, or learning how to cooperate."

The Oklahoma story also teaches us how a state's political culture determines the kinds of reforms that can legitimately be made and the reform ideas that slide off the table. Its proponents pitched making preschools universally available, for example, as a way to raise and equalize the quality of early education. But given the lack of diversity and cultural understanding among many of Tulsa's elites, their socialization agenda for young children has implicitly taken on dominant linguistic and social norms. The idea of engaging the city's Asian, Latino, and Native American parents—to explore alternative forms of pedagogy, knowledge, or bilingual instruction—is almost unheard of in these polite circles.

Head Start leaders express growing concern about the possibility of a two-tiered preschool system in Oklahoma. It's a bedeviling dilemma. School superintendents are faced with scarce classroom space and realize that Head Start and other CBOs have rich local knowledge. Contracting out preschool to CBOs not only frees up district resources for middle-class communities but also passes the buck to these community agencies to provide health services, engage parents, and worry about the shortage of bilingual teachers. One of the wisest liberals I know in Washington, Mark Greenberg, once told me: "If I had a blank slate, I wouldn't design a (preschool) system just for the poor."[53] But with school systems continuing to favor their middle-class constituencies, should we expect school-based preschools to do any differently? Once preschools are handed over to school systems, like kindergartens, won't the fate of young children be shaped by the unequal political-economy of public education?

But we should stay tuned. The Oklahoma story continues to unfold. One piece of good news, perhaps, is that preschool enrollments are leveling off. "I'm not sure our enrollments are going to get much higher; we have a preschool on every corner," Tulsa school superintendent Sawyer told me. He was already shifting his attention to how to "improve services" for children and families. Perhaps once the UPK institution is fully legitimated and completely built out, the essential question of how Oklahoma's diverse parents really want to raise and teach their children will come into sharper focus. Basic academic skills will likely remain a central thrust. But as civic activists in Tulsa realize that the city's population is becoming more diverse and even better organized, a more sensitive discussion about how families hope to raise their children may result that might challenge the ideological positions of skilling proponents and liberal-humanists alike.

* * *

In the next chapter, we travel to the wild west of the universal preschool movement—the state of California—to explore how local conditions there have affected the timing and social organization of early education reform. California offers a vastly different political scene, a colorful array of ethnic communities, seasoned activists, many of whom run child care programs, and a spirited debate over how best to raise children. We discover the way that deep-seated economic and institutional forces are animating civic leaders and grassroots enthusiasts in the wide-open political culture of the Golden State.

CHAPTER FIVE

California—Preschool with Pluralism

Terri Robison, a preschool teacher on the blue-collar west side of Long Beach, savors her child care options. "She just loves school," she told me, referring to Brianna, her three-year-old granddaughter. "She wants to go on weekends. It's so home-like . . . Rosario's love spreads wide and far and deep."[1] Brianna's "school" is actually a family child care home, run by Rosario Gutierrez, just a mile from Garfield Elementary, where the soft-spoken Robison works, surrounded by tidy 1950s-era cottages with faux-hacienda façades.

The demographics of neighborhood—"just off the 710 (freeway)," as Los Angeles residents say—have shifted since World War II. After the war, black families like Robison's arrived over two generations, when jobs in the aerospace industry were plentiful here and in neighboring yet mostly white Lakewood. There are few trees, and the day I visited the school the glare overhead was intense, the sun trying to erase the moist haze drifting inland from the harbor. But that didn't slow the enthusiasm of the hundreds of mostly Latino kids as they zoomed about the playground, a concrete rendition of a

Mexican plaza, but bordered by rectangular classroom blocks rather than a majestic church.

"I like hands-on with the kids . . . My life is just kids," Robison told me. She entered the early education field at age eighteen as a classroom aide. Twenty-four years later, she works as a lead teacher for the Long Beach schools. Robison became a mother of sorts for the second time in her early forties when her daughter, Chanell, entered the military and left for Kuwait, leaving Brianna in the care of her grandmother. For Brianna, she said, "I was looking for a family thing. I didn't want her to be in an environment like a school setting, like here with forty kids." "It's just four kids over there (at Gutierrez's licensed home). She likes being read to, she tells me all the time, 'It's reading time.' But it's a bigger scale at a center. I know she needs to see more kids and adults . . . she's almost ready."

Framing the Child Development Problem

While Robison was weighing options for Brianna, California's largest teachers union and Rob Reiner were licking their wounds. Together, they had drafted a $4.5 billion ballot initiative to create a universal preschool system to be run by local school districts. It would have incorporated nonprofit preschools and their teachers into the public schools and the union, similar to Oklahoma's system. But in early 2004, under the weight of opposition from moderate churches, ethnic leaders, and a rookie governor named Schwarzenegger, Reiner crumpled.

Meanwhile, Los Angeles and three counties in northern California were busy creating regional UPK initiatives that advanced a wider set of early education options for families, including a mixed market of centers and licensed homes like Rosario Gutierrez's. "You have people with the 5–0 perspective, (where) the child is in school and my job is to make sure the child learns within the four walls," said Neal Kaufman, then the director of pediatrics at Cedars Sinai Hospital; he is also a persuasive member of the L.A. Children and Families Commission, which had set aside $600 million for UPK. "And you have people who think 0–5, you start with the fetus prenatally, and the child needs to develop in the family . . . How much does the construct include preschools as centers of the neighborhood?"[2]

Kaufman is a flag-bearer for those who start with the child's surrounding social environment—the home and the neighborhood—and ask how the preschool and allied child care organizations can strengthen the child's everyday settings. His conception of the problem is rooted not only in the liberal-humanist conception of the individual child acquiring discrete skills, absent his or her immediate environs; also, he perhaps unknowingly provides a contemporary voice for Arnold Gesell's view that until home and neighborhood environs improve significantly, child development won't markedly advance. But the rhetoric of Reiner's allies and some public educators continues to focus on the infant's brain and embedding skills. The preschool thus becomes a discrete treatment that is applied to a lone youngster situated within a bounded classroom.

Some UPK advocates find salvation in states like Georgia or Oklahoma, where institution building has unfolded with comparative ease. But when we look at California, with its colorful demography and politics, we see evidence of a new kind of culture war. The contest is between strong players who advance differing ideas about how young children should be raised, and by whom. They ask whether one universal institution can match the state's diversity of families. This chapter focuses on Los Angeles County, the nation's most populous metropolitan area, where two in every five children enter kindergarten with little or no proficiency in English. In 2002, 29 percent of the state's young children lived in Los Angeles.[3]

As in Oklahoma, in the Golden State a circle of civic activists—including progressive children's advocates and Republican moderates—have attempted to coordinate the institution-building process. Regions like Los Angeles and San Francisco have their own political cultures, different institutional histories when it comes to child care, and seasoned advocates from various professional and ethnic communities. Differing conditions have led to differing ways of framing the problem and variations in the local timing of early education reforms.

This chapter locates the major players on a geopolitical map of sorts, situated inside or along the edges of this civic circle. These actors, as we saw in Oklahoma, both ride deeper social-economic currents and attempt to alter them. We begin with a bit of history, sketching how ideals regarding child development, the economic divisions that fracture California society, and the government's interest in early childhood have, since the 1940s, come to energize the wider child care movement.

Diverse Children, Pluralist Politics

During my Oklahoma sojourn I never met anyone quite like Yolie Flores Aguilar. But to grasp Los Angeles' bewildering mix of cultural forces, local identities, and sometimes rugged politics there is no better teacher.

Before moving to southern California, Aguilar's father milked cows in El Paso to feed his wife and young children. He found work close to Lakewood in the 1960s, sanding down the metal sheets that formed the shiny skins of jetliners, and Aguilar's mother worked sorting vitamins into plastic bottles. "I didn't even know anyone who went to college, except the landlord's son," Aguilar told me. "I remember feeling I couldn't even talk to him." But after a high school biology teacher took her to visit Occidental College, within an hour from home, she succeeded in winning a scholarship. Because she was the eldest of four children, Aguilar's parents opposed her leaving for college. "I actually left without their permission. It was a very painful experience."

"Where I get the slight radicalness, I don't know," Aguilar told me. However, L.A. insiders never confuse her petite stature and riveting smile for softness or a willingness to toe the line. "We don't want to create a (universal preschool) system that no one will use, a straight middle-class system," she told me.[4] She heads the Los Angeles County Children's Planning Council (CPC), not to be confused with the county's Children and Families Commission, which kick-started L.A.'s own preschool initiative using tobacco tax revenues.

Over the past decade, Aguilar artfully organized neighborhood councils in each of eight so-called "service planning areas" (thus the ironic acronym, SPAs), which serve to unify neighborhood activists and ethnic leaders. Referring to one member of the small civic circle that guided the UPK design in Los Angeles, Aguilar commented demurely that he "may have been threatened by the CPC's ability to get 3,000 parents to show up."

After the core UPK planning group floated preschool quality standards that would have excluded some community-based programs that lacked the resources to upgrade their teachers, Aguilar made sure that new support dollars were included in the $600 million budget. When the group discussed inclusion of family child care homes (FCCHs) that met certain quality standards (a plank included in no other UPK state), she pushed hard for this measure and won. And when the planning co-chair, Nancy Daly Riordan (wife of the former mayor, Republican Richard Riordan), resisted inclusion of parents on the governing board, Aguilar compromised but secured two out of the eleven seats for parents. She moves easily between talking with county supervisors about child care issues and speaking before a crowd of nine hundred–plus Asian, Latino, and black activists at the Carson Convention Center, pulled together to create an agenda for early education and public school reform.

In contrast to Latinos in places like Oklahoma, in Los Angeles the Latino community is politically dynamic and highly effective. Antonio Villaraigosa was elected mayor in 2005, the first Latino to head the city since 1872. Campaigning two weeks before election day, he read *Rainbow Fish* to a class of curious four-year-olds as Daly Riordan and Reiner looked on. Villaraigosa promised to expand preschooling, attempting to draw a contrast to his opponent, incumbent James Hahn, who allegedly was "missing in action" when it came to school reform.[5]

Beyond the role of CBOs and parents in any new preschool initiative, well-placed Latino leaders like Aguilar worry that UPK is often pushed as a way to raise test scores. This emphasis could lead to assessing three- and four-year-olds in English (already begun in Head Start) or promoting English immersion (already felt in school-based preschools). There's a pervasive distrust of the unwieldy, often ineffectual Los Angeles Unified School District. An activist attending the Carson political rally told me: "Why would we want to hand our young children over to *that* system a year earlier (for the pre-k year)."

Ideals and Realities

The Yolie Aguilars of Los Angeles epitomize the cultural pluralism and organizational diversity that are energizing contemporary politics. The state's wild and woolly political culture—*democratic* is another adjective that comes to mind—reflects the optimism and the economic roller coaster that characterize the Golden State. Indeed, California's mixture of cultural and linguistic groups is somehow different: Californians are supposed to live on the cutting edge, creating something bolder for their children.

The state has long been marked by sharp economic disparities, but of late with incomes displaying an hourglass structure, there's an apartheid-like separation between rich and poor. The struggle over early education is but one location in which civic activists try to equalize opportunity across local communities that live in separate realities. Attending a ceremony to mark the one-hundredth preschool to receive funding from the city's UPK program in the fall of 2005, L.A.'s newly elected Mayor Villaraigosa proclaimed that "this experience, make no mistake, will give these kids a level playing field, that fighting chance to make it in this city of dreams."[6]

One of California's dreams is that somehow opportunity will be arranged more fairly, compared with the old world ways "back East." One of the state's earliest philosophers, Josiah Royce, looking east from San Francisco in the late 1870s, asked whether conforming Americans simply "read the same daily news, to share the same general ideas, to submit to the same masterminding social forces, to live in the same external fashions, to discourage individuality."[7] He would later complain of California's lack of social coherence and depart for Cambridge, recruited to Harvard College by William James. Royce had concluded that "there is no philosophy . . . from the Golden Gate to the summit of the Sierras."

Californians would come to pride themselves on rejecting the East's affection for preserving caste and old cultural forms, instead valuing the pioneering spirit and hoping for egalitarian social relations. Writer Joan Didion recalled her eighth-grade graduation speech, delivered in 1948 at Arden School, outside Sacramento. Her punch line: "We must live up to our heritage, go on to do better and greater things for California." Didion has written of how this innovative spirit was embraced by men and women who left their kin, pulled up roots, risking disease or death on the uncertain journey to California. The first immigrants arrived by boat or covered wagon in a land that promised gold, cheap land, a fresh start—and a looser social fabric. In philosopher Royce's words: "Nowhere else were we driven so hastily to improvise a government for a large body of strangers."[8]

A TORTILLA CURTAIN

At the turn into the twentieth century, the journalist and playwright John Steven McGroarty helped to create a fresh identity for Los Angeles, then still seen as a ragged city playing second fiddle to San Francisco up north. He settled on this: "The old new land of promise . . . the City of Destiny." Yet one problem constrained this drive for progress: how to assimilate the growing number of Mexican and Chinese families. "California is no longer a Territory of the United States, and legally, Los Angeles no longer a Mexican pueblo," wrote historian James Miller Guinn in 1901. But, he added, the "process of Americanizing the people was no easy undertaking."[9]

In Los Angeles, residents of Latino origin made up about four-fifths of the population in the 1850s, falling to just one-fifth by century's end. But the "Mexican problem" was worsening, in the eyes of civic elites, and undercut its freshly marketed profile. The outskirts of downtown, around Aliso and Los Angeles streets, were described by one commentator: "Crooked, unpaved streets; low, lean, rickety, adobe houses . . . here and there an indolent native, hugging the inside of a blanket, or burying his head in a gigantic watermelon, were the most notable features of this quondam Mexican town."[10] In the 1890s civic leaders, including the growing count of real estate agents, came up with the idea of creating *La Fiesta de Los Angeles*, with an annual parade in which various ethnic groups built floats and marched through downtown. Photos of the parade were used by developers to recruit investors by projecting L.A.'s apparent social harmony.

The city boosters who organized *La Fiesta* could not have dreamed of their eventual success. By the year 2000, the combined Los Angeles and Long Beach metropolitan area was home to over 9.5 million people, 45 percent of whom were of Latino origin. Beginning in 2001, a majority of newborns in California once again have at least one Latino parent.[11] The count of Latinos *doubled* in Los Angeles between 1980 and 2000, rising to over 4.2 million.

The Latino middle class, too, has grown dramatically over the past two generations. Almost one-third of all Latinos live in suburban areas, not the inner city.[12] One-third of the residents of Ventura County, once a lily-white region to the northwest, are now of Latino descent. Across all suburban residents, 24 percent are foreign-born.[13] And the southern California basin is huge geographically. Stretched across 4,100 square miles, it's twice the size of New York City and its six surrounding counties.[14]

Even so, the centrifugal spread of ethnic communities has come to segregate peoples throughout much of the region.[15] The upscale west side of Los Angeles, which includes Beverly Hills, Malibu, and Santa Monica, is 63 percent white and 16 percent Latino; 58 percent of all adults there have attended college. A half-hour south on the 405 in the Long Beach and Lakewood area, just one-third of residents are white, 35 percent are Latino, and 16 percent are black. A flat, economically desolate stretch between the 605 and the 710 is home to a colorful range of families, speaking at least thirty-nine different languages. The better-known south-central region of poverty—Compton and Watts, which experienced severe rioting in the 1960s and again following the Rodney King verdict—is now 60 percent Latino and one-third African American.[16] In four in every five zip codes of Los Angeles, the residents speak more than twenty languages.[17]

The Southern California writer T. C. Boyle captures the separation that marks daily life in Los Angeles. Delaney, the white and affluent protagonist of Boyle's novel *Tortilla Curtain*, reflects: "They are everywhere, these (Latino) men, ubiquitous, silently going about their business, whether it be mopping up the floors at McDonald's, inverting trash cans in the alley . . . or moving purposively behind the rakes and blowers that combed the pristine lawns of Arroyo Blanco."[18] In Orange County, one-third of the housing developments built a decade ago were designed as gated communities.[19]

The suburbanization of California, and the widening gaps between rich and poor, undercuts idealized images of social integration. Los Angeles didn't invent the idea of suburbs, of course, but developers took the notion to extremes during the postwar boom. In April 1950, some 25,000 people lined up in front of one Lakewood real estate office to bid on two-bedroom homes costing $7,575 each. Over 17,500 houses were sold by one developer, and in what was then the world's largest shopping center, parking was constructed for 10,000 cars.[20] In one picture of a pristine Lakewood, countless rows of square cottages appear, dotting a perfect grid of treeless streets. To this day, Lakewood's city-limits sign proclaims: "Tomorrow's City Today."

RAISING CHILDREN IN A ROLLER-COASTER ECONOMY

Californians enjoyed a suburban nirvana for two generations at most. The economic restructuring that hit the nation's rust belt in the 1980s soon arrived in California, sending its automotive, steel, and tire industries—enterprises that provided union-level wages in places like Long Beach and the East Bay up north—into a tailspin. Aerospace rose and fell before going into permanent decline in the early 1990s, with massive job losses for middle-class workers.

At the same time, the high-tech industry, entertainment firms, and international trade were booming—reshaping the structure of jobs available to semi-skilled workers. The garment sector continued to expand, reflecting a new production model in which countless small firms began to fill specific niches; these jobs typically paid low wages, freezing out unions, and rarely offered health insurance. Currently, a quarter of all undocumented Latinas in Los Angeles work in these textile firms, the sector employing 140,000 workers overall.[21] One need only stop for coffee in tony Westwood to see the gulf between laptop-gazing scientists from UCLA and the Spanish-speaking clerks who take orders for their lattes. In Los Angeles, there is a greater share of adults who have never finished high school (24 percent) than in any other metropolis nationwide; 11 percent of adults have never finished the sixth grade.[22]

Still, in much of California, upward mobility persists. Of the state's middle-class families with young children, those hovering on either side of the state's median income, fully 47 percent are now Latino.[23] However, sharp disparities in children's daily environments map onto the state's hourglass structure of work and family income.

These disparities lead to recurring calls for bolder policy action on children's issues. The share of L.A. County residents living in poverty rose from 11 percent in 1970 to 18 percent in 2000, and family poverty, no longer contained to the inner city, continues to seep outward.[24] The share of suburban neighborhoods in the region experiencing high poverty rates quadrupled between 1970 and 2000. And the segregation of families by ethnicity, language, and social class is remarkable. Just one in six children lived in poverty on the west side of Los Angeles in 1999, whereas half of the children in South Central (Watts) and a fourth of youngsters in Long Beach (where just half are fluent in English) did so.[25]

But in the 1990s paradise was not yet lost, to paraphrase veteran journalist Peter Schrag. The dot-com industry was booming up north in Silicon Valley, and southern California's economy was remaking itself, struggling to adapt better to global flows of labor and capital and to new technologies. State government revenues, fueled by the frenetic trading of stock options by electronics industry moguls, climbed by $21 billion in 2000, when it supported one-fifth of the burgeoning state budget. This influx allowed Republican governor Pete Wilson, and then Democrat Gray Davis, to nearly quadruple outlays for child care and preschool centers, which reached $3.1 billion annually by 1999. The legislature's women's and Latino caucuses also played an increasingly influential role (the former chaired by Deborah Ortiz). At one point, female legislators staged a sit-in at Governor Davis's office, refusing to leave until he agreed to another hefty augmentation of child care funds.

Those heady days proved to be short lived. As the dot-com boom turned to bust, it blasted a hole in the state budget and brought down Gray Davis, who lost to Arnold Schwarzenegger in a 2003 recall election. The new governor tried, some claimed half-heartedly, to protect school spending, but a $12 billion budget deficit meant that child care and other family supports would be slashed. These cuts would reinforce the claim by UPK advocates that a wider base of support was necessary, and public dollars should be targeted to the middle class rather than only on the poor.

It seemed that the California of a bold, unbridled future was being pulled down by economic divisions and fractured politics. If there ever was a time for idealism, for defining an uplifting public project, it was now, and Rob Reiner—filmmaker, liberal stalwart—had a grand dream in mind. He wanted to tax wealthy Californians to the tune of $24 billion over the coming decade to finance free, high quality preschool for all four-year-olds.

Early Education Comes of Age

California's idealism and its deep economic divisions can make for a combustible mix. The cultural battles that have flared up in the Golden State often turn on questions of how children are to be raised or taught in school. Voters passed a succession of ballot initiatives in the 1990s—to immerse school children in English-only classrooms; to limit affirmative action; and to cut off social services to immigrant families (the latter was thrown out by the state supreme court). California's nativist impulse—the desire of many, mainly white, voters to conserve one language and one way of life—will likely fade as California moves into an era with no one ethnic group forming a demographic majority.

Still, among civic activists—from moderate business leaders pushing school reform to ethnic neighborhood leaders running preschools—the tough challenge is to build a consensus about who should run early education, and by what means. Part of the problem is institutional: Los Angeles County alone contains 88 cities, 82 school districts, and over 1,100 nonprofit agencies; combined, they spend over $18 billion on children's services each year.[26] By the mid-1990s child care had become a major public policy issue in Los Angeles and up in Sacramento, where Governor Wilson talked of "preventative policies," including expansion of state-run preschools and the legislature considered new child care options as welfare-to-work mandates led to a surge in demand.

CHILD CARE BECOMES A PUBLIC ISSUE

Wilson Riles first moved early education to the center of school reform in 1972. As California's first-ever black schools chief, Superintendent Riles proposed, and the legislature approved, what he called *early childhood education* (ECE). This initiative consolidated and infused new dollars into various child care efforts, including a dramatic expansion of the state's half-day preschool program, which had been created in 1965 and was modeled after Head Start. Children's advocates also convinced the legislature that the state education department, not the welfare agency, be designated to oversee the ECE initiative, given its focus on educational quality and support for blue-collar working families, not only for quick child care placements to help move mothers from welfare to work.

California's education department had long overseen the preschool centers established by the federal Lanham Act. These were begun in 1943, when thousands of women took jobs at factories and military bases to aid the war effort. Each center established a sliding fee schedule pegged to family income and was to give "special consideration . . . to women whose husbands were killed or maimed in the war."[27] (The woman worker "Rosie the Riveter" was originally popularized at the Richmond shipyards just north of Berkeley.)

The state legislature began licensing "day nurseries" even earlier, in 1927, about a decade after creation of the federal Children's Bureau to advance national standards. The first two centers licensed in California were the Grace Day Home in Sacramento, run by the Franciscan order, and the Colored Children's Home and Day Nursery in Oakland. California also began to experiment with child care vouchers early, in the 1970s, spearheaded by liberal activists. The experiment offered local "resource and referral agencies" to better inform parents of their options. The idea was to empower parents to make better-informed choices, picking among a wide array of child care choices. By 2002, the state education department had contracts with over 1,300 local agencies—well over half of them CBOs—to run state preschools and centers.[28]

Berkeley, of course, was ground zero for the student revolt in the 1960s, and sparked all sorts of creative political actions by young feminists. One group in 1969, for example, demanded that the administration replace the ROTC office with a women's studies department. Historian Ruth Rosen recalls when she and her comrades took over the already-leftist KPFA radio station in Berkeley, agitating for more coverage of women's news, literature, and poetry.[29] Young mothers in Berkeley like Betty Cohen and Patty Siegel came to focus on the issue of child care. Frustrated by the lack of options, they turned their living rooms into day care co-ops and created a hotline for other mothers seeking care.

In 1973, Cohen founded Bananas, one of the first resource and referral agencies for parents and child care providers, sparking what became a national movement. Siegel created a statewide network of these local agencies in the early 1980s and became California's preeminent advocate for state funding for child care.[30] If you ask capital insiders why the state child care and preschool budget nearly quadrupled in the late 1990s, Siegel's name inevitably comes up. Down south in Los Angeles, two black community leaders—Alice Walker Duff and Karen Hill-Scott—created Crystal Stairs Inc. in 1980, which would become a mammoth agency supporting families in the impoverished South Central district.

Two episodes back in Washington would pump fresh funding and political enthusiasm into child care in California in the early 1990s. The first was

George H. W. Bush's agreement on the new child care block grant in 1990. Federal child care funding—much of which went to preschools via parent vouchers—then rose dramatically in the wake of the 1996 federal welfare reforms, the second episode that shook the early childhood field.[31] The number of California families drawing cash aid had fallen by half by 2000. This policy success was sustained by rising child care support, which allowed single mothers to work. Governor Pete Wilson signed legislation in 1997 to implement the federal reforms; included was a major expansion of state-funded preschool and child care programs, which had been pushed by advocate Siegel and the women's caucus. The next logical question then emerged: why couldn't hard-working blue-collar and middle-class families benefit from skyrocketing public funding?

RESEARCHERS AND REPORTERS

The political debate was no longer over *whether* government should help shoulder the child care burden, but over *which kinds* of child care settings should be endorsed by the state—presumably in response to parents' own preferences—and *how wide* a swath of families should benefit from public financing. By the mid-1990s, the media were furiously covering the early brain development story and asking whether welfare reform would hurt young children. The widening public debate moved government agencies and major foundations to fund new studies of how young children's development was spurred or hampered by different kinds of child care. The release of fresh findings in support of preschool's ability to boost the cognitive and language proficiencies of poor children sparked greater interest in that institution.

By the late 1990s, another result of feminist progress came to play a strong role in California. Persuasive women now staffed the state's leading editorial boards, including Susanna Cooper and Pia Lopez at the *Sacramento Bee*, Patty Fisher at the *San Jose Mercury News*, and Karin Klein of the *Los Angeles Times*. And education reporters—were focusing on young children's development and the pressures facing young families; led by the pioneering Susan Chira at the *New York Times*, Linda Jacobson at the national paper *Education Week*, and Carla Rivera of the *L.A. Times*. These women offered in-depth reporting and careful analysis of young children's daily lives and how public agencies might improve the early childhood experience.

In 1997 California's welfare agency asked my research center to detail the supply of preschools and home-based care across the state's counties, down to zip-code areas. This research would help the agency to figure out how to distribute new dollars to expanding programs. The study was jointly funded by President Clinton's child care bureau and was conducted with Patty Siegel's network. When it was published in 1998, our work revealed vast disparities between poor and affluent communities in the supply of preschool centers. The story was covered in detail by the statewide press. When we updated our research in 2002, the results revealed that the robust growth in parent vouchers had boosted the number of informal care arrangements but had failed to spur growth in preschools. The *Los Angeles Times* ran this headline: "Southern California Need for Preschools Is Acute."[32] The research report, covered by the *Times*'s Rivera, came out just a month after Reiner had urged the county to set aside $100 million for universal preschool.

In the late 1990s, the National Institute of Child Health and Human Development (NICHD) funded a neighborhood study, headed by sociologist Anne Pebley, that mapped how demographics and the structure of jobs in Los Angeles shape disparities in children's development. The results of the study, involving two rounds of interviews with 3,010 families across sixty-five neighborhoods, are eye-opening. Among mothers who failed to complete high school, disproportionately Latinas, just one-fourth reported reading with their young child (three- to five-years-old) at least three times a week. Among mothers who attended college, almost 80 percent read to their child with this frequency. Among parents residing in very poor neighborhoods (median household income, $23,391) just over half reported that their preschooler had at least ten children's books, whereas in non-poor communities (median, $55,378), 89 percent did. Importantly, the study found that low-income and Latino parents displayed similar levels of warmth and affection toward their young children.[33]

Public concern over young children grew, alongside these fresh findings. This helped set the conditions for effective advocacy. Voter approval of Proposition 10, in the fall of 1998, was another bolt of lightning to hit the early education field. Crafted by Reiner, "Prop. 10" added a fifty-cent tax on every pack of cigarettes sold, initially raising over $700 million per year. The bulk of the proceeds continue to flow to local First 5 Children and Family commissions—fifty-eight of them, one per county—to support early learning, child health, and programs for parents of children zero to five. Governor Davis appointed Reiner chair of the statewide First 5 Commission; he in turn recruited Jane Henderson, a savvy and meticulous Sacramento veteran, as executive director.

Reiner's earlier focus on infants and toddlers was now history. The cause had gained little traction in the young network of county First 5 commissions. Several studies had confirmed what young parents often say across the back fence: they preferred to place their toddlers with a home-based caregiver, someone they know and trust. The question of what *parents* actually preferred for their small children would soon preoccupy Reiner's commission and spark contentious debate among key players in Los Angeles.

Another line of research proved controversial as UPK efforts got under way in California. State politicians like Assemblymember Wilma Chan were being recruited into the fold. She asked the legislature's research arm to estimate current enrollment rates. The number that came back was 47 percent: under half of all *three- and four-year-olds* were enrolled in a preschool center.[34] But when Berkeley's Margaret Bridges calculated enrollment rates for the state's *four year-olds*—the exclusive focus of Reiner's new ballot initiative— she found that 62 percent were attending a preschool center in 1998, based on federal data. RAND researcher Lynn Karoly put the figure at almost 65 percent, drawing from a second, and more recent, source.[35] These numbers proved troublesome for movement leaders, since in Georgia and Oklahoma, enrollments were topping out at or below 70 percent. How should the argument for "universal" access be framed, if enrollment rates were already quite high?

Fusing the Preschool "Vaccine" to School Reform

Within two months of his 1998 gubernatorial election, Governor Gray Davis proposed an ambitious "public schools accountability act," which followed similar measures in Kentucky and Texas. California children's reading scores had fallen toward the bottom nationally and were just ahead of scores in Alabama and Mississippi. In the mayoral race of 1993, just one-fifth of Los Angeles voters had called education their top worry. By 2001, 47 percent of voters did so.[36]

In response, Davis pressed for more frequent testing, more attention to the progress of ethnic subgroups, and a barrage of carrots and sticks for schools that showed growth or still fell behind. The legislature moved quickly on Davis's platform, approving most elements of it by the summer of 1999; this was more than two years before Washington would up the school-accountability ante by passing NCLB. And with dot-com–related revenues still pouring into the state treasury, Sacramento pumped more than $2 billion in additional yearly funding into the schools, including expansion of the state preschool program.

The logic of *systemic reform*—replete with state-specified learning objectives, curricular standards, and cognitive assessments of children—was seeping down into kindergarten and preschool classrooms. Delaine Eastin, who served as state schools chief for most of the 1990s, assembled a pair of blue-ribbon panels. They signaled the coming of age of the issue of early education among the state's political leaders, and the growing popularity of aligning preschool classrooms with the K-12 accountability agenda.

The first commission, which was financed by the Packard Foundation, released its report in March 1998; it detailed a ten-year plan to build a universal preschool system and recommended that fifteen hundred new centers be built each year.[37] "It's like finding out there's an effective polio vaccine," Eastin said. "Once you've seen the research, the evidence of what preschool can do for children, it becomes almost obscene not to call for universal preschool."[38] The chair of the task force was Karen Hill-Scott, the former UCLA professor who had co-founded Crystal Stairs.

This task force proved to be ahead of its time, a warm-up for more focused planning a few years later. It signaled the rising state interest in engineering more formal settings for young children—implying a system run from Sacramento. This approach worried older-line advocates. One group, Parent Voices, was concerned that "kids as young as three years old will be tested," said Rowena Pineda. Referring to her young son and echoing the ideals of Froebel or Piaget—not to mention national surveys that said parents' foremost worry is over social development—Pineda added: "I just want to make sure that he's getting the social skills that will be helpful and that he's having fun."[39]

Superintendent Eastin asked a second panel to devise learning standards for state-funded preschools; the panel included developmentalists like Susan Holloway, Sam Meisels, Marlene Zepeda, and Ed Zigler. When she released the first-ever, non-binding curricular guidelines, Eastin proclaimed that "universal preschool is the next big idea that our nation must embrace . . . more important than putting a man on the moon."[40] The task force issued a carefully balanced set of learning objectives and classroom practices, and urged preschool teachers to create a "variety of experiences that will stimulate their (young children's) cognitive, social, physical, and emotional growth." Classroom learning activities were to take into account the state's new kindergarten standards and address youngsters' social and emotional growth, not to mention "the role of play in children's learning." Traditional socialization goals, such as "self-regulation of emotions," were listed, along with "creativity and self-expression."

However, policymakers can lose track of the varied capacities of young children—or these subtleties can be eclipsed by the press in favor of school accountability. "By 2001 there was quite a lot of interest in having an all-school-district system," chair Hill-Scott told me, in a disapproving tone. That year, Sacramento Democrats were pushing to fuse early education to their aggressive school-accountability efforts. In 2002, just weeks before his re-election, Governor Davis issued a statement emphasizing that "child care programs and preschool programs should focus on the skills that children will need to be successful in kindergarten."[41] Eastin's successor as schools chief, legislator Jack O'Connell, would later ratchet up this logic, pushing a bill that specified the cognitive skills that all three- and four-year-olds should acquire, including knowing the responsibilities of citizenship and grasping the sacred importance of "national symbols."

At the same time Reiner's fledgling Children and Families Commission (later renamed First 5 California) had come under attack. Ned Roscoe, head of the drive-by tobacco chain Cigarettes Cheaper, organized a ballot initiative to repeal Prop. 10. "Don't let Rob Reiner be your kid's mom," argued Roscoe; "What kids really need is the love of their parents." The voters defeated Roscoe's initiative.[42] By 2001 the state commission had kicked into high gear, committing $206.5 million for local school readiness programs that aimed to unite child care providers, preschool teachers, and kindergarten managers inside the public schools. It also funded salary incentives for preschool teachers pursuing further training and experimental preservice training. The commission also contracted with an L.A. public relations firm for a barrage of media messages, in part talking up the virtues of preschool. This move would come back to haunt Reiner.[43]

The other effort lending form and legitimacy to California's fledgling UPK movement came in 2001, when state legislators appointed a committee to develop a new master plan for what some now called "pre-K to 12" education; it was no longer just K–12 in policy parlance. Reiner's state commission then volunteered to pay for a "school readiness working group" of over fifty members and chaired again by Hill-Scott. Sharon Lynn Kagan at Yale was asked to serve as the principal consultant, and Rima Shore, who had penned the earlier reviews of infant brain research, would draft much of this blueprint.

The second pitch for universal preschool was published in early 2002, four years after the first task force. This plan was more detailed and breathtakingly ambitious—at the very moment that state revenues were dwindling, along with the dot-com bust. It urged that infants and toddlers be given "guaranteed access to high quality child development services . . . beginning at birth," and that universal preschool be provided to all three- and four-year-olds.[44] The earlier panel's focus on infants and toddlers was back on the table, given the panoramic range of ideals being put forward.

Yale's Kagan also pushed the radical notion that schools need to get ready for young children, not vice versa, recommending that a "ready schools plan" be drafted by every school district to ensure a "rich, standards-based curriculum . . . and continuous family supports and services through the primary grades," a return to Gesell's holistic conception of development. The panel's family-oriented subcommittee urged the legislature to "provide incentives for paid family leave and (employers) to create family-friendly practices."

As the state's budget deficit ballooned and Schwarzenegger replaced Davis as governor, Reiner moved his road show to Los Angeles. This tactic proved effective in keeping alive the UPK embers, and soon sparked a diversity of county-level programs for extending access and improving preschool quality. The idea of hitching a large preschool system to Democratic leaders' push for K-12 school accountability was now firmly in place. A tighter, more loyal circle of advocates, led intellectually by Hill-Scott, had emerged. Reiner would hire a young political operative from the Clinton White House, Ben Austin, to sort out the pieces to the political puzzle, which proved to be more befuddling and explosive than these activists had ever imagined.

The Cultural Politics of Universal Preschool

Since its 1999 birth, the L.A. Children and Families Commission had undertaken not one, but two, strategic planning exercises to shape its priorities. A plan finally emerged. They came up with a crisper name, First 5 LA. But what was most notable in Reiner's mind was that the commission wasn't spending their money. Their initial sluggishness had led to a burgeoning savings account, with about $165 million in annual tobacco tax revenues steadily accumulating. This was politically risky, given the earlier attack on the state First 5 agency by the tobacco industry. Stymied in Sacramento, Reiner came together in early 2002 with progressive advocates and moderate Republicans in L.A. to build greater momentum.

THE PLAYERS AND THEIR POLICY FRAMES

Before making his pitch to the First 5 LA commission, Reiner did his homework. He met with two key players; the first was Zev Yaroslavsky, a veteran member of the county board of supervisors (which governs the vast Los Angeles metropolis) and the chair of the commission. Yaroslavsky wanted to use the First 5 dollars to extend child health insurance to blue-collar families, working parents who earned too much to qualify for federal Medicaid coverage, but whose jobs provided no health benefits. Ben Austin estimated at the time that $95 to $140 million would be required to extend half-day preschooling to the 78,000 four-year-olds in Los Angeles not currently enrolled.[45] A deal was cut with key commission members to split the accumulated revenues between health insurance and universal preschool.

Involvement by powerful county supervisors would continue to challenge Reiner and his inner circle. Two years later, when county politicians pushed to require that the UPK governing board be subject to open-meeting statutes and allocate grants equally across legislative districts, Hill-Scott said: "It saddens me that it takes so much struggle to agree on issues of control and governance . . . This in a way was sort of like a political campaign."[46] Supervisor Don Knabe, who had become chair of First 5 LA, remarked, however, that "at the end of the day, they (the voters) are not going to hold the LA-UP (Los Angeles Universal Preschool) board to account, they are going to hold the political establishment accountable."[47]

The second key player Reiner met with was Roy Romer, the former Colorado governor, who now ran the L.A. Unified School District. When I talked to Reiner the week before his initial pitch, he said: "Romer will back us on the bond issue (including dollars for preschool facilities within a new revenue bond), but he seemed overwhelmed with everything else." Romer was never really drawn into the UPK movement. According to Hill-Scott, he "stood up in 2002 and said, 'we don't have any business in preschool.'" School board president Caprice Young, who was a rising star in former mayor Richard Riordan's circle of moderates, did attend the First 5 LA meeting to support Reiner's call. But she also warned that most overcrowded elementary schools did not have space to add preschool classrooms.

In part based on Romer's tepid support and because of a memo from UCLA's Neal Halfon waving Reiner off backing a school-based system, the proposal advanced in June 2002 "would stress early reading and math skills and mainly use existing child care centers in both the private and public sectors rather than develop a new string of government-built schools."[48] Just sixteen months later, Reiner veered back to a school-based system, arm in arm with the California Teachers Association (CTA), advancing the first rendition of his UPK ballot initiative. But in the pluralistic politics of Los Angeles, "the challenge is the sheer number of perspectives and groups and people that need to be a part of this," according to Jacquelyn McCroskey, a First 5 commissioner and USC social welfare professor.[49]

Reiner successfully put together the votes, and First 5 LA directed its staff to design a countywide universal system and set aside $100 million as a down payment. Hill-Scott and her consulting firm were named to lead the planning effort the following November. She "will be seeking to unite an often fractious assortment of community leaders, child care advocates, educators, and parents to complete the project," as *L.A. Times* reporter Carla Rivera put it.[50]

The curtain went up in early 2003 on designing L.A.'s regional UPK initiative, and a colorful array of players came on stage, not always playing their roles harmoniously. The theater metaphor fits well, given that Hill-Scott artfully proceeded on two levels: frontstage and backstage. First came a sustained political pep rally: over a hundred fifty local politicians, child care stakeholders and community organizations, school officials, and academics; they convened eight times, occasionally within the new, $189 million Catholic cathedral, Our Lady of the Angels. Polite quips surrounded the elegant meals catered by Hill-Scott's firm, perhaps arranged to fit the spiritually rich and palatial surroundings. "It was a traveling circus," one participant said. The task force's co-chairs, Daly Riordan and mayoral hopeful Robert Hertzberg, sat up front, watching over the proceedings on a raised platform (reminiscent of the high table at Cambridge University).

At the mid-summer meeting, Reiner arose from the high table to admonish the task force members, seated at some eighteen round tables in the Catholic hall. The group was to "put aside the internecine fights," he said. He and Hill-Scott were being pressed to include infants and toddlers in the UPK plan. But the "two areas that the public understands and supports . . . are preschool and health care," he told the assembled crowd. The plan was to focus on four-year-olds. "Let's get this investment to build public will," Reiner said. "L.A. is the linchpin to build a real infrastructure for early childhood education."[51] Later that day, we were asked to vote on whether teachers under the new preschool system should be required to have a bachelor's degree, or something less. The assembly was urged to shape other consequential policies through New England–style direct democracy.

At a second, backstage, level, Hill-Scott organized subcommittees to dig carefully into the key features of the UPK design. Should First 5 fund a half-day or a full-day program? Which agencies should run preschools? Which possible quality standards were truly related to children's development? How would parents be involved? The "community outreach committee" proved a base from which Yolie Aguilar and her neighborhood allies began to move the L.A. blueprint toward a remarkably inclusive program: a range of community- and school-based centers—including licensed family child care homes (FCCHs)—would eventually be able to run UPK programs.[52] "I saw it as my job to respond, to be inclusive, to not have fights with people," Hill-Scott said in our interview. "I thought you couldn't have a school district just sweep in and take over," harking back to her own CBO roots at Crystal Stairs. "I found a monolithic, one system as the easy way out," she said. "It doesn't make it responsive, culturally sensitive."

The issue of who would get to run neighborhood preschools became prickly throughout the planning year. First, which county agency should run the UPK effort, in light of scant political support of the L.A. schools to take over administration? This question looped back to the broader framing of the raison d'être of preschool. Should this human-scale institution focus on a narrow instructional mission—focusing on academic knowledge and plugging four-year-olds into school? Or should it be conceived more broadly, in the vision of Aguilar or Kaufman—an organization that looks at child rearing more holistically and serves to pull together parents and unite neighborhoods?

Second, if the public schools did not run the L.A. system, how would quality benchmarks or curricular guidelines be set? Should the county system rely on proxies of quality, such as maximum class sizes, staffing ratios, or teacher credential levels? Or should the implementing agency promote a particular classroom approach, as in Oklahoma, where academic skilling and the logic of NCLB were taking root? Georgia and New Jersey have both put forward a variety of curricular packages from which preschool directors choose. The L.A. school district, for its own network of preschools, was implementing in 2003 a semi-scripted package called Developmental Learning Materials Express, which "could be correlated to California's pre-k curriculum guidelines," as district administrator Imelda Foley told me. "Thinking of No Child Left Behind, even though it doesn't apply (to preschools) . . . we want to align teacher credentials (and curricular practices) to it."[53]

One feature of Hill-Scott's plan was never contested within the pluralistic politics of Los Angeles. There was quick consensus that the UPK initiative should focus on identified "hot zones," defined as zip codes with high poverty levels and few preschools. A controversy briefly emerged when it became clear that half of the hot zones, based on these criteria and mapped by UCLA demographer Leo Estrada, turned out to be in the district of supervisor Gloria Molina, a long-time advocate of community-based child care. In the end, the two hundred first-round "preschool" sites (half of which were actually FCCHs) were distributed more equally across each of the five supervisor districts. But the initial allocations from the implementing agency did, in fact, focus on lower income communities. "Universal" preschool remains progressively targeted on low-income families in Los Angeles.

WHICH ORGANIZATIONS GET TO PLAY?

A clear distinction between *child care* and *preschool* had emerged in the minds of UPK advocates by the late 1990s. The tandem study panels in Sacramento pitched the phrase "school readiness" and talked of high quality. Advocate

Libby Doggett's argument in Washington was worth remembering: "I think we made a huge mistake in child care. Even if it means slow growth in (preschool) enrollment, we shouldn't compromise quality." The small circle of national advocates wanted to sell something new, something only seen before in boutique experiments like the Perry Preschool. They also wished to distance themselves from the sizable gains in child care funding in the 1990s made by the earlier generation of advocates, many of whom weren't jumping on the UPK bandwagon.

Yet as Hill-Scott's planning effort moved forward she was reminded of this earlier view: given parents' varied work schedules and preferences when it comes to caregivers, families desire options. The pro-choice policy frame, which had come to dominate the field by the early 1990s, fit the L.A. political culture quite well—especially given the diversity of organizations that served children across L.A. Kathy Malaske-Samu, the county's child care director, put it like this: "I think Rob and some school districts saw it as a school-based program. This (early childhood) community just couldn't accept that. There are advantages of having different options. The numbers are just too big (to accommodate enrollment growth in schools alone)." She also emphasized that a half-day program inside a school would require, for parents working full time, moving four-year-olds to another center or caregiver in the afternoon.

First 5 LA already was battling its parent commission in Sacramento and Reiner's executive director Henderson over whether funding should go to schools or to community-based organizations. Henderson had held a senior post in the state education department when the federal Healthy Start initiative expanding child and maternal health services via public schools came down. "She hated the CBO ones," one First 5 LA commissioner told me. Another pro-CBO activist reported that Henderson saw "school as the universal link . . . UPK becomes part of school, it starts at four rather than five." When the state commission provided matching grants for school readiness hubs, linking public schools and child care providers, they "rejected CBO proposals . . . A majority (of the awards) went to school districts," said Mary Hammer, a leader of the Long Beach neighborhood council.

Several key actors emerged in 2003 to advance a mixed-market arrangement, pushing for a wide mix of neighborhood organizations that would qualify for UPK funding. One front was to ensure that centers run by community nonprofits, churches, and even for-profit firms could participate in the new L.A. program. Local FCCH associations also got into the act, participating in Hill-Scott's work groups and at times allying themselves with Aguilar and the local SPA councils. As Nancy Wyatt, head of the San Fernando Valley association said, "Family child care providers in other states have had the bad experience of being promised an opportunity to participate (in UPK) and being disappointed."[54] Midway through the planning year, another activist, Inglewood psychologist Colleen Mooney, protested: "Child development people feel they know what's best for all kids. This is not a program that honors parent choice . . . They have a clear bias for institutional settings."

The teacher unions, perhaps unintentionally, were driving a wedge between multifaceted child care options and the push to attach preschool to public schools. The CTA's magazine ran a piece in 2001 with this subtitle: "Once looked upon as child's play, preschool education is now serious business."[55] When Reiner joined with the CTA to advance his first version of a UPK ballot proposal in fall 2003, the union contributed an organizer and legal staff to this short-lived effort. Similarly, the American Federation of Teachers (AFT, the rival to the CTA's parent union, the National Education Association) flew out a staffer from Washington in early 2005 when Reiner's caucus regrouped to draft a new ballot initiative. And the pro-UPK foundations would come to fund public school lobbies to advance the cause. In California the Packard Foundation, for example, provided a grant to the California School Boards Association to publicize the issue with local members.

The advocates also zeroed in on a shared interpretation of their polling data. When Reiner's state First 5 commission had first gauged public opinion in 2001, pro-UPK enthusiasm looked soft, especially among Latino families.[56] They hired a new pollster, Peter D. Hart in Washington, and new questions were devised, including one which asked whether "organized education should be made available at age four or younger." Favorable responses climbed when the question was asked this way, without the ambiguities of other forms of child care.[57] The respondents were a random sample of possible voters, not parents. They were nervous about government involvement when it came to infants and toddlers. County child care director Malaske-Samu and others were trying to focus policy attention on the entire zero-to-five period, but she reported that "Reiner's polling said that's not where the public's mind is at." She added: "But they do get school readiness for four-year-olds."

What *do* parents prefer when it comes to child care options? This question was the subject of recurring debate throughout Hill-Scott's planning process. One earlier study, by Raymond Buriel and Maria Hurtado-Ortiz at Pomona College, found that less than one-sixth of Latino parents, whether native or foreign born, had selected a preschool for their young child under five.[58] Wen Chang and I analyzed NICHD parent survey data from Los Angeles and found a similar pattern across the county, with a slightly higher propensity for Latino parents to select FCCHs.[59] Our work demonstrated a classic chicken-and-egg dynamic, however: if parents could not find any affordable, or publicly funded, preschool slots in their neighborhood, then preschool was not really a credible option.

To become better informed about the issue of parental preferences, Hill-Scott asked UCLA's Estrada to facilitate a series of focus groups. The answer came back: across social classes, there apparently was strong support for preschool centers. However, Yolie Aguilar and her neighborhood council leaders, more focused on parental choice, were not convinced. So, in the summer of 2003, midway through the planning year, Aguilar obtained First 5 funding to make a broader survey, of 3,201 parents, to be administered by staff and volunteers from the local SPA councils.

Almost 48 percent of the parents with young children in the survey were non-English speakers, and 47 percent availed themselves of some form of nonparental child care. In the latter group, 28 percent of children under six attended a preschool center; another 10 percent attended an FCCH. Parents in all ethnic groups expressed interest in enrolling their child, beginning at age three or four. A significant slice, about 12 percent, said they preferred to use an FCCH provider. Most parents emphasized the importance of both pre-literacy skills and social development. Many reported understanding the message that pre-literacy skills were important for their child's later school performance.[60]

Other players encouraged Hill-Scott to build from L.A.'s colorful pastiche of organizations. The FCCH associations argued that they had many vacancies in their licensed homes, just under 4,000 enrollment slots according to Malaske-Samu's earlier county-wide analysis.[61] A child care workgroup in the SPA that stretches from the Los Angeles airport south to Long Beach issued a position statement proclaiming that "we reject the notion that at the age of four all children should be relocated to an institutionalized, formal educational setting. One of the chief benefits of family child care is that it honors the right of parents to choose from a variety of programs."[62]

This statement echoed the sentiments of Michelle Cerecerez, a union child care organizer, who told me: "In terms of facilities . . . there's no way under God's green earth that you can get every kid in L.A. into a school-based center. These ladies (running FCCHs) really need help and resources . . . people in the industry realize that you can't put these people off any more."[63] Other L.A. groups also had been organizing FCCH providers, among them John Jackson, at the Association of Community Organizations for Reform Now (ACORN). "To see LAUSD (L.A. Unified School District) as the saving grace, it's just another nail in the coffin," Jackson told me. "They can't now deliver everything that's on their plate."[64] Another CBO advocate said: "I don't think Karen Hill-Scott understands grassroots organizations . . . she is far from these communities."

Yet some neighborhood activists may have misjudged Hill-Scott. Her first academic writings in the 1970s focused on how black families had long relied on kith and kin for child care. She wrote: "Child care should not be seen as an end in itself, but rather as the means by which public policies can create the appropriate kinds of services to meet diverse family needs."[65] Her final plan for universal preschool was dramatically inclusive, making CBO programs and FCCHs eligible for universal preschool funding. "I know people around the country thought I was crazy . . . but it's all a big experiment," she told me.

Others pushed for child care options as well. One of them was Renatta Cooper, a persuasive First 5 commissioner, who reported that the planning group focused on preschool for four-year-olds because "that's what the polling data said . . . (but there is) a strong class bias around who goes to preschool, (and) who goes to child care."[66] The inclusiveness of Los Angeles' final design was shaped also by Kara Dukakis, who staffed Hill-Scott's subcommittee as an Oakland-based policy analyst for Children Now. "We're talking about high quality family day care that can compete," Dukakis told me. "Even the CTA was saying we can't accomplish this without a mixed delivery system."

In the end, those who saw UPK as strengthening the wider community-building agenda were pleased with the blueprint that emerged in early 2004.

"We are very, very interested in how neighborhoods help children's development and well-being . . . from prenatal, to preschool, to community the child grows up in this context," said First 5's Kaufman, adding, "It's an ecological approach, how to create better environments for children. The plan that Karen Hill-Scott created is quite ecological." Don Knabe, the county supervisor who chaired First 5 LA when the plan was approved in February 2004, told me: "We have to look at what we have (already). I saw opportunities (for) existing community-based programs and to build from them. I don't think we should build new buildings."

HOW TO BUILD QUALITY PRESCHOOLS

As the planning committees rallied around an inclusive range of organizations, the pivotal question of how to build quality preschools became complicated substantively and politically. At first, many worried that Reiner had in mind something like the Hope Street Family Center downtown, an expensive comprehensive-services model that few mom-and-pop nonprofits could afford to replicate. "We don't want it (UPK) to be another white elephant program . . . like Cinderella, so special, precious that it will just fit into the shoe," said veteran child care advocate Patty Siegel.[67] Others were concerned about the rhetoric of "school readiness" and the drift toward a narrow set of academic skills, in part because the L.A. school district was implementing their new preschool curriculum in alignment with Open Court, the phonics-based curriculum.

Still other activists feared that quality standards befitting affluent suburban preschools—those employing more teachers with bachelor's degrees— might lead to less diversity—linguistically and culturally—in the teachers entering the field. Having less diverse teachers, in turn, might homogenize the content and the pedagogical strategies used in classrooms. These fears were not unfounded. Early on, Malaske-Samu's office began shaping a five-star quality system, distributing more UPK dollars per child to programs that employed more highly credentialed teachers; it eventually was adopted. I visited one new program in Pasadena, which initially was given just three stars, where the lead teacher—who had seventeen years of teaching experience but lacked a bachelor's degree—was completing her credential by taking classes on the Web. But the question persists: empirically, do such training mandates have much to do with children's growth over time?

The diversity of the child care workforce in the long term remains a major worry in California, where a majority of newborns have at least one Latino parent. Evaluating a forty-eight–county in-service training effort supported by Reiner's First 5 commission, the University of Virginia's Bridget Hamre found that 47 percent of preschool staff were non-Latino whites. This result is explained by the community-based nature of federal Head Start and state preschool programs going back to the 1940s. In stark contrast, 74 percent of the state's public school teachers were white in 2002.[68] Thus, worries of a whiter, more monolingual, workforce persist. Such a workforce could discourage enrollment growth among the very children who most benefit from quality preschool.

In fact, "more and more immigrant children are being enrolled in programs in which teachers possess little knowledge of their family culture and language . . . (with an) increasing emphasis on rigid and narrowly defined academic goals for very young children," according to Laurie Olsen of the civic group California Tomorrow.[69] This trend cuts to a core question: what social norms, cultural values, and languages should characterize preschool classrooms? Paraphrasing one parent, early childhood specialist Antonia Lopez said, "I don't want them teaching my child to negotiate with her grandmother."[70]

The question of whether the programs propagated should be half-day or full-day was also being debated during the planning year. The grassroots group Parent Voices urged that full-day programs be emphasized, "so that children do not have to move from location to location throughout the day."[71] But less than a third of parents in the L.A. area reported preferring a full-day preschool; the majority preferred a half-day preschool with the option of wrap-around care, according to Aguilar's survey. Hill-Scott's plan eventually fit this preference, also driven by cost considerations.

One potentially controversial topic drew little interest during the planning year: How should classroom activities or a formal curriculum be structured for L.A.'s four-year-olds? "I think we're dancing around it," Malaske-Samu told me one afternoon, at a downtown open-air market, adding: "With the quality rating system we chose not to get into the curriculum." But, I asked, how could the school district be so aggressively implementing a fairly scripted "basic skills" curriculum in their preschools while the Hill-Scott process was punting? "Carmen (Schroeder, the school district's preschool chief) is in communities where test scores are a real problem . . . (but) it would be a sin if we capitulate on that—the opportunity to get rich classroom experiences—if we boil it down to something so small," Malaske-Samu answered.

Hill-Scott did believe that suggesting a range of curricular packages, as Ellen Frede had done in managing New Jersey's UPK effort, might help to structure classroom activities. "If I look at High/Scope or Creative Curriculum, they look at various domains . . . social, emotional, High/Scope even does carpentry," Hill-Scott said in our 2005 interview. "I'm not denying that I didn't impose some thinking about this, to look at some theory about the curriculum," as a means to advance quality, she said; "as an embedded way (of) professional development." Hill-Scott's instinct, reflecting back on the planning year, was to advance developmentally appropriate classroom practices in the liberal-humanist vein. "But the curriculum committee saw it as putting dollars in the pockets of the producers," Hill-Scott said.

L.A. parents, like L.A. planners, preferred that preschool teachers attend to the children's social and emotional growth, rather than focus one-sidedly on pre-literacy skilling. Aguilar's survey revealed that families preferred a balance. The three "most important" learning goals among parents were to "listen to the teacher and respect adults," to "cooperate and share with other children," and to "develop self-confidence."[72] These responses were reminiscent of the national polling data that Doggett in Washington had been dogged by; talking about social-emotional growth didn't really help in wooing school-accountability hawks. The parents in Aguilar's study, 61 percent of whom were Latinos, however, cared about whether their child would "learn to use more words," or be able to write her name before entering kindergarten. Two-thirds of the parents Aguilar interviewed expressed support for their child's learning a second language at preschool; only the white parents downplayed this priority.

In the end, Hill-Scott's plan for Los Angeles resembled pieces of the two earlier blueprints that she had designed in Sacramento. Yet the L.A. design, reviewed and approved by the First 5 LA commission in February 2004, focused clearly on low-income families and was remarkably accepting of school- and CBO-based centers; it was even open to funding family child care homes if they met quality standards. In a sense, "universal preschool" in Los Angeles was to be neither universal nor limited to preschools.[73] This unprecedented design mirrored the unique, colorfully inclusive political culture of Los Angeles.

WHO RUNS UNIVERSAL PRESCHOOL?

As the plan moved back to First 5 LA for final approval, it hit two final snags. First was the question of whether the commission itself would try to run this massive, now $600 million, enterprise. If not, who would run it, and how could they be held accountable? As commissioner Kaufman put it, "It was a difficult, third trimester birth."

Hill-Scott's blueprint had been warmly embraced by the First 5 commission and the inner circle of civic elites, who would enthusiastically endorse the UPK plan. She had built strong trust with Reiner, who would appear occasionally for key votes or for a well-engineered photo-op. By spring 2004, however, it became clear that First 5 LA did not want to direct this huge effort. The inner circle, coordinated by Hill-Scott, came to support the idea of an independent non-profit agency (in reality, a massive CBO) to manage the initiative. It would come to be called Los Angeles Universal Preschool (LA-UP), and was to be run by civic and corporate elites, who could raise new dollars and sustain high-profile political support.

Hill-Scott didn't want it to become a bureaucratic agency, and continued to advance a more dynamic corporate image. The well-heeled side of this civic coalition had long had stylistic differences with the more grassroots groups. Some, like Aguilar, worried about elite control of the entire UPK enterprise. Referring to potential board members, Aguilar said: "They had to have the ability to raise $40 million as an individual. These were the Westside, Hollywood types, almost all rich Anglos making decisions for a system serving other people." This elite originally included Daly Riordan, who was appointed co-chair of the LA-UP board. But after learning that as a public official she would have to submit financial and conflict-of-interest reports, she quickly resigned.

The related question of how to afford LA-UP a degree of independence from county government while ensuring public accountability proved to be nettlesome. One downside of tightly tying the UPK initiative to the First 5 commission was that the initiative might be subject to political pressure—for instance, to distribute dollars evenly across supervisor districts. Well over a half billion public dollars were at stake, and some members of the inner circle pushed for a high, thick wall of political separation. This was rejected by First 5 commission chair Don Knabe. "I had a hard time with a group that would not be held accountable," he told me. "At the end of the day, as a member of the commission, I was going to be held accountable. If this didn't work, given the interests of community organizations, they (LA-UP board members) couldn't go in some little room with no windows and make decisions." "It had to be a public entity," Kaufman said, and that was the decision made by First 5 at its July 2004 meeting.[74]

In the fall of 2004, Graciela Italiano-Thomas was appointed the first executive director of LA-UP, arriving with a long history of working inside community organizations and Head Start. The following spring her agency announced its first grants to local programs, aiming at creating additional enrollment slots and improving quality across a diverse mix of a hundred preschool centers and a hundred FCCHs. Just two years after Reiner had nudged his local offspring—the First 5 LA commission—to move forward, the highly participatory politics of Los Angeles had yielded the most organizationally inclusive UPK model in the nation, aiming to serve a kaleidoscopic array of children and families. Little was said about what four-year-olds were supposed to be learning or how preschools would complement parents' own child-rearing goals. But UPK had arrived in Los Angeles.[75]

A Statewide Campaign

Los Angeles was a victorious front in the California-wide battle for universal preschool. In October 2003, as her L.A. plan was taking shape, Hill-Scott e-mailed a celebratory memo to her large advisory panel, reporting that "today the California Teachers Association (CTA) is announcing an Initiative . . . to raise money for two major programs: class size reduction throughout the K-12 system and Universal Preschool for four year old children. Rob Reiner . . . has partnered with the CTA in preparing this Initiative."[76] The measure was formally submitted two weeks later, and the union began circulating petitions to place it on the statewide ballot. It aimed to raise commercial property taxes by $4.5 billion, with a third of the take to finance universal preschool.[77]

DIFFERING STATEWIDE DYNAMICS

This second episode—a story that ended in a political setback for Reiner and the teacher unions—tellingly illustrates how much particular cultural and political context matters, when it comes to formulating early education reforms. The UPK system originally sketched in the CTA-Reiner initiative was rather monolithic, giving local school districts control of all pre-kindergarten programs, and thus a radical departure from the organizationally inclusive program that was emerging from Hill-Scott's design process. In California, direct democracy isn't cheap. It takes lots of money to gather signatures, buy television ads, and combat the anti-tax groups. Reiner's first rendition of a UPK ballot initiative would have undone a key element of the infamous Proposition 13 and set a slightly higher tax rate on commercial property. To win, Reiner needed access to the CTA's campaign war chest.

Thus it was Bob Cherry, the union's seasoned policy director, who called many of the shots in producing this version of the initiative. It called for public schooling to be extended down to four-year-olds. It allowed local school boards to contract with CBOs to offer preschool slots, but would force CBO employees to become school district employees, and thus members of the union. It required that all preschools, even those run by churches, Montessori practitioners, and other nonprofits, use a structured curriculum approved by their school district. Since it required all districts to operate free preschool programs, it would have driven many nonprofits out of business, especially those in suburban communities that operated solely on parental fees. Ironically, if this first rendition of Reiner's initiative had gained traction, the more inclusive, more democratic L.A. model that targeted lower-income communities would have been emasculated.

Reiner's willingness to abandon the L.A. model, given the demands of a statewide campaign, punctuated how fluid and uncertain the institution of preschooling remained. Sociologists study the way in which inchoate fields come to cohere and become institutionalized over time—as, for instance, with the growth of public schooling or the bureaucratization of health care. The contrasts we have seen between Oklahoma and California point out the importance of local conditions, which give rise to different, politically constructed institutions to provide early education. These conditions tell us which social collectives inside neighborhoods are deemed a "preschool," and whether it is a public effort to aid poor children or an entitlement offered to all.

Given Sacramento's fiscal woes, many advocates were in the doldrums, especially after the booming 1990s, which had spurred dramatic growth in public child care spending. But now the mood had shifted. "We don't have a George Bush or an Arnold Schwarzenegger," Patty Siegel complained one evening; adding, "no one else but Rob is standing up for young children." "The most effective ways to improve education," CTA president Barbara Kerr declared, "include sending kids to schools with smaller classes . . . and by providing access to universal preschool, our children will be prepared when they enter kindergarten."[78]

Without missing a beat, the business lobbies came unglued. The state chamber of commerce, along with manufacturing and technology groups, came out in opposition to the measure. But what Reiner's inner circle didn't anticipate was the opposition that arose among moderate groups, including the California Council of Churches and the National Council for La Raza (NCLR). In a note to the field Hill-Scott tried to explain why the statewide UPK system needed to be embedded in the public schools: "Becoming a public system is the price of the ticket for admission, because the CTA is a public employees union, and by law, all instructional employees must be employed by school districts."

A small group, worried about the fate of nonprofit preschools and the likely political fallout, urged Reiner's inner circle to delay submitting the initiative language. When I inquired about the state of play, Hill-Scott e-mailed back: "First of all, it's not ME that's driving the Initiative, Rob, or anything else. If it were me, this would be an open process with plenty of participation from my colleagues in the child development community."[79] Her stance was consistent with how she had guided the L.A. blueprint. Cherry, the CTA's policy thinker, dismissed these worries in a phone conversation, concluding: "we are going to move ahead." The language of the ballot measure that emerged two weeks later still required that teachers in nonprofit preschools or churches become school employees. The initiative aimed to raise the enrollment rate to 70 percent of all four-year-olds and would require that all teachers obtain a bachelor's degree.

The debates in Los Angeles were civil, compared with the hardball played by Reiner's operatives. Austin, the young policy adviser, e-mailed me: "Talk to Karen about it. I'm not the conduit to the CTA on this. All I can say is that if 'progressives' want to be against $1.5 billion for preschool . . . because they don't agree with the process, that's their choice."[80] Since the process of drafting this first rendition had been entirely secret, I was becoming perturbed. When a reporter asked me to comment, I said: "Given that three-quarters of preschools are based at churches and community organizations now, the current draft would jeopardize the vitality of those programs."[81] Austin let me know that "your comments to the press have really pissed off Rob." The unions promised $1.8 million for the initiative campaign, with the National Education Association (the CTA's parent organization) contributing $1 million.

PLURALISTIC IDEALS AND CULTURAL INTERESTS

The concern being expressed by Antonia Lopez at NCLR, along with Libby Sholes at the moderate council of churches, based in Sacramento, was tied to the ideal of community action, so effectively advanced in Los Angeles by people like Aguilar and Kaufman. Many of NCLR's local members were Latino leaders based in CBOs, Head Start agencies, or charter schools, which served many families with young children. These leaders had grown suspicious of big urban school districts. They also saw the initiative's mandate that all obtain a bachelor's degree as a threat to the livelihood of preschool teachers of color. This, at the very same time that NCLR, NAACP, and other groups were responding to the two-year degree requirement placed on Head Start teachers by the Bush Administration.

The CTA–Reiner initiative also required that all preschools adopt "a curriculum that is age and developmentally appropriate and aligned with statewide standards for elementary schools."[82] The juxtaposition of the two competing philosophies, so ironic when viewed through an historical lens, seemed perfectly sensible to the initiative's drafters. A related classroom issue deeply troubled staff at NCLR and the Mexican American Legal Defense and Education Fund (MALDEF). If preschools were to be part of the public school system—even sanctioned by the state constitution—wouldn't the state's English-immersion mandate, required by state Proposition 227 for all school children, now apply to four-year-olds?

On April Fools Day, 2004, Lopez and Cristina Huezo at NCLR, along with MALDEF's Jimena Vasquez, hosted a meeting in Sacramento. Also present were backers of the initiative, including Maryann O'Sullivan from the Packard-created group Preschool California, and a growing list of constituencies who were quietly expressing reservations, including moderate church groups, the NAACP, and the Child Care Law Center in San Francisco. Yolie Aguilar and the SPA councils sent delegates from Los Angeles as well. In total thirteen concerns about the Reiner proposal were advanced, ranging from how school districts would find sufficient facilities to how CBOs would be involved in collective bargaining to whether the English-immersion mandate would indeed apply to preschool classrooms.[83]

The following week, a story from the Associated Press catalogued these worries, as voiced by some of the same groups. Beyond the arguments made by anti-tax groups, reporter Jennifer Coleman quoted Aguilar as arguing: "It's hard to take this position because we need more resources for preschool . . . (but) if you're going to create a system in the public education system, that will drive people out of business."[84] The California Charter Schools Association, now headed by Caprice Young, announced its opposition, in light of the credentialing and unionization requirements, which she said would obliterate pre-k programs run by charter schools.

The next day, the CTA announced that they were dropping the initiative. "Now that director-activist Rob Reiner and the state's largest teachers union have pulled their joint initiative from the November ballot, they should learn from their mistake of writing a proposition behind closed doors to fit a narrow agenda," wrote Karin Klein in a *Los Angeles Times* editorial.[85] Reiner beamed an e-mail out to the field saying that he would be back another day. He made good on that promise.

Reiner's Resurrection

The activist filmmaker, along with his equally driven policy adviser, Ben Austin, did learn from their missteps. In the year following the sudden collapse of their initial rendition of "preschool for all," they reached out to civil rights leaders, statewide child care associations, and labor unions. Reiner hosted strategy sessions and pep rallies in his spacious Hollywood home. A small circle of preschool and labor activists began negotiating the contours of a second ballot initiative.

Meanwhile, the Packard Foundation ramped up grants to a variety of groups—including those that had raised sharp concerns with the first ballot measure, like NCLR and the NAACP—to support forums with local members across the state. The elite shock troops housed within Oakland-based Preschool California were funded by Packard, as well, and "charged with coordinating statewide preschool for all advocacy and communications," wrote Lois Salisbury, the civil rights lawyer turned foundation official.[86] Austin, along with Preschool for All's executive director, Maryann O'Sullivan, went about securing endorsements from leading Democrats, and even from a handful of chambers of commerce. Reiner was ready by November 2005 to announce at a San Francisco press conference, accompanied by the obligatory photo-op sitting with preschoolers, that over a million signatures had been gathered for his new ballot measure, what came to known as Proposition 82.

Reiner's new version of UPK differed from the first in significant ways. Community-based preschools would no longer be necessarily fused to local school districts, a concession to the CBO sector that would cool off the enthusiam (and campaign cash) offered by the teacher unions. Still, community nonprofits would have to compete with local school districts for their share of $2.4 billion in annual funding under Proposition 82, a process to be controlled by California's fifty-eight county education offices. Rather than taxing business and taking on California's sacred Proposition 13 to pay for his ambitious program, Reiner chose to tax the wealthiest one percent of the state's citizens, those citizens who had benefited handsomely from the Bush II tax cuts.

The other consequential shift—stemming from interpretations of fresh polling data by Reiner's inner circle—was to define preschool expansion as a hardcore school reform. "This is truly no child left behind," Reiner said at the San Francisco press event. "This levels the playing field."[87] Democratic leaders began rallying around identical phrases. State schools chief O'Connell, in Riverside County to christen a new preschool, read from the same script: "I really believe that preschool will be the great equalizer in terms of educational opportunity for students."[88]

The head of California's Assembly, L.A. legislator Fabian Nuñez, announced his support of Reiner's Proposition 82 a month before it qualified for the (June 2006) statewide ballot. After being flown to France and Sweden by an unknown donor, Nuñez became convinced of the benefits of universal preschool. "I'm convinced that if we really want to talk about public education as being the great equalizer, we have to start talking about prekindergarten," he said, appearing with Reiner at a Los Angeles preschool. Everyone's talking points were in order: Mayor Villaraigosa, appearing at a

South Central preschool, agreed with Nuñez: "this experience, make no mistake, will give these kids a level playing field."[89]

The Reiner camp, even after reaching out to the CBO sector and ethnic leaders, had decided to fuse preschool to the public schools. And this was not only to advance children's academic skills and eventually raise their test scores. UPK would now somehow transform the institution of public schooling as well. This heightened rhetoric was starting to worry the original designers of L.A.'s universal preschool system, however. Just as Reiner's new campaign was getting under way in fall 2005, several of them met to critically review an early draft of this chapter.[90] "The message from Head Start in the sixties was the improvement of early experience, and now it's shifted to early academics," Hill-Scott emphasized. Italiano-Thomas talked about recent history, including the 1998 Head Start mandate that all children learn any ten letters of the alphabet, adding, "I find it disturbing that we've split the child . . . It's been a political decision." Meanwhile, Reiner's speech writers were doing just that.

At first the question framed by Reiner seemed like a no-brainer to many Californians: Why shouldn't we tax the very rich to provide free preschool to all four-year-olds? By February 2006 two-thirds of likely voters surveyed by the Public Policy Institute of California said they supported Proposition 82.[91] "This thing is going to pass," pollster Mark Baldassare told me.

Yet just as Reiner was feeling real lift-off from his political resurrection, he came crashing to earth once again. During the first three months following Reiner's November 2005 announcement that Proposition 82 had qualified for the ballot, the state First 5 Commission, chaired by Reiner, had spent $23 million on public service announcements that advanced the virtues of preschool, a remarkable development uncovered by *L.A. Times* writer Dan Morain.[92] The commission had funded similar messages, across various media, regarding the healthy development of children, zero to five years of age. But apparently no one in Reiner's camp had reflected on the questionable timing of the current contract with GMMB Inc., the L.A. public relations firm that produced the pro-preschool ads and had run Reiner's earlier campaign.[93] A memo drafted by a staffer at GMMB Inc. also talked of "creating demand" for preschool via public efforts.[94] In addition, Austin had moved back and forth between the state payroll and the new Proposition 82 campaign. He became the immediate fall guy, resigning in early March. Then, by month's end Reiner stepped down from chairing the state First 5 Commission. Still claiming that he had done nothing wrong, it was Reiner himself who had become the issue, not the merits of Proposition 82, which soon slipped eight points in statewide polls.

AN UNUSUAL CAST — HOLLYWOOD ACTORS
AND SCHOLARS ENTER THE FRAY

"We've seen first hand how the opposition campaign to Proposition 82 is being run," said Mark Fabiani, a veteran Democratic strategist. "It is being run against Rob, not against preschool."[95] But within the contentious *realpolitik* that quickly unfolded, no one really argued against the idea of extending quality preschool to more families. Yes, the predictable array of opponents arose, including the state chamber of commerce and the California Business Roundtable, a moderate group advocating for more effective public schools. John Fisher, heir to the Gap clothing empire, led the charge of wealthy individuals that bankrolled the No on Proposition 82 campaign. But unexpected critics of a state-run, more uniform preschool system also began to raise questions.

Debate over the substantive elements of Proposition 82—appearing in the major dailies and on the airwaves—came to eclipse the simple messages sharpened by both sides of this vigorous campaign. One bone of contention pertained to which children would truly benefit from universal financing in a state where almost two-thirds of all four-year-olds already attended a preschool center. Enrollments had reached 334,000 four-year-olds in 2003, including 141,000 who benefited from public funding via federal Head Start or much larger state programs that supported preschool centers.[96] RAND researchers Lynn Karoly and James Bigelow estimated that universal funding would boost the enrollment rate to 80 percent of California's four-year-olds. But it would pull in more children from families in the upper half of the state's family income distribution (about 32,000) than from the poorer half (about 26,000).

The net effect would be that $1.2 to $1.4 billion of the measure's $2.4 billion annual cost would go to families who already could afford to pay for preschool. When the *L.A. Times* came out against Proposition 82 two weeks before the June 2006 election, the editorial board complained that "in order to pay for 25,000 to 50,000 additional children in preschool, taxpayers would foot the bill for the 325,000 other four year olds already in preschool.[97]

The related question was whether middle-class children would discernibly benefit from a half-day program at age four, as proposed in Proposition 82. Leading Democrats were arguing—with a curious twist of logic—that universal preschool would help all children and close early achievement gaps. Those devising crisp pitches, like advocate O'Sullivan, also claimed that "the state would gain $2.62 for every dollar invested in preschool for all."[98] This figure came from the Packard-purchased RAND analysis and was based on returns to the Chicago Child-Parent Centers, which operated two decades ago, exclusively serving poor black children (Chapter 6). The advocates repeatedly generalized these findings to California's middle classes, a huge inferential leap of faith.

Two months before the election, the Packard Foundation flew in the Chicago program evaluator, Arthur Reynolds, along with Yale's Edward Zigler, Rutgers's Steve Barnett, and William Gormley, Jr., who directed the Oklahoma UPK evaluation. Only reporters were allowed to ask questions during this conference, hosted by UPK convert and faculty colleague David Kirp, at Berkeley, the home of the Free Speech Movement. Each scholar spoke persuasively about how children from poor or blue-collar families benefit from quality preschool. But the spin put on their research papers was that *all* children would benefit if Proposition 82 were to pass. Just four months earlier, the National Institute of Child Health and Human Development (NICHD) had reported how initial cognitive and language gains stemming from middle-class children's exposure to preschool had faded out by third grade (Chapter 6). But these findings were kept under wraps.

Reiner's decision to not target preschool aid on lower-income communities proved costly. A group of veteran child care activists, including Nancy Strohl of the San Francisco–based Child Care Law Center, had urged Reiner to include strong, progressive targeting language in early drafts of Proposition 82.[99] He denied this request. In response, Oakland's local First 5 commission refused to endorse Proposition 82. Equally telling, the Democratic leader of the state senate, Don Perata, switched sides, coming out against the Reiner initiative, saying it "wouldn't improve access to those who need it most: poor, disadvantaged, and English learners." Then, Governor Schwarzenegger, within a month of the June election, proposed a much smaller but highly targeted program to expand preschool in communities with the lowest-performing students.[100]

Directors of community preschools, including those fearing competition from the free school-based centers envisioned by Proposition 82, were beginning to speak up. Austin, O'Sullivan, and Reiner's inner circle had won the backing of statewide associations of subsidized preschools, since their existing funding streams were explicitly preserved. Reiner's additional $2.4 billion per year would allow these centers to further expand and upgrade quality. But preschools out in the suburbs charging fees—and three-fifths of California's four-year-olds were enrolled in these self-sufficient programs—feared severe price competition. Pamela Zell Rigg, director of the state association of Montessori preschools told the *L.A. Times* that Proposition 82 was a "wolf in sheep's clothing. We're serving 100,000 children in California, and parents see us as a strong . . . choice. But by the standards of the initiative, we will not be one of the choices."[101]

The possibility that all preschools—whether government-subsidized or independent and nonprofit—would now be attached to the state education department was worrisome to many. *L.A. Times* writer Klein penned in a signed column that "Reiner's preschool utopia would force the state to set 'content standards,' and take oversight on such matters as whether to read 'Pat the Bunny' or 'Goodnight Moon' away from parents and preschools and give it to education officials."[102] Proposition 82 also said that all preschool directors must align their classroom activities to the state's curricular standards for elementary school, a mandate that a clear majority of community preschool directors opposed in one pre-election survey.[103] Daffodil Altan, an editor for New America Media, objected to the state's normative push for a single form of child care and wrote: "There's something wrong with telling parents, who are 'disadvantaged' . . . that their kids may end up on coke and in juvenile hall if they don't go to preschool."[104]

As it became clear that Proposition 82 would boost preschool enrollments only modestly, the Reiner crew tacked in another direction, arguing that $2.4 billion a year would buy big gains in quality. An engaging flyer mailed to voters, displaying a riveting photo of a toddler tugging on a toe, read: "This little kiddie went to preschool . . . the other four kiddies had none." The fine print inside, all paid for by the CTA, clarified that four in five preschoolers attended low-quality programs. Where this statistic came from never surfaced.

Some said that only preschools staffed by teachers with a bachelor's degree display high quality. But at least two surveys had found that one-third had attained a four-year college degree.[105] The empirical evidence remains very thin that a bachelor's degree raises children's developmental trajectories, after taking into account the class backgrounds of children and teachers (Chapter 6).

We earlier saw how the research community had played a distinguished role in elevating early childhood issues, including the potential punch of preschool, over the past four decades. Now as the Proposition 82 campaign heated up, it often sounded more like a spirited academic seminar than a typical dumbed-down political tussle. Reynolds, Zigler, and I each wrote dueling op-eds, politely debating what we knew empirically about the preschool's effects on differing groups of children and how best to improve quality. The professional campaigners were not always so civil. Advocate O'Sullivan even crashed a conference call our research center arranged to brief journalists on our technical analysis of Proposition 82, attempting to discredit anyone who veered from the party line.[106]

At the same time, the selling of Proposition 82 mobilized several well-heeled Hollywood activists. The Reiner family and their star-studded friends bankrolled much of the campaign. Reiner, along with his wife, Michelle, and father, Carl, spent $5.8 million to buy television spots and mass mailings. Martin Sheen of *West Wing* fame contributed cash and appeared in television ads in the weeks before the election. Financial backers included Candace Bergen, Al Franken, Jamie Lee Curtis, and Norman Lear. By election day the Service Employees International Union, which had long been organizing child care workers, chipped in $15.7 million. Along with $2.5 million from California's two teacher unions, the proponents of Proposition 82 outspent their opponents by almost four to one.[107] If any skepticism remains that the cause of universal preschool is drawing attention from major education interest groups, one needs only to scan the list of major donors to Proposition 82.

DEMOCRATIC DOUBTS

Despite all the political juice and unrelenting media pitches, doubts were growing over Proposition 82. By late April a bare majority of likely voters (52 percent) said they supported the ballot measure, although 56 percent still reported knowing little about the Reiner initiative. Then, as more likely voters read more, they became more worried about the devil in the details. By the final week prior to the June 6 election, the yes vote had shrunk to 41 percent, with 46 percent now opposed, including souring affection among Democrats.[108] A total of forty-three California newspapers had editorialized against the initiative, expressing concern over the lack of focus on poor children, the possible state takeover of nonprofit preschools, and the wisdom of locking down within the state constitution $2.4 billion of the state budget for a single purpose, forever. Even historically Democratic papers, like the *L.A. Times*, the *Sacramento Bee*, and the *San Francisco Chronicle*, stayed off the bandwagon, arguing that Proposition 82 was too cumbersome and insufficiently focused.

Proposition 82 was rejected by 61 percent of California voters on the first Tuesday in June, 2006, despite a lopsided turnout of Democrats, who flocked to the polls to choose between a pair of would-be Democratic challengers to Schwarzenegger in the fall elections. Exit interviews by the *L.A. Times* revealed that it was well-educated Democrats who walked into the voting booth with too many doubts over Reiner's rendition of universal preschool. Three-fifths of self-identified moderates voted against Proposition 82.[109]

Inside Preschools, Seeing the Difference

By 8:45 just under ninety toddlers and preschoolers were merrily running through sprinklers, in and out of shallow vinyl pools, occasionally letting loose jubilant squeals. There was no shortage of water play at the All Saints Children's Center this hot July morning; it was already nearing 80 degrees in downtown Pasadena.

The daily news voiced by children at circle time in Room 5 was upbeat as well. Sure, a couple of their four-year-old classmates were home sick, and Genai reported that "yesterday I twisted my ankle." Nicholas, however, said he was "gonna tell my dad if we can go surfing." Everyone stood to recite the Pledge of Allegiance, and then had a quiet snack at their low-lying tables. Caitlin's tummy didn't feel quite right, but it was remedied by a long hug from lead teacher Sandy Ahlstrand. Then nets and paper bags were efficiently organized, and it was back outside for a bug hunt.

Though they don't know it, this group of twenty four-year-olds is part of a vanguard of kids in Los Angeles' intriguing experiment with universal preschool. One of the few lucky centers, All Saints was drawn out of a hat in a consequential lottery in which 100 centers were selected from the over 400 that applied. Adjacent to a gracious stone church built in 1923 by Episcopalians, the preschool sits just a block from the old city hall. All Saints preschool, founded in 1966, once served children from Pasadena's inner-city black community. But the program went deeply in debt and was unable to pay teachers "a living wage," as one staffer put it, if it served only this community. The restructured preschool now serves mainly children from upper middle-class families, who pay about $1,000 a month for a full-day program. "We have come a long way," assistant director Marti Rood told me.

All Saints, although situated in a lovely spiritual setting, couldn't be more secular and humanist in its philosophy. "To implement our philosophy, we care for children in a developmentally appropriate environment," the preschool's mission statement reads. "Children are given choices. They can experiment and explore with activities designed to meet their needs . . . by the teachers to offer choices designed to encourage physical skills, cognitive learning, problem-solving and independence."

It's too early to make firm judgments about the early impacts of UPK in Los Angeles. The ambitious effort had been under way for less than eighteen months as this book went to press. However, after visiting a handful of "LA-UP classrooms," as one Long Beach director put it, I could see several benefits, and important questions were beginning to surface.

EXPANDING ENROLLMENT, IMPROVING QUALITY

LA-UP's blueprint promises to create tens of thousands of new places to serve four-year-olds across Los Angeles county. Thus, the young agency allocated dollars to All Saints for a three-and-one-half-hour morning program to serve twenty youngsters, provided that a ratio of six children per adult not be exceeded, that the program submit to a classroom assessment, and—given that All Saints had only earned a three-star rating from LA-UP—that teaching staff pursue higher credentials.

The center receives about $5,280 per child for their twelve-month program. But if they rise to five-star rating, All Saints will get $6,600 per child from LA-UP—this is before subtracting the "parent investment fee," which equals $400 annually. All Saints is located in a middle-class Zip code, but serves a large proportion of affluent Pasadena families. This sliding-fee schedule is similar to the one used by Georgia's decade-old pre-k program.[110] The LA-UP subvention allows All Saints to cut by half the normal $12,000 annual tuition charge for parents with four-year-olds.

Lead teacher Ahlstrand told me that in the prior year, before LA-UP funding arrived, there were about eighteen kids in Room 5, a mix of three- and four-year-olds. In other words, while LA-UP is funding twenty kids, the enrollment increase actually equals two kids. This was in the initial year of implementation.

The same was true at the Long Beach Montessori School, located a few minutes' south of Lakewood on the 710. There, what director Barbara Stalle McClean calls "the LA-UP classroom" serves twenty-four four-year-olds, which McClean said was "a little bump up" from the prior year's count. In this lively classroom, a diverse array of youngsters were free to engage in a variety of activities, from dressing up as a French baker to comparing lengths of wooden rods to solving puzzles ("Now I like the easier ones," Carmen admitted matter-of-factly). The largely middle-class parents served by Long Beach Montessori were paying $550 monthly for a full-day program. The fee charged to parents of the fourteen additional children served under LA-UP is lower, $380 per month, again for the full-day program. McLean said that they would like to find the space to serve additional children, but "we're limited by our state license," as well as by space limitations, being squeezed into two trailers on the church's edge.

The LA-UP managers see the first batch of 100 centers as demonstration programs that benefit from "enhancement funds," according to All Saints' Rood. In a sense, LA-UP is testing its own organizational legs, creating a premier network of universal preschool sites. The young agency understands that growing more enrollment slots will be difficult. There are high institutional hurdles, including scarce and expensive urban space, the expense of building new facilities, and bottlenecks in the state licensing process.

LA-UP funding presently supports an array of quality improvements. Even after reducing parents' tuition payments at All Saints, now subsidized by their LA-UP grant, Ahlstrand still had fresh dollars to buy new classroom materials, enrich how she implements her own rendition of the Creative Curriculum, along with organizing a wider array of field trips. "We go and see two plays, the *Nutcracker* at Christmas, the *Festival of Culture* . . . so LA-UP will fund part of that," Ahlstrand said. Down in Long Beach, director McClean was able to purchase a fresh set of Montessori-style manipulatives and instructional materials.

Ray Hernandez oversees the LA-UP funding that flows into his community organization, Para los Niños. It is an impressive CBO with headquarters in the Pico-Union district, a stone's throw from downtown. His agency runs a network of eight state-funded preschools in Los Angeles county. LA-UP is supporting the Vermont Street center, "Enhancing two classrooms that we have . . . and I want to buy (new) computers," Hernandez told me.

Almost all children attending Vermont Street come from Spanish-speaking homes, and live in small rickety cottages on the edges of the downtown garment district. Hernandez was painting the walls of every classroom in a uniform set of four inviting colors, except, he said, "Oh, that maroon, we've got to work on that." He also was creatively expanding training opportunities for his lead teachers and classroom aides. "They are excited about it and interested," Hernandez said. He warned against moving too fast on the bachelor's degree mandate under LA-UP's five-star system. "It's unfortunate that they're really gonna do it," Hernandez said. "Unless they raise the salaries, you'll lose teachers to K-12."

STANDARDIZING A CLASSROOM PHILOSOPHY

One feature of early implementation of universal preschool in Los Angeles that vividly stands out is the strong commitment to older-line developmental principles, rooted in liberal-humanist ideals. This approach may have been driven by Hill-Scott's own history, since she came from the child development field, not from the public school, and from Italiano-Thomas's deep history in Head Start. Early education curriculum specialists, including those working within the L.A. school system, have never exerted much influence.

For whatever reason, LA-UP's attempt to move local programs toward a more uniform set of "developmentally appropriate practices" somewhat reminiscent of the PreKare network, adds a dash of irony to the story. To date, LA-UP leaders, especially Italiano-Thomas, have not pushed any particular curricular package. But, like the UPK leaders in New Jersey, LA-UP gently promotes a developmentalist viewpoint, requiring all centers to respect the symbols of quality contained in the Early Childhood Environment Rating Scale (ECERS), a classroom assessment tool, and placing faith in higher college degrees for teachers.

When LA-UP staff visited the Long Beach Montessori preschool, they assessed McClean's class of four-year-olds using the ECERS observation tool. Because she was negotiating the initial year of funding, they suggested that "dress-up and blocks (be) integrated into the classroom, whereas we would (previously) reserve that for play time," McClean said. "Normally we would bring out music" as a discrete, purposeful activity true to the Montessori method. "But now if they (the children) want to choose it . . . ," she added, and sure enough, an endearing African American girl walked around the classroom ringing a metal triangle.

The Montessori method—stretching back almost a century in America—calls for "more focus (on discrete activities), what's called a normalized kind of concentration, with opportunities to choose," McClean said. "They (LA-UP staff) adhere to the ECERS, but we still have a lot of freedom . . . They're a little over the top on hand washing," she added, but "they want them to be independent, pouring their own water, their own snacks." The LA-UP assessor complained to McClean that activity centers were strewn around the classroom, leaving a long open space in the middle across which kids might be tempted to dash. "But on weekends the church uses the room for Sunday school, and we don't want to keep moving the furniture around," McClean said.

Back at All Saints in Pasadena, teacher Ahlstrand had endorsed the developmentalist framework long before the LA-UP assessor showed up. "We let our kids do a lot of exploring on their own," Ahlstrand reported. "Social and emotional development is first in my book (and getting) socially and emotionally ready for the challenges of kindergarten." Her classroom approach is a motivating fusion of liberal-humanist ideals and a caring rendition of boot camp. "In kindergarten they don't have a lot of teachers to help, (so) we help them learn to stand up for their rights, how they talk to their friends. They are pretty much working out their own problems. They can prepare their own meals, pour their own juice . . . we want them to be as self-reliant as possible."

A more costly form of pressure from LA-UP aims to nudge teachers and preschool staff toward a two-year or four-year college degree. As classroom staffers attain higher degrees, preschools can win that savored fourth or fifth star in the county's quality rating system. Ahlstrand's center is fully accredited by the National Association for the Education of Young Children, a mark of quality that some UPK states reward through higher per child allocations. All Saints, however, will remain a three-star program until Ahlstrand receives her B.A. degree. She takes a general education course from Phoenix University online, and she told me: "I already have my child development courses. It's called distance learning . . . I talk to my counselor (online) once a week," and there's a chat room attached to each course.

NEIGHBORHOOD CONDITIONS, INSTITUTIONAL CHANGE

It's too early to make any inferences about the benefits of UPK in Los Angeles. The early focus on quality improvement rather than expanding enrollment may help LA-UP become more firmly established. It also buys time as strategies are devised for building new facilities. The determination of its leading architects, such as Hill-Scott and Italiano-Thomas, to hold out against the incursion of narrow academic skilling—at the very time that Los Angeles' schools are pressing a softly scripted curricular routine down into their preschools—also distinguishes the L.A. model.

The broader question—foreshadowed by Reiner's original worry over the disparate nature of child care and early education—is whether the LA-UP version of universal preschool will address such underlying economic and institutional conditions. Reiner, Hill-Scott, and their inner circle are banking on the virtues of universal access. But this means that new funds will flow to places like All Saints and Long Beach Montessori, which already served families who could afford to pay for high-quality programs. "The culture in Pasadena is if you can afford a private school, you do that," said All Saints' Rood. "Generally my parents get into one of their (private school kindergarten) choices. Some are giving five applications for (their) child . . . It's worse than going to college."

Meanwhile, at Para los Niños in South Central, Ray Hernandez says he just hopes to get his classroom aides up to "the permit level," meaning just four college-level courses in child development. This is progress for sure, but not enough to boost his funding level. The concern is that such incentives for improving quality, although well-meaning, may reinforce the already stratified character of preschools.

The LA-UP funds already are viewed as yet another separate stream of funding arriving with its own goals and rules, not unlike the myriad programs that send down dollars from Sacramento or child care vouchers disbursed by other local agencies. "It's really like running a program in a program," Rood said. The early educators I visited saw their organizations as having "LA-UP classrooms," and then other classrooms. When I asked about her ability to serve children from low-income families, Montessori's McClean said: "We do support kids on what's called alternative payments (vouchers) but not on LA-UP, since it's a totally different contract." How UPK will leverage movement toward an easier-to-access network of local preschools, simplifying Sacramento's fragmented, $3 billion annual investment, remains an open question. Universal preschool in Los Angeles may remain an elegant and flexible tail wagged by a still-gangly dog.

Lessons Learned

Getting ahead remains an uncertain challenge for many in California's disparate society, perhaps united by that promise of Tomorrow Land. Against this backdrop, California's once-gleaming public schools still offer hope and optimism for millions of parents and employers alike. And affordable, high quality preschool has become part of the school-reform story line. If kids can receive a potent head start from preschool, this may propel them into a more hopeful future. State schools chief Jack O'Connell, in the campaign for Proposition 82, claimed that UPK would be "the great equalizer."

Like the Oklahoma story, that of California illustrates how long-running historical forces shape both the timing and the way early education is organized, situating it within local political and cultural conditions. In Los Angeles, we saw how civic leaders remained committed to a liberal-humanist approach, despite being in an expansive county dominated by poor and blue-collar families. But when shifted to a statewide campaign for UPK, that approach was suddenly eclipsed by the *political interests* of state leaders eager to fuse preschool to boosting test scores, and educational interests desperate for any reform strategy that might relieve pressure on local educators to raise test scores. Labor unions and their legislative allies acted out of *economic interests*, no matter how benevolent their intentions, in order to expand the (dues-paying) teacher work force and thereby strengthen their political position.

Perhaps in reaction to the conservative era in which the movement emerged, UPK advocates at times seemed willing to pay any price to win, even if it meant shrinking our conception of how young children develop. If it would gain the support of militant backers of school accountability and standardized testing, then so be it. They viewed child care options and parental choice as impediments to building a tighter state-run *system*. Such a system promises to bring more uniform benchmarks of quality and equitable access. If it happens also to disempower community agencies or homogenize classroom activities and curricula, again, that's a small price to pay.

While bent ideals and shrewd tactics seemed to characterize much of Reiner's statewide crusade, the democratic deliberation led by Hill-Scott in Los Angeles yielded a quite different organizational model. Though broad historical forces continue to drive policy action at the state level in California, local politics and cultural forces are proving influential in local settings. Despite backing a shift in the balance of control to the public schools when pitching state-level reform, Reiner agreed to a wildly mixed market of preschool organizations in Los Angeles. The city's feisty politics, along with its cultural variety and organizational diversity, would simply not support such a centralized, school-dominated system. It's reminiscent of Jürgen Habermas's image of a "decentered society," in which "this concept of democracy no longer needs to operate with the notion of a social whole centered in the state."[111]

During Hill-Scott's planning year, no credible advocate seriously suggested that the L.A. school system should run UPK. When I asked Ray Hernandez at Para los Niños why a downtown parent would choose a CBO-based preschool over one situated in an elementary school, he let loose with a loud laugh and said, "Do you really want me to answer that question?" Still, when Reiner sought political legitimacy and capital to fund his statewide campaign, he went straight to the unions, whose price was to nest preschool firmly within the public schools.

LA-UP is mounting an intriguing experiment, supporting preschool classrooms in poor and well-off communities alike, delivering early education through a wide mix of community- and school-based programs, and even funding licensed child care homes. By tying preschool quality to traditional developmental theory, rooted in the best of liberal-humanist philosophy, the LA-UP leaders are taking a stand. Whether this tack succeeds in weaving around the shoals of academic skilling and proves responsive to the area's diverse parents remains to be seen. Will it continue to be tolerated when LA-UP faces the same accountability pressures that have beset the public schools?

Josiah Royce complained in the nineteenth century that California's people were so dispersed, so diverse, so rough around the edges that no coherent *public philosophy* could be pasted together and pursued over time. To their credit, Reiner and the small circle of elites that he mobilized have defined a hopeful public project, drawing on Enlightenment ideals while aiming to improve the life chances of young children. Such *institutional liberals* seek salvation through a unified system, run largely by experts and professionals. We see such a system in the centralized definition of quality, the unions' desire to control the character of teachers and the social organization of classrooms, and Sacramento's desire to hold young children to standardized learning aims and testing.

In vivid contrast, *decentralized progressives* are rooted in the ideals of community action and sensitive to how young children grow within particular cultural and linguistic contexts. Preschools cast within this frame offer a human-scale place for uniting parents and sustaining community organizing, as we heard described by Aguilar and Kaufman. When I asked Hernandez why South Central's Latinos didn't prefer pre-k programs in the public schools, after he stopped laughing, he said: "All our teachers, 98 percent, are Latina. They're really conscious of the children's culture."

Well, can the public project of UPK proceed in a cantankerous society like California's, in a form that advances more enriching environs for young children without disempowering parents and the human-scale organizations that lend cohesion to their communities? Perhaps. What's most encouraging about the L.A. story thus far is the success that democratizing movements have realized in this breathtakingly diverse metropolis. Just four decades ago, people like Yolie Aguilar, Rosario Gutierrez, and Terri Robison had no voice and little place in the civil society of Los Angeles. They do now, and their views and ideals are shaping the social organization of early education. Maybe the long-term political and culture challenge is not so much to ignite "a thousand points of light," as the senior Bush so eagerly pitched, but to get them to shine in the same direction, illuminating a shared public project that's responsive to human variety.

*   *   *

We have heard many advocates and policymakers cite evidence of one sort or another. As I traveled about the country, phrases like "the research shows that preschool helps all children" kept popping up, or, that UPK will advance "research-based practices." It's refreshing when proponents of a worthy cause turn to empirical findings, although facts are frequently styled and spun to match a particular party line.

Next, Margaret Bridges and I take stock of the empirical literature, matching key claims of UPK advocates to scientific work conducted to date. We will focus on what we know about preschool's influence on children's early development and on ways to make its benefits more widely felt.

CHAPTER SIX

Which Children Benefit from Preschool?

WITH MARGARET BRIDGES

No self-respecting advocate pitching universal preschool forgets to invoke the phrase, "The research shows that. . . . " Thus, the research shows allegedly that all children benefit from preschool. Or, the research shows that preschool's early boost persists throughout a child's life. Or, the research justifies requiring all teachers to obtain a bachelor's degree. And so on. It's permissible to substitute the phrase, "research-based practices," but the allusion is typically to a stable, sacred truth that science has unambiguously revealed.

The promises made about the benefits of universal preschool are reaching unparalleled heights. The venerable Brookings economist Isabel Sawhill, for instance, at a 2006 pep rally in Manhattan, promised that if UPK spread nationwide, the gross domestic product would climb by $988 billion within sixty years.[1] And after the L.A. chamber of commerce agreed to back Rob Reiner's latest ballot initiative, its president, Rusty Hammer, declared that "preschool is the single best way to ensure that children enter school ready to succeed, which researchers have found translates into higher test scores and higher graduation rates."[2] As if that was not enough, Hammer went on to allege that UPK would "give California and L.A. a critical educational advantage in the global economy."

Such statements offer more illusion than measured consideration of what's known empirically. The new generation of advocates—several trained as lawyers—tend to assert facts as fixed and unalterable. However, child development, like any mature field of study, manifests an intellectual dialectic, with existing, contested data and new findings steadily emerging from stronger data sets and study designs.

Using, and misusing, scientific findings is not new in the world of education politics of course. But the leading UPK advocates crank it up a notch, trying to stay "on message" and shape public opinion. By overstating the returns on this growing public investment, or harping on one particular aspect of preschool quality, advocates risk wasting billions of public dollars. The didactic deployment of selected findings has characterized the UPK hawks, and their approach has failed to inform parents and policymakers about their options, and even kept them from knowing of the *existence* of differing schools of thought about how young children might be nurtured.

When action by the state proves efficacious and makes a clear difference—from raising test scores to lowering teen pregnancy rates to moving poor parents from welfare to work—the citizenry comes to trust that policymakers know what they are doing. Our starting point is not to discourage the vital interplay between the research community and civic debate. Instead, we want to ensure that all the evidence is on the table when it comes to early education—not just one advantageous slice—and that this evidence be in the service of democratic dialogue.

We need to examine how each assertion stacks up against what the research shows to date. In some cases, we don't know what the empirical truth really is, and more careful research is urgently required. This does not mean that we must wait until all the puzzle pieces can be put in place. It does suggest that policymakers might move more cautiously, instead of going so far beyond what's known that they risk contributing to the public's recurring cynicism over careless government action.

First, we want to focus on the postulate that attending preschool benefits *all* three- and four-year-olds, across major domains of child development, and that this head start persists over time. Second, we will examine the argument made by UPK advocates and many policymakers that because preschool is such a potent intervention, more of it is always better—from full-day programs to moving toddlers into classrooms even before they shed those damp diapers. Third, we examine the growing body of evidence on how best to improve the quality of preschools and look at how money has been misspent on symbolic forms of quality. The issue of school effectiveness—what materials, teaching practices, and organizational features pay off most handsomely—has preoccupied education researchers for the past half-century. Those working in the early childhood field are catching up.

Do All Children Benefit from Preschool?

The pamphlets that UPK advocates spread across the land—full of riveting photos of cute youngsters and impressive graphics—typically claim that preschool yields remarkable gains for all children, gains that are experienced throughout life. One brochure displays a chart with the title, "Quality preschool linked to fewer multiple arrests at age 27."[3] When I asked Sue Urahn, a major funder of the movement at the Pew Charitable Trusts, about this, she told me: "We had a research base, an empirical reason to go in (to the preschool sector in 2001)."[4] The movement, in part, sprouted from the growing evidence that preschool can have a meaningful effect, at least for some children.

But does this organization called preschool advance the development of all children, after we take into account the influence of parenting practices and home environment? How long do its benefits persist, and do long-term streams of school or home environs help to sustain these benefits? Can massive, large-scale statewide or national programs replicate the gains that children experience in carefully engineered preschool experiments?

BOUTIQUE PRESCHOOLS SERVING POOR CHILDREN

The story in many ways begins with the Perry Preschool, the earliest and most widely recognized small-scale experiment in early education. This remarkable effort began in 1962, when the first cluster of black children from poor families began an intensive, meticulously designed half-day preschool and home visiting program in Ypsilanti, Michigan. Four small cohorts of children, each one involving three-year-olds, joined the study between 1962 and 1965. Each youngster and mother were randomly assigned to either the Perry experimental classroom or a control group, which received no preschooling and no parenting education. The Perry program differs from the kind of universal preschool envisioned by contemporary advocates in one crucial respect: the Perry designers included a regular home visit, made by the classroom teacher, that engaged the mother and child for one and a half hours each week.[5]

Over the Perry experiment's three-year lifespan, ten female teachers filled the treatment group's four teaching posts. A curriculum package was designed and used in each classroom; it focused on cognitive skill development, since the project aimed to raise the I.Q. of these young black children (see Chapter 2). The children attended the program for thirty weeks of one or two years, depending on their age. Each teacher held at least a four-year degree and was certified by Michigan authorities to teach at the elementary or early childhood level. Each teacher "received extensive managerial supervision and inservice training," according to the program designers.[6] The average ratio of children per adult in the classroom was under six to one, well below the average staffing levels of contemporary preschools. Lawrence Schweinhart estimated the per child cost of Perry Preschool at $15,166 (in 2000 dollars), twice what Head Start spends per pupil and almost four times what Oklahoma spends on its UPK program.[7]

The Perry Preschool's widely reported benefits—now holding mythical status in the minds of many—remained notable as the program's graduates moved through public school and into adulthood. Those experiencing the Perry treatment were about 20 percent more likely to have graduated from college, they were less likely to have been arrested, and the girls experienced fewer pregnancies as teens, compared with the control group. Note that though Perry effects are invoked when UPK is debated, some of these outcome measures would not be relevant in detecting effects for middle-class children.

In discussing Perry's place in the preschool movement's history back in Chapter 2, we emphasized the small number of families that participated. For instance, a 20 percent difference in any outcome actually means that about 10 Perry graduates took a positive pathway, compared with the path taken by members of the control group. The other nagging worry with the Perry results is that, once we get past the press releases and summaries, we find that some differences are not statistically significant, apply only to girls, not boys, or fade away. In the mid-1960s, the control-group parents had few other child-care options, a rare condition nowadays, thanks to the intervening four decades of growth in centers serving poor families. The benefits of Perry are comparable only to a control group consisting of poor black children who largely stay at home.

Still, the fact that time has not dimmed certain effects suggests that if the enriched quality of Perry Preschool could be replicated, and if classroom activities could be matched with intensive work with mothers, larger, statewide programs might be able to yield comparable benefits. These are two big ifs, however, that are linked to institutional and policy dynamics, not to the virtues of Perry.

The High/Scope Foundation, run by the architects of the Perry Preschool, published its most recent assessment in 2005, when the original Perry graduates turned forty. High/Scope's Schweinhart and his colleagues, including Rutgers's Steve Barnett, candidly reported that exposure to Perry explains less than 3 percent of all the variation in earnings at age forty, and about 4 percent of the variability in school attainment levels. It's notable that differences could be detected this far out, but the practical implications are modest at best.[8] At nineteen years of age, Perry graduates' school-attainment benefits and rate of special education placement were statistically significant for girls, but not for boys. Reduction in the total number of criminal arrests was significant in some years and not for others; at age forty it was significant for males, but not for females. In short, findings for some key outcomes are inconsistent across years, and alleged benefits reported in the popular media fade out in terms of statistical significance.

So, what does the Perry Preschool experience say about the likely benefits—at least for poor children—attending large, statewide preschool systems in which key features such as cost and quality are rarely replicated? Certainly, generalizing from such tiny experiments is difficult. When RAND researchers endeavored to estimate the economic return likely to result from a massive statewide preschool initiative for California, they rightfully set aside the Perry experiment, and instead turned to the Chicago Child-Parent Centers, which served over 4,000 youngsters in the mid-1980s. This program had a heavier parent-training component and cost less than half what Perry cost.

Some program elements that Perry pioneered, such as better training for teachers and a coherent, developmentally appropriate curriculum, are being replicated in contemporary efforts. They may be paying off, as we see with the encouraging evaluation results in Tulsa, where children of poor and blue-collar parents have shown clear cognitive gains. But other elements sacred to Perry have not yielded replicable results: in Georgia, the bachelor's degree has not yielded returns beyond focused training in child development. Still, the tiny experiment at Perry yielded a huge demonstration effect, becoming a central icon for the early childhood field, like Newton dropping the apple.

A second notable hot-house experiment was the Carolina Abecedarian Project. Its designers, based at the University of North Carolina, recruited 111 children from low-income families between 1972 and 1977, just months after they were born. The average participating mother was under twenty years of age and had completed just ten years of schooling. Most were single African Americans.

The Abecedarian intervention was even more intensive than Perry Preschool. The design allowed the evaluation of four groups—two treatment, a comparison, and a control group. The first treatment group had infant through pre-k care; the second had infant through pre-k care as well as a home-visiting enrichment program. The initial infant-per-adult ratio in the center was three-to-one, and increased to six-to-one in the preschool classrooms. The preschool was a year-round, full-day program, so presumably it offered a stronger dosage of intervention than Perry did. In contrast, the comparison-group children participated only in a post-k after-school program and the home-visiting enrichment program. The home-visiting program lasted for the children's first three years of primary school, and mothers in this group received instruction from a home visitor about how to create stimulating pre-literacy activities, among other instructional goals. Finally, the control group received free iron-fortified formula and diapers, but no care or visiting program.

Children who experienced the infant-through-preschool intervention displayed the greatest gains in cognitive skills, such as early language development and reading skills—especially the girls. Frances Campbell and her colleagues found that test score effects persisted through age twenty-one, the final point at which participating children were assessed. Those who had participated in the preschool component were less likely to have repeated a grade in school or to have been placed in special education; they were more likely to be enrolled in a four-year college, compared with the comparison and control groups.[9]

Steve Barnett has calculated that for every dollar spent on Abecedarian, the participants or society at large would gain four dollars in benefits. This rate of return wasn't as high as the eight dollar return from the Perry experiment, also calculated by Barnett for one particular follow-up period.[10] The Perry estimate was revised downward to four dollars for every dollar invested when economist Lynn Karoly excluded "intangible losses to victims of crime," which Barnett had included.[11] Abecedarian's rate of return looks higher than the $2.62 returned per dollar spent at the much larger Chicago Child-Parent Centers, to which we turn shortly.

Overall, when we consider Perry or Abecedarian, these economic analyses help only a little in estimating the likely benefits of massive preschool programs. It's like looking at the cognitive acumen or earnings of Harvard graduates, and then using this rate of return to justify building more community colleges. The benefits realized by these small, model programs are not generalizable to apply to mass preschool systems. No state is contemplating spending over $16,000 per child (in current dollars) for a preschool and home-visiting program, as was done in the Perry Preschool project, nor the $34,476 per child (in 2000 dollars) spent by the Abecedarian experiment.[12]

This has not stopped UPK advocates from advancing exaggerated claims about the effects of preschool. In promoting its session at the California School Boards Association's 2005 convention in San Diego, the Packard Foundation's ad claimed: "Children who attend high-quality preschools have higher rates of school readiness, better language ability and math skills, and fewer behavior problems, suggest many longitudinal studies."[13] Only three longitudinal studies of high-quality preschools have been completed, two of which we just reviewed. These studies do show encouraging effects—but at a cost that no state, nor Head Start after forty years, has been able to afford. In addition, both Perry and Abecedarian engaged mothers and the home environment, rather than targeting their intervention solely on classrooms.

We must emphasize that demonstration experiments like Perry's and Abecedarian's were not conducted in order to justify, or be generalized to, large-scale, statewide programs. They were created to demonstrate that young kids' cognitive capacities could be enlarged through "early intervention." The deeply committed architects of these programs combated the claim that nature trumped nurture—that poor children lacked the inborn ability to achieve at high levels—and they succeeded in doing so.

LARGE-SCALE PROGRAMS SERVING POOR CHILDREN

Beginning in the mid-1980s, a younger generation of researchers, attempting to establish generalizable results, began to follow young children from infancy or toddlerhood, through preschools, and into elementary schools. Rather than demonstrating that small, boutique preschools yield marked effects, these researchers asked whether preschool programs implemented on a wider scale would pack a similar punch.

These large-scale studies came in two varieties. First, over the past decade they assessed specific programs that serve children from poor and working-class families. Perhaps the most detailed results in this genre stem from the Chicago Child-Parent Centers (CPC) effort, which has operated in the Chicago public schools since 1967. During a period of intensive study in the mid-1980s by the University of Wisconsin's Arthur Reynolds, this program offered preschool in largely black neighborhoods. The Chicago effort, like Perry and Abecedarian, included elements that went beyond the preschool classroom. Parent education and home visits often began at age two; participating children entered preschool at three years of age; for some, enrichment activities and parent involvement continued through third grade.

The CPC's preschool element remains a half-day program (three hours in length) that focuses on children's early language, pre-literacy, and mathematical skills. Lead teachers have both the bachelor's degree and specialized Illinois certification in child development. Teachers and classroom aides are employees of the Chicago public schools. The staffing ratio is typically seventeen three- or four-year-olds in a classroom with two adults. CPC staff members are trained to encourage parent involvement, such as organizing learning activities in the home. The comprehensive services provided during the 1980s evaluation period included health screening, immunizations, and free meals—similar to federal Head Start. The follow-up program through third grade included smaller classes and intensive efforts to keep parents involved in their children's learning and social development at home.[14]

The director of CPC, Sonja Griffin, told me: "Parents realize we are an academic program. We effectively went into the scientifically based practices . . . Standards are the backbone of our curriculum."[15] At the same time, some centers retain the spirit of parental empowerment. Edith Allen-Coleman, the principal of Lorraine Hansberry Elementary School, when she helped to create their pre-k center in 1967 tried to ensure that poor parents saw themselves as full-fledged members of the school community, as she puts it: "to know the office staff, to see the principal, what the teacher does."

Allen-Coleman told me that the full-time parent educator at Hansberry school doesn't just teach parents that they should read with their child, but shows them "how to raise their voices, to get excited about the story . . . to tell the story if they can't read." Despite recent budget cuts and the closure of several of the centers, as Cabrini Green and other housing projects came down, CPC's holistic approach to child and family development appears to be working well.

Professor Reynolds and his colleagues attempted to gauge the long-term effects of the CPC initiative by following a cohort of 1,539 children who moved into (program-bolstered) kindergartens in twenty-five sites during the 1985–86 school year. The sample included many children who had not attended a CPC preschool (although one-fifth had gone to a Head Start preschool) and some who did not enter the first-through-third-grade follow-up program.

Selection bias could be operating, that is, prior home or parenting factors might have influenced which children started and stayed in CPC programs, and these factors, rather than exposure to the intervention per se, may also explain developmental gains. For this reason, researchers prefer true experiments, although we have seen how they can yield findings of limited generalizability. Reynolds did examine how families differed across the treatment conditions and found few differences. This finding may have been due to the fact that enrollment rates across Chicago's poor neighborhoods were related more to the mere presence of a nearby CPC than to features of the individual families that expressed demand for preschool.

Participating children were living in impoverished communities. Two-fifths of the parents involved in the study had not finished high school. Seventy-six percent of the children lived in a single-parent family, and 84 percent were eligible for subsidized lunches under federal poverty guidelines. Those attending a CPC preschool scored significantly higher on a test of cognitive proficiencies at age five than youngsters who did not attend, with an effect size of 0.21 of a standard deviation (SD).[16] This level of magnitude approximates the effect observed in Tennessee's class-size reduction initiative in kindergarten and early elementary grades, which also focused on children from poor families.[17]

What's most impressive about the CPC results is that the moderate effect on cognitive growth stemming from the preschool component (one and half years in preschool for the average child) was sustained over time. Participating children's reading scores were still 0.19 SD higher at age nine, and 0.16 SD higher at age fourteen than those of youngsters who had not attended the CPC preschool component. By age eighteen, just over 14 percent of CPC graduates had been referred to a special education program, compared to 24 percent of the control group. The propensity to repeat grade levels was lower among CPC participants as well, and they graduated from high school at a modestly higher rate (49 percent, compared with 38 percent of the control group). CPC participants also had lower rates of delinquency and criminal activity. For boys, however, these positive effects tended to fade, unless they remained in enriched classrooms after graduating from preschool.

Program benefits were significantly stronger for children whose parents participated more consistently in the preschool and elementary school components. Reynolds reported that participating children "get up to six years of intervention from age three to nine (with) really a heavy emphasis on family social services." He went on to detail the forms of parental engagement that paid off, including "classroom volunteering, parent room activities, educational workshops and training, and home visiting activities."

Reynolds attributed fully one-quarter of the program's effects to variation in (primarily) mothers' engagement and training. "The 25 percent or so would be the contribution of parent involvement, generally, to the effect on educational attainment estimated as the contribution to the indirect effect of CPC on the (child) outcomes. This would include home visits," he told me. "This estimate may be somewhat low since it is based on one measure. Examining achievement, it would be higher." This point is pivotal in the design of wide-scale UPK programs, which often lack a determined focus on parents and home practices (Chapter 7).

Reynolds estimates that Chicago's CPC program cost $6,692 per child (in 1998 dollars)—lower than the Perry Preschool but about 40 percent higher than spending per child for UPK in Georgia (in current dollars) and over twice Oklahoma's spending level. Child-care options available to control-group parents in poor black communities in the mid-1980s may well have been more limited than what they are today. We should be careful in generalizing from the estimated effects of any one program.

HEAD START'S HOPEFUL BENEFITS

A much larger type of program is, of course, the $6 billion federal Head Start initiative, which focuses on children from poor families. Its origins hark back to the Great Society; in this context Head Start has sparked four decades of vociferous debate over its community-based and holistic philosophy, and in turn about its potential benefits for children and parents. Head Start's rocky road since the 1960s has yielded ample empirical results regarding children, especially about what kinds of investments and quality factors elevate children's developmental trajectories. Institutional lessons abound, as well, as this originally human-scale preschool has grown into a massive, far-flung network of local programs.

Initial empirical results were downright depressing. The original evaluation, published in 1969 by the Westinghouse Learning Corporation and Ohio University, found few sustainable effects when the earliest cohorts of Head Start graduates were assessed in their first years of elementary school.[18] The modest tracking studies done in the following decade were equally discouraging. In 1985, when Ruth Hubbell McKey reviewed the initial generation of empirical work for the federal government, she concluded that for poor children, Head Start preschools were sparking discernible cognitive benefits, which quickly faded, however, once they entered elementary school.[19]

But recent findings from the carefully designed Head Start Impact Study (HSIS), which involved randomly assigning poor children to a treatment or control condition, have revealed significant benefits in the cognitive and social development of the participating three- and four-year-olds.[20] It's too early to discern whether these modest gains will persist or fade as youngsters enter elementary schools of uneven quality. Still, the boost to early learning and development is consistent with earlier results published in 2003, detailed in the federal Family and Child Experiences Survey (FACES), that showed steady developmental progress for Head Start children over the one, two, or three years during which they attended preschool.[21]

At the same time, John Love, Ellen Eliason Kisker, and colleagues at Mathematica Policy Research in Princeton found robust benefits for toddlers and parents participating in the federal Early Head Start program. This inventive study, begun in the 1990s, emphasized work with mothers in their homes, along with time in high-quality centers for infants and toddlers. The Mathematica evaluation revealed modest effects for infants' responsiveness to their mothers and for toddlers' early language and social development in programs that combined steady engagement with mothers and involvement of young children in center-based programs. Effect sizes ranged from 0.15 SD in early cognitive and language growth to 0.43 SD in mother-child engagement during play situations.[22]

The most recent Head Start findings are also cause for guarded optimism. The Westat-based research team, a respected evaluation firm outside of Washington, D.C, assessed three- and four-year-old children enrolling in a Head Start preschool for the first time. Each youngster was assessed at the beginning and the end of his or her first nine months in the program. Growth rates could then be compared between children randomly assigned to Head Start and those who remained at home or those entering other child-care settings. Because many of the children in the control group entered other preschool centers, the estimated effects of Head Start are relative to a range of child care environments.[23]

Exposure to one year of Head Start raised children's pre-reading and emergent literacy skills by about one-fifth of a standard deviation higher than that of the control group. This level of magnitude is quite similar to the benefit of the Chicago CPCs (using the comparison group that faced few child care options). Head Start's effects on youngsters' vocabulary and pre-writing skills, though statistically significant, were half as strong. Overall cognitive gains were significantly greater for Head Start children coming from English-speaking households than for Latino children from Spanish-speaking homes. This finding suggests that classroom practices may be less effective for the latter group, or perhaps that Head Start preschools serving monolingual Spanish youngsters are lower in quality overall.

The HSIS study team also examined possible benefits in the domain of social and behavioral development. Exposure to nine months of Head Start was found to reduce children's problem behaviors such as aggressive social interactions, although only by a small 0.13 SD. Reduction of hyperactive behavior was also observed (with a 0.18 SD effect size). These positive results were observed most consistently for three-year-olds; four-year-olds experienced similar benefits, but at lower magnitudes. Parents with three-year-olds attending a Head Start preschool reported that their children were healthier, on average, than those in the control group. Head Start children received more regular dental care than did non-participants. In particular Latino parents whose children attended Head Start reported higher levels of child health than did the control group.

The comprehensive nature of Head Start program components—in contrast to some state UPK programs—appears to spark more robust parenting practices, at least in the short run. Head Start parents reported reading with their children more frequently, and Head Start three-year-olds were exposed to more educational outings, such as visiting a museum or zoo, than the control group children. Parents of three-year-olds reported less reliance on spanking or hitting as a disciplinary method. In contrast, many state preschools are classroom-bound, as we saw in Oklahoma, perhaps limiting the benefits that accrue to children through improved home practices.

INITIAL EVALUATIONS OF STATE PRESCHOOL INITIATIVES

Sound assessments of first-generation state UPK efforts are beginning to emerge. We detailed the encouraging benefits of Tulsa's version of universal preschool in Chapter 4, with gains experienced by children from poor and blue-collar families. In Georgia, a study by Gary Henry and colleagues tracked 466 four-year-olds through three types of preschool and into kindergarten. These programs include Georgia's decade-old pre-k program, Head Start, and other nonprofit or private preschools.[24]

There was stark segmentation among families in the three sub-sectors in Georgia. Just 5 percent of mothers enrolling their children in Head Start held a four-year college degree, compared with 29 percent of those enrolling in the new UPK program and 49 percent of mothers selecting other community preschools. There were no discernible differences for children in Georgia's UPK effort, compared with those attending preschool in either of the other two sub-sectors. No comparison group of non-preschool children was available for this study. This study highlights the importance of specifying an appropriate comparison group. Remember, with two-thirds of all four-year-olds currently attending preschool nationwide, comparing UPK attendees to children who have never gone to preschool has become an exercise of diminishing utility.

In New Jersey, the UPK effort in the so-called Abbott school districts has had a marked effect on the cognitive growth of young, mainly poor, children. Westat's Gary Resnick followed a large cohort of children over two years during the program's early years in the late 1990s, and he found a significant rise in growth curves, compared with normal rates of early learning. At the same time he discovered far more variation in children's growth among kids *within* classrooms than *across* classrooms.

So, although New Jersey preschools overall offer promise, the influence of family background and home practices continues to eclipse the effects of quality differences among preschool classrooms and teachers. That is, after realizing the gains of simply attending preschool—of fairly high quality preschool in the initial years of the Abbott reforms—variability in quality measures doesn't explain much more of the variance in children's outcomes. This conclusion is consistent with recent findings from the NICHD longitudinal study of child-care effects.[25] We return later in the chapter to this question of how much difference quality makes, after the encouraging—at least in the short-term—effects of attending or not attending preschool are taken into account.

Steve Barnett and colleagues recently assessed child-level effects of large-scale preschool programs spread across five states, including the Tulsa sample. These efforts focused on children from low-income families in all but one state, West Virginia; in the Tulsa sample there were also a smattering of middle-class children. In a yet to be peer-reviewed paper, Barnett employed the same regression-discontinuity design used by Gormley and Phillips in their Tulsa study, detailed in Chapter 4. The reported effects were modest overall. Before adjusting for the child's age in months, preschool attendees scored 0.21 SD higher on early language development and 0.34 higher on math concepts.[26]

The magnitude of these differences shrank considerably when Barnett focused on age-adjusted mean differences. Although preschool attendees did score higher on knowledge of print materials, no differences were detected in phonological awareness. Even though state preschool programs exhibited high quality standards and most of children served were from poor or blue collar families, the effects were uneven and generally modest.

BROADER FAMILY POLICY REFORMS

Fresh evidence about the effects of preschool and child care has emerged from assessments of allied policy changes that affect children's daily lives—most notably the nation's decade-long experiment with welfare reform. A study conducted by Sharon Lynn Kagan, Susanna Loeb, and me of 927 young children, as they moved through various forms of child care, has revealed strong effects on children's cognitive growth when mothers move from welfare to work.

The majority of these youngsters spent varying amounts of time in preschool centers between the ages of two and a half and five. Participating children in California and Florida displayed growth in the Bracken test of cognitive skills and related school readiness measures in the range of 0.32 to 0.57 SD.[27] These effects stemming from exposure to preschool centers actually exceeded the magnitude of the effect that mothers' verbal capacities and home practices, such as reading together, had on the children. We found no consistent effect of preschool exposure on children's social development.

We also found that the gains linked to preschool attendance could still be observed in second and third grade, although the growth trajectories flattened considerably between four and a half and seven and a half years of age. Still, the findings for cognitive growth were striking, given our ability to control the child's prior proficiency levels, which were directly assessed by our field staff. Noteworthy cognitive effects also have been observed at varying levels of magnitude across five random-assignment experiments involving mothers moving from welfare to work. Reforms in state and county welfare have varied greatly, especially in the extent to which preschool slots are available for young children, and the extent to which mothers must rely on kith and kin for child care as they move into jobs.

CHILDREN MOVING THROUGH GARDEN-VARIETY PRESCHOOLS

The second genre of studies—moving beyond boutique experiments and larger preschool programs—consists of longitudinal studies, which follow large samples of young children over time. Doing so enables researchers to investigate a variety of questions including how the benefits of preschool vary among children of differing social classes, among various ethnic or linguistic groups, and between girls and boys.

Columbia University economist Janet Currie has led the most careful and illuminating research in this arena, which examined the sustained effects of Head Start. Her earlier papers in the 1990s with Duncan Thomas showed that poor children who attended Head Start preschools displayed stronger achievement in elementary school, especially white children and Latino youngsters coming from homes with better educated mothers, than children who did not attend preschool.[28] Youngsters from non-English speaking households experienced weaker gains, a similar finding to the recent HSIS results. These results suggest that home environments, especially in their language practices, may interact with preschool settings to shape developmental trajectories. Currie also detected longer-term benefits for poor children in terms of educational attainment, earnings, and reduced reliance on welfare.[29]

Drawing on longitudinal data from the national Panel Study of Income Dynamics, Currie found that low-income whites who had attended Head Start completed high school and entered college at higher rates than those who never attended preschool. For blacks, long-term educational effects could not be identified; however, Head Start graduates overall had less contact with the criminal justice system. Currie addressed methodological concerns, verifying her models for families in which one sibling graduated from Head Start and another did not. Doing so helped to rule out the possibility of selection bias, a problem that has undercut confidence in the inferences of some earlier studies. In selection bias, the prior attributes or practices of parents may be driving the greater likelihood of selecting a preschool *and* child outcomes. The researcher, observing a correlation between preschool exposure and developmental outcomes, may mistakenly infer that it's the preschool that is causally boosting child development, when it may be the home factors. By controlling for the *fixed effects* of family membership and then pinpointing Head Start's effects on siblings, Currie avoids this issue.

Currie has begun to clarify the conditions under which the initial bump from preschool can be sustained into and throughout elementary school. She found that African American children graduating from Head Start generally move into lower-quality public schools than white children completing Head Start do.[30] This conclusion is consistent with Katherine Magnuson's recent finding that the positive benefits of preschool experienced by low-income children are more strongly sustained for those who enter schools with stronger instructional programs.[31]

This line of research, which draws on nationally representative samples of young children, also enables researchers to weigh a pivotal claim made by UPK advocates—that preschool benefits all children, including those from language-rich families in middle-class or affluent suburbs. When I asked UPK benefactor Sue Urahn of the Pew Charitable Trusts why government should subsidize preschools for all families, rich or poor, she acknowledged that "you probably won't get the degree of benefit for middle-class children that you would for poor kids." But, she added, universality may bolster the political will to widen children's access to, and to improve the quality of, preschool. "What do people say? 'Programs only for the poor make for poor programs,'" she said.

Given that their most appealing pitch is to claim, like Urahn, that preschool will give all children an early boost, UPK advocates seem somewhat confused. California schools chief O'Connell started calling universal preschool "the great equalizer," purporting that it narrows achievement gaps, as discussed in Chapter 5. But it's difficult to argue both that an intervention will help all children *and* that it will narrow disparities in early learning. The only way this could happen is if poor children derive a dramatically higher benefit from it than do middle-class kids. If so, then over time the former group would catch up to the latter group. However, the evidence shows that middle-class youngsters do not benefit much from preschool. If that is the case, what is the rationale for preschooling middle-class kids, and shifting public investment away from the children who benefit the most?

Findings from the national study of early child care done in concert with the National Institute of Child Health and Human Development (NICHD) do help to inform this debate. This research team began recruiting parents and their newborns in 1991. The study would become the most ambitious longitudinal study ever attempted to assess the influence of youngsters' child-care settings on their cognitive, social, and health development well into elementary and secondary school.

Perhaps unintentionally, the NICHD team ended up with a sample of 1,364 families that was largely middle-class. Non-English speaking parents were excluded from the study. But it was fortuitous in one sense: this large sample is a rich one for gauging the effects of middle-class children's exposure to preschool on a range of developmental outcomes. The families remaining in the study were 79 percent white and mothers reported over two years of college on average. When children turned three years of age, 27 percent were attending a center-based program; the figure rose to 54 percent at age four and a half.[32]

Northwestern University economist Greg Duncan helped the NICHD team carefully control prior selection factors to isolate the effect of exposure to preschool centers on cognitive development, taking into account parents' education levels, social class, the mother's mental health, parenting practices, and child temperament and separation anxiety. Duncan found that one standard deviation of additional time spent in a preschool center between the ages of twenty-seven and fifty-four months (rather than time cared for at home or within a less formal child-care arrangement) was associated with about a 0.27 SD advantage in cognitive proficiencies and academic scores, a level of magnitude similar to earlier studies focusing on children from poor families.

At the same time, the NICHD team found a small but significant elevation in children's aggressive social behavior after spending long hours in preschool, an issue to which we return. Duncan found very small benefits of higher levels of preschool quality after taking into account the basic effect of attending a center-based program. Overall, however, the news was good: exposure to preschool centers yielded short-term benefits for this largely middle-class sample of children.

Working with Stanford's Susanna Loeb and Daphna Bassok, we analyzed the much larger Early Childhood Longitudinal Survey data (ECLS-K), which involved direct assessment of over 22,000 kindergartners nationwide. Parents reported detailed data on the kinds and duration of child-care settings utilized since their child's birth. We found that Latino children who were enrolled in preschool during the year before kindergarten entry, typically at age four, displayed a 0.23 SD advantage in early language and pre-reading skills, compared with all children who did not attend a preschool.[33]

Equally intriguing, we found that the magnitude of this advantage was over one-third smaller for white children, an effect size of just 0.14 SD. For whites the benefits in terms of learning mathematical concepts and counting were slightly stronger than in terms of early reading; Latinos showed the strongest magnitude of benefit in the math domain across ethnic groups. In short, our analysis showed weaker benefits for middle-class and affluent white children than for youngsters from Latino families.

For middle-class children, it appears that benefits largely fade by third grade. A paper completed by the NICHD team in 2005 found that the cognitive benefits stemming from more time in preschool centers had faded by third grade, falling to about 0.07 SD, depending on the specific measure reported.[34] Two independent analyses of the large ECLS-K child sample have found a similar pattern: there were some sustained cognitive benefits for poor children, especially those going to higher quality elementary schools, but a substantial fade-out for middle-class children.[35]

Children from low-income families appear to have realized more sustainable advantages, according to Magnuson's recent analysis. All disadvantaged children, either from poor families or with a parent who dropped out of high school, scored at the 33rd percentile in reading in first grade. However, the subset that had attended preschool prior to kindergarten scored at the 44th percentile. Unfortunately the negative effect on social development persisted for many children, with poor children rising to the 69th percentile on the problem-behaviors index by the end of first grade, as reported by their teachers. "The authors conclude," wrote one academic reviewer, "that for maximum effectiveness, further expansion of pre-kindergarten should be mainly focused on children who are disadvantaged or who will go on to attend low (performing) schools."[36]

Advocates rightfully point out that if preschool quality could be raised to the levels attained in the Perry or Abecedarian experiments, the magnitude of benefits could grow and be sustained through elementary school. But the evidence to date on an additional boost from quality gains, beyond exposure to preschool, is not especially encouraging, and the institutional question of how to "go to scale" while protecting quality continues to befuddle many would-be reformers.

DOES PRESCHOOL HAVE DETRIMENTAL
EFFECTS ON SOCIAL DEVELOPMENT?

Even though studies show that preschool's effect on cognitive proficiencies is positive, these same studies also confirm that children's social development can be slowed, especially for those spending long hours daily in a formal program. Developmentalist Jay Belsky, a member of the NICHD team, published controversial findings in 2003 showing that spending many hours in preschool each week may raise the incidence of behavior problems exhibited by white and black children.[37] The hours question has been a long-running issue in the child-care field. Fellow developmentalist Ron Haskins—who later helped to craft welfare reform as a Republican congressional staffer—in a 1985 paper showed that the children in the Abecedarian experiment displayed more aggressive behavior, as reported by their elementary school teachers. The finding prompted a quick adjustment in the program's curriculum.[38]

Magnuson and her colleagues, again analyzing data from the large ECLS-K family sample, observed the same slowdown in social development. Our analysis with Loeb and Bassok replicated the Magnuson finding, but we also learned that spending more time in preschool each week was not detrimental to the pace of social development of Latino children, as assessed by their kindergarten teachers at age five. In short, the preschool's influence on rates of social development may vary across large subgroups of children.

COULD UNIVERSAL PRESCHOOL
REINFORCE EARLY LEARNING GAPS?

Important findings have resulted from these studies. First, the short-term effects of preschooling—despite widely varying quality—on poor children's cognitive growth are well established. This finding has been replicated in a variety of studies, drawing from different samples of youngsters. The magnitude of these effects tends to be higher when poor children enter higher quality preschools, but studies have not established that quality has any added boost for middle-class children. The general effect of size—even for poor children—ranges from one-fifth to one-third of a standard deviation. It is a notable level of magnitude, though not as dramatic as the advocates would have us think.

Second, significant benefits accrue to children from middle-class households, but at considerably lower levels of magnitude. The only exception may be in states like California, where almost half the middle class is of Latino origin; there we found the effects of preschool exposure to be somewhat stronger than the more modest effects experienced by white middle-class children nationwide, as evidenced by the independent analyses of the ECLS-K data.

Overall, how expanding universal access would close yawning gaps in young children's early learning and social development is still unclear. Even before the ingredients of preschool quality—such as better-trained teachers, or perhaps richer instructional materials—are distributed under a UPK system, children from upper middle-class homes display short-term gains. Without a careful targeting of dollars to raise the quality of preschooling for poor children, the stronger teachers may migrate to better-off communities, as has happened in the labor market for kindergarten teachers. Children from poor families would have to display very strong gains indeed—well beyond the 0.20 to 0.35 SD effect sizes found in recent work—to close the current disparities in early cognitive development. And if state governments abandon the targeting of resources on preschools in low-income communities, there would be an even more negative effect on social development for children who spend many hours in preschool each week, further setting back already-disadvantaged children. As for how preschooling—perhaps in combination with home-visiting efforts—is advancing the health status of young children, we know much less, although the initial results from the Head Start Impact Study are encouraging.[39]

Is More Preschool Better?

If attending preschool gives poor and some middle-class children an advantage, does longer exposure boost the magnitude of benefits? Let's review this literature from two angles. First, we are finding that children who *enter preschool earlier*—at age two or three—display somewhat stronger cognitive and social developmental effects than those entering at age four—although the effects are not always positive. Second, the *intensity* of children's exposure during a typical week, measured in the number of hours per day or week the child is attending, is being examined in the recent studies.

The phrase "early intervention" seems to imply that the sooner a two-year-old toddles into a formal organization, the sooner parents are engaged by public agencies, the better. Yet, the empirical results to date do not clearly bear out such a conclusion. We recently found that children entering preschool between the ages of two and three years, and attending at least fifteen hours per week, displayed the strongest cognitive gains, compared with children who remained at home or attended a less formal setting.[40] Even so, Belsky's analysis, focusing on social-emotional development, found that long hours spent in preschool centers (and other forms of nonparental care) were predictive of slightly elevated levels of aggression and just plain crankiness. He argues that any form of child care in the first year of life, attended continuously, puts the child at risk for externalizing behaviors.[41] Our own analysis, based on the much larger ECLS-K family sample, found the one exception noted above: when Latino children enter preschool early and attend for more than three hours per day, they do not exhibit this slowing of social-emotional development.

These results relate to a second question about preschool exposure that is often asked by parents: do the returns of preschool top out, or do they diminish after a certain number of hours of attendance per week? The costs of full-day programs are much greater than half-day programs—setting aside the need of many working families for full-day coverage of some kind. As it turns out, greater intensity during the week is not necessarily better. Our recent findings showed that attending preschool about fifteen hours per week boosts children's cognitive outcomes, but attending for additional hours adds little, at least given present levels of quality. And the slowdown in social-emotional development, which has even been detected for children attending preschool for fifteen hours, doubled in magnitude for children spending thirty hours or more per week in a preschool center.

We discovered different patterns of associations for different subgroups of children beyond the Latino pattern. For children from poor families, the greater intensity of exposure was related to stronger cognitive growth in a linear fashion: spending more hours per week was better for pre-reading and math skills. And these children did not display greater levels of aggression when spending all day in preschool. It was white and middle-class children whose social competence lagged behind most notably when they attended preschool more than fifteen hours per week, even though they benefited in terms of greater cognitive growth.

Moreover, among children from affluent homes, the decrements to social behavior were three times greater when children attended preschool more than three hours per day, compared to otherwise similar children who were home with a parent for part of the day. African-American children did not display a greater incidence of behavioral problems when attending full-time, beyond the decrement associated with attending half-time, when compared with similar children who did not attend a preschool center.

Belsky's analysis posited a linear or continuous relationship between preschool exposure and behavioral outcomes: spending more hours yields steady declines in social behavior. He found no threshold number of hours, prior to which social development was advanced or simply unaffected by preschool. He reported that children attending preschool at high levels—for thirty or more hours per week, typical for children of full-time working mothers—exhibited higher rates of externalizing behavior than other children, as reported by teachers, mothers, and independent researchers.

Given that all observers agreed, Belsky's finding does not appear to be an artifact of biased reporting. His conclusions must be qualified, however. Remember that the NICHD family sample was generally white and middle-class—the group for which detrimental social effects from intensive preschool exposure were found, according to our own analysis.

More research is certainly needed in the crucial area of social-emotional development and its relation to preschool exposure. True experimental designs, perhaps focusing on varied approaches to advancing social development, would be optimal. We also need to learn more about which families are more likely to select full-day preschooling, rather than mixing part-day programs with some other kind of child care. Many parents are eager to find ways to spend more time with their youngsters, and researchers may not adequately capture their combinations of preschool and home care. Nor do we know much about how facets of preschool quality and classroom practice might mitigate the slowdown in social-emotional growth.

Reynolds's long-term study of the Chicago Child-Parent Centers also examined the effects of one year versus two years of preschool attendance.[42] Children who attended preschool for two years were found to outperform those who attended just one year when assessed at the end of kindergarten. Effect sizes for the one additional year of preschool equaled 0.28 SD for reading and 0.23 SD for math at kindergarten. The children with two years of exposure maintained their boost initially, yet those attending just one year largely caught up by first grade, and the two-year advantage faded by sixth grade. This phenomenon punctuates the importance of improving the quality of elementary schools, and perhaps of working with parents, to sustain the preschool benefits.

Researchers are examining the mechanisms by which spending more time in child care influences development—in particular, why social-emotional growth tends to falter. Exposure to preschool, along with earlier child-care experiences, appears to interact with parents' involvement during infancy and early toddlerhood. One research group, led by Jane Waldfogel and Jeanne Brooks-Gunn at Columbia University, analyzed another national data set containing information on children of the adults participating in the National Longitudinal Survey of Youth.[43]

These investigators found that children whose mothers worked within the *first nine months* of life, a factor presumably linked to the mother's own involvement in child care, showed higher rates of externalizing behavior by seven and eight years of age. Given that the association they discovered is between maternal work—not child care—and children's acting out, the mechanism that spurs behavior problems may not be participation in preschool per se, but longer periods of separation from parents.

At the same time, they observed cognitive benefits for white children when their mothers labored outside the home during the *second and third year* of the child's life, effects that were not discernible among black and Latino children.[44] The question of why and how causal mechanisms might vary by ethnic group—perhaps being linked to voluntary versus involuntary maternal employment, or to the quality of child-care settings selected—remains unanswered. Brooks-Gunn points out, however, that the negative effect of maternal employment early in a toddler's life appears to be linked more to the home environment than to variation in the quality of child care.

Part of this mystery may involve differences in children's temperament and how they react to formal classroom settings. When they spend extensive hours with same-age peers, very young children appear to have more trouble with self-regulation than older children do. Susan Crockenberg and her University of Vermont team recently found that children's temperament moderated the effects of long hours in child care: youngsters prone to frustration who attended centers for thirty hours or more per week were more likely to have exhibited externalizing behaviors as toddlers.[45] In contrast, children who were highly distressed by novelty and spent long hours in centers were more likely to experience internalizing behaviors such as withdrawal from others and anxiety as toddlers.

The causal pathways have been further illuminated by research into children's cortisol levels—indicators of the flow of stress hormones throughout the human body—which provide physiological information about how one is experiencing the social environment. Three- and four-year-old children in all-day child care experienced rising levels of cortisol over the course of the day, reported Kathryn Tout and her colleagues.[46] Generally speaking, children at home and not in child care settings display a circadian decrease in hormone levels when at home.

Attending child care appears to cause stress for some (but not all) youngsters, stress that is then linked to negative social behavior. Poor self-control and aggression, and shyness for boys, were associated with increases in cortisol when children were observed in organized child care by a second research group.[47] Young children, in contrast to school-age children, and those with immature social competence, also experienced this increase in cortisol levels when attending child care, along with the negative social-behavioral effects previously discussed.

How Do We Raise Preschool Quality?

Can significant gains in quality raise the magnitude of benefits tied to preschool attendance? If so, what particular ways of boosting quality yield gains cost-effectively? These tandem questions have preoccupied researchers studying public schools over the past half-century. We know that attending school yields real average gains in literacy, for example. But beyond these mean levels of school quality, additional increments of teacher training, better instructional materials, or other "inputs" often yield quite modest effects.

When it comes to preschooling, the empirical answer may prove to be the same, according to economist Duncan's analysis of the NICHD data. After including an array of quality measures—linked to preschool and less formal kinds of child care—to estimate children's cognitive development, the additional effect (beyond attending a preschool) was a tiny effect size of 0.04 to 0.08 SD.[48] This effect equals only about ten to twenty days of acquiring new pre-literacy skills inside the average kindergarten classroom.

North Carolina's David Blau found slightly stronger effects from particular quality factors, drawing from a national data set focused exclusively on preschool centers. These included benefits in the 0.20 SD range from having teachers with specialized pre-service training in child development, and even from in-service training.[49] Even so, the overall effects from additional increments of conventional measures of quality were modest.

Again, remember that the NICHD sample was largely made up of middle-class families. When we followed the over four hundred children from low-income households participating in the Growing Up in Poverty Project in California and Florida, we found that for children attending preschools with teachers holding two-year college degrees and displaying more responsive interactions involving more language, there were sizable effects on cognitive development and knowledge of print materials like storybooks, compared with children enrolled in lower-quality preschool centers over a two-year period. Effect sizes reached 0.30 SD for some cognitive outcomes. These more encouraging effects from quality factors—for children from poor families—also were found with regard to language growth for black and Latino children.[50]

Which attributes of preschool organizations, including teacher characteristics, most directly shape children's learning? The debate continues. One reason this topic is so contentious is that some alleged features of quality—such as requiring that teachers obtain four-year degrees—are costly and yield questionable benefits for young children. But we are getting ahead of the story. Let's turn now to the most prominent benchmarks of quality.

STAFFING RATIOS

The number of children in a classroom relative to the number of adults has long been used to gauge quality; state governments have earnestly regulated this easy-to-observe proxy. Several studies have confirmed that lower children-per-adult ratios offer a solid starting point for improving the quality of child care. Martha Zaslow, reviewing the literature for the National Research Council in 1990, concluded that lower staffing ratios are associated with stronger child outcomes.[51]

This pattern has been further substantiated with the NICHD family sample, which confirmed that employing more adults to serve fewer children in preschool centers yields slightly more robust cognitive outcomes.[52] Nonetheless, as team member Alison Clarke-Stewart emphasizes, "These associations between child care quality and children's abilities are statistically significant . . . (but) they are not very large. It's probably unreasonable to expect that the quality of child care would have a stronger effect than the quality of parenting."[53] To understand if certain kinds of parents are better able to access preschools that have stronger staffing ratios, more work is required. Scholars need to report actual effect sizes, to identify the magnitude of these benefits, compared with other ingredients of quality.

Some progress has been made in uncovering the human processes by which lower child-teacher ratios advance youngsters' early development. Margaret Burchinal and colleagues at the University of North Carolina found that teachers and classroom aides are more responsive to children's utterances and expressed desires when the staffing ratio is stronger.[54] Similarly in Britain, Blatchford's research team found that smaller class sizes for four- and five-year-olds were associated with higher quality interactions between children and adults and stronger academic outcomes later.[55] In this way, facets of quality reflected in the organizational *structure* of preschools overlap with the responsiveness of teachers and human *processes* inside classrooms.

DOES CURRICULUM MATTER?

The structure of classroom activities—guided by a certain philosophy, operationalized via specific materials and practices—may further contribute to the preschool's developmental effects. With the rising emphasis on academic skills and "school-ready" social behaviors, thinner slices of knowledge and classroom routines are embodied by commercial curricular packages. They fit in with the desire of UPK advocates to roll out a more standard program across diverse communities, aiming to yield universal buoyancy in test scores. Nevertheless, early educators know little about which curriculum packages are most effective for which kinds of young children. Underlying the trusty phrase "research-based practices" are a set of evaluations typically funded by the firms that are pitching the glossy packages.

Proponents of *developmentally appropriate practices* (DAP)—advanced by the liberal-humanist old guard as led by the National Association for the Education of Young Children—and the oddly avant-garde adherents of *direct instruction* each claim that their approach is more beneficial. The provocative results of the Perry and Abecedarian experiments stemmed from—their architects argue—an active-learning approach replete with developmentally appropriate practices and creative activities, which nurture the child's natural curiosity and place pre-literacy skills within this wider developmental agenda.[56]

Stanford's Deborah Stipek has found that DAP-like practices, sometimes called *child centered*, do spark stronger enthusiasm among children to engage in learning activities, compared with direct instructional methods, which are focused on narrower academic skills—although the latter method can yield stronger short-term gains in the cognitive domain. At the same time, Stipek's research team detected higher levels of stress among children attending direct-instruction classrooms than among children in the child-centered program.[57] We return in Chapter 7 to the issue of contingency between the kind of children being served and the pedagogical approach chosen.

Richard Marcon designed a true experiment to assess the relative benefits of these two instructional strategies; he included a third condition that offered a blended approach, reminiscent of the way teachers in California and Oklahoma tried to mix both. His team found that both the child-directed and the intense academic skilling strategy boosted children's language and social outcomes more than the blended approach did.[58] Children in the child-centered program scored highest in early math skills at school entry and displayed higher grades in middle school, suggesting sustained effects.

PARENTS AS TRUE PARTNERS

Another promising line of work focuses on getting parents to read with their children, drawing on the same materials that are used in preschool classrooms. This effort is sometimes part of the staff's work with parents to help them understand that child development is an explicit, sometimes complex project, which involves paying attention to pre-literacy activities and the child's emotional well-being. A series of studies have evaluated the Little Books program used in many Head Start programs; some of them have shown impressive gains in pre-reading skills and, not surprisingly, in knowledge of print materials.[59] Less is known about how such social interactions reinforce the quality of parents' relationships with their children, or about the potentially rich language that emanates from such activities.

Child psychologist Grover Whitehurst, who more recently served as Bush II's chief education researcher, designed a useful experiment, randomly assigning children with limited English who attended New York preschools to one of three conditions: a storybook reading program delivered solely by the preschool teacher, the same activity with a parent-reading component at home, and a control group. After just six weeks of exposure to the "preschool plus home" condition, the children displayed significant gains in expressive vocabulary, and this boost persisted over the following year.[60] This work shows that fairly modest activities that meaningfully link parents to the preschool can yield significant benefits, at least in terms of cognitive and early literacy development.

TEACHER EDUCATION AND VERBAL SKILLS

Another basic feature of the classroom—the skills or credentials held by the teacher—has received considerable attention from developmentalists over the past three decades. Unfortunately, the earlier research designs were weak, typically failing to control for the teacher's own social-class background (which can be confounded with the individual's school attainment and credentials) and inadequately controlling for children's background (often correlated with the credential levels of teachers working in their preschools and neighborhoods).

We know that teachers who come to the job with more formal education provide higher quality care to children. So the question of credentialing has led to great worries in policy circles, given the low levels of formal education of much of the preschool workforce. The rush to a remedy has been focused on jacking up credential levels—whether or not spending more time in college actually yields stronger verbal skills or adds to the caring sensitivity associated with stronger child development.

The Head Start administration, for example, now requires that half its teachers have a two-year community college degree, ideally including training in child development. Congressional staffers on Capitol Hill talk of requiring a four-year bachelor's degree, we recall from Chapter 2. About one-third of the nation's preschool teachers have bachelor's degrees, but disparities in teacher preparation from one locale to another remain stark.[61]

Debate continues over whether this formal pre-service training delivers the skills and caring qualities that contribute to children's early development.

Three decades ago Norton Grubb and Marvin Lazerson warned of the dilemmas around "the drive within centers for higher status vis-à-vis the elementary school . . . the trade-off between more distant professional behavior and more affectionate, nurturing behavior, tending to make child-care settings more formal and institutional."[62] Even now, theoretical and empirical work specifying the skills and character that effective preschool teachers exhibit—and how training programs impart such attributes—remains primitive. Again, "effective" can have several facets of meaning, depending on one's philosophical position.

Teacher education levels are consistently linked to more global quality measures, such as the richness of classroom materials, the structure of children's learning centers, and the quality of physical facilities (tapped by quality gauges like the Early Childhood Environment Rating Scale, or ECERS). After taking into account collateral quality benchmarks, such as staffing ratios or even parental fees (a proxy for the preschool's surrounding neighborhood and their families' social-class positions), the discrete effect of teacher credentials largely disappears.[63] So-called selection biases are rampant in the early studies, which attempted to show discernible benefits accruing to children exposed to teachers holding bachelor's degrees. The problem is that teachers with stronger credentials tend to migrate to preschools that serve better-off families, and thus display higher quality levels overall.[64]

In recent years, more carefully designed studies have drawn on stronger data sets, helping to distinguish what forms of pre-service teacher preparation are more likely to advance children's early learning. The NICHD study team, for instance, found that, after adjusting for staffing ratios, class size, and teachers' own child-rearing beliefs, such as being more authoritarian or liberal in their orientation, the teacher's overall educational attainment was related to positive caregiving.[65] The more focused training in child development of a two- or four-year degree program also has been associated with more sensitive and responsive caregiving.[66]

Currie and Matthew Neidell looked at whether Head Start children displayed stronger growth when they had teachers with bachelor's degrees, but found no effect.[67] Given the ample evidence that the character of child-adult interactions is key to a child's development, it's curious that credentials cannot consistently be related to richer social processes observed inside preschool classrooms.[68]

The debate also hinges on the comparative utility of specialized training in child development, since employing this more focused strategy would be much less costly than requiring a bachelor's degree. UCLA's Carollee Howes and colleagues, for example, compared a group of teachers who had obtained bachelor's degrees and had early childhood (ECE) training with a second group of teachers with bachelor's degrees but no specialized preparation.[69] No statistically significant differences were found in teacher sensitivity, harshness, or detachment between the two groups.

Teachers with a bachelor's degree *and* those with ECE training but no B.A. were found to be more sensitive and less harsh with children than teachers with little formalized education. Teachers with a bachelor's degree and ECE training were rated higher than those with a bachelor's degree but no ECE training. These findings suggest that specialized training contributes significantly to child outcomes among teachers with less than a four-year degree, and that the additional investment in a bachelor's degree may not yield an additional boost for preschoolers.

Preschool teachers who hold a bachelor's degree in ECE did tend to provide high quality programs, but those with a two-year degree and early childhood training displayed equally sensitive and rich care within their classrooms. The lack of a significant difference has now been found in several studies, drawing on a variety of preschool and family samples.[70] In Georgia, economist Henry found no difference in children's growth between those attending classrooms with teachers holding a bachelor's degree and those with teachers holding a two-year degree focused on child development. The latter is required by the Georgia UPK program. Henry attributes this null finding to the amount of in-service training and teacher mentoring that's built into the state program.[71]

Recently Diane Early and colleagues at the University of North Carolina painstakingly re-analyzed data from seven different studies of thousands of local preschool programs to ascertain the associations of teachers' education level, college degrees, and dimensions of classroom quality, as well as effects on children's development. Their methodology was rigorous: all constructs were operationalized in identical ways, and the same statistical approach—which included stringent controls for the prior background features of children and teachers alike—was used. The results are noteworthy because at last the results of these major studies could be compared directly. Better yet, most (five) of the samples were nationally representative, so findings can be generalized more widely than previously.

This research team found few associations between teachers' overall education level or attainment of a bachelor's degree and the quality of early care and education they provided. Children's developmental trajectories were no steeper when their preschool teacher had earned a B.A. degree. Two of the studies did find that having a teacher with a B.A. or more was related to higher quality, one found that it was related to lower quality, and four found no relation. The links to child outcomes were no more promising. Only six studies included a pre-reading measure and two of them found a positive association between having a B.A. and reading scores; the rest found no relation. For math, five studies found no association between teachers' degree status and early math skills, and the remaining two studies found associations but in opposing directions.

Still, researchers have also found that preschool teachers or child-care providers with low levels of education—such as those with only a high school diploma (who can legally work inside classrooms in several states)—displayed less sensitive care and were often characterized by impoverished language and colorless classroom activities. Repeatedly this factor has been shown to suppress the development of thousands of young children.[72]

TEACHER-CHILD INTERACTION

While staffing ratios, curricular approaches, and pre-service teacher training—fundamental structural ingredients of classrooms—have received the bulk of attention from researchers and state regulators alike, more recent investigations have examined the character of interactions between children and adults. How teachers engineer peer relations among children and approach their own interactions, along with the richness of their language and the instructive challenges they pose for youngsters, are likely social mechanisms for pacing the early learning that unfolds inside preschools.

Robert Pianta at the University of Virginia is a leading American researcher attempting to illuminate the variety of child-teacher relationships and interactions that unfold in preschool and kindergarten classrooms. He has discovered certain kinds of interactions that help to predict children's later development in cognitive and social domains.[73] For example, drawing from the NICHD data, Pianta and his colleagues are finding that teachers who offer young children steady feedback and express care and responsiveness with emotional support are yielding stronger benefits for youngsters in both the cognitive and the social-developmental domains.[74] His work relates to Jeff Arnett's earlier research into how the teacher's responsiveness, in caring tones, to young children's utterances and questions and greater complexity in language and cognitive demands (such as in reasoning through problems with youngsters) also help to predict youngsters' intellectual growth and social maturity.

In the Growing Up in Poverty Project, we used Arnett's measures, finding that when children were exposed to teachers who reasoned with them when problems arose and hunkered down to their level to listen and talk about their problem or to celebrate their success on a task, children displayed stronger language and cognitive growth over time.[75] Their pace of development flagged when their teachers were insensitive, detached, or failed to deploy more complex language when problems or questions arose. In addition, children who experienced a stable, longer-running relationship with teachers in the same preschool predictably had stronger cognitive outcomes.

Sensitive caregiving may be a particularly relevant factor when teachers are serving children from diverse social-class and ethnic backgrounds. Howes and her colleagues found that when responsive caregiving included practices used in children's own ethnic communities, the quality of teacher-child relationships fostered positive developmental outcomes among children.[76] These practices include use of language, forms of authority, and social rules recognizable by the children. Utilizing such practices, preschool centers were supportive and welcoming to local families, both respecting their beliefs and values and getting their children ready for school.

It is difficult to legislate or regulate from afar legal policies that markedly improve the smallest social interactions inside preschool classrooms. But an essential step in making preschool more effective appears to be figuring out what sorts of classrooms, child groupings, curricula, and teacher education will result in more supportive conditions for richer social interactions, more complex language, and stronger emotional support. Even though making classroom practices fit elaborate curricular standards set in the state capital, or testing three- and four-year-olds more intensively, may sound good in the contemporary policy climate, such surface measures may do little to increase the preschool's human benefits for children or for their families.

Who Should Run Preschools?

One final question that has received the attention of researchers lately is whether public school–based preschooling is more effective than the CBO-based preschooling. The literature on this topic is still quite young. But to date few differences have been detected, perhaps because both school- and CBO-based preschools are operated under the same quality standards set by UPK legislation—or, in pioneering states like New Jersey and Oklahoma, by education departments. Further research is certainly required to determine if public schools are better positioned to run early education programs. We do know that public school programs tend to attract more teachers with four-year degrees, but thus far this difference has yet to be shown to influence children's developmental trajectories.[77]

In Georgia, evaluation of its decade-old UPK program was thoughtfully designed so as to compare the quality and effects of three sets of preschools: those funded under Governor Zell Miller's original initiative, Head Start preschools, and nonprofit or private programs, including those financed through parental fees in better-off suburbs. The evaluation team, headed by Gary Henry, determined that 54 percent of all teachers in the Georgia pre-K program had attained a four-year degree by 2002. In contrast, just 20 percent of teachers in nonprofit and private preschools had a bachelor's degree, and only 13 percent in Head Start programs. This finding mirrors the ethnic segmentation of teaching staff across programs, as mentioned above. Three-fourths of Georgia pre-K teachers were white in 2002, and 22 percent were African American. The pattern was reversed in Head Start programs: 69 percent were black and 28 percent, white.[78]

Focusing only on the state's UPK program, Henry and his colleagues found that almost two-thirds of participating children were attending preschool in a nonprofit or private organization and one-third attended preschool within a public school. In terms of children's growth over two years, the research team initially found no differences between these two subsectors from preschool through the end of kindergarten. Across eleven different cognitive proficiencies and three social-behavioral measures, Henry found just one difference in those attending a school versus a CBO program: attending a school-based preschool was associated with a slower rate of growth in expressive vocabulary.

A more recent analysis by Henry and his colleague Craig Gordon tracked participating children through third grade in CBO- and school-based preschools within each of Georgia's counties.[79] Henry and Gordon theorized that children might perform better in counties where a vibrant CBO sub-sector effectively competed for stronger teachers and convinced parents that their programs were of stronger quality than the school-based programs. They found that theory borne out: children at nonprofit and for-profit preschools did display steeper developmental trajectories as shown by higher language scores and lower retention at third grade.

In fact, they found that all preschools that operated in a more richly competitive mixed market showed higher child outcomes. Effect sizes for test score benefits were only about 0.14 SD, although comparable to the earlier studies that looked at sustained effects in elementary school. Part of the advantage, according to Henry, appears to rest in the ability of CBO programs to attract younger, well-trained teachers who have avoided, or didn't survive, working in public school programs.

In New Jersey, early evaluation of their UPK initiative reported similar results in the generally low-income Abbott school districts. Just under 70 percent of all children were attending CBO preschools when I visited in 2003. The evaluation team, led by Gary Resnick at Westat, found no consistent differences in children's cognitive or social development between school-based and community programs.[80] The New Jersey education department under Ellen Frede set demanding quality standards for all programs, including a major push for all teachers to gain bachelor's degrees, regardless of the program's auspices. In Oklahoma, although just 18 percent of all children were attending CBO-based programs in 2004, an ongoing evaluation should be able to examine differences between the two subsectors.

Building Robust Theory for Effective Preschools

The benefits accruing to poor children from preschool attendance are encouraging, although they are not as dramatic as some advocates would have us believe. The effects on middle-class children look hopeful as well, though they are more modest. But while both groups of children appear to benefit, publicly financing universal access would not necessarily close gaps in youngsters' early development—even if levels of quality remained the same across communities. One nagging concern is, as we have seen, that middle-class children attending long hours each week will show depressed levels of social development, even as their cognitive proficiency inches upward. This is not such a concern for advocates, who argue that more money will help to raise preschool quality.

The benefits of preschool for children and families might increase if we knew more about what facets inside and outside this institution explain its effects. The field of early education could certainly benefit from a more precise causal account of what works for which subgroups of children. And experts of various stripes and colors might show greater humility, along with respect for parents, when we all reflect on the question of *how* the preschool is attempting to raise and shape young children.

The new UPK advocates often reduce the discussion to promotion of a narrow band of cognitive skills and academic knowledge. But the evidence that social development is being stalled for many middle-class kids when they spend long hours in preschool should be setting off alarms in state capitals and professional associations. This is the domain that parents care about the most, yet it's been largely ignored in the current policy debate.

Recent findings from the NICHD team, led by Virginia's Pianta, are forging new ground in this regard. His findings linking the intensity of teachers' caring and emotional support to children's social and cognitive growth should be instructive for early educators and policymakers alike. In a sense, we need more research that is policy *irrelevant*, setting aside the simple causal models favored by advocates and politicians as they assert that state curricular standards and alignment with elementary school standards will spur cognitive development and higher test scores. Pianta's efforts vividly show how leaving out the teacher—and her affection, feedback, and encouragement in the classroom—represents a huge conceptual mistake.

This new line of research moves us well beyond the debates over credentialing or child-staff ratios. Such findings have important implications for the kinds of expensive teacher training programs that state governments are embarking on. This research does not deny the importance of enriching classrooms with stronger pre-literacy content, but it does suggest that inattention to the character of human relationships may prove costly.

It is also still too early to know much about how differing preschool models, including the new state UPK programs, will actually influence parents' commitment to their children's early learning. One recent review of Head Start evaluations was suggestive of benefits. Yet this first generation of studies suffers from unknown selection effects: were the low-income parents who entered into a Head Start program already more inclined to be involved in their child's development prior to the intervention than those who didn't enter?[81]

Child health represents another domain in which we just don't know which preschool models will truly pay off. And, as the political economy of preschool organizations grows—spreading across rich and poor neighborhoods—we will also need to gauge the employment and economic benefits accruing to these communities. In theory, Head Start was supposed to help invigorate local economies and organize young parents. Evidence remains scarce on this score.

How to sustain the initial benefits of preschool is turning out to be a pivotal question. Even if quality gains yield modest improvements in children's trajectories, a bump of one-fifth to one-fourth of a standard deviation initially isn't likely to persist very far into elementary school. It will be swamped by the disparate effects of children's home environments, which often mirror the quality of elementary schools entered.

We have some evidence that when Head Start children find their way into elementary schools that display significantly stronger levels of quality, the preschool's effect does persist. Yet we are still in the dark in understanding how public-school quality interacts with whatever advantage children have gained prior to kindergarten. This interdependence between preschool and elementary school makes the preschool-effectiveness question even more pressing: advocates may well push for quality measures that have little effect on young children, squandering public dollars that could have been used to boost the quality of kindergarten or early elementary grades.

Another frontier for building stronger theory is at the cusp between the preschool as an *institution* and the practices and early learning found inside classrooms. Claims abound, for example, about the benefits of CBO-run preschools. Do more responsive teachers, for instance, attract parents, especially those who are skeptical of formal agencies? But beyond learning that there is no overall difference in child-level effects between public school–based preschools and those situated in CBOs, we really don't know whether there are any advantages accruing from where this institution is located.

Finally, the past half-century of empirical work largely ignored the question of parents. How do parents' goals and daily practices vary across cultural and linguistic groups—and what are the implications for how classroom activities are designed? It's an issue that must be raised in any pluralistic society. Theorists in child development assume, like those working in physics or biology, that there are regularized actions, emotions, or social rules enacted by adults will yield universal results across all kinds of young children. However, the rise of cross-cultural psychology and sociological studies of home practices over the past generation has sharply challenged the validity of universal theories. This is the pressing topic to which we next turn in Chapter 7.

CHAPTER SEVEN

Early Learning in Latino Communities

WITH ALEJANDRA LIVAS AND SEETA PAI

"Hispanic families use alternatives to day care, study finds," the *New York Times* headline reported. It added: "The liberal view of institutionalized care is challenged."[1] Our own fresh findings, reported by Susan Chira in 1994, revealed that Latino children, age three to five, with a working mother, were much less likely to attend preschool than children in other ethnic groups. These results were greeted with perhaps predictable enthusiasm by the political Right, including Douglas Besharov at the American Enterprise Institute, who said: "I think the conservatives were right . . . it may not only be the most financially economical way (to support child care), but it may be the most socially appropriate way."

The following month Michael Levine, a very smart and unusually well-tailored early childhood specialist from the Carnegie Corporation, came up to Cambridge from New York City. We met for coffee near Harvard Square. I was curious about his Carnegie task force, which would soon hatch the *Starting Points* report and spark a flurry of civic debate over the not-so-new brain research. But Michael had another agenda: he was trying to figure out my motivation for publishing these findings. He opened by asking, with a wry grin, if I was surprised by how the findings had "upset the Head Start community."

We had discovered—working with Harvard colleagues Susan Holloway, Xiaoyan Liang, and Judith Singer—that, after taking into account the mother's employment status, Latino children were fully 23 percentage points less likely to enroll in a preschool center before starting kindergarten than African American youngsters, and were 11 percentage points lower than whites.[2] Head Start leaders claimed that we were questioning their resolve to serve Latino families, given the program's origins and deep roots in black communities. At the time, the Clinton Administration was eager to expand Head Start, and our findings suggested a distinct softness in family demand. Instead, many Latino parents relied on kith and kin for child care, indirectly supporting the parental choice position that had earlier been taken by the Bush I White House. Our aim was simply to inject fresh findings into the public domain for debate. Levine politely probed to see whether I was truly so naïve.

This episode sparked a decade-long quest to better understand how Latino families—including a diverse range of parents—weigh different kinds of child care, including preschool. Our research group also began to disaggregate how different Latino subgroups, living in varied communities, make different "choices." Government has, over the past generation, vigorously pressed its own ideas and institutional preferences, extending Head Start preschools as well as child care vouchers into Latino communities. These divergent policy strategies were founded on assumptions about parents' *capacity* and *resources* to make wise decisions in raising their children. They also continue to manifest the intensifying struggle over what groups and individuals hold authority over child rearing—the battle now being waged by parents, experts, advocates, and early educators when it comes to universal preschool.

Latino Families—Terminally at Risk or All American?

Ever since anthropologist Oscar Lewis put forward the dismal image of a "culture of poverty" to characterize poor Mexican and Puerto Rican families in his 1965 book, *La Vida*, social reformers have continued to accept this portrayal. Lewis wrote: "By the time slum children are six or seven, they have usually absorbed the basic values and attitudes of their subculture, and are not psychologically geared to take full advantage of . . . increased opportunities."[3] Latino parents were allegedly embedded in a "traditional society" that displayed a sense of resignation, fatalism, an inability to plan for the future. Michael Harrington would speak of poverty as "a culture, an institution, a way of life." Lisbeth Schorr more recently wrote: "These families are so devoid of structure, or organization, they can disorganize you!"[4] And William Julius Wilson talked of "the tangle of pathology in the inner city."[5]

Latino families were treated as abstract entities into the 1980s, often being cast by researchers and reformers as "at risk" of various maladies. As the phrase "culturally deprived" faded, the medical metaphor, being "at risk" or "disadvantaged," was used to mean that a young child displayed a limited English vocabulary or somehow wasn't "ready for school," that she was guilty of being unable to sit still, resisting those miniature metal desks with Formica tops. Latino parents, it was alleged, were in need of a new religion: they needed formal institutions to help raise and properly socialize their young children. One California advocacy group argues that the magic of universal preschool will rescue "linguistically isolated" children, and eventually lower their rates of divorce or incarceration.[6]

Antonia Lopez, early childhood specialist for the National Council for La Raza, points out that "in some of the school readiness rhetoric there's an undercurrent of belief that the problem of low achievement is rooted in something deficient about the students." She adds: "They think that our children have such an inadequate early growing experience, that parents . . . aren't competent to give them what they need, that someone has to step in and take on the 'material' that makes it to kindergarten."[7]

But what share of Latino parents and children actually do display such maladies? In what ways do Latino parents lack the economic or social resources so necessary in raising robust young children—and for which Latino subgroups? What forms of early education might build upon the strengths of Latino communities? These are the questions that motivate this chapter.

The question we started with, how to advance Latino children's early development, also prompts us to be more aware of the cross-cultural revolution in learning theory. Developmentalists, cultural psychologists, and sociologists have been detailing how young children grow and learn within *particular communities*, demarcated by social class, ethnicity, and language. This scholarly work, begun over eight decades ago, moves beyond the biological emphasis of Piaget and the neuroscientists. And cultural psychologists place on a wider, more colorful pallet the individualistic and liberal-humanist assumptions of enlightened European thinkers, which they regard as situated within bounded culture as well.

In modern times, the aim of civic leaders and government schools has been to move children up and out of their local communities. The goal of assimilation into the abstract nation-state was to be expedited by a shared language and literacy skills, along with a social commitment to the modern sector, leaving backward, parochial ways behind. Thus we arrive at an important question: whether institutions of early learning should act to advance forms of knowledge, language, and social behavior that are valued by reformers, but still feel rather foreign to parents and their local communities.

Just beneath the cultural tensions surrounding this question are the regulatory and standardizing habits of the bureaucratic state, which seems tacitly intent on rationalizing various domains of economic and social life. The early education field has become the stage upon which the political culture of the modern state—an agenda set by well-meaning elites—confronts the moral tenets and forms of parenting that may characterize particular communities. An intense *cultural* democratization now flourishes across America, along with an *organizational* democratization, which is seen in the wide range of well-established community agencies that are legitimate political players, as was so vividly illustrated in the case of Los Angeles.

Thus to rationalize early childhood holds real advantages for some, but doing so discounts what German idealists once called the *geist*, the particular spirit, values, and cultural fabric of particular groups.[8] In the Enlightenment, the state sought to wrench the child out of the village's backward ways, including its confined notions of the youngster's developmental potentials. In Lockean terms, the child had the capacity to become a logical, reasoning creature with the autonomy to break from the group's interests. The same logic can be seen today when universal preschool advocates earnestly seek to rescue Latino children from their somehow "at risk" households.

But will the push by UPK elites to save Latino children by means of an institutional fix unravel the very fabric that lends coherence and strength to Latino communities? Can collective action, implemented by public agencies, effectively bolster the communities and human-scale organizations that provide stability and economic resources for parents and young children alike? As we dig into these questions, we must keep in mind the words of the late Talcott Parsons, that the arguments of both the *cultural idealists* and the *rational utilitarians* can be informed by empirical analysis.[9] We must push beyond the ideals of community agencies and the promises of government to empirically assess how, or under what conditions, differing organizing strategies truly advance the family's robust character and the child's development.

The Paradoxes of Latino Child Development

Latino parents in general place great value on schooling, believing that it will prepare their children for better jobs and happier lives. In a 2004 poll for the National Council for La Raza, when Latino adults were asked to name "the most important issue for the Latino community," public education topped the list. Nearly three-quarters of the respondents said government spends "too little" on education, and 77 percent agreed that the nation "should spend more to ensure all children have access to preschool education and services."[10]

Nevertheless, the school attainment of Latino children lags far behind other groups. In 2003 fully 30 percent of all Latinos had not completed high school by age twenty-four, compared with 11 percent of blacks and 7 percent of whites. Among first-generation Latino youths, 43 percent left school without a diploma.[11] And these disparities are strikingly apparent before young children enter kindergarten. In California, we found that even Latino kindergartners with minimal English proficiency are about 0.60 of a standard deviation (SD) below whites in pre-reading skills and almost 0.90 SD (close to a full year) behind in their understanding of numbers and mathematical concepts. These gulfs in early cognitive development equal the achievement gap observed between white and Latino fourth graders.[12]

If Latino parents are so deeply committed to schooling, what factors account for these lags in the *cognitive* and *linguistic* aspects of children's early development? Should we attribute them to children's language environments, parenting practices (weak literacy traditions, maybe), or family poverty and social disorganization? Have researchers observed the same kinds of developmental gaps when it comes to *physical health* or *social-emotional* well-being?

Our assumptions about the causal dynamics are pivotal, since the new preschool advocates assume that something is lacking in children's everyday environments, including, possibly, the weak capacities of their parents.

Let's begin this search for causal explanations by examining America's demographic revolution. We look at the new scholarship on the vibrant family values and social assets that undergird child rearing in many Latino families. We also detail Latinos' diversity, with differences in country of origin, social class, level of education, and degree of acculturation.

A DEMOGRAPHIC REVOLUTION

Skyrocketing growth across Latino groups means that millions of additional children will be entering kindergarten, many with limited oral proficiency in English. The overall Latino population residing in the United States grew fivefold between 1960 and 2000, becoming our society's largest minority group in 2003.[13] The number of Latino youngsters under five is projected to grow from 4.2 million in 2006 to 8.6 million in 2050, a rise from 21 percent to 32 percent of all young children nationwide.[14]

This growth may slow as school attainment rises for Latino mothers and acculturation brings middle-class norms, especially those related to fertility and family size. In California, the fertility rate dropped from 3.4 to 2.6 births per woman just between 1990 and 2003 (the non-Latino white fertility rate was 1.9 in 2000).[15] Even so, the flood of youngsters with limited English into the schools will probably continue unabated for decades to come. In California just over 39 percent of all children five or younger speak a language other than English at home, according to the 2000 census. More than a million children with limited English now attend California schools, fully one-quarter of all children enrolled.[16] The share with limited English—which includes all linguistic groups, not just Spanish-speakers—equals 31 percent of all children in Texas, 28 percent in New York, and about one-fifth in Florida, Illinois, and Massachusetts.[17] In Los Angeles County, just under two of every three births are to Latino parents.[18]

The diversity of language patterns today is especially important to grasp. Well over half (57 percent) of all Latino students, kindergarten through twelfth grade, spoke mostly English at home in the late 1990s nationwide. Another 17 percent reported speaking English and Spanish equally in their household. Nearly three-fourths of the students who spoke mostly English at home had a mother who was born in the United States. Conversely, the 92 percent of the Latino students who spoke mainly Spanish at home had mothers who were born outside the states.[19] Mexicans comprise the largest Latino subgroup nationwide. Just over two-thirds of all Latino children under five were of Mexican origin in 2000. In the city of Los Angeles, residents of Mexican origin account for almost a third of the total population and 63 percent of the Latino population. In Chicago, 71 percent of the Latino population has roots in Mexico.

THE FAMILY'S ECONOMIC RESOURCES

The share of Latino children living below the federal poverty line—with parents earning about $16,000 for a family of four—equaled 22 percent in 2002. This figure was comparable to that for blacks (24 percent), but almost three times higher than for whites (8 percent). When sociologist Don Hernandez looked at Mexican-origin families, he found that fully 48 percent of third- and later-generation children lived in households with earnings under twice the poverty line; the figure was 69 percent for children in immigrant Mexican-American families.[20]

In California, the share of Latino adults living in poverty fell significantly as Great Society initiatives kicked in during the 1960s; then it drifted upward and reached a plateau of about one-fifth after 1980. One-fourth of all California Latinos were first-generation immigrants in 1970, but after three decades of steady migration from Mexico and parts south this share climbed to 57 percent by 2000. The share of Latino first-generation immigrants nationwide in 2020 will fall to just one-quarter, given slowing immigration and birth rates.[21] Among immigrant Latinos in California in their forties, just over 77 percent report that Spanish is their preferred language; among U.S.-born Latinos in the same age cohort, only 13 percent prefer speaking Spanish.[22]

SOCIAL FOUNDATIONS

Do low-income Latino households suffer from the same fragility displayed by other, generally low-income, groups? Latino family structures are changing from one generation to the next. However, most families remain intact, and serve as cultural cornerstones that are firmer than those of contemporary (non-Latino) white families in America. Almost three-fourths (73 percent) of first-generation Mexican families include a married couple; the figure declines to 66 percent among second-generation families. The mean number of persons residing in a first-generation Mexican household is 4.4, and 3.6 in second-generation homes. This smaller size is related to the declining number of children and co-resident kin members. In contrast, 36 percent of all Puerto Rican families were headed by a single mother in 2000, This figure is 18 percent for Cuban-Americans, compared with 45 percent for blacks and 14 percent for whites.[23]

Since the 1940s, "Latinos have behaved more like members of the 'American' middle class than middle-class 'Americans' themselves have," argues David Hayes-Bautista, a UCLA professor of medicine.[24] This statement echoes demographer Nancy Landale's conclusion that "Hispanics exhibit higher levels of familism than non-Hispanics on most demographic indicators."[25] Hayes-Batista's analysis stretches back over the past half-century, focusing on families of Mexican heritage in California. He shows that a higher share of these adults have been employed than any other ethnic group over the past six decades, and a lower fraction have drawn welfare benefits. The incidence of infant death and low birth weight is lower for Latino offspring than for African Americans and other low-income groups. Latino adults also live longer than other groups. He attributes strong maternal and child health outcomes to Latinos' healthier diets, including steady consumption of fresh fruits and vegetables.

First-generation Mexican mothers are more likely to breastfeed their infants than whites, although this healthful practice declines for second- and third-generation mothers. Unwed low-income Mexican couples are less likely to break up following a birth than white or black unwed couples.[26] Also, developmentalists have shown that certain parenting behaviors, including levels of affection and time spent with children, are stronger or comparable to middle-class white parents along several measures.[27] Children of immigrant parents are twice as likely to live in a home with at least one grandparent as second-generation children of non-immigrant parents.[28]

In short, Latino infants and toddlers, along with their mothers, show robust health, nutrition, and social indicators; nonetheless, by age three or four these youngsters lag behind other groups in terms of certain cognitive skills and pre-literacy proficiencies. The numbers paint a rather paradoxical portrait. However, pasting labels such as "disadvantaged" or "at risk" onto Latino parents and children ignores both the culturally situated strengths and social assets held by most families and differences observed across subgroups.

RETHINKING LATINO FAMILIES

The Latino experience in general is unlike the historical routes taken by immigrant whites or African Americans. As the late anthropologist John Ogbu so forcefully argued, it makes a difference whether one's family voluntarily migrated to get ahead, or were captured and brought to the United States involuntarily.[29] Economic opportunities, levels of racial discrimination, the civil rights movement have been experienced differently for black and Latino communities over the past half-century. The persisting coherence of families and kin networks among most Latino subgroups and resulting levels of social support depart markedly from the overall African American experience. These historical differences hold implications for how we think about the capacity of Latino parents to raise their children within two-parent households and a coherent set of cultural norms.

Researchers continue to detail how Latino parents express a strong commitment to familism, including the hierarchical nature of social authority, with clear role obligations for siblings, parents, and kin members. Sociologists Angela Valenzuela and Sandy Dornbusch argue that these resilient social mores, while sometimes conceiving of the child's individual ambition and eventual mobility differently, bring coherence and structure to everyday life.[30] The renewed attention among scholars to the notion of social capital and the way in which cooperative family networks help to buffer the exigencies of economic poverty also cast Latino family structure and Latino values in a positive light.[31]

Contradictions do emerge. Our own work has shown that, when a grandparent or kin member lives in the household, Latino parents select preschool at a lower rate. In this situation, immediate supports reproduce the family's social norms and linguistic patterns, at the same time limiting the child's exposure to a wider range of cognitive demands and social behaviors.[32]

We find another paradox when we try to interpret Latino families' capacity to raise healthy and robust children. From work with Bridges, Russ Rumberger, and Loan Tran, we know that five-year-olds from low-income Latino families enter kindergarten with considerably lower pre-reading proficiencies than four-year-olds from middle-class Latino families (when isolating on those with basic English proficiency). But by high school, the pattern flips, and first-generation students report higher grade point averages than third-generation students nationally (although prior schooling in Mexico also plays a contributing role).[33] These findings suggest that parenting practices and home language are at work when children are young, but, over time, local peer and community norms within low-income settings start to pack a punch. The parents' own reported endorsement of the school's utility remains invariant and strong across generations. But other actors and the family's economic resources often put constraints on the direct influence exerted by parents, even when cultural expectations remain strong.[34]

Among Latino families—as in all households—young children are faced with a variety of activities that make cognitive and social demands. And the kinds of activities and behaviors that adults tacitly expect often differ across cultural or social-class groups. Not all types of parents are bent on scheduling play dates or zooming to the nearest chain bookstore to pick up a new children's book. Toddlers and preschoolers may play with siblings, learn how to have fun with grandma, and soon play video games or bake with their mother.

Cross-cultural psychologists and anthropologists over the past half century have been detailing such human-scale contexts, and looking at how young children glean meaning and acquire skills within home settings. Doing so may occasionally call for didactic teaching by a parent; mostly, however, it involves the child's observing, mimicking behaviors, or diving into a collective activity. And these settings can vary systematically across ethnic and social-class groups. This kind of work by cultural psychologists has led to a revolution in how we think about early learning across diverse families. It has strong implications for how we create more effective preschools, and, indeed, how we define what "effectiveness" means when early education is formally organized within a particular community.

The Cultural Revolution in Early Learning

Developmentalist Gary Resnick made an intriguing discovery when he was assessing New Jersey's initial move toward UPK in the late 1990s. He found that white children who attended the new pre-k classrooms located inside public schools showed notable gains in *English* vocabulary and productive language capacities. Equally impressive were the gains for Latino children in their vocabulary and pre-literacy skills in *Spanish* when they attended CBO-based preschools. The community preschools employed a large share of bilingual teachers, and the two sets of organizations held different philosophies about what language, or languages, of instruction should be deployed.[35] The power of organizational context, along with the character of developmental benefits, proved remarkable.

A couple of years earlier David Dickinson published results from a study that followed Latino children whose home language was Spanish into either English-medium or Spanish-medium preschools. Youngsters placed in the English-speaking classrooms displayed significantly more behavioral problems than those in classrooms in which Spanish was the dominant medium. Weaker social relationships with English-speaking teachers and uneven peer relations helped to explain kids' slower acquisition of cognitive and pre-literacy skills. Summing up this study, Harvard sociolinguist Catherine Snow wrote: "Given the power of preschool children's social development to predict long-range outcomes, including literacy, these results are striking."[36]

The particular context in which young children learn—including the degree of continuity between the family and preschool classroom—influences a youngster's ability to acquire mainstream cognitive skills and behaviors valued in school. This claim is pivotal, from the vantage point of cultural psychologists and learning theorists. Rather than viewing the preschool as a purposefully foreign organization, aiming to modernize the young child, these scholars emphasize that the cognitive demands and social norms found inside the homes of Latino children offer preschool teachers a scaffold for building new levels of development.

Indeed, Piaget's idea that adults must calibrate their practices to the child's developmental stage remains widely accepted among early educators, despite the rising pitch for disembodied skills. Teachers working with special-needs children also employ this basic strategy day in and day out. But when it comes to children with cultural or linguistic differences and strengths, normative psychology has often trumped any serious attempt at scaffolding. Policy-makers and many practitioners simply aim to *fix* these differences, be they the lack of English vocabulary or the "shy" child's reticence to speak up.

This revolutionary notion recognizes that the child's mind doesn't develop in a social vacuum. Instead, it develops through social interaction, acquiring the cognitive tools, social norms, and emotional dispositions expected of young members within a particular community. This idea can be traced back to Herder's eighteenth-century postulate that "to be a member of a group is to think and act in a certain way, in the light of particular goals, values, pictures of the world . . . and to think and act so as to belong to a group."[37] Cultural psychologists have long been digging into how material conditions, social norms, and symbolic systems (including language and moral beliefs about behavior) shape different ways of thinking and acting. Only recently, however, has this third perspective on early development attracted a growing following, at the same time that civic elites and the state intensify their efforts to somehow repair or compensate for the way "at risk" Latino and other non-mainstream children are raised and educated at home.

It's impossible, of course, to generalize about Latino children, a vastly diverse group. Many do not grow up exclusively within the boundaries of one cultural or linguistic group. Indeed, demographer Don Hernandez, analyzing data from the 2000 household census, found that just over 40 percent of Latino children five to eight years old are fluent in Spanish and also speak English "very well."[38]

BIOLOGICAL AND CULTURAL
DETERMINANTS OF DEVELOPMENT

Cross-cultural scholars do not discount the biological stages that characterize the maturation of the child's brain and body. But these organic forces don't explain why young children speak different languages, or why some Latino children rarely challenge the authority of adults, infrequently flip through a book, or prefer not to sit alone to finger paint. Variability in youngsters' linguistic and social proficiencies, so consequential to behavior inside a classroom, is shaped by culturally bounded practices, not simply emergent through biological maturation.

UCLA anthropologist Patricia Greenfield talks about the universal sign-posts that appear along the path of development, including the toddler's ability to learn about primary social relationships with peers and parents, or how adolescents in all cultures must reason through independence from their parents to varying degrees.[39] The contours of basic mechanisms may be quite similar. For example, we know that young children's pre-literacy skills in Spanish are stronger when their parents read to them in Spanish at home.[40] But what a first- or second-generation Latino child is learning—from the cognitive symbols linked to language to the social and moral norms that are tacitly learned—will likely depart from what a white child in a middle-class family is learning.

As Santa Cruz psychologist Barbara Rogoff puts it, "Cognitive development occurs as new generations collaborate with older generations in varying forms of interpersonal engagement and institutional practices." She adds: "The conceptual shift (is) from individual to sociocultural activity as the unit of analysis . . . to move from thinking of cognition as a property of individuals to thinking of cognition as an aspect of human sociocultural activity."[41] It follows that when preschool teachers pursue "developmentally appropriate practices," or bore phonemes and numbers into children's minds, or allow youngsters to freely choose among activities, they are pressing distinctive cognitive demands and norms that equip children to operate within a *particular* context. Whether a linkage operates between the requisite knowledge and cognitive demands of the classroom's organization—from encouraging children to go wild in the dress-up corner, or having them sketch their names within a bounded rectangle on the page—and the child's socialization at home remains a crucial question for culturally sensitive learning theorists.

In the early 1970s, as parents' reliance on child care and preschool accelerated, an interwoven fabric of scientific work emerged. A rising number of young children were growing up in *multiple environments* with a mix of adults and with more time spent in formal institutions like preschools. The earliest child care scholars, notably Greta Fine and Alison Clarke-Stewart, moved from Urie Bronfenbrenner's ecological framework to detail how toddlers and preschoolers were learning in novel settings about how to become members of different groups: the family and child-care settings placed differing cognitive demands, social rules, even health practices on young children.[42] My son Dylan by age two, for example, was exuberantly praying out loud in Spanish at the dinner table. His skills stemmed not from his parents but from Gloria Marín, his dedicated and religious caregiver. In these ways, toddlers and preschoolers are apprenticed, acquiring normative, expected forms of behavior and belief.

The family's position in society, historically and culturally, also drives the kind of cognitive demands and social norms that many Latino parents make and expect, especially as they try to bridge two cultural logics. The settings and small-scale organizations that their children then encounter, as activity theorists like Michael Cole argue, present differing tasks, which require particular cognitive skills and social rules of participation. Thus we return to the broader, macro forces that condition the nature of childhood in any society. "Cultural and contextual factors that influence early socialization experiences and goals for African American and Latino children are different from those of their White counterparts," as Deborah Johnson, Suzanne Randolph, and others working on the NICHD child care study emphasize.[43] "The demographic and ideological factors that converged to initiate and shape early child care research in the last two decades were primarily relevant to middle-class, European American families," they write in a recent paper. But "families use (their) primary cultural values to inform their parenting practices and child care choices."

IMPLICATIONS FOR LATINO CHILD REARING

By ignoring how parents and caregivers adapt to surrounding conditions, "developmental science has resulted in a literature on minority children and their families that concentrates on explaining developmental deviations in comparison to white middle class populations rather than examining normative development processes and outcomes" within particular communities, Brown University psychologist Cynthia García Coll argues.[44] Her findings show that Latino children who acquire bicultural cognitive and social proficiencies are "less likely to experience school and family conflicts." As Beatrice and John Whiting wrote a generation earlier, "If children are studied within the confines of a single culture, many events are taken as natural. It is only when it is discovered that other peoples do not follow these practices . . . that they are adopted as variables."[45]

Recent discoveries illuminate the ways in which Latino parents try to prepare their children to operate within a dominant culture that often discounts their home language and cultural mores. Leslie Reese's discussions with first-generation Mexican parents in Los Angeles revealed that many see America as a land of economic opportunity devoid of any strong moral compass. Thus, they reach back to their native country for lessons and tales to pass along to young children to define their identity in opposition to white society.[46]

Similarly, when Nurit Sheinberg at Harvard talked with Latino mothers about how they define good parenting, they mentioned various models they used: some saw themselves as protectors and mediators between their child and a hostile outside world; others sought to shape *niños educados*, ensuring that youngsters would display the proper demeanor and dignity to command respect and meet the family's obligations. A few talked of using didactic, teacher-like practices, such as helping their children do well in school and instructing children in their cultural mores.[47] Again, we see how home practices are nested within, and adapt to, the broader forces of the child's immediate community. The specific child-rearing strategy flows from the parent's way of adapting to the family's position in the dominant culture, defined in terms of language, social class, and their posture toward acculturation.

Born in the same year as Piaget, 1896, Lev Vygotsky was a pioneer in learning theory who placed a consequential cornerstone, by revealing how young children acquire knowledge, language, and social understandings situated in particular contexts. He did not argue against the influence of physiological development, nor against the behaviorists' emphasis on discrete incentives (or negative sanctions) in the socialization process. But he argued that neither model sufficiently accounted for why young children were motivated to learn and to construct meaning out of early social interactions. Vygotsky's work unfolded in the Soviet Union and did not take hold in the United States until the 1980s.

"In child development," he wrote, "along with the processes of organic growth and maturation, a second level of development is clearly distinguished— the cultural growth of behavior. It is based on the mastery of devices and means of cultural behavior and thinking."[48] Detailing Vygotsky's account of development, James Wertsch writes: "higher mental processes in the individual have their origin in social processes, (and) mental processes can be understood only if we understand the tools and signs that mediate them." Rogoff adds: "Babies enter the world equipped with patterns of action from their genes and prenatal experience, as well as with caregivers who structure their biological and social worlds in ways deriving from their own . . . cultural histories."[49]

Vygotsky moved from Karl Marx's premise that human beings have no fixed nature but that we adjust our consciousness and social behavior according to evolving material demands and the social organization of work. He became interested in how parenting practices in one generation stemmed from the economic context and dominant activities of the previous generation, the rudiments of an ecological account of children's changing environments. He and A. R. Luria emphasized that the rise of industrial organizations altered daily activity and forms of cognition—that is, that institutional forms and norms evolve over time and thus alter how children are tacitly apprenticed in settings conditioned by parents' class position.

Vygotsky and Luria studied, for instance, how literate groups in Central Asia invoked symbols and abstract ideas more readily than nonliterate communities, and how the cognitive tools required by novel institutions and the modernizing organization of work led to "new forms of thinking."[50] As Sylvia Scribner and Michael Cole summarized a generation ago, "According to Vygotsky, basic psychological processes (abstraction, generalization, inference) are universal and common to all humankind; but their functional organization will vary, depending on the nature of the symbol systems available in different historical epochs and societies . . . Language is a universal symbol system . . . but other symbol systems are not universal and introduce culture-specific differences in the way higher (cognitive) processes are organized."[51]

Like Piaget, Vygotsky was fascinated with how young children learn the meaning of certain social signs within their immediate context. One oft-repeated example is the way a toddler constructs the meaning of gesturing toward a block or teddy bear—without intentionally pointing to it—only after a caregiver observes the child's random arm movement and hands the object to the child. The sign becomes intersubjectively understood through this (non-didactic) interaction between child and adult. This interaction is similar, for example, to how peers model mutual obligations of support within many Latino families, or how activity corners in preschools signal the opportunity to play inventively and at times cooperatively. The meaningful signs are linked to cognitive demands, and this fusion of symbol, thought, and be-havior holds meaning in a particular context, guided by the mentoring of adults or peers.

Vygotsky argued that this learning would occur only if the new informa-tion or cognitive tool was within the child's "zone of proximal development," where the child held enough prior knowledge to make meaning of the new social sign or to resolve the novel cognitive problem. This process is similar to learning a new language, where new grammatical structures or complex sentences can be comprehended only with sufficient prior knowledge. Piaget, similarly, argued that children learn to cooperate and pursue a task together by moving from a disagreement or conflicting strategies to negotiating a shared course of action. And the pathway to intersubjective consensus is con-ditioned by children's sharing a common language, with shared meaning at-tached to symbols and behavioral scripts that contribute to solving the issue at hand.[52]

John Dewey in his progressive pedagogical thinking would come to share Piaget's and Vygotsky's view that development is advanced when the child is an active participant engaged in solving cognitive or social challenges that come to hold meaning in context. Adults or peers can lend some structure and constitutive rules to the setting, but the child inevitably constructs his or her understanding of the forces and symbols at play.

"Learners inevitably participate in communities of practitioners," as Jean Lave and Etienne Wenger, theorists of culturally situated learning, put it.[53] Blending their earlier work on how learning occurs through apprenticeship and social learning theory (from psychology), Lave and Wenger distinguish between didactically transmitted information that is passively received and active participation in real activities that involve a "master craftsman" of sorts, from the fine tailor to the careful preschool teacher who deploys cognitive scaffolds *and* encourages children to tackle their own tasks. Their framework for "situated learning" draws heavily from activity theory and Vygotskian roots, and they emphasize that apprenticing learning is easier said than done. It involves the careful weaving together of discrete skills with social engage-ment, and it views learners and facilitators as collaboratively involved in the same work. In fact, this framework departs from liberal-humanist ideals in that it sees learning not as something that clicks in the isolated child's mind, learning to reason or explore with maximum autonomy, but instead it sees "how practice grounds learning . . . in certain forms of social co-participation," as learning theorist William Hanks says.[54]

MOVING CHILDREN OUTSIDE LOCAL CONTEXTS

The critics of situated conceptions of development raise an important point: by reproducing social and cognitive forms, Latino children may remain less equipped to deal with the broader society or operate in an impersonal economy. Bilingual preschools will only delay acquisition of the most valued language in the dominant culture, English, these critics argue. Thus we return to Talcott Parsons's preoccupation with how to balance the idealism and zeitgeist of the native community with the utilitarianism inherent within capitalist economies and instrumental governments.

As psychologist Robert Sternberg stressed in his 2004 presidential address to the American Psychological Association on culture and intelligence, "children may develop contextually important skills at the expense of academic ones."[55] But of course, academic skills are not acquired in a culture-free zone. The ways in which children conform to the social rules and meritorious forms of behavior that are valued by the public schools are rich in cultural meaning and instrumentally tied to advancement in a liberal economy and stratified class structure. To deny access to higher-status forms of language or cognition does a disservice to any child of color, of course. The collateral question, however, is how to build from culturally situated forms of child development, moving from the youngster's original social foundations in ways that do not erode them.

Vygotsky himself examined this question, sparking original thinking on what Wertsch calls "the decontextualization of the mediational means."[56] Vygotsky highlighted that the methods and symbolic systems of mathematical calculation are no longer attached to an immediate context; they are portable as tools that can be readily applied to various situations. This notion of portability is tied to García Coll's point that some Latino parents explicitly coach their children on how to behave differently in their native and white cultural settings. Different behaviors, symbols, and language become deployed in a versatile and contingent way. The odds that a child will acquire decontextualized forms of knowledge, however, depends upon the adults and caregivers that enter her or his daily environment.

Overall, Vygotsky and his contemporary disciples bring institutions into sharp focus, seeing organizations as linked to the nature of work and industrial-like forms, which manifest particular cognitive demands and social norms that hold utility in the wider social system. Vygotskian thought allows us to link institutional change to the kinds of cognitive tools, curricula, and cultural mores that are enacted inside classrooms and are variably infused with status and legitimacy by the state and the economy.

What Do Parents Want?

Not only children but parents, too, must negotiate the situated agenda advanced by the preschool institution, deciding whether to enroll their youngster, or whether to rely on old-fashioned kinds of child care. We know that Latino children coming from poor families who attend Head Start preschools benefit significantly in terms of cognitive and language development (Chapter 6). Given these benefits, at least within cognitive and linguistic domains of learning, why do some Latino subgroups continue to shy away from preschools?

Researchers have pursued two lines of investigation to find the answer, focusing on family attributes that contribute to variation in *demand* for preschool and factors that suppress or enhance neighborhood *supply*. Both sets of factors may interact to shape the perceived legitimacy of the preschool institution in the eyes of Latino parents located in varying circumstances.

PRESCHOOL DEMAND AMONG LATINO FAMILIES

Fact number one, on the demand side, is that a smaller share of Latina mothers work outside the home than women in other ethnic groups. Among married mothers with a child under six, 46 percent of Latina mothers were in the labor force in 2004, compared with 58 percent of comparable white mothers. Just over 75 percent of African American mothers were in the paid labor force that year.[57] (Maternal employment rates among black women have been comparatively high for at least the past century.)[58]

Indeed, maternal employment is a strong predictor of a child's propensity to attend a preschool at age three or four, although many children of stay-at-home mothers go to preschool as well. Even after we take into account maternal employment status, Latino children are still about one-fourth less likely to enter a preschool center than children in other groups. But ethnic membership likely masks fine-grained features of families or child socialization patterns that may further explain lower preschool enrollment among Latino subgroups.

Family income, for instance, co-varies with children's preschool enrollment rates, but the patterns of association turn out to be somewhat counterintuitive. Figure 7.1 shows how preschool enrollment rates among *four-year-olds* are similar for children from poor and middle-class families. In fact, enrollments also dip for lower middle-class white and Latino families. Our earlier work details how first-generation and Spanish-speaking children are less likely to enter preschool as detailed below. Latino children also display lower enrollment rates across the middle-income range than either African American or white children; this is explained in part by lower maternal employment. Enrollment levels then climb steadily for children of increasingly affluent families at the eighth decile and above. Among *three-year-olds*, the

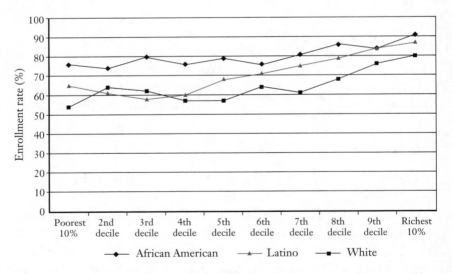

Figure 7.1 National enrollment rates in preschool centers among four-year-olds by socioeconomic status and ethnic group. ECLS-K data for 1997–98, National Center for Educational Statistics. Original tabulations by Daphna Bassok, Stanford University.

Latino disparity is more stark: just one-fifth attended a preschool nationwide, compared with 42 percent of white and 44 percent of black three-year-olds in the late 1990s.[59]

The fact that poor children now attend preschool at rates approximating middle-class youngsters is good news. Yet it highlights the widening gap in access that blue-collar families face. The disparity is explained by a combination of forces: the success of Head Start and state preschool programs in boosting enrollment since the 1960s; the scarcity of preschools in blue-collar communities where families can neither qualify for subsidies nor afford costly preschool fees; and softer demand for preschool among blue-collar and middle-class Latino parents than for whites in states like California or Texas.[60] The squeeze felt by the lower middle-class also arises in the health sector, where these families often earn too much for public support but too little to buy quality health care or basic insurance on the open market.[61]

SOCIOCULTURAL DETERMINANTS OF PRESCHOOL DEMAND

Certain demographic features of Latino families related to kin support, family size, and language further explain the enrollment gap. Among mothers who give birth to a third child, for example, we found that their likelihood of selecting any form of nonparental child care diminishes significantly.[62] This effect may be linked to the rising cost of child rearing in larger families, class-based beliefs about maternal employment, or a decision to invest in fewer offspring. Culturally bounded beliefs also are at play: *marianismo* is very much alive in many Latino communities, based on the Catholic ideal of the Virgin Mary and defining the woman's role as self-sacrificing mother.[63] We also found that grandparents or other kin are more likely to be co-resident with Latino (and black) parents than with white families, reducing demand for institutional forms of child care.[64]

Immigrant Latinas, however, report having fewer kin members co-resident or living close by. Still, they are 19 percent less likely to select a preschool program for their child than other Latinos, after taking into account ethnic membership, family income, and a variety of other factors, according to another recent analysis.[65] This study team also found that married couples are half as likely to use preschools, compared with single-parent families, after taking other factors into account. Non-English speaking Latino and Vietnamese parents were less likely to select preschools than their English-speaking counterparts, according to a recent California study.[66]

In these ways the softer demand for preschool expressed by Latino parents is linked to acculturation and accompanying shifts in child-rearing beliefs. Some features of the preschool itself, as well, likely influence how inviting this institution appears in the eyes of parents. As Harvard anthropologist Robert LeVine emphasizes, not all cultures or subgroups view child rearing as a discrete and intense project, certainly not one that requires pre-literacy training or encouraging individual autonomy before a child enters school. Yet as child-rearing experts or public messages encourage parents to emulate the role of teacher and prepare the child in ways valued by the school, home practices can change over time. In turn, Latino mothers with more schooling tend to structure activities for young children that mirror the teacher's behavior, setting aside reading time, practicing counting or reciting the alphabet, sitting at a table to complete art projects.

Harvard graduate student Xiaoyan Liang, building from Susan Holloway's earlier work at Berkeley, tested whether parents' beliefs about child rearing and home practices help to explain their propensity to enroll their child in preschool.[67] She employed indicators of pre-literacy activities structured by parents, and looked at the importance that parents placed on cooperation and sharing and other socialization goals. Before she entered these parental practices and beliefs into the estimation model, it appeared that children from Spanish-speaking homes were significantly less likely to enter preschool. But once Liang found that pre-literacy activities, parents' emphasis on cooperation, and amount of television viewing were associated (the latter, negatively) with the likelihood of attending preschool, she discovered that the effect of home language disappeared, becoming statistically insignificant.

These results confirmed that immigrant and Spanish-speaking Latinos engage less in teacher-like practices with their children *and* express softer demand for preschool than do English-speaking parents of Latino origin. However, the latter group of Latinos approximates the practices of white middle-class parents. Thus, it's not that Spanish-speaking parents care less about their youngster's early development; instead, they have less experience in acting like teachers at home, explicitly structuring activities that pass on academic and linguistic knowledge in Anglo-like ways. These home practices change over generations, with acculturation, depending in part on the degree to which parents adapt to middle-class norms related to cognitive demands and helping one's child achieve in school.

IF WE BUILD NEW PRESCHOOLS, WILL LATINOS COME?

I would answer: Yes, it's a good bet overall. But the children who would benefit most—those from first-generation and blue-collar Latino families—may not show up. Enrollment of low-income Latino children has grown steadily; they presently equal two-thirds of the 113,052 children enrolled in California's Head Start preschools, one-third of the 52,158 attending Head Start in New York, and 63 percent of 74,927 in Texas. Poor Latino parents also have responded to state-funded preschool initiatives in recent years: 63 percent of the additional 120,948 children served in California's state-funded centers are of Latino origin. In contrast, one-third of parents drawing child care vouchers that enable their child to enter either a preschool center or a home-based arrangement, are Latino.[68] A recent analysis by Stanford's Susanna Loeb shows that black children remain significantly more likely to enter a Head Start preschool nationally than Latino or white youngsters from similarly low-income families, perhaps harking back to the program's historical roots in poor southern states.[69]

Persisting cultural values and the odd-hour jobs that many Latina mothers are forced to take may constrain their demand response to a rising supply of preschools. Holloway and I followed fourteen Latina women over a three-year period in Boston, and heard much from them about the cultural disconnects between home and institutional care. Beatriz, referring to *marianismo* ideals, preferred to stay at home with her two sons, age two and six. Becoming a mother, she said, is "a sacrifice of oneself because no one can take care of a child like his mother." Another Latina mother, Delmi, told us: "A mother is completely dedicated or given (*darle*) to the child, sacrificed. It's something special."

When she did return to the workforce, Delmi relied on her mother and three nearby sisters to care for her daughter, age four. To reciprocate, Delmi would help clean their apartments on weekends. Beatriz took her voucher to a Honduran family child care provider, where she found a warm atmosphere within the provider's home. "They sing, she records their voices, she has them paint, she has lots of things to do," Beatriz told us. When she worked afternoons, Beatriz would pay the provider's husband to pick up her school-age son after school.[70]

Delmi's daughter entered a preschool later during the course of our study, but she complained that "kids in this country (are) very independent, so they don't take studying seriously. They have different [switching momentarily to English] free-choice activities [returning to Spanish] where the child chooses where she's going (and) what she's doing . . . I see that they play more than work." This notion that white children are raised to be "free" and "independent" came up in conversation with other mothers in the study. They see the preschool as the first organization in which this foreign behavior arises. In addition, a study by Purdue developmentalist Karen Diamond drew from a large national survey; she found that many Latino parents see preschool as a place to acquire basic academic knowledge, including learning one's colors, numbers, and the rudiments of written language.[71] It's supposed to be more like school, in their eyes. At times the liberal behavioral norms—even when justified as developmentally appropriate—don't feel appropriate within the cultural frames of many Latino parents.

The Latina women in our Boston study also complained about a lack of Spanish-speaking teachers and staff. In one preschool, just a single classroom aide was available to read with one mother's four-year-old daughter. Another mother complained of gaps in basic quality, such as when teachers plopped the children down to watch videos for more than an hour at a stretch. These discontinuities between home and preschool norms are not peculiar to New England, where Latino populations began to grow in the 1980s. Recall the California preschool classroom in Chapter 3, where in a room filled with rambunctious Latino children neither the lead teacher nor the aide spoke Spanish. The shortage of bilingual teachers only gets worse when universal preschool advocates ratchet up credentialing requirements, as we saw so vividly in Oklahoma.

TACIT NOTIONS OF HOW CHILDREN DEVELOP

The concept of small-scale yet widely shared *cultural models* further illuminates the disconnects between Latina mothers and formal preschool institutions. Cultural models represent persisting understandings or scripts of behavior shared by members of bounded groups. For instance, Latina mothers may act from taken-for-granted notions like being self-sacrificing and *cariñosa* (attentive and affectionate), or aiming to raise a child who is respectful (*con respeto*) and is respected by family members (*buen comportamiento*). At times, these scripts or expected attributes are discussed, even contested, especially when acculturation brings new cultural forms into view, including higher-status ways in which children are to behave as defined within foreign yet dominant cultural circles.

Such scripts of how social relations should work inside a community "are presupposed, taken-for-granted models of the world which are widely shared . . . by members of a society and that play an enormous role in their understanding of that world and behavior in it," as anthropologists Naomi Quinn and Dorothy Holland put it.[72] Reese and Gallimore emphasize that "cultural models are so familiar and mundane that they are invisible and unnoticed by those who hold them."[73] Clifford Geertz talks about such tacit models of action as a map of what constitutes "common sense" within a bounded group, scripted forms of action that often remain practical and shared at the surface level of social life. The problem arises when parents are urged to join a preschool in which the cultural models of child rearing are distant from their own models that are enacted inside the home, as the ethnographic literature so vividly details.

PRESCHOOL SUPPLY AND PARENTAL CHOICE

The stark disparities in preschool supply mean, for many Latino families, that preschool is not even an option, as UPK advocates have rightly emphasized. Consider the situation in Los Angeles, for instance.

If you are a Latino parent with a four-year-old and live in East Los Angeles—the generally impoverished home of many immigrant and second-generation Latinos—you face a set of preschools that are able to serve just one in every five young children. But if you have moved up to the middle-class San Gabriel Valley, you face a richer supply of preschool programs, with the capacity to serve one out of three young children. Pockets of each region are home to concentrations of first-generation Latinos; one is South El Monte, where preschools are so scarce that only one out of fourteen children can find an enrollment slot. When Diane Hirshberg, Danny Huang, and Kathy Malaske-Samu surveyed just over one thousand of them in 2000,

East L.A. preschool directors reported much longer waiting lists. They found that in East L.A., one family was on a waiting list for every two children enrolled, compared to the San Gabriel Valley, where one family was waiting for every four children attending preschool.[74]

The analysis of national data sets, including my work with Loeb and Annelie Strath, reveals similar inequities in the range of child care options available to many Latino families. We found that in predominately Latino communities the average count of preschool teachers is about two-thirds smaller per capita than in white communities.[75] Education levels of these teachers were no lower in Latino communities, however, suggesting that targeted public support and quality regulations are working, despite a lower preschool supply. We showed in a second study that African American preschool teachers outnumber Latino teachers four to one in the poorest quarter of the nation's zip codes.[76]

Latino Child Development—Shared Models, Varied Adaptations

The window into Latino families, at least as seen through the eyes of curious researchers, has opened more widely in recent years. Let's consider what ethnographers and quantitatively inclined scholars have been learning about socialization practices.

All parents hold "commonsense folk models," in D'Andrade and Strauss's phrase, about how best to raise children and the attributes that parents desire for their youngsters. These models involve parents' socialization beliefs and goals and a constellation of parenting practices, from enforcing strict respect for adults to asking one's child stimulating questions at the dinner table. These cultural models of child rearing—whether one raises a child on Manhattan's upper east side, in the rural Midwest, or in gray and gritty East L.A.—are often enacted tacitly, inherited from one's own parents or the surrounding community. Yet acculturation and social change, or contact with formal institutions that advance dominant cultural forms such as preschools, bring tacit parenting practices into sharp relief.

Indeed, we are learning much about variation across Latino subgroups and individual families. "There are regularities in the ways cultural groups participate in the everyday practices of their respective communities," write Kris

Gutiérrez and Barbara Rogoff; "however, the relatively stable characteristics of these environments are in constant tension with the emergent goals and practices participants construct."[77] It's crucial that we get a fix on the distinctive qualities of Latino child development, while recognizing variation among families and change within households, as parents acculturate and youngsters bring home new social practices, even a new language.

Researchers, of course, hold their own notions of what proper child rearing should look like. NICHD investigators—as part of their longitudinal study of child care—aimed to measure variation in the socialization goals and discipline practices displayed by parents that might help to predict more robust child development. One set of questions the NICHD team posed to parents drew from what's called the Modernity Scale, a thirty-item index "describing parents' ideas about children and the parenting role."[78] It intends to gauge "traditional beliefs," including an "emphasis on child obedience and parental authority." (Greater intensity is bad, less is good.)

The NICHD group also employed the "harsh control subscale" from the Raising Children Checklist, which includes items like "Do you expect your child to obey the first time you say something?" (Also bad.) There's something quaint in how this stellar group of developmentalists sought to dichotomize parenting practices between "traditional" versus "modern" forms. But the conceptualization ignored the past half-century of ethnographic and sociological research conducted inside nonwhite families.[79]

ALTERNATIVE PORTRAYALS OF LATINO CHILD REARING

When it comes to sketching the cultural models that pattern child rearing inside Latino families, three interpretive lines of research have emerged. Early on, researchers juxtaposed the *interdependent, cooperative* character of many Latino families against the more individualistic and liberal forms enacted by white middle-class parents. Patricia Greenfield emphasizes the agrarian roots of Latin American societies and the importance of economic cooperation, large families, and socializing children to contribute to the household. "In collectivist societies that value group harmony and cooperation . . . helping can be perceived at a different level of urgency and obligation," writes Greenfield.[80]

In one study she contrasts these family values with how a kindergarten teacher in Los Angeles is told by her supervisor not to insist that children share a single cup of crayons, but instead to give each child his or her *own* crayons. The teacher, whose classroom was filled with children from Mexican-origin and Central American families, had been encouraging the children to take good care of the crayons, so that everyone would benefit. This model of child rearing emphasizes the group's unity and harmony as the fundamental goal. The child's obligation to the household's well-being then becomes the paramount value in which the youngster's own interests are couched (*familismo*). Greenfield writes: "The primary goal of socialization in (the Anglo-European) model is an autonomous, self-fulfilled individual who enters into social relationships and responsibilities by personal choice. In the (Latino) model, the preferred endpoint of development is interdependence."

Related studies by Ray Buriel and Concha Delgado-Gaitán and others emphasize high levels of respect for adult authority (*respeto*) and an emphasis on moral socialization, emphasizing the family's integrity and one's obligations to it.[81] Robin Harwood similarly details how Puerto Rican mothers stress the inculcation of proper demeanor: "the concern that a child be respectful, obedient, and accepted by the larger community," in contrast to white mothers, who emphasize how to maximize the child's knowledge and self-expression.[82]

This coherent bundle of cultural expectations implicates grandparents and other kin, who are expected to watch after and guide the child's development. Similarly, the role of older siblings, especially girls, in caring for younger sibs is reinforced and reproduced in cultural circles. Language inside the home also comes into play, since the authority of Spanish-speaking adults may diminish as children bring English into the household, and then translate for adults and mediate contact with the outside world. "Parents may even believe that they are harming their kids by using their home language, so they communicate less," Berkeley's Lily Wong Fillmore found in her studies of first-generation Latinos. "Think about that—parents and children communicate less."[83]

This core emphasis on interdependence leads to particular characteristics that many Latino parents try to inculcate in their young children. Good manners (*buenos modales*) and respectful ways of behaving (*comportamiento*), for instance, are highly valued by first-generation Mexican-American parents. As one father told UCLA researchers, "One always has to try to walk the straight path. It would be impossible to get into the university if one doesn't have good behavior, if one isn't taught to respect others."[84] The UCLA team, led by Ron Gallimore, Claude Goldenberg, and Leslie Reese, followed 121 Spanish-speaking parents in Los Angeles for several years, initially as their children were entering kindergarten. Gesturing to her five-year-old and the daughter's siblings one mother said, "That is the most important thing. Respecting those close to them and themselves . . . we respect the opinions of each person."

Other researchers have detailed how the notion of *bien educado* refers not so much to the child's being well schooled, but to her being dutiful, respectful, and well-mannered, the youth who is respected by family and community. Another mother, asked about how she would like her five-year-old to grow up, said: "I'd like him to study and above all to be upright, to have good behavior, to become (*que llegara a ser*) a person of respect and to be respectful of others as well." Robin Harwood has detailed a similar set of moral commitments among Puerto Rican families, stressing proper demeanor and winning the respect of the extended family.

A second interpretive frame draws on Diana Baumrind's classic typology of socialization, which sorts parents into those who deploy *permissive, authoritative*, or *authoritarian* parenting practices. She derived these types from empirical patterns observed among many families, detailing variations in parenting goals and methods within each category as well. Baumrind found that child outcomes were more robust when parents acted authoritatively, offering guidance and information to children without being overbearing, in the best of the liberal-humanist tradition.

Scholars working in the Baumrind vein have attempted to predict variable developmental trajectories or later school achievement from these parenting patterns. Many Latino parents appear to follow more *authoritarian* forms of parenting, exhibited by steady monitoring of children's behavior and directive forms of discipline. These parents sometimes score low along Baumrind's archetypal sorting of parents, which tends to map better onto the liberal, middle-class versus non-modern dichotomy of parenting, as do the measures used by the NICHD researchers. Baumrind herself did not place value judgments on her empirically informed categories, however. Nor did she claim that the framework was pegged to child rearing priorities across different cultural groups.

In their longitudinal study of school-age Latinos, Valenzuela and Dornbusch did not find that authoritarian parenting was associated with flatter developmental trajectories. Similarly, ethnographers have reported that some Latino mothers combine a steady attention to their youngster's behavior with a "relatively relaxed child rearing style . . . consonant with Hispanic socio-centric cultural values that encourage family member interdependence rather than independence and individuation," in Cynthia García Coll's words.[85]

What might be seen as illiberal parenting—say, through tight oversight of home work or strict compliance with adult authority—can help to predict school success in many Latino families, according to psychologists Buriel and Ross Parke.[86] The efficacy of particular home practices must be judged in the context of community norms, and how such parenting equips a Latino child to perform in what's first seen as a foreign setting. Similarly, anthropologist Tom Weisner has shown that Latino children, who are steadily engaged in household chores and family social activities, display higher achievement levels after starting school than children who have fewer family obligations or great autonomy to disengage from collective obligations.[87] Nor is such a directive approach in a Latino context empirically associated with harsh forms of discipline or punishment. It's often accompanied with warmth and steady interaction between mother and child.

A third framing moves away from the notion that parental child-rearing practices can be sorted into categories, especially across diverse subgroups. This more recent work attempts to identify discrete home practices or models of socialization that cluster together but not necessarily along static cultural models or Baumrind's typology. This approach emphasizes how many Latino parents—as acculturation unfolds in diverse neighborhoods—adapt to dominant forms of child rearing, including school-like cognitive demands. Adaptation may unfold within families or as successive generations move up in the social-class structure. And the preschool—an institution that young Latino parents contend with—becomes an agent of respect or cultural imposition along the way.

From this viewpoint, first-generation Latina mothers do not act solely from tacitly held parenting practices but instead have a "dual point of reference," which is ecologically driven. "Cultural dissonance forces immigrant mothers to constantly negotiate their role as mothers and redefine their cultural model of parenting to meet their present society's expectations (in the United States) and helps their children navigate both cultural worlds," Nurit Sheinberg emphasizes in her doctoral thesis, working with Harvard's Catherine Snow and

Patton Tabors.[88] Sheinberg also draws from the work of Gallimore, Goldenberg, and Reese, who found that many Latino parents "cast themselves in a morally superior position relative to those who succumb to what they perceive as the libertine and corrupting lifestyles of Los Angeles."[89] For example, parents relay stories of families who returned to Mexico to get their children out of gang-infested high schools, or families heading south every December "because the mother wants her children to learn and experience the Mexican traditions."[90]

Sheinberg went about measuring a variety of discrete parenting practices and socialization beliefs through interviews and in-home observations. She concludes that what might be seen as authoritarian parenting was manifest in parents' more intense engagement with their children, which was often mixed with warm affect and responsiveness. More highly educated immigrant or first-generation mothers spent more time with their young children, made sure that school-age kids finished their homework, had clear expectations for when young children would reach developmental benchmarks, and managed more smoothly functioning households. These mothers exercised parental authority firmly and more consistently. Parents who displayed permissive or authoritative tendencies proved to be less engaged in their children's lives overall and attended less to their youngster's experiences in school.

This way of empirically sketching Latino parenting and conceptions of proper child development is consistent with more dynamic ecological and bi-cultural perspectives. First-generation parents often see the family as a haven in a heartless world. They view the homeland as preferable in terms of stronger family values and collective obligations. Spanish-speaking parents and kin advance a stiff, protective dose of socialization, nurturing inviolable family expectations, subordination of self to the household, mutual *respeto*, and a child who unfolds as *buen educado*. When mothers identified more strongly with their country of origin, they also reported a stronger desire for their young children to keep speaking Spanish in the home. Through the reproduction of Spanish, one generation passes on essential values, family obligations, and a coherent personal identity to the next. As one mother said, "Later if he or she speaks more English, they will forget who they are in reality, their culture."[91] For others, the family's social ecology varies. And the preschool may come to help Latino parents negotiate hybrid, perhaps parallel, ways of raising their children.

This ecological framework sees Latino families as situated in highly variable local communities, from deeply impoverished immigrant areas to blue-collar suburbs that ring urban centers. The developmental niches that emerge for young children are viewed as open systems. That is, parents must adapt their child rearing practices, from keeping toddlers inside to avoid danger, to accommodating job and child care options that arise in the environment. Persisting, resilient cultural models and norms may add to the family's cohesion, but the ecological perspective emphasizes that the inability to adapt to new economic and social surroundings can limit opportunity for parent and child alike.[92]

Cultural Models of Cognitive Growth

Latino parents also express their own beliefs about their youngster's cognitive capacities and have their own conceptions of how young children grow and mature. Blasting Beethoven in utero or taping up the alphabet in the child's bedroom is not part of the Latino heritage. But Latino mothers and fathers hold clear, and certainly diverse, beliefs about how "development" should unfold.

DEVELOPMENTAL EXPECTATIONS

Initial findings suggest that many Latino parents conceive of "intelligence" and the engineered "development" or plasticity of the child's cognitive skills somewhat differently than middle-class whites do. One study team led by Moira Inkelas at UCLA's medical school interviewed 4,801 parents in 2001, each with at least one child, age zero to five. Inkelas's aim was to learn how different groups think about child development. Parents were asked to respond to the statement: "A child's capacity to learn is pretty much set from birth and cannot be greatly increased or decreased by how parents interact with them." White parents—indicating strong disagreement with a value 1.0, strong agreement with a 10—averaged just 2.4 in their responses, weakly endorsing the notion of inborn intelligence. In contrast, Latino parents scored this item at 5.8 on average.[93] Marlene Zepeda's work in Los Angeles also reveals that Latino parents, in general, think that certain motor skills and language abilities emerge later in their toddler's life than do white parents.[94]

Parents in Inkelas's survey also were asked how much they agreed with the statement: "It doesn't really matter whether a child learns the alphabet, can count or is able to write their name before he or she begins kindergarten." Latino parents agreed, on balance, scoring this item at 6.4, compared with largely disagreeing white parents, who scored it 3.7 on average. This result fits a set of earlier independent studies by Gallimore, Delgado Gaitán, and Guadalupe Valdés, showing that many Latino parents do not sit and read, or practice reciting the alphabet, with their toddlers. Reading and learning the alphabet are seen as academic knowledge, which is taught by teachers once the child starts school. The formal classroom represents to them a quite different, modernizing setting for learning new forms of knowledge, one that is perhaps disconnected from the socialization principles on which Latino parents are so keenly focused.

The idea that school institutions hold distinct authority and a sharply demarcated role in the child's life persists in many Latino communities. When Lisa López at Harvard asked Latina mothers why they enrolled their child in a Head Start preschool, one mother told her: "I wanted her to learn how to be with other children, how to communicate with other children. I wanted her to learn to write her name, to learn the colors . . . to learn everything one needs to learn in school."[95] These skills are seen as tied to the formal school and represent cognitive demands placed on children after they enter school.

FAMILY ACTIVITIES AND COGNITIVE DEMANDS

Within the flow of daily activities in Latino homes, pre-literacy practices are not as frequently observed as in middle-class white families. Latino parents do vary in the extent to which they organize time to read storybooks with their young children, engage in "explanatory talk" around the dinner table, or display imaginative narratives rich in vocabulary when playing with their children, as David Dickinson and Patton Tabors have observed.[96] The extent to which reading with one's child is viewed as a didactic or interrogatory and expressive activity also varies across parents independent of ethnicity. Yet since reading is tacitly seen as involving skills acquired at school, Latino parents often believe that reading proficiency is reached after repeated practice and after a sufficient time attending school.

Latina mothers told Iliana Reyes, a sociolinguist at the University of Arizona, that while they rely on the schools to teach their children English, they prefer to focus on acquisition of Spanish as the medium of cultural and behavioral views.[97] Reyes also observed diversity among Latino parents: those who used literacy skills in their jobs emphasized familiarity with print materials and decoding written words with their young children more strongly than those who did not. This pattern reminds us of Vygotsky's argument, that children's development is couched within the cognitive demands that parents themselves face.[98]

The overall incidence of reading with young children or arranging educational outings (such as frequenting libraries or museums) is markedly lower for Latino families than for other groups, even after taking their social class into account. Child psychologist Robert Bradley, after compiling years of interview data from the National Longitudinal Survey of Youth, found that just over 29 percent of poor Latino parents, and 49 percent of non-poor, read with their child (age three to five) at least three times per week. For whites, reading with one's child this often was reported by 55 percent of low-income parents, and 71 percent of non-poor parents.[99] About a third of poor Latino parents reported that their preschooler had more than ten children's books in the home, compared with three-quarters of poor white parents.

Latino parents' uneven attention to pre-literacy practices appears to be linked to the mother's bounded role when it comes to cognitive growth. As one mother told UCLA's Leslie Reese, "It's more necessary to educate children morally than academically . . . if a teacher is given a child who doesn't have moral principles, or who isn't morally prepared, it will be difficult to teach this child academic things. A child will learn more easily if he already knows how to respect and treat others."[100] Historically Latino parents have held teachers in high regard. "*La maestra es la segunda mamá*" (The teacher is the second mother) is an oft-heard phrase in Latino communities. Children are to respect and never challenge the teacher's authority, as if she were literally a second mother. Some research shows that parents show their respect for teachers by not raising questions and keeping a distance from the modern school institution. This behavior prompts misunderstandings, as preschool teachers may infer that Latino parents are not committed to the enterprise.[101] One study found that Latino parents rank respect for teacher authority considerably higher in importance than do kindergarten teachers.[102]

Latino parents vary in the value they place on learning English, compared to being proficient in Spanish. When Lisa López asked one mother why she had selected a bilingual Head Start classroom for her son, she said: "He knows a little bit of English, but I expect that when he starts kindergarten he will learn it better . . . I put him in bilingual because that way he can maintain his Spanish and learn English." Other mothers reported on the usefulness of their children's learning to speak English, within their bicultural world in Boston. "I go to my appointments, and I don't know to say a word, and so I ask Clara, 'How do you say this in English,' and she gets me out of problems." Another mother told López: "Imagine that, when I go to my appointments in the hospital, and I bring him (her five-year-old son) with me . . . incredible, he serves as my interpreter."[103]

Early Educators' Models of Development

Preschool teachers bring their own tacit ideals about the nature of children's development into classrooms and what and how youngsters should be learning. We already have heard much from early educators and advocates in this regard based on their liberal-humanist, skilling, or culturally situated notions of child development. At times they blend the models in fascinating ways. One dedicated preschool teacher I visited in Pasadena, for instance, emphasized the inculcation of "self-reliance" in her charges. But she also argued that four-year-olds should "learn to recite the pledge of allegiance," and added, "I don't let them wear their hats backwards."

Researchers have begun to assess teachers' own cultural models of development—a young literature that takes us back to the ethical and empirical question of whether the preschool institution acts to tighten or to fray the social fabric of Latino families.

TEACHERS' MODELS OF EARLY LEARNING

Alison Wishard, Carollee Howes, and colleagues—developmental psychologists at UCLA—recently completed a fascinating study of how preschool teachers think about and enact differing conceptions of "quality" preschooling, including how classroom activities are arranged to promote certain cognitive demands and social patterns. They noted that "practices, more than (structural indicators of) quality, appear to be deeply embedded within value and belief systems that are rooted in ethnicity, community, and social class . . . programs that emphasize individual needs over collective experience or child initiated learning over didactic learning have been criticized as not reflecting the values and beliefs of other than affluent, white culture."[104] Howes and her research group went about disentangling how diverse teachers defined their developmental goals for children, getting beneath the state-regulated aspects of quality, such as maximum class size or the physical dimensions of classrooms.

The preschool teachers in California and North Carolina that they sampled expressed various goals for what children should be learning inside their classrooms. As the research team interviewed teachers and sat in their classrooms, certain domains emerged, including an emphasis on culturally specific forms of knowledge, peer relations, and favored pedagogical approaches. The latter domain broke into three classroom strategies: a "child-initiated" or Piagetian approach, more structured scaffolding of children's activities, and "direct instruction" of academic skills.

Black teachers strongly emphasized teaching preschoolers the ideals and social obligations of African American culture, and endorsed direct-instruction methods more enthusiastically than teachers from other ethnic groups. Black teachers with more Latino preschoolers in their classrooms stressed the acquisition of English proficiencies more than white or Latino teachers who served similar mixes of children did. Latino teachers created classrooms that allowed for more child-initiated activities than did black teachers.

Equally intriguing, Latino preschoolers in classrooms led by Latino teachers displayed stronger peer relations and social skills than did Latino children in classrooms led by other teachers. Wishard and Howes's work highlights how teachers bring into the preschool their own models of early learning, and how the match between child and teacher may influence youngsters' developmental trajectories.

LANGUAGE AND PRESCHOOL CLASSROOMS

Little is known about the comparative effectiveness of bilingual and monolingual preschool classrooms, or how cognitive and social-developmental effects vary across Latino subgroups. When they are carefully implemented, bilingual programs for elementary-age children do appear to be more effective in raising writing and reading proficiencies in English among Spanish-speaking children than English-only instruction, according to one careful study by Robert Slavin and Alan Cheung at Johns Hopkins University. This is a young and complicated area of research, in part because the children who gain access to sound bilingual programs may differ systematically from those placed in English immersion. Both kinds of programs are implemented at varying levels of quality, with teachers holding uneven skills. And researchers also must confront government's contested cultural agenda: Slavin resigned from a Bush Administration panel studying bilingual education when the federal education department asked him to delay publication of his findings.[105]

The jury may remain out for several years on the question of whether bilingual preschools yield stronger language development *and* social development than monolingual programs. One experimental study compared the linguistic growth of Spanish-speaking Mexican-American children who entered a bilingual preschool for one year to a control group that did not attend preschool. James Rodriguez and his colleagues found that although both groups made significant progress in oral dimensions of Spanish, including receptive vocabulary and the retelling of short stories, the treatment group far outpaced the control group in terms of English proficiency, with no decrement in their pre-literacy skills in Spanish.[106]

Ethnographic studies are illuminating how children with limited English engage language opportunities and interact with their peers in preschool or kindergarten classrooms. Thus far, it appears that young Latinos quickly grasp the rudiments of oral and written English, such as naming and writing letters of the alphabet, reading short words, and becoming familiar with storybooks and print materials in English. However, they have difficult in tackling more complex uses of English, such as rhyming words, or predicting events in situations that they don't fully comprehend.[107] Even less is known about peer relations and whether language discontinuities between teacher and child undercut motivation.

Beyond language, the cognitive demands and social rules of classroom activities can be consistent with, or distant from, Latino children's home experiences. Here Vygotsky's principle, that if a novel task is not within the child's zone of proximal development, comprehension and thus motivation will suffer, applies. Ann Eisenberg, for example, created an ingenious experiment where working- and middle-class Mexican-American mothers were asked to work with their four-year-old on a block-building task and then on a simple baking project. She found that mothers asked more questions of their children during the block task, but that more complex concepts and language were deployed in the baking project. On both tasks, the working-class mothers were more directive and used less complex language than did middle-class Latina mothers.[108]

Another study shared this Vygotskian framework. Angela Willson-Quayle created three pedagogical conditions at predominately Latino preschools; each involved building a Lego structure. Children were allowed to work freely on their own in one experimental condition, while teachers either scaffolded from what children were able to do or, in the second and third conditions, simply directed children to build a tower in a prescribed way. She and colleague Adam Winsler found, based on the coding of videotaped talk among the children, that they were more engaged, happier, and persisted longer under the scaffolding condition. The authors inferred that some degree of teacher structure and careful scaffolding may be more effective for these children than a purely "learning-through-play" approach.[109]

Over the past two decades, Stanford psychologist Deborah Stipek has been investigating whether the more child-centered (liberal-humanist) model of pedagogy is most motivating for all young children. She quotes Piaget's goals for early education: "to form minds which can be critical, can verify, and not accept everything that is offered . . . who learn early to find out for themselves."[110] But this starting principle may conflict with the priority placed on collective socialization and cognitive learning that characterizes many Latino families.

Stipek is curious about whether social-class differences, rather than ethnicity per se, may account for differences in parenting practices and early literacy activities. She finds that working-class families report greater use of didactic exercises with children, such as reciting the alphabet or counting out loud, but engage less frequently in activities that involve reading together, use of rich language, or discussions of print material. Rather than promoting a universal theory of classroom practice, Stipek emphasizes the *contingency* between how cognitive demands and social norms are expressed at home, and how learning activities are structured at school.

Stipek then tests whether basic knowledge must be mastered by young children from lower-income families before more complex forms of problem-solving or constructivist pedagogies can be effectively deployed. Parents in poor communities generally express a preference for didactic or traditional forms of teaching, even in kindergarten, compared with middle-class parents, who have a more developmental, exploratory, and pro-social conception of early learning.[111] And more scripted pedagogies may be more practical for a preschool workforce that remains unevenly trained.

After observing 314 kindergarten and first-grade classrooms in three states, Stipek could strongly predict the teachers' use of direct instruction based on student demographics, teachers' own instructional goals, and their views of children's capacities at entry into school. Many children in this sample were from low-income black families.[112] Digging further into the what motivates children in preschool or kindergarten, Stipek looked at a variety of classrooms serving a total of 123 four- and five-year-olds. She found that the more didactic, skilling-oriented programs did advance children's letter and word recognition, but that children attending more child-centered programs displayed higher levels of motivation, which was in part seen from their more eager and sustained engagement in learning tasks.[113]

One can criticize Stipek's viewpoint, arguing that it is a self-fulfilling logic that encourages teachers to underestimate children's capacities based on markers of their social class. But Stipek's basic notion of contingency between home and early learning settings and her rigor in empirically testing claims central to her framework hold great relevance for designing effective preschools for Latino youngsters.

Gaps between home and preschool also arise in when we look at how Latino children expect to participate, talk, and contribute to groups. Anthropologist Greenfield and her colleagues found that preschool teachers often complain that Latino children don't speak up enough in class. But at home, these children are taught that saying to an adult "Why should I do this?" or "I don't understand what you are telling me" is considered disrespectful. In turn, young children may have very strong oral language and comprehension skills but have little practice in producing language—certainly not utterances that probe, question, or critique the flow of events inside the home or classroom. Greenfield also cites the growing body of work on cooperative learning tasks deployed in classrooms, encouraging teachers to use lateral forms of participation and recognize group accomplishments, rather than publicly highlighting individual performance.[114]

Inventive activities and curricular tools are being developed to build from what young Latino children already know. Mari Riojas-Cortéz, for example, is experimenting with dramatic play structured by preschool teachers around episodes and events found at home or involving family members. She found that preschoolers could readily tap into parents' core values or moral lessons— even how conflict is mediated inside the home. By creating simple and comfortable theatrical performances, children and teachers can explore new cognitive demands and social-emotional feelings about episodes that bubble up from children's own everyday experience.[115]

PARTNERING WITH PARENTS

Early educators struggle with how to move beyond lip service to the idea of meaningfully involving parents day to day. Program developers working inside preschools have devised simple approaches to connect with Latino parents at deep levels. UCLA's Gallimore and Goldenberg, for example, in the Vygotskian vein, created a series of small books, simply called *Libros*, for Latino kindergartners that are inviting and accessible for parents, grandparents, and older siblings to read. During one trial of these materials, the school district also sent home basic worksheets for parents and children to work on together, covering phonics and the sounding-out of words, along with vocabulary practice, in English.

The Libros initiative quickly became popular with parents and significantly contributed to gains in children's early literacy skills by year's end. But it was the worksheets that were used most consistently by parents, further boosting children's proficiency levels. Goldenberg and colleagues discovered during home visits that the worksheets better fit parents' "bottom up" model of how literacy skills are supposed to be acquired: children move from letters, sounds, syllables, and words, through repeated practice, to acquiring school-related literacy. The Libros were entertaining and fun to read with one's five-year-old. Yet they were poor tools with which to drill and recite phonemes and pieces of language.[116] This episode vividly illustrates Stipek's point about the power of contingency—the fit between parents' tacit model of early learning and how preschool teachers structure activities inside classrooms.

Still, early educators do not consistently reach out to parents, especially when the teachers differ markedly from the families they are trying to serve. The level of mutual respect often runs low. Anthropologist Delgado-Gaitán has done extensive work to understand this relationship between parents and early educators, in her decade-long investigation within the Latino community of Carpinteria, in northern California. Since the school remains a foreign institution in the eyes of many first-generation parents, she found that parents often deferred to their six-year-olds when it came to understanding how much time was required to complete homework and when they should do it.[117]

Parents were often unaware of how their children were doing in school, or why the worksheets and tasks that came home were exclusively in Spanish, with little English being introduced. When teachers failed to reach out to parents or communication broke down, parents sought information from relatives and friends at church or over meals. Eventually, after communication between teachers and parents had ruptured, a Latino community action agency became involved to advocate on the parents' behalf. School authorities remained unaware of the range and depth of miscommunication between teachers and parents.

Lessons — Preschools that Scaffold Up from Family Practices

The Latino question, broadly conceived, highlights the importance of situating child development within communities, to understand how daily activities, cognitive demands, and social scripts are reproduced in bounded contexts. The ecology of children's development, among many Latino families, is characterized by parents who are actively adapting to novel, often dominating, messages about how to raise one's child, and to the normative messages beamed from institutions, like the preschool, or the signals of experts and the media, all advancing a rather foreign bundle of norms.

We know that Latino families make up the largest set of clients for early educators in many regions of the nation, from central cities to aging suburbs to rural areas. The presence of Latino children will continue to grow dramatically throughout this century. Any respectful effort to advance preschooling cannot ignore how diverse Latino parents hope to raise their children, as well as what social relations inside classrooms advance local values. Early educators will be challenged to understand the distinctive features of Latino child development, while becoming sensitive to variation among families and subgroups.

The rhetoric of individual differences will come in handy for teachers, while being attentive to children's collective obligations, stricter social roles, and more limited exposure to academic skills in the home. That is, preschool teachers must be sensitive to variation in the conditions in which Latino children are being raised, while grasping how these youngsters will likely differ, on balance, from those raised in white middle-class suburbs. At present, one initial challenge is to build from the strengths of Latino families, rather than stigmatizing differences as symptoms of being "at risk" for some ill-defined malady.

The past generation of empirical work suggests that Latino parents desire *options*, not a single, homogeneous institution. This desire is driven not only by the forms of child care that feel comfortable to them—often relying on kin members or the *niñera* down the street—but also by how low-wage jobs are structured in America's capitalist economy. Preschools do not serve parents who work irregular shifts or weekends well. Children can certainly attend preschool when their mother is at home—millions already do. But maternal employment will continue to drive the likelihood that Latino parents seek out a preschool program. With acculturation, upwardly mobile Latino parents will increasingly select preschools for their young children that are inviting to them, and staffed by teachers who share their own models of how young children are to be raised. It is vital for UPK enthusiasts to understand these preferences; otherwise, they risk building preschools to which few Latino families will come, not to mention disregarding the imperious manner in which UPK advocates often ignore parents' own conceptions of child development.

The cultural revolution in learning theory is teaching us much about how *all* young children learn, situated in particular community contexts. For Latino youngsters, the context often consists of being raised in monolingual Spanish or bilingual households, and learning to be respectful of, and deferential to, the authority of adults and older siblings. The Euro-American commitment to literacy and written text, and to individual autonomy and creative expression, may be weaker in Latino homes overall. Even so, the Latino commitment to respectful comportment, to the family's well-being, and to the cognitive proficiencies necessary for advancing cooperative action will continue to be strong. What we understand less well is how practices of preschool teachers can scaffold up from what Latino children already know and the strong social norms they acquire at home.

These rich lines of empirical research can inform, but not resolve, the intensifying contention over how "non-mainstream children" should be nurtured and taught in publicly funded institutions, especially in preschools that are becoming increasingly standardized—even serving as pedagogical agents of a monochromatic state.

Thus, we come back to fundamental human questions: For whose community are young children being raised? And who decides what they should learn and what forms of social behavior are expected? The ethical quandaries become even more difficult in states or regions where Latino children are the *majority* of youngsters filing into preschool, and where no single "mainstream" way of raising and teaching young children truly exists outside the minds of elite reformers. In a sense, the earnest advocates who guide the UPK movement would freeze their own cultural assumptions in the preschool institution, which will increasingly serve children who come from very different cultural worlds.

The three conceptions of child development—the liberal-humanist, the skilling, and the culturally situated frame—lend order to the debate over how government and activists should craft preschools for America's pluralistic society. The claims about causation that are embedded in each ideology should be studied rigorously. For instance, it may be that culturally situated scaffolding can advance Latino children's early literacy skills in English. Or, the active and constructivist traditions may in fact undercut the motivation of some preschoolers, compared with what direct instruction does. We are just beginning to understand the empirical validity of such claims for Latino subgroups and to disentangle scientific from philosophical questions, especially in defining what cognitive and socialization outcomes preschools are to emphasize.

These debates over how young Latino children are to be raised—and by whom—represent a new battleground in America's ongoing fight between cultural democratization and a rough-edged, impersonal approach toward social integration. The evidence is clear that many Latino parents, with acculturation, become eager to advance their youngsters' English proficiency and school achievement. Many others, including more comfortable middle-class Latinos, struggle for a balance between culturally situated family values and an assurance that their children will acquire the skills necessary for doing well in school (and then in the labor force).[118] One intriguing trend is how middle-class Latino parents increasingly are giving their offspring Aztec names. Other urban families no longer trust the moribund, even dangerous, public schools to impart much of anything. To many Latino parents, the nation's unrelenting celebration of self-expression, individual entitlement, and the shared rejection of central authority, not to mention the capitalist impulse to commercialize childhood, feels coarse and foreign.

Taking sides in these cultural disputes over child rearing is difficult, since it's hard to tell the good guys from the bad guys. It's not a simple friction of differing philosophies, bi-coastal liberals against Midwestern conservatives. The new contests at times pit preschool reformers and old-line mandarins of child development against Latino parents and activists, who often express differing views of how young children are to be raised.

Conservatives, at least the white ones, now see the utility of preschool for shaping the language and instrumental skills of young children. Institutional liberals advance a kinder and gentler form of social integration, yet they too pitch a universalist agenda, one that focuses on equitably advancing the same, uniform skills, to boost the individual's competitiveness in the labor market.

Rarely does either of these camps slow down to talk respectfully and at length with Latino parents about how *they* hope to raise their children—what cognitive skills, expected behaviors, and human virtues they see as truly basic.

CHAPTER EIGHT

Moving Forward—Stronger Families, Richer Childhoods

The unrelenting charge of the UPK faithful brings to mind an episode in another time and place. Liberating western Europe from the pagans about a millennium ago, resurgent Catholics eagerly built huge Romanesque cathedrals. These towering edifices broke away from architectural tradition in order to squeeze in more pilgrims; they were newly designed with expansive stone floors and fewer pillars to impede the congregation's views forward. These radical changes, however, required walls of unprecedented thickness to support the tons of masonry high overhead. So, just a few tiny windows could be cut into each wall to protect its structural integrity. Thousands of additional worshipers were accommodated, but they enjoyed their religious instruction largely in the dark.

A similar rush by the modern state and its experts to build yet another mass institution may result in rather dull illumination as well. The Enlightenment offered us upbeat postulates about the young child's inner nature, along with brighter ideals for how to improve the environs of childhood. The modern state took from the church its bureaucratic means of social regulation, including a uniform (now-secular) catechism, which came to guide instruction inside the common school. Textbooks replaced hymnals. Rows of classroom desks replaced pews. Encrusted forms of organization persisted.

The nineteenth-century state's quest for standard instruction and secular social commitments yielded a one-best system of public education. It took over a century, and the upheavals of the 1960s, for government and elite planners to realize that families had been the objects of reform, long seen as impediments to the task of modernizing their children. Meanwhile many pilgrims, perhaps tired of being educated in the dark, sought alternative forms of schooling, allowing them to break away from this often unresponsive institution of mass schooling. Seeking both efficiency and equity, the public schools had delivered homogenized content and stultifying didactics.

The rising UPK movement is gaining adherents, as we have seen. But it has also hit a raw nerve for many parents and politicians, as diverse children and a variety of neighborhood preschools are to fit now into large school systems. The tension prompts a dilemma for the modern state. On the one hand, political leaders feel unrelenting pressure to demonstrate that public institutions can show real results—from advancing economic competitiveness for the nation, to ensuring a more fair society that offers brighter futures for all children.

But at the same time that politicians try to exact accountability from public institutions, many citizens are expressing skepticism over the impersonal workings of mass organizations. "Why would I want to turn my four-year-old over to that (school) system," we remember a Long Beach community activist saying back in Chapter 5. As the issue of young children has been pulled onto the public stage, we have seen a pushback from others, who worry about public schooling's downward seep, and the standardization of childhood.

When feminist icon Betty Friedan died recently at age eighty-five, many returned to her classic 1963 book *The Feminine Mystique*, part academic musings, part pragmatic blueprint for the women's movement. Her thesis was not simply that women had become isolated and demoralized, as postwar nirvana spurred the growth of suburban culture and consumerism. Men, too, were similarly alienated by working as mid-level managers, as "organization men," in sociologist William Whyte's phrase. Friedan cited Whyte's work, along with David Reisman's criticisms of American conformity and the mindless, instrumental service to corporations, in his 1950s classic *The Lonely Crowd*.[1]

In the four decades following Friedan's call to arms, maternal employment rates climbed dramatically, as did the economic well-being of families with two working parents. Tailing right behind this radical change in women's roles have been expanding child care options and preschool slots, spreading with equal voracity. One result is that two-thirds of American parents report wishing they had more time to spend with their children.[2] Mothers worry about the inevitable "second shift," caring for the family after coming home from their day job, and ask whether their own aspirations and economic exigencies may be subverting how their youngsters are growing up. Maternal employment rates actually have ticked downward a couple of notches in recent years, with mothers now spending a few hours more each week with their children than they did in 1995.[3]

Still, some parents labor in regimented or bureaucratic jobs and then return home to hear about the equally cold, unresponsive public schools in which their children labor each day. Education reformers have been speaking to this concern over the past generation, successfully creating human-scale institutions, like charter schools and small high schools. The struggle against alienating institutions continues, for instance, in the push to move students beyond passive roles in classrooms and in teachers' resistance to centralized efforts to regiment their work, undercutting their own passion for teaching, for helping to raise our children.

Our liberal-humanist instincts, in short, continue to push against the creation of a new lonely crowd, brought to you by a government apparatus that is earnestly trying to do the right thing. Parents similarly hunger for ways to create safer, warmer, more engaging environments for their young children. They do not necessarily endorse the assumption that rising public support of early education should narrow how we conceive of young children's potential and inquisitive spirit. Few parents are telling researchers that preschool should focus on memorizing the alphabet, learning how to stand in line, or sitting still in those tiny desks with vanilla-colored Formica tops.

Raising Children for the State or for the Community?

The new campaign to expand and improve preschooling is seductive and has been welcomed by important constituencies. Children should benefit from equal access to warm and stimulating environments; the ability to enter a quality preschool should no longer be driven by where a family lives or their capacity to pay high fees. At the same time, the assumption that a centrally regulated, mass institution can be responsive to America's rainbow of families is no longer tenable. But the elite organizers of the UPK movement, typically liberal in their social ideals, paradoxically continue to drift from their humanistic, democratic moorings. Rather than asking parents and early educators how diverse children's settings should be organized, they press forward with their own solution, often worried more about tactics than about substance, more about winning in the halls of state capitols than carefully building up from neighborhoods.

This chapter sketches how we might return to first principles: nurturing a democratic discussion over how to strengthen the *capacity of families* to raise their own children, especially how the nation's employers and big institutions can support a more healthy balance between work and child rearing. This task will necessarily involve finding a middle ground on several fronts, including a form of statecraft that advances equity and quality without imposing just one set of cultural assumptions about how young children are to be raised locally. The evidence we have reviewed in earlier chapters shows that respectful partnering with parents—from home visits to involvement in classrooms to learning about and respecting their means of socialization—can yield stronger benefits for children. Meanwhile, the institutional liberals continue to place their trust in highly credentialed professionals, and threaten to replicate in preschool the yawning distance that has opened up between teachers and parents in so many public schools.

As implementation unfolds in the early UPK states, we heard the worries of preschool teachers in California and Oklahoma, now under heavy pressure to push the recitation of phonemes, counting out loud, and following pedagogical scripts. Meanwhile, advocates claim that requiring teachers to have a four-year degree will yield thinking, discerning professionals able to exercise discretion—in classrooms that ironically are becoming highly regimented. Why do we need teachers with more professional wisdom and discretion, if classrooms are to become more routinized? Don't get me wrong: preschool teachers and caregivers can do much more to enrich the oral and written language environments as they help to raise young children. But to disempower teachers and parents alike—inviting them less frequently to participate in crafting improvements that affect children's everyday settings—can only exacerbate alienation.

The tactics by which the new generation of advocates have packaged and sold UPK also betray this fatal drift away from the democratic, grassroots origins of the feminist and child care movements. These elite organizers discover through national surveys that most parents worry about their child's social and emotional growth, but since defining the problem as "school readiness" and boosting first-grade test scores adds more political girth, that's how they define it. The "new" brain research reveals "critical windows" of development, so at first proponents advocated for public initiatives to aid infants and toddlers. But that cause gained little traction by the late 1990s, so now they have recast the brain research to somehow justify a universal institution for preschoolers. Then, the advocates' pollsters discovered that the word "universal" is a turn-off for many voters, so they rename the entire movement "preschool for all." Most bewilderingly, the advocates claim that universal access will allegedly boost learning for all children *and* simultaneously close gaps between youngsters from rich and poor families, ignoring the logical contradiction.

Some of my progressive friends may say, Well, what's wrong with a little spin, if it helps the cause? Or, as one advocate reported earlier, that the school-readiness line, while admittedly narrow, buys political legitimacy. Don't worry, the preschool as an institution will be fixed later. But many Americans have grown tired of, and conservatives have exploited, hugely expensive social programs that fail to live up to the bold promises made by their original architects. Lowering class size in several states, which is costing billions each year, was to reduce achievement gaps—as was universal kindergarten, a century ago. Huge tax breaks for the wealthy are to spur economic growth, trickling down to all. When these overly optimistic reforms don't work, public resources and political will are squandered. At the very same time that government is under pressure to exact accountability, its failed remedies breed more skepticism over the efficacy of public action.

Early education reform does not have to unfold this way. The fact that UPK in Los Angeles looks a lot different than UPK in Oklahoma, which departs from New Jersey's approach, manifests a healthy aspect of our federal system. As R. W. Apple, Jr., wrote within another context, the state might aspire to be "experimental, questioning, hard to satisfy . . . solidly anchored in local tradition."[4] Such a spirit sharply contrasts the homogenized brave new world that UPK advocates envision for a more engineered form of childhood. Instead of falling for such proposals, we should keep our eye on the long-term prize: to enrich children's lives and learning in settings that families have helped shape. Building a more unified network of preschools that are rooted in diverse communities, rather than incorporated into an already overburdened public school system, could be a significant part of the solution.

Returning to Democratic Foundations

The most fundamental public interest turns on helping families raise their own young children in materially secure and developmentally rich ways. *How* to pursue this goal through public action forms the persistent (philosophical) question, to paraphrase Heidegger.[5] The state already plays a crucial role in pursuing this public aim, especially in financing a variety of preschool and child care options for America's families. Yet the state now finds itself at a junction in the policy road: (a) to discourage civic participation locally, turning preschool settings over to central agencies and schools, or (b) to nurture decentralized organizations that help to strengthen civil society. Wise government might also get employers more involved in addressing the imbalance between work and family, a huge lesson that we should take from Europe.

Certain UPK initiatives are already sprouting from deep roots in their communities and are truly dedicated to local participation, as we have seen in Los Angeles and with New Jersey's balanced reliance on CBOs and local schools. Indeed, universal preschool holds the potential for enriching the range and quality of the local organizations that enable parents and early educators to enrich young children's daily environments. This enrichment should continue to unfold in dialogue with researchers and the variety of experts who speak to parents.

The early childhood field as a whole, including the push for universal preschool, has been strongly influenced by a half-century of scientific attention. Few public initiatives have been studied more rigorously, including child care programs of various stripes and colors. But the rising dominance of expert voices should not eclipse a first principle: the need to create human-scale organizations that advance quality and respond to the variety of child-rearing philosophies and practices held by families. Their ways of raising young children will not remain static, but they will continue to hold far greater consequences than the influence of formal institutions.

The neoclassically liberal state—bent on sanctifying and protecting the individual's rights—has done much to shake off oppressive forms of social control, whether political or industrial in nature. Government should certainly ensure that children acquire discrete skills that eventually equip them for a competitive labor market. But the cornerstones of civil society must also include initiatives that strengthen families and the neighborhood organizations that enrich the lives of young children. At certain historic moments— from the New Deal to the Great Society's rekindling of community action to the pro-social spirit of feminism—government has devised ways of nurturing collective action locally.

Balancing Work and Family

UPK advocates often cite France or Scandinavia as models of how strong central states have advanced quality preschooling. Fair enough. But what the proponents ignore is that early education is couched within broader policies that allow parents to better balance work and child rearing. Even America's individualistic society, with its sacred commitment to "personal responsibility," has made progress in recent years in offering family leave and economic supports for poor households and financing child care for middle-class parents.

It's understandable that during a largely conservative era in America's social history, advocates would focus on one piece of the work-family puzzle. But by aligning the fledgling preschool with the public schools and centralized dictates by a regulatory state, UPK leaders detract from the broader debate over economic security and the quality of family life within a capitalist economy. Preschool alone will never come close to lessening the damage done to young children by growing up in poor homes and hazardous cities or, increasingly, declining suburbs. Until our society becomes committed to distributing work and income more equitably, education reforms will hold little effect.

Middle-class families seek greater economic stability, and many mothers and fathers struggle to balance their own aspirations against spending enough time with their children. Expanding preschooling will free up women's labor power, but it also relieves pressure on business leaders to actually deliver on their recurring family-friendly rhetoric. The welfare state has long served as a convenient device promising that social institutions—like schools—will alone fix the deeper inequalities in the way America organizes work, income, and social status.

Universal preschool advocates rightfully point out that our society lags behind many nations in Europe and Asia when it comes to support for early education. France, for instance, has become the poster-child for UPK enthusiasts; over 90 percent of France's four-year-olds were enrolled, and even two-fifths of all two-year-olds, by the mid-1980s.[6] Even so, after tracking teachers dressed in white lab coats, looking more like fastidious nurses than on-the-floor preschool teachers, a delegation of American early childhood specialists found a number of aspects of the French preschools that they "wouldn't necessarily want to replicate in the United States: large classes, teacher-directed teaching style, little parental involvement, and emphasis on French cultural immersion rather than sensitivity to cultural differences."[7]

Across much of western Europe, government leaders and employers support preschool as one part of a wider commitment to child rearing vis-à-vis work. "Imagine a world in which mothers and fathers could choose to work part-time until their children are in primary school without changing employers or losing their health benefits," write Janet Gornick of Baruch College and Marcia Meyers of the University of Washington.[8] They continue: "It is a reality . . . for parents in several countries in Europe (benefiting) from public policies that distribute the costs of caring for children across society and require employers to accommodate parents' caregiving responsibilities."

Faced with a slowing birth rate and a growing labor shortage in 1963, the Swedish government provided six months of paid maternity leave for women who were employed before giving birth.[9] Ever since the 1930s, social critics such as Alva and Gunnar Myrdal had been writing about the importance of stronger public involvement in child care, especially if working-class parents were to make good on Scandinavians' egalitarian aspirations.[10] By the late 1990s, Denmark, Finland, and Sweden were offering at least fifty-two weeks of paid leave, sometimes split between mother and father. Even Britain offers eighteen weeks of partially paid maternity leave. The cost is not borne directly by employers; it's distributed across all workers through social insurance reserves.[11] In 2003 Tony Blair's government pushed through a flex-time policy that gives any parent with a child under six the right to request a change in work hours—be it a four-day work week, telecommuting, or job sharing—and employers must respond to such requests. After the first year, fully one-quarter of eligible employees—about 800,000 parents—had reached an agreement with their employers.[12]

The United States has been catching up, although in baby steps, when it comes to policies supporting young families. A decade after President Clinton signed the Family and Medical Leave Act, over 35 million workers had taken unpaid time off to care for young children or family members. This direct adjustment to the balance between work and family has raised mothers' average time off after giving birth from three weeks to seven, even though most leaves remain unpaid.[13] When the Department of Labor surveyed employers nationally, 85 percent reported neutral or positive benefits for their employees in general.[14]

Clearly, more remains to be done in the United States, especially in providing paid leave to parents who cannot afford to forgo earnings for several weeks after a child is born. Jeff Bond and Ellen Galinsky at the Families and Work Institute in New York found that women from affluent and middle-class families were much more aware of family leave options than those in low-income families.[15] Still, such policies are expanding the amount of time that parents can spend with their young children, rather than placing youngsters in preschool institutions for longer and longer hours.

Other inventive U.S. policies encourage part-time employment without loss of health or retirement benefits, and boost wages for low-income parents. Almost 3,800 American firms now draw on unemployment insurance funds—similar to how European nations finance paid family leave to share work through part-time jobs—rather then laying off white- and blue-collar employees.[16] Since Baltimore led the way in 1994, half of the nation's twenty largest cities now have living-wage statutes, affecting two-fifths of urban workers nationwide. These initiatives improve the quality of families' lives, going beyond the minimum-wage floor set by federal and state governments. Initial evidence suggests that under such initiatives the count of jobs may decline for the least skilled, yet overall these policies are lifting millions out of poverty.[17]

Work-family policies only partially ease the time and economic demands that beset parents with preschool-age children. A more reliable, higher quality network of preschools and child care options is certainly a key piece needed to solve this puzzle. Within U.S. political culture, government may not assume the fiscal burdens shouldered by the European welfare state, but governors and state legislatures have displayed a willingness to broaden the revenue base of social insurance funds to aid families with young children. These measures bring broad-based adjustments to how work and income are structured in our society, instead of assuming that an extension of mass public schooling to younger children can somehow lessen inequality in America.

The intersection between family and early education offers another promising terrain for policy innovations and offers a way to boost parents' own efficacy in raising their children. The original punch of the Perry Preschool experiment may well have been tied to weekly home visits with mothers. We saw, too, how the larger Chicago initiative and Early Head Start programs were more effective when parents were intensively engaged.

Family Options, Parent Voices

The leaders of the new UPK campaign have typically dodged the essential human question: how do parents want to raise their young children? They seem to be preoccupied instead with political tactics: pumping up youngsters with pre-literacy and math skills—to get them ready for real school—in hopes of boosting test scores. Working in a tightly disciplined movement, these proponents have been understandably frustrated by the dispersed politics of child care. Yet there has been little room for recognizing cultural and linguistic differences, or for honestly asking whether "school readiness" is understood or valued by parents.

At times the new alignment between preschool proponents and the central state has been downright silly. Chicago's downtown schools office has developed a seemingly useful "early literacy framework" for their child-parent centers and state preschools that even includes benchmarks for meeting "State Goal 30: Use the target language to make connections and reinforce knowledge and skills across academic, vocational, and technical disciplines."[18] Remember that this framework pertains to three- and four-year-olds; does it aim, perhaps, to infuse more utilitarian meaning into young children building Lego garages or creating productive kitchen scenes inside their pre-k classrooms? When I asked Sonja Griffin, director of Chicago's centers, whether any guidelines were available for teachers in the social and emotional domain (after pressing pre-literacy, math, and science standards since 2002), she replied that it was "still an important ingredient, (but) we haven't had to write a framework yet."

When it comes to the social organization of preschool classrooms and the degree of fit they have with family's own conceptions of development, plenty of middle ground remains to be explored. Susan Neuman, an early-reading scholar at the University of Michigan, reports on how one well-intentioned preschool teacher corralled her increasingly antsy four-year-olds on the rug for over seventy-five minutes, first having them chant the daily schedule, "we will eat breakfast, we will go to centers," and then drilling them on words that start with an N, as in "night, nuts, noodles," aided by a puppet named Nina. As the youngsters got increasingly rowdy, the teacher gave them the predictable admonishment, "Hands are for holding up!" School officials chose this school as exemplary in its approach to pre-literacy; it is in a district that assesses each preschooler six times during the year using six different instruments.[19] Neuman, while lead architect of the Bush II Reading First initiative, had urged that policy conditions should encourage more balanced and motivating teaching practices.

Many teachers are doing just that, bringing to life the classroom methods of Rheta DeVries and others, who spell out how cooking and musical exercises can be used to help children grasp elements of measurement, geometric relationships, even reasoning and causality. Classroom designers like DeVries and Neuman also advance the teacher's capacity to embed richer pre-literacy content into socially engaging classroom activities and create cooperative tasks that are thick with oral language and warm relationships.[20] In coming decades, as early education becomes more institutional, the struggle may center on how the development and learning of young children is structured in classrooms, and whether parents have much say in shaping it.

It is striking how many of the otherwise-liberal UPK hawks decry the doctrinaire and nativist cultural bent of conservative activists. At the same time that they are backing the ideology of academic skilling—narrowing child development down to pieces of language, numbers, and knowledge—their own surveys are telling them that parents care more about their child's self-confidence and socialization, and their youngster's ability to make friends and work with others. Here, too, there's plenty of middle ground to be tilled. But, with advocates and political leaders beginning to cement the institutional foundations—for example, by aligning preschool classrooms to standardized test items in elementary school or aligning what four-year-olds are to learn with how seven-year-olds are tested, and making English the single language of instruction—practices that are more respectful of families and communities may become relics of the past.

Another irony is that UPK enthusiasts' affection for school accountability and testing—even when simply feigned to win political support—may prove to be expedient in the short run and explosive in the long run. Over one-third of Americans polled in 2005 by Phi Delta Kappa, the association of educators, and by Gallup, said there is too much testing, while two-fifths said the current level is about right. Well over half (58 percent) said that the current focus on annual testing of students is leading teachers to teach to the test.[21] So, do parents really want to see the pressure of standardized tests and regimented curricula trickle down into the everyday lives of preschoolers?

Early Education Rooted in Communities

Federal child care policy over the past four decades has largely responded to how families express demand, and they have pursued a variety of child care settings. Government has tried, by financing vouchers and preschools for the working poor and tax credits for the middle class, to make child care more affordable. Nevertheless, this mixed-market orientation has failed to equalize families' access to quality care, as we examined in Chapter 1.

Still, America's increasingly colorful families, presently served by a decentralized array of human-scale organizations, are not reporting that they desire welfare state remedies, replete with uniform institutions and central regulation. The underlying tensions that beset the child care and born-again preschool movements may be related to the breakdown of what Princeton sociologist Robert Wuthnow calls the modernization story line.[22] Decentralized social institutions like the public schools of the early nineteenth century or the health care organizations of the late twentieth faced unrelenting pressure from a modernizing, unifying state. The state's aim was make such decentralized institutions work more like an integrated system, with a uniform view of what the craft must look like inside, with universal routines for all clients and uniform gauges of quality. Thus the modern state was supposed to rationalize and lend order to pluralistic societies via bureaucratic mechanisms. Gerald LeTendre and David Baker at Pennsylvania State University put a sharp interpretive point on this issue: "Rationality as a pervasive cultural product . . . of the historical rise of Western ideas serves to bureaucratize, marketize, individuate, and homogenize the institutions of the world."[23]

During certain historical moments, enforcing centralized rules has certainly been just and necessary, as with the desegregation of schools in the South, or in focusing public resources on low-performing students and holding local schools more accountable. But when today the majority of youngsters are served by community-based organizations that are directly accountable to parents, the burden should be on the state to argue the virtues of rationalizing these human-scale organizations for all youngsters. As preschools come to be financed and controlled by central government, life inside classrooms will likely become more uniform and less subject to the preferences of their surrounding communities.

State and federal governments must decide whether to continue down the modernizing, Weberian pathway, codifying what young children are to learn; to regulate the settings in which they are normatively supposed to spend over eight hours a day; *or*, taking a more Hegelian tack, to strengthen the colorful array of CBOs that operate alongside local schools to offer preschooling. These small public firms can be rightfully asked to meet higher quality benchmarks, while continuing to advance differing ideals and practices. This would resemble the current struggle to advance locally rooted and effective charter schools.[24] Some UPK leaders, such as the early educators we observed in Los Angeles, are elaborating this more inclusive, community situated model. As historian Barbara Beatty has argued, "Advocacy that both emphasizes public access to programs (rather than direct provision of services) and encourages participation of public and private preschools has a greater chance of being effective."[25]

How might government and professional associations avoid uniform and pallid notions of child development, while delivering a robust assortment of high quality preschools? This involves new conceptions of how the state can strengthen local institutions without alienating these organizations from the very families they purport to serve.

A Resourceful, Surgical State

The UPK advocates' pitch is convincing on one point: if we are to achieve more equal access to quality preschools, it will require stronger public investment. On the financing side, it seems fair to ask wealthy Americans to help pay for this long-term investment in the next generation, given the ample benefits they have received under federal tax reforms. Some pro-business lobbies, such as the Los Angeles Chamber of Commerce and the New York–based Committee for Economic Development, have backed this position. They might extend the conversation on preschool to their corporate colleagues, who have so far contributed mainly rhetorical support.

Yet money alone will not ensure a fairer distribution of preschool opportunity. What is needed as well is to craft the state government's role carefully, to focus on more equitable financing across communities, to advance elements of quality that truly promote youngsters' growth, and to strengthen local governance. Rather than trying to pull young children into the institution of mass schooling, government could devise—and in some cases already is devising—strong partnerships with community organizations.

Policymakers need to act in surgical fashion, focusing public resources on the children who will benefit the most from quality preschool. Some advocates say that "programs for the poor make for poor programs," but the evidence does not bear them out. For example, the recent results from the Head Start experimental study (Chapter 6) reveal benefits that rival the magnitude of early literacy benefits stemming from the Tennessee class-size reduction experiment, also focused on poor children. Admittedly, Head Start preschools are of mixed quality, but given current efforts to boost teachers' ability to enhance children's social and cognitive development, we can expect stronger benefits. And the recent findings from Tulsa, with its healthy investment in teacher quality, showed the strong benefit of preschool attendance for poor and working-class children.

In contrast, for children from middle-class and affluent families, few sustained benefits from preschool have been observed. Most of these children have the benefit of growing up in stimulating and nurturing homes. The head start from preschool that they display in kindergarten is encouraging; it may rise in magnitude as preschool quality improves. But the school performance of middle-class preschool graduates will likely drift to average levels early in elementary school. If the "U" in UPK simply stands for a clever political strategy—to gain the pivotal votes of middle-class voters—then advocates should be candid on this point. To date, the promise that all children will benefit markedly from preschool is simply not backed by the evidence. Proponents who claim preschooling can narrow early learning gaps are operating closer to the evidence. But narrowing gaps will require that preschool pack a stronger punch for poor children, and will also require higher-quality elementary schools, to sustain these youngsters' head start.

To give entitlements to all families is politically attractive, but it is infamously ineffective in closing achievement gaps. Entitlements are often sold as policy remedies that will reduce educational inequality. But, in fact, they rarely close disparities in children's learning. The Tennessee effort that shrunk class sizes in predominately black elementary schools did succeed in narrowing achievement gaps. But a decade after California capped class size at twenty children in the early grades, those from low-income families lag behind to the same degree as before.[26] Initial analyses have shown that No Child Left Behind may help sustain the momentum begun by states in raising test scores at the elementary level. But achievement gaps among ethnic groups have failed to close overall.[27] Of course, public policies must aim to advance the schooling and life chances of middle-class children. But that may become the sole effect—and at quite modest levels of magnitude—until UPK advocates and policy leaders focus their effects on poor children.

UPK advocates rightfully criticize the mishmash of financing mechanisms and funding streams that trickles down to local government and preschools, and the confusion it creates for parents. The mix of direct institutional funding (such as Head Start and state pre-k efforts), market-oriented vouchers, and tax credits will likely continue at the federal level. Conservatives will resist giving up on vouchers for low-income families, since about half of this support goes to home-based caregivers. Consolidating the over $18 billion in public support into one stream of funding to preschool organizations and a single voucher program, and then decentralizing management to local counties, could lead to an easier-to-access, higher-quality network of organizations and caregivers.

Long-term public support for pro-family policies, including preschool expansion, will grow stronger if parental choice is preserved and enhanced. It's difficult to conclude from the history of America's century-old kindergarten movement that a takeover by the public schools has led to a colorful spectrum of kindergarten settings for five-year-olds—indeed it has not. Nor has this aging organizational innovation helped to close early learning gaps. Once the kindergarten was incorporated into the public schools, it took on much of the character of the K-12 system—and all of the inequities in finance and teacher quality that beset it. At the spectrum's opposite end, the largely unregulated growth of child care vouchers offers income support for low-income communities, but often by supporting uninspired caregivers.

The dilemma is how to both enrich options and simplify how families enter public preschools. The solution must involve widening eligibility in ways that detach preschool from its welfare history. Blue-collar families won't believe preschool is for them until the image of public support becomes more inclusive. This has worked in broadening family eligibility for health care.

Preserving and enhancing options, including the choice of home-based settings that meet higher quality standards, will make early education more responsive to varying family preferences as we saw in Los Angeles' UPK experiment. In this same light, such measures as expanding federal tax credits for businesses that install preschools at worksites or offer child care reimbursements as part of benefit plans can advance parental choice, and may even lower the cost of fringe benefits for employers.[28] By the late 1990s about 56 percent of major employers had extended child care benefits, and 13 percent had created a preschool center, according to one national survey.[29] The federal government provides another $2.7 billion annually in tax credits to middle-class families to help cover child care expenses.

Investments in quality should be driven by evidence that an organizational strategy truly boosts children's development and not by symbols of quality—regardless of how much appeal the latter may hold for professional groups or labor unions. The fact that expensive "improvements" such as mandating four-year college degrees don't actually help children further undercuts the state's legitimacy.

Oddly, some liberal advocates now seem to discourage lively democratic discourse about the nature of work in America, the well-being of families, and how to strengthen parents' capacity to raise their own children. Somehow conservative writers seem to hold more wisdom about parents and the shortcomings of know-it-all institutions, like the *New York Times*' David Brooks, who writes: "Human beings are not simply organisms within systems, but have minds and inclinations of their own that usually defy planners. You can give people mosquito nets to prevent malaria, but they might use them instead to catch a fish."[30]

It behooves government, certainly, to be more resourceful in raising public investment and strengthening empirically justified improvements in quality. But political leaders must also recognize that post-federalist innovations in statecraft are sorely needed. The fact that the states, not the federal government, are taking the lead on early education reform has sparked a range of UPK experiments, as we have explored. Even so, a more pluralistic model of civil society already has emerged, driven by cultural diversity and the democratization of local organizations across America's kaleidoscope of neighborhoods. Almost a quarter-century ago, Norton Grubb and Marvin Lazerson warned that the "negative conception of *parens patriae* (the state as parent) was coming to characterize some child care initiatives," rather than strengthening the nonprofit sector and thickening civil society to more firmly undergird families.[31] It's a lesson that some UPK advocates fail to appreciate.

The melting-pot metaphor will persist, along with assimilationist impulses across American society. At the same time, the contemporary building blocks of cities and suburbs obviously are communities bounded largely by class, ethnicity, and language. It's this "persisting importance of group membership" that's so relevant to the quandary over how to organize public efforts to improve the upbringing of children. What's vital is an emphasis on the "solidarities rooted in economic situations and interests . . . the notion that children can draw . . . advantages from the group's cultural and socioeconomic resources," in the words of sociologists Richard Alba and Victor Nee.[32] These localized dynamics challenge anew the standardizing and regulatory habits of government.

The state must neither hesitate to keep defining common public projects across the nation's disparate communities, from improving health care and social security to advancing early education. Nor should it mindlessly attempt to impose particular cultural forms or ways of raising young children; these elements are central to the authority of parents and the social mores of communities. As William Galston and other political theorists now argue, educating children to be autonomous and individualistic makes sense for the market, but it threatens to unravel the social fabric.[33] Their contemporary plea is reminiscent of the community-situated views of child development advanced by Dewey, Gesell, and Vygotsky.

One way to get *beneath* the state is to center governance at the local level, whether housed in school offices or wider community-level boards, collectivities operating closer to the ground than far-away government officials. This position is expressed in California's county-led UPK initiatives, which are among the most inclusive and respectful of the nonprofit sector. State governments should then hold local councils accountable to demonstrate gains in young children's cognitive, social, and healthful development. The role played by parents in bolstering children's gains should be tracked as well. State governments might provide more equitable funding, planning data, and creative ideas, so that county managers and early educators can adapt them for children and families in their own settings—while demonstrating how local practices and classroom strategies contribute to the child's multifaceted development.[34]

Let me be clear that the current, very mixed market of preschool organizations is not only insufficient; it's distressingly unfair. I have detailed how the contemporary population of preschools is driven largely by the purchasing power of parents—in the number of enrollment slots available and in teacher quality. If political leaders were to try to arrange the location of public schools based on what parents could afford to pay, rioting in the streets undoubtedly would ensue. Distributing quality preschooling on such market principles sadly characterizes much of the early education sector. Yet allowing overburdened public schools to take over the rich array of community-based preschools and jumping to a centralized remedy would be enormously risky. Instead, the present market of public and private preschools needs, therefore, to become less mixed in quality and cost, and more vibrant and responsive to America's diverse range of families.

Advancing Theory—How to Organize Young Children's Lives?

Finally, what have we learned about the forces that shape the new preschool institution? After looking at all the numbers, the debates over philosophy and evidence, the implementation in various states, cannot we predict whether or not childhood is about to change for millions of youngsters? Ideally, we would like to advance a sociology of child development that ties the rise of formal institutions to the well-being and early learning of young children.

We are making progress in illuminating the forces that shape three kinds of causal events, operating at three levels of analysis. First, as this volume has detailed, are enduring economic and social forces, which variably push state and metropolitan governments to formalize preschool, prompting a push-back from strong, locally rooted elements of civil society. Second are institutional changes, which affect the character of social relations found inside preschool classrooms. Third are changes in policies and organizations, which variously benefit or constrain children's early development.

To more clearly track this trio of causal actions, it's instructive to start by encircling the expansive field of child care and early education, comprised of the UPK activists, funders, political leaders within the state, and grassroots advocates. This book has focused on the intensifying effort by UPK proponents and, of late, education reformers to formalize and regulate the *preschool sector*, one coalescing territory within the wider child care field.

This basic story line involves strong economic and political interests motivating governors and state school chiefs to craft a reform that promises to raise test scores, along with K-12 associations and unions eager for more funding for the public schools, not to mention adding union members. Wide-eyed and wealthy men also enter the story, like Reiner in California, George Kaiser in Oklahoma, and David Lawrence, the former *Miami Herald* publisher. They show little patience for a loosely coupled, politically weak array of child care activists—nor do they care for shades of gray when it comes to how young children might be motivated and nurtured inside classrooms. They are men of action.

The newly drawn boundaries of the preschool sector and advocates' thirst for popular legitimacy have led to the borrowing of certain forms and symbols from neighboring sectors, especially the public schools. This process is what Stanford sociologist John W. Meyer calls the search and instantiation of *ritualized categories*. What would any earnest advocate of UPK, struggling for traction inside state political circles, where the imperative to raise student test scores has become sacred, try to do? Well, how about pressing for a tidier, more centrally regulated preschool system, then promising that "school readiness" will boost test scores when four-year-olds turn six or seven? Sure, this means shifting away from what we know about how young children engage their social environs, how they learn. But step number one for the advocates has been to gain political traction and fuse UPK to the wider school-accountability movement. So, they import the language and scripts from the K-12 policy discourse—whether or not the new institutional forms match what parents actually prefer, or offer the most effective ways of nurturing child development.[35]

As this strategy coheres and political stars come into alignment, UPK initiatives are moving ahead. But another notable lesson is that widely varying forms of "universal preschool" are taking hold across the pioneering states and regions of the country. We discovered, for example, how the innovative experiment in Los Angeles is neither universal nor really preschool. Initial investments are highly targeted on low-income communities, and even family child-care homes are included in the "preschool" network, part of a widely mixed market of early education organizations. In contrast, in Oklahoma UPK is seen as simply "adding another grade onto school." Oklahoma's state funding moves down through school districts. The bulk of young children are enrolled in public schools, and their teachers report there is considerable pressure on them to attend to pre-literacy guidelines and strict pacing schedules. Thus, we see how much local political and cultural conditions—and the ability of grassroots leaders to mobilize against or with civic elites—matter in shaping the new preschool institution.

Local political cultures are also shaping the character of the early education workforce and the practices that teachers enact inside their classrooms. The community-rooted history of Head Start and alternative entry requirements have invited many teachers of color and many with bilingual skills into the field. At the same time, these lower training bars have resulted in highly uneven classroom quality, especially within for-profit preschools that populate many middle-class neighborhoods. Thus, attempts to raise credential levels or to install particular curricula within preschool classrooms are unfolding in organizations that vary dramatically in the complexion, philosophy, and competency of teachers. In this context, one pressing theoretical question holding practical implications is, What are the mechanisms that most directly affect teachers' pedagogical practices and beliefs about children's development? That is, *how* do UPK policies and institutional formalization seep down into preschools, and even into parents' own ideas about child rearing?

We heard from many teachers who feel the push to address preschoolers' early literacy and math skills from the state; the push is bolstered by local school leaders under pressure to raise test scores. In Oklahoma, young teachers are trying to follow the learning goals and scripts handed to them by school principals, while remaining true to the developmental practices they acquired in their university training. Meanwhile, just blocks away at Head Start, teachers were being coached to cover eight, not just one, developmental domains, true to their holistic philosophy. And we heard from L.A. teachers and preschool directors continuing to work from their philosophies and to use native languages inside their classrooms.

This is another pivotal area where a middle ground is being explored by early education thinkers. The developmentalist Ellen Frede, who ran New Jersey's UPK effort, explicitly avoided content standards. She feared that pressing academic knowledge alone would lead to "testing each child all the time."[36] Instead, the state education department requires that local programs, whether run by school districts or CBOs, adopt one of five approved curricular packages, which range from highly scripted packages stressing pre-literacy skills to fully constructivist sets of classroom activities for young children. Frede also devised an observational or "portfolio" assessment procedure that guides teachers to check each child's knowledge in particular areas, along with the youngster's social skills and emotional well-being. "We did it because it informs teaching, it helps teachers," Frede said. The New Jersey approach is quite similar to the holistic yet specific approach to child assessment that the California department of education has been refining, the method that would have been set aside under Reiner's failed UPK plan.

Other thinkers, like Sharon Lynn Kagan at Teachers College in New York, are exploring the middle ground as well. "We have to separate the pre-k movement from pedagogical and curriculum issues," she said.[37] "With the nation's literacy rate declining we must address early language and literacy skills. But I would never condone an assessment system that doesn't look at all domains of development." I asked Kagan whether this stance might be politically naïve, given the ongoing pressure to raise test scores. "Not if we do our job well," she responded. "That's where I think early educators should stand tall. We know a lot about child development, we can maybe influence what's going on in kindergarten, first, second grade."

These artful ways by which the state might require more rigorous structuring of classroom activities and careful assessment of children's progress—while allowing local practitioners to move from their own pedagogical ideals and experience—represent what I have called *selective coupling*. That is, the state doesn't simply regulate along proxies of quality that hold little empirical relationship with child development, such as credential levels of teachers. Instead, it works with local organizations to enrich and organize classrooms in ways that build from what we know about the motivation and curiosity of young children. Rather than enforcing tight and regimented couplings between the bureaucracy and the classroom, the state can be more selective and resourceful as it moves to improve classroom practices. This approach is also democratic and participatory in spirit, encouraging preschool directors and teachers to think through differing learning activities that are both effective and appropriate to local preferences. Thoughtful forms of child assessment, as New Jersey and California, encourage teachers to clearly see and carefully track children's multifaceted forms of development.

We now come to the final causal step in building a sound theory of action: how formulated policies and local implementation benefit, or constrain, the early development of children. Reviewing the past four decades of empirical research we saw how the exposure of poor children to preschool moderately boosts early cognitive development and familiarity with print materials. But research has found few discernible effects on children's social and emotional growth, except for the slightly negative effect of spending long hours in preschool (at present levels of quality).

Yet clearer theory and thicker empirical work are sorely needed to clarify *how* the cognitive benefits come about within preschool classrooms, effects that persist for the most potent experiments, and why they diminish in magnitude among middle-class children. Beyond crude proxies for "quality," like the ratio of children to adults in the classroom, or whether a teacher has a college degree, we know surprisingly little about the fine-grain actions and utterances of adults who work with young children—and the differing effects experienced by America's diverse youngsters. These effects likely stem not only from highly variable teaching practices and the character of social relationship inside classrooms, but also how home practices interact with the child's time in preschool. The science of child development continues to separate the social processes that unfold in home versus those that unfold in preschool; in reality this is more than just parallel play.

Nor do we know much about how children themselves make sense of what's going on inside their preschool classrooms. Those who now press for pre-literacy skills rarely consider the social rules and forms of interaction that their narrow content threatens to imply. Few researchers have focused on how the pedagogical forms tied to skilling and drilling may be motivating for some children and stultifying for others. The work of Stanford's Deborah Stipek is one notable exception, as discussed in Chapter 7. Just a few program evaluations point to the added punch that comes from deeply involving parents. Scholars need to look more carefully at this component of the new preschool initiatives, and how parental engagement may advance children's cognitive and social growth.

Democratic Child Development

In tracing how the preschool institution attempts to touch the lives of children and parents, we quickly realize that this story involves many characters, recurring tensions, even a bit of suspense. Indeed, early education has become a field that hosts a variety of education interest groups, community groups, church activists, and politicians. Under modern logics of statecraft we see government struggling to act from broad public ideals, be it equalizing school finance, creating market pressures on health care providers, or advancing the nation's security. The state's perennial challenge to create civic will for public projects, in contemporary times, runs into a counter-faith in the market and the wonders of self-reliance.

This battle between market and state, however consequential, should not eclipse the fact that when it comes to raising young children, the localized actors—CBOs, preschool teachers, or parents—turn out to be the most influential. Yes, it's true that "research-based practice" and "the research shows . . . " are phrases we hear often, as if Tourette's syndrome had beset UPK advocates. But the guiding frames of the early education debate—whether liberal-humanist, or academic skilling, or cross-cultural conceptions of development—remain *philosophical* claims about the nature of young children and the kinds of social organization that advance their early learning. And it's care-givers on the ground, not state officials, who will blend their philosophy and practices with the greatest consequences for their young charges.

Each guiding set of ideals was first articulated by elite thinkers or popu-larized experts. University researchers and professional groups will continue to inform the debate. But today it's from the grassroots where contestation, including the push-back on central government, is contributing fresh energy to the public discussion over early education, as largely decentralized orga-nizations host democratic discourse on the ground.[38]

Thus, neoliberals—including UPK advocates as they push to fuse pre-school to the state—may push a human capital or skilling notion of what chil-dren should be taught inside classrooms. Yet early educators or caregivers (not to mention middle-class parents)—since most were raised within either a liberal-humanist or another cultural tradition—can be expected to resist such notions. We heard of the parallel struggle, reported by some preschool teachers, as they try to balance the new regimentation against their profes-sional commitment to nurturing children's self-confidence or that impulse to explore. Or, when a teacher remains committed to advancing a child's Latino identity or bilingual proficiencies, she will likely find ways to buffer the work-sheets and drills advanced by state officials. Still, we have much to learn from early educators regarding how they rebuff or accommodate intensifying pol-icy signals from above.

One haunting question is whether the modern state really wants to strengthen democratic social organizations on the ground. Today we see politicians across the ideological spectrum eager to raise test scores and ma-nipulate a variety of centralized policies levers to further regiment class-rooms—even to radically narrow how we conceive of young children's po-tentials. A modern state that aims to integrate diverse groups must devise uni-form rules and symbols, even endorse a shared, often dominating language. This neo-classical function of the political apparatus can serve to equalize economic opportunities while paradoxically legitimating dominant forms of work and culture and pressing them onto diverse families over time.

But given the horizontal distribution of community organizations that now serve young children, and the nation's burgeoning pluralism, central rules will be contested from below. When policymakers attempt to homogenize institutional forms, set uniform gauges of quality, or impose one way for organizing classrooms (implying a homogenized relationship between teacher and child), this push-back will come with considerable force, as we saw in the colorful political culture of Los Angeles. The rise of cross-cultural conceptions of child development presents yet another challenge to the regulatory habits of the central state.

We see, then, the modern, vertical imagery that has long portrayed policy-making and political authority—with focus on heads of state at the top of the body politic—giving way. Perhaps the beast now lies horizontally, sustained by de-centered fields of human-scale organizations and multiple nodes of social or "public" authority. The two-thirds of all nonprofit preschools that are supported mainly by parental fees have operated largely free of government oversight or funding, until now. Even preschools that depend on state funding were free to devise their own curricular and teaching philosophies—until UPK advocates and their allies began to stress the academic skilling agenda. This has not been entirely unwelcome, given the unevenness of preschool quality.

One difficulty is that the de-centered arrangement of early education organizations constrains the central state's own presence in the field—a point on which UPK advocates rightfully harp. In conservative Oklahoma, a few political actors had to sneak through the monumental finance reform for UPK. In California, it took a Rob Reiner, who could command media attention and help bankroll a statewide ballot measure, to circumvent a hog-tied legislature and a hesitant series of governors. Meanwhile, conservative leaders have become quite adept at pushing market remedies for public problems—advancing a smaller, less efficacious state.

Caught in between are institutional liberals trying to rekindle modern faith in big systems, promoting a Weberian nirvana where government becomes the chief architect of ever-expanding institutions. To look accountable and equitable, they specify uniform learning goals, routinize didactics, and test children with standardized exams. If test scores do rise, then maybe taxpayers' faith in government will grow, offering up richer tithes to feed the beast. Herein lies the UPK advocates' strategy for standardizing childhood. Under the modern logic of mass society—assuming this story of progress continues to draw believers—building a tighter, more uniform way of raising young children sounds so right.

The field of early education now enjoys clearer, more expansive borders, rooted in richer soil, watered and, shall I say, fertilized by many of the same interest groups and bureaucratic forms that support the public schools. The past generation of research has helped to encircle and detail this far-flung network of preschool organizations and individual caregivers, and reveal what's so unfair about who gains access to high-quality child care. The new empirical work and fresh theoretical accounts of decentralized social action help to clarify the consequential choices that now confront political leaders and local educators. Indeed, much is at stake in this unfolding debate over universal preschool—differing pathways for how Americans choose to raise their youngsters, the settings in which they grow up, and even for how we understand a young child's human potential.

In coming decades, public resources will be marshaled, perhaps, to enrich the democratic arrangement of organizations that aid parents in this essential task of child rearing. Or, the political apparatus may decide to concentrate authority in a more uniform institution, augmenting the public schools. The scenario will play out differently across the states and among metropolitan regions. We confront a telling choice. Where will America place its faith: in the state, in the market, or perhaps in a civil society populated by stronger neighborhood organizations? How we move from this juncture forward will test our shared resolve to improve the most fundamental of all human endeavors, nurturing the next generation.

The Research Team, Methods, and Many Thanks

From this project's inception Margaret Bridges, Seeta Pai, and I aimed to clarify the philosophical fissures that characterize American society on the essential question of how we raise young children. The contest of ideals—as we have examined it across diverse communities—speaks to how we conceive of young children's potentials and how we try to enrich their daily settings. Contemporary developmental scientists often try to set aside ideological considerations to focus on discovering universal relationships that lead to stronger childhoods. But core learning and developmental outcomes are a mix of universal facets like robust physiological growth and culturally situated tasks, cognitive demands, and social norms. We realized that the rising political battle over universal preschool accents how institutions and interests rival developmental science in shaping early education in America.

As we corralled these two lines of research, one philosophical and one positivist in character, our own empirical work proceeded as well. I spent two years interviewing key actors in California, New Jersey, Oklahoma, and Washington, D.C. These included preschool teachers, community activists, school officials, researchers, and state and federal policymakers. Certainly ideals and intellectual history alone do not power major education reforms—people do. Our ethnographic work unfolded inside preschools, as did our surveys of parents. We followed young children through various child care options, and analyzed populations of preschool organizations. Burrowing more deeply into the UPK movement, I became intrigued with how evidence was being appropriated to bolster the advocates' case and their contemporary push for a more standardized childhood.

The Spanish artist Joan Miró often worked on a large canvass, inviting our imagination to interpret great swaths of color or abstract strokes ranging across a textured surface. Yet he was equally passionate about capturing the meaning of the details. "Everyone has painted only the great masses of trees and mountains, without paying any attention to the small flowers and blades of grass," he wrote.[1] This book, certainly with a less evocative palette, attempted to capture the broad historical and cultural forces, then illuminate how individuals and groups—each expressing heartfelt ideals, often with a dash of stylized facts—bring these broader forces to life.

After pulling apart this cobweb of philosophical claims and scientific findings, we should disclose our own intellectual roots and the roles we played in crafting the perspectives and assembling the evidence that appears in this book. When I speak in the second person, invoking the royal *we*, I refer to my colleagues, Margaret Bridges and Seeta Pai. This volume stems from our collective research program, conducted over the past few years. Seeta led the ethnographic work inside preschools detailed in Chapter 3. Margaret contributed greatly to the review of empirical research reported in Chapter 6. Seeta arrived at Berkeley as a remarkably sensitive and rigorous post-doctoral scholar, having trained in cross-cultural human development with Robert LeVine at Harvard. She presently serves as the research director at Sesame Workshop in New York City. Margaret is a developmental psychologist trained at the University of Virginia.

Much of our empirical work on the supply of preschool programs and the effects of these human-scale organizations on child development has been conducted with other colleagues. Sharon Lynn Kagan, Susanna Loeb, and I co-directed the Growing Up in Poverty Project, a study that followed 927 low-income mothers and their young children in three states over a five-year period.

Doctoral student Alejandra Livas contributed much to this volume, adding the rich viewpoint of a former bilingual kindergarten teacher in Compton, California. She dug out various facts and statistics and contributed heavily to Chapter 7. Alejandra's own interviews with California kindergarten teachers informed our qualitative research. Sally Serafim masterfully edited the manuscript, finding the many bugs in my pesky prose. Allison Chen, Katie Gesicki, and Krystal Mincey helped with fact checking and searching out reference materials. April Alvarez organized focus groups with a variety of Latina mothers and pulled together countless journal articles.

Some of the lines of argument explored in this book were advanced by a pioneering set of scholars working at the intersection of philosophy, science, and cross-cultural child development. They include Cynthia García Coll, William Corsaro, Eugene García, Carol Joffe, Susan Holloway, Robert and Sarah LeVine, Sally Lubeck, Barbara Rogoff, and Julia Wrigley. We are indebted to each of them. I also want to warmly thank historian David Tyack, who taught me years ago about the benefits and risks associated with trying to advance a one-best system of schooling for a pluralistic society.

Several people generously reviewed earlier drafts of chapters, helping to correct factual errors and offering a reality check on our interpretations. In this regard, I want to especially thank Andy McKensie, who also hosted my three stays in Tulsa, along with his wife Janet. They were always warm, candid, and patient in pointing to weak spots in my analysis. Karen Hill-Scott was a wonderful colleague in this regard as well. She read multiple chapters, attended review meetings, and proved to be a most engaging foil, always with grace, often with humor. Bob Harbison spent hours with me, talking through historical details and making sure that every fact was correct. William Gormley, Jr., offered detailed comments on the Oklahoma chapter.

Ellen Frede, the thoughtful developmentalist who ran New Jersey's UPK program for several years, was always available, and her comments were candid and insightful. Steve Barnett patiently responded to my prickly questions about the evidence. Janet Currie spent considerable time checking and gently correcting our review of the empirical literature. Paul Miller and Patty Siegel in California have been available and supportive always, even when we disagreed. A pair of wonderful editors, Kate Wahl and Elizabeth Knoll, helped to conceptualize and guide this project, steadily nudging me to focus on the basic human questions. The comments of four anonymous reviewers guided revisions. Susan Dauber at the Spencer Foundation has long supported our work with low-income Latino families, sharpening our thinking with her typical candor and warmth. In Chicago, Sonja Griffin spent loads of time teaching me about the impressive child-parent centers, and Arthur Reynolds freely clarified his findings.

Conversations with and feedback from many other individuals were invaluable in teaching me about local dynamics out in the states. In Oklahoma, special thanks are due Steven Dow, Pam Brooks, Maria Carlota Palacios, Joe Eddins, Judy Feary, Cindy Lance, Ramona Paul, Harriett Patterson, Leslie Porter, and Carol Rowland. In California, several people spent hours with me, piecing together recent history, writing brilliantly on local details, and weighing the contributions of key players in Los Angeles and in California statewide. Warm thanks are due Yolie Aguilar, Sandy Ahlstrand, Renatta Cooper, Sue Curtis, Laura Escobedo, Karin Klein, Graciela Italiano-Thomas, Neal Kaufman, Kathy Malaske-Sumu, Barbara McLean, Carla Rivera, and Marti Rood. Jacquelyn McCroskey helped me sort out the complicated dynamics of L.A. politics on several occasions.

Our heartfelt thanks are extended to the public agencies and foundations that have supported the research over the years. Their generosity allowed us to spend months inside preschools, follow families over time, and analyze national data. The support of private foundations is crucial for any scholar asking questions about a politically charged issue. In this regard, the Spencer Foundation financed Seeta's ethnographic work and currently supports our study of Latino children in and outside preschools. My research on poor families and child care options has been backed by the Spencer Foundation, along with the David and Lucile Packard Foundation, for almost fifteen years. Steady support from three civic-minded Haas families in San Francisco has been crucial, as well. Special thanks go to Hedy Chang, Susan Dauber, Amanda Feinstein, Deanna Gomby, Cheryl Polk, Wei-min Wang, and Marie Young for their tough questions and encouragement over the years. Our long-term tracking study, the Growing Up in Poverty Project, has been funded by the U.S. Department of Education and the Department of Health and Human Services, the Haas family funds, and the Casey, MacArthur, and Spencer foundations. Pia Divine, Laurie Garduque, Naomi Karp, Mike Laracy, and Joan Lombardi were early and steady supporters of this work.

Margaret's original work on the preschool and child care workforce was funded by the California First 5 Children and Families Commission. The Packard Foundation funded her research with Russ Rumberger and Loan Tran on the persisting effects of preschooling for different children. The University of California supported a truly inspiring sabbatical in Barcelona with my family, where I wrote much of this book.

None of these agencies or foundations necessarily agrees with the arguments put forward in this volume. Nor do Margaret and Seeta always concur—just one reason why I love working with them. Any errors of fact or interpretation are mine alone.

I warmly dedicate this book to Susan Holloway, my intellectual soul mate and gentle partner in the unpredictable adventure of raising our two children, Caitlin and Dylan. Each continues to tease me about being logged on or reading late into the night, always claiming that it just can't wait. Susan is a developmental psychologist, and she helps to keep me grounded in children's own experiences whenever I drift toward the curious behavior of grown-ups. She got me into all this, somewhat to her chagrin. It's impossible to thank Susan fully for all that she has contributed to my life, my growth, and our shared ideas. Thank you all.

BRUCE FULLER

BERKELEY

List of Acronyms

CAP	Community Action Program, Tulsa, Oklahoma
CBO	Community-based organization, nonprofit
ECLS	Federal Early Childhood Longitudinal Study (family data set)
FCCH	Licensed family child care home
First 5 LA	First 5 Children and Families Commission of Los Angeles County
LA-UP	Los Angeles Universal Preschool
NAEYC	National Association for the Education of Young Children
NCLB	No Child Left Behind Act of 2001
NICHD	National Institute for Child Health and Human Development
SRA	Scientific Reading Associates (owned by McGraw Hill Publishers)
TPS	Tulsa Public Schools
UPK	Universal pre-kindergarten programs, universal preschool

Notes

1. The labels for local organizations—child care *center* and *preschool*—have become synonymous, while the term *nursery school* has largely faded into history. Estimate based on census data. Kristen Smith, *Who's Minding the Kids? Child Care Arrangements*, Report No. P70-70 (Washington, D.C.: U.S. Census Bureau, 2000).

2. In a study conducted with Margaret Bridges and Russell Rumberger, we found that over 80 percent of the gap in fourth-grade reading scores between Latino and white children observed in California was quite apparent in their pre-reading skills, assessed in kindergarten. See Margaret Bridges, Bruce Fuller, Russell Rumberger, and Loan Tran, "Preschool for California's Children: Promising Benefits, Unequal Access" (Working Paper Series 05-1, Policy Analysis for California Education, Berkeley, 2005).

3. U.S. Government Accounting Office, *Prekindergarten: Four Selected States Expanded Access by Relying on Schools and Existing Providers of Early Education and Care to Provide Services* (Washington, D.C.: U.S. Government Accounting Office, 2004); Douglas Besharov and Nazanin Samari, "Child Care After Welfare Reform," in *The New World of Welfare*, ed. R. Blank and R. Haskins (Washington, D.C.: 2001).

4. Marketdata Enterprises, *U.S. Child Day Care Services: An Industry Analysis* (Tampa, Fla.: Marketdata Enterprises, 2005).

5. State data appear in U.S. Government Accounting Office, *Prekindergarten: Four Selected States Expanded Access by Relying on Schools*. California estimates appear in Bridges et al., *Preschool for California's Children*.

6. Quoted by Jennifer Coleman, "Schools' Chief Calls Preschool a Priority," *Contra Costa Times*, December 30, 2004.

7. Quoted by Nancy Trejos, "Time May Be Up for Naps in Pre-K Class," *Washington Post*, March 15, 2003, http://www.washpost.com.

8. Susanna Cooper and Kara Dukakis, *Kids Can't Wait to Learn: Achieving Voluntary Preschool for All in California* (Oakland: Preschool for All, 2004), 14. The reference to sitting at desks and the ability to focus on text stems from school readiness measures used in national surveys.

9. Janet Napolitano, "Remarks to Supporters of the National Task Force on Public Education" (Washington, D.C.: Mayflower Hotel, April 22, 2004). Interview with Darcy Olsen.

10. Historian Barbara Beatty discusses how the preschool issue has risen on the agenda of mainstream education lobbies. Barbara Beatty, "The Politics of Preschool Advocacy: Lessons from Three Pioneering Organizations," in *Who Speaks for America's Children?*, ed. Carol De Vita and Rachel Mosher-Williams, 191–208 (Washington, D.C.: Urban Institute Press, 2001).

11. David Brooks, "Reacquaint the Republican Party with Republican Traditions," *New York Times Magazine*, August 29, 2004, 37–38.

12. Jean Lave and Etienne Wenger, *Situated Learning: Legitimate Peripheral Participation* (New York: Cambridge University Press, 1991), 47.

13. Deborah Phillips, interview by author, January 10, 2005.

14. Susanna Loeb, Margaret Bridges, Daphna Bassok, Bruce Fuller, and Russ Rumberger, "How Much Is Too Much? The Effects of Duration and Intensity of Child Care Experiences," *Economics of Education Review* (forthcoming).

CHAPTER I

1. The original research on this episode was conducted by Barbara Beatty; see her *Preschool Education in America: The Culture of Young Children from the Colonial Era to the Present* (New Haven: Yale University Press, 1995).

2. John Harrison, *Utopianism and Education: Robert Owen and the Twenties* (New York: Teachers College Press, 1968), 145–46.

3. Beatty, *Preschool Education in America*.

4. Quoted by Caroline Winterer, "Avoiding a 'Hothouse System of Education': Nineteenth-Century Early Childhood Education from the Infant Schools to the Kindergartens," *History of Education Quarterly* 32 (1992): 289–314.

5. Steven Mintz, *Huck's Raft: A History of American Childhood* (Cambridge, Mass.: Belknap Press of Harvard University Press, 2004).

6. Catherine Beecher, *Treatise on the Domestic Economy* (Boston: Marsh, Capen, Lyon, & Webb, 1841).

7. The unrelenting nature of policy talk, and how it occasionally powers new policy and some institutional change, is discussed by David Tyack and Larry Cuban, in *Tinkering Toward Utopia: A Century of Public School Reform* (Cambridge, Mass.: Harvard University Press, 1995).

8. Thomas Popkewitz, "Governing the Child and Pedagogicalization of the Parent," in *Governing Children, Families, and Education*, ed. Marianne Bloch, Kerstin Holmlund, Ingeborg Moqvist, and Thomas Popkewitz (New York: Palgrave, 2003), 35–61.

9. See, for example, Colin Gordon, ed., *Power/Knowledge: Selected Interviews and Other Writing, 1972–1977* (New York: Pantheon Books, 1980).

10. Tamar Levin, "The Need to Invest in Young Children," *New York Times*, January 11, 2006.

11. Amended Assembly Bill, *Sacramento California Legislature Assembly Bill 1246* (July 11, 2005).

12. Initiative language as submitted by Attorney General's Office, *Preschool for All Act* (Sacramento, 2005) 17.

13. I use the terms *child care center* and *preschool* synonymously throughout the book. Preschool historically connoted a half-day, more enriched educational program, similar to earlier nursery schools. But many parents, through fees, and public agencies support high-quality, center-based programs. Conversely, the quality of some "preschool" programs is weak. A 1990 national study of center-based programs by the U.S. Department of Education found that the two labels *center* and *preschool* no longer reliably distinguished programs.

14. Personal communication via e-mail from anonymous source, February 10, 2006.

15. Ellen Kisker, Sandra Hofferth, Deborah Phillips, and Ellen Farquhar, *A Profile of Child Care Settings: Early Education and Care in 1990* (Princeton, N.J.: Mathematica Policy Research, Inc., 1991).

16. Julia Overturf Johnson, *Who's Minding the Kids? Child Care Arrangements: Winter 2002* (Washington, D.C.: U.S. Census Bureau, 2005), 70–101.

17. Estimates from the Survey of Income and Program Participation, conducted for the National Research Council's Committee on Family and Work Policies. See Eugene Smolensky and Jennifer Appleton Gootman, eds., *Working Families and Growing Kids: Caring for Children and Adolescents* (Washington, D.C.: National Academies Press, 2003).

18. Abby Cohen, "A Brief History of Federal Financing of Child Care in the United States," *Future of Children* 6 (1996): 26–40.

19. Estimates of the supply of preschools and family child care homes are discussed in Smolensky and Gootman, *Working Families and Growing Kids*; Bruce Fuller, Susanna Loeb, Annelie Strath, and Bidemi Abioseh Carrol, "State Formation of the Child Care Sector: Family Demand and Policy Action," *Sociology of Education* 77 (2004): 337–58.

20. Bruce Fuller, Shelly Waters Boots, Emiliano Castillo, and Diane Hirshberg, *A Stark Plateau: California Families See Little Growth in Child Care Centers* (Berkeley: University of California, Policy Analysis for California Education, 2002).

21. Bruce Fuller, Stephen Raudenbush, Li-ming Wei, and Susan Holloway, "Can Government Raise Child Care Quality? The Influence of Family Demand, Poverty, and Policy," *Educational Evaluation and Policy Analysis* 15 (1993): 255–78.

22. National Center for Educational Statistics, "Survey of Classes that Serve Children Prior to Kindergarten in the Public Schools, 2000–2001" (Report FRSS-78, U.S. Department of Education, Washington D.C., 2001).

23. For a careful review of these data, see the monograph by Lynn Karoly and James Bigelow, *The Economics of Investing in Universal Preschool in California* (Santa Monica: RAND Corporation, 2004).

24. These basic data appear in Bridges et al., "Preschool for California's Children."

25. For discussion of the role of CBOs, see Rachel Schumacher, Danielle Ewen, Katherine Hart, and Joan Lombardi, "All Together Now: State Experiences in Using Community-Based Child Care to Provide Pre-kindergarten" (working paper, Washington, D.C.: Center for Law and Social Policy, 2005).

26. Sandra L. Hofferth, Kimberlee A. Shauman, Robert R. Henke, and Jerry West, *Characteristics of Children's Early Care and Education Programs* (Washington, D.C.: National Center for Educational Statistics, 1998).

27. Bridges et al., "Preschool for California's Children."

28. Original tabulations from the Early Childhood Longitudinal Study; see Margaret Bridges and Loan Tran, "Kindergarten Class of 1998–1999." Detailed findings appear in Loeb et al., "How Much Is Too Much?" (forthcoming).

29. Bruce Fuller, Susan Holloway, and Xiaoyan Liang, "Family Selection of Child Care Centers: The Influence of Household Support, Ethnicity, and Parental Practices," *Child Development* 67 (1996): 3320–37.

30. Karoly and Bigelow, *The Economics of Investing in Universal Preschool in California*.

31. Bridges et al., "Preschool for California's Children."

32. This gap for working-class families did not narrow after taking into account average enrollment size. See Bruce Fuller and Annelie Strath, "The Child Care and Preschool Workforce: Demographics, Earnings, and Unequal Distribution," *Educational Evaluation and Policy Analysis* 23 (2001): 37–55.

33. Rachel Gordon and Lindsay Chase-Lansdale, "Availability of Child Care in the United States: A Description and Analysis of Data Sources," *Demography* 38 (2001): 299–316.

34. Fuller et al., "Can Government Raise Child Care Quality?"

35. Victoria Goldman, "The Baby Ivies: Preschool Pedagogy, for up to $15,000," *New York Times Magazine*, January 12, 2003, 22–25.

36. Arthur Reynolds, Suh-Ruu Ou, and James Topitzes, "Paths of Effects of Early Childhood Intervention on Educational Attainment and Delinquency: A Confirmatory Analysis of the Chicago Child-Parent Centers," *Child Development* 75 (September/October 2004): 1299–1328.

37. The study team relied heavily on the Early Childhood Environment Rating Scale. See Suzanne Helburn, Mary L. Culkin, John Morris, Naci Mocan, Carollee Howes, Leslie Phillipsen, Donna Bryant, Richard Clifford, Debby Cryer, Ellen Peisner-Feinberg, Margaret Burchinal, Sharon Lynn Kagan, and Jean Rustici, *Cost, Quality and Child Outcomes in Child Care Centers: Technical Report* (Denver: University of Colorado, Department of Economics, 1995).

38. Bruce Fuller, Sharon Lynn Kagan, Susanna Loeb, and Yueh-Wen Chang, "Child Care Quality: Centers and Home Settings that Serve Poor Families," *Early Childhood Research Quarterly* 19 (2004): 505–27.

39. Telephone interview with Deborah Phillips, chair of psychology at Georgetown University, January 10, 2004.

40. Anthony Bryk, Penny Bender Sebring, David Kerbow, Sharon Rollow, and John Easton, *Charting Chicago School Reform: Democratic Localism as a Lever for Change* (Boulder, Colo.: Westview Press, 1999).

41. Deborah Phillips, Michelle Voran, Ellen Kisker, Carollee Howes, and Marcy Whitebook, "Child Care for Children in Poverty: Opportunity or Inequity?" *Child Development* 65 (1994): 472–92.

42. Bruce Fuller, Susan Holloway, Laurie Bozzi, Elizabeth Burr, Nancy Cohen, and Sawako Suzuki, "Explaining Local Variability in Child Care Quality: State Funding and Regulation in California," *Early Education and Development* 14 (2003): 47–66.

43. Fuller et al., "Child Care Quality."

44. This idea is developed further in Bruce Fuller, *Government Confronts Culture* (New York: Taylor & Francis, 1999).

45. Fuller et al., "State Formation of the Child Care Sector"; similar results were derived from a second data set, the 1990 survey of preschool centers conducted by Mathematica Policy Research, Inc. See Fuller et al., "Can Government Raise Child Care Quality?"

46. Beatty writes: "Advocacy that both emphasizes public access to programs (rather than direct provision of services) and encourages the participation of public and private preschools has a greater chance of being effective." See Beatty, "The Politics of Preschool Advocacy: Lessons from Three Pioneering Organizations," in *Who Speaks for America's Children? The Role of Child Advocates in Public Policy*, ed. Carol De Vita and Rachel Mosher-Williams, 165–90 (Washington, D.C.: Urban Institute Press, 2001).

47. Alejandra Livas, *Analytic Memo from California Kindergarten Teacher Interviews* (Berkeley: University of California, 2005).

48. Edward Zigler and Sally Styco, eds., *The Head Start Debates* (Baltimore, Md.: Brookes Publishing, 2004).

49. Quoted from an article by Dana Hull, "Rob Reiner Pitches Preschool Plan to Leaders," *San Jose Mercury News*, December 14, 2005, B4.

50. Sue Urahn, interview by telephone, August 23, 2005.

51. Letter from Lois Salisbury, "Brief on the Children, Families, and Communities Program of the David and Lucile Packard Foundation" (Los Altos, Calif., April 14, 2004).

52. Theda Skocpol and Jillian Dickert detail how the post-1950s growth of national nonprofit organizations in education and child health has been dominated by non-membership groups with small staffs who conduct research and lobby on

specific issues. See Skocpol and Dickert, "Speaking for Families and Children in a Changing Civic America," in *Who Speaks for America's Children? The Role of Child Advocates in Public Policy*, ed. Carol J. De Vita and Rachel Mosher-Williams, 137–64 (Washington, D.C.: Urban Institute Press, 2001).

CHAPTER 2

1. Richard Coley, *An Uneven Start: Indicators of Inequality in School Readiness* (Princeton, N.J.: Educational Testing Service, Policy Information Center, 2002).

2. For a broader conception, see Huey-ling Lin, Frank Lawrence, and Jeffrey Gorrell, "Kindergarten Teachers' Views of Children's Readiness for School," *Early Childhood Research Quarterly* 18 (2003): 225–37.

3. For historical details on Froebel's schools and writings, see Beatty, *Preschool Education in America*. See also Henry Barnard, ed., *Kindergarten and Child Culture Papers: Papers on Froebel's Kindergarten* (Hartford, Conn.: Office of Barnard's American Journal of Education, 1890), 21–48.

4. Raymond Williams, *Keywords* (New York: Oxford University Press, 1973).

5. Michael Cole, "Cultural Psychology: Some General Principles and a Concrete Example," in *Perspectives on Activity Theory*, ed. Yrjö Engeström, Reijo Miettinen, and Raija-Leena Punamäki (New York: Cambridge University Press, 1999), 87–106.

6. Paraphrasing Mill in editor George Sher's introduction to *Utilitarianism: John Stuart Mill* (Indianapolis, Ind.: Hackett Publishing, 2001), viii.

7. Quotations from original sources appear in Beatty, *Preschool Education in America*, 40–45.

8. Additional details on his pedagogical techniques appear in Joachim Liebschner, *A Child's Work: Freedom and Guidance in Froebel's Educational Theory and Practice* (Cambridge: Lutterworth Press, 1992); quote is on p. ii.

9. These passages appear in John Axtell, ed., *The Educational Writings of John Locke* (Cambridge: Cambridge University Press, 1968).

10. Marianne Block, "Global and Local Analyses of the Construction of 'Family-child Welfare,'" in *Governing Children, Families, and Education: Restructuring the Welfare State*, ed. Marianne Bloch, Kerstin Holmlund, Ingeborg Moqvist, and Thomas Popkewitz, 195–230 (New York: Palgrave Macmillan, 2003).

11. Quoted and paraphrased by Deborah Stipek in Deborah Stipek, Sharon Milburn, Darlene Clements, and Denise Daniels, "Parents' Beliefs About Appropriate Education for Young Children," *Journal of Applied Developmental Psychology* 13 (1992): 293–310.

12. Sue Bredekamp and Carol Copple, *Developmentally Appropriate Practice in Early Childhood Programs* (Washington, D.C.: National Association for the Education of Young Children, 1997).

13. Rheta DeVries, "Understanding Constructivist Education," in *Developing Constructivist Early Childhood Curriculum*, ed. Rheta DeVries, Betty Zan, Carolyn

Hildebrandt, Rebecca Edmiaston, and Christina Sales, 3 (New York: Teachers College Press, 2002).

14. Victoria Getis and Maris Vinovskis, "History of Child Care in the United States Before 1950," in *Child Care in Context*, ed. Michael Lamb, Kathleen Sternberg, Carl-Philip Hwang, and Anders Broberg (Hillsdale, N.J.: Erlbaum, 1992), 185–206.

15. Elizabeth Peabody, *Guide to the Kindergarten and Intermediate Class* (New York: Steiger, 1877), quoted in Beatty, *Preschool Education in America*.

16. Jill Walston and Jerry West, *Full-day and Half-day Kindergarten in the United States* (Report 2004-078, National Center for Educational Statistics, Washington, D.C., 2004).

17. Elizabeth Peabody, "Report of the Sixth Meeting of the American Froebel Union," *Kindergarten Messenger and the New Education* 3 (1879): 1.

18. Marvin Lazerson, "Urban Reform and the Schools: Kindergarten in Massachusetts, 1870–1915," *History of Education Quarterly* 11 (1971): 115–42.

19. Evelyn Weber, *The Kindergarten: Its Encounter with Educational Thought in America* (New York: Teachers College Press, 1969).

20. Larry Cuban, "Why Some Reforms Last: The Case of Kindergarten," *American Journal of Education* 100 (1992): 166–94.

21. Jennifer Russell, "Changing Conceptions of Kindergarten Teaching: Loss of Control in an Era of Accountability" (manuscript, Graduate School of Education, University of California, Berkeley), 19, 21.

22. Mintz, *Huck's Raft*.

23. For a review of parenting guides and experts, see Ann Hulbert, *Raising America: Experts, Parents, and a Century of Advice* (New York: Knopf, 2003).

24. Kieran Egan, *Getting It Wrong from the Beginning: Our Progressive Inheritance from Herbert Spencer, John Dewey, and Jean Piaget* (New Haven: Yale University Press, 2002), 5–6.

25. Herbert Spencer, *The Works of Herbert Spencer*, vol. 16 (Osnabrück, Germany: Otto Zeller Publisher, 1966).

26. Arnold Gesell, *The Pre-school Child* (New York: Houghton Mifflin, 1923), i.

27. Mintz, *Huck's Raft*, 219.

28. Gesell, *The Pre-school Child*, 84, 185, 189.

29. Arnold Gesell and Frances Ilg, *Infant and Child in the Culture of Today: The Guidance of Development in Home and Nursery School* (New York: Harper & Brothers, 1943), 271–72, 358.

30. Gesell and Ilg, *Infant and Child in the Culture of Today*, 10, 258–59.

31. Jean Piaget, *Understanding Causality* (New York: W. W. Norton, 1974), 121.

32. Jean Piaget, *The Child and Reality*, trans. Arnold Rosin (New York: Grossman, 1973), 2.

33. Jean Piaget, "The Significance of John Amos Comenius at the Present Time," in *John Amos Comenius on Education* (New York: Teachers College Press, 1967), 1–31.

34. Piaget, "The Significance of John Amos Comenius," 15–16.

35. Jacques Prévot, *L'Utopie Educative de Comenius* (Paris: Belin, 1981), 157.

36. Copple and Bredekamp, *Developmentally Appropriate Practice.*

37. Robert D. Hess, Susan D. Holloway, W. Patrick Dickson, and Gary G. Price, "Maternal Variables as Predictors of Children's School Readiness and Later Achievement in Vocabulary and Mathematics in Sixth Grade," *Child Development* 55 (1984): 1902–12.

38. Maris Vinovskis, *The Birth of Head Start: Preschool Education Policies in the Kennedy and Johnson Administrations* (Chicago: University of Chicago Press, 2005).

39. Quoted in an interview with David Kirp, "Life Way After Head Start," *New York Times Magazine*, November 21, 2004, 32.

40. Lawrence Schweinhart, *The High/Scope Perry Preschool Study Through Age 40* (Ypsilanti, Mich.: High/Scope Educational Research Foundation, 2005).

41. For a review of economic returns, see Robert Lynch, *Exceptional Returns: Economic, Fiscal, and Social Benefits in Early Childhood Development* (Washington, D.C.: Economic Policy Institute, 2004).

42. The NAEYC has warned against moving standardized testing into kindergarten and preschool. See David Hoff, "Made to Measure," *Education Week* (June 16, 1999): 21–28.

43. Preschool California, *California Kids Can't Wait to Learn: Preschool Opportunity for All* (Oakland, Calif., Preschool California, 2004), 1.

44. From an interview of Kotulak by John Bruer detailed in Bruer, *The Myth of the First Three Years: A New Understanding of Early Brain Development and Lifelong Learning* (New York: Free Press, 1999), 40–42.

45. See D. R. Neuspiel, "Starting Points: Meeting the Needs of Our Youngest Children" (book review), *Journal of the American Medical Association* 272 (1994): 1301.

46. Quoted in Bruer, *The Myth of the First Three Years,* 62.

47. Rima Shore, *Rethinking the Brain: New Insights into Early Development* (New York: Families and Work Institute, 1997), 39.

48. Charles Nelson and Floyd Bloom, "Child Development and Neuroscience," *Child Development* 68 (1997): 970–87; W. T. Greenough, "We Can't Just Focus on Ages Zero to Three," *Monitor* 28 (1997): 19–22.

49. Quoted from an interview in Bruer, *The Myth of the First Three Years.*

50. Joan Lombardi, *Time to Care: Redesigning Child Care to Promote Education, Support Families, and Build Communities* (Philadelphia, Pa.: Temple University Press, 2003), 46–47.

51. Detailed in Ruth Rosen, *The World Split Open: How the Modern Women's Movement Changed America* (New York: Viking, 2000).

52. Lombardi, *Time to Care,* 37.

53. Lynne Casper and Suzanne Bianchi, *Continuity and Change in the American Family* (Thousand Oaks, Calif.: Russell Sage, 2002).

54. Linda Waite and Mark Nielsen, "The Rise of the Dual-Earner Family, 1963–1997," in *Working Families: The Transformation of the American Home*, ed. Rosanna Hertz and Nancy Marshall, 23–41 (Berkeley: University of California Press, 2001).

55. Harriet Presser, *Working in a 24/7 Economy: Challenges for American Families* (New York: Russell Sage, 2003).

56. Liana Sayer, Suzanne Bianchi, and John Robinson, "Are Parents Investing Less in Children? Trends in Mothers' and Fathers' Time with Children," *American Journal of Sociology* 110 (2004): 1–43.

57. Sonya Michel, *Children's Interests, Mothers' Rights: The Shaping of America's Child Care Policy* (New Haven: Yale University Press, 1999).

58. Judith Warner, *Perfect Madness: Motherhood in the Age of Anxiety* (New York: Riverhead Books, 2005).

59. Suzanne Bianchi, "Maternal Employment and Time with Children: Dramatic Change or Surprising Continuity," *Demography* 37 (2000): 401–14.

60. Jane Waldfogel, Wen-Jui Han, and Jeanne Brooks-Gunn, "The Effects of Maternal Employment on Child Cognitive Development," *Demography* 39, no. 2 (2002): 369–92.

61. NICHD Early Child Care Research Network and Greg Duncan, "Modeling the Impacts of Child Care Quality on Children's Preschool Cognitive Development," *Child Development* 74, no. 5 (2003): 1454–75.

62. Rosemarie Putnam Tong, *Feminist Thought: A More Comprehensive Introduction* (Boulder, Colo.: Westview Press, 1998), 154–60.

63. Clare Ungerson, "Cash in Care," in *Care Work: Gender, Labor, and the Welfare State*, ed. Madonna Harrington Meyer, 68–88 (New York: Routledge, 2000).

64. Daniel Patrick Moynihan, *Maximum Feasible Misunderstanding: Community Action in the War on Poverty* (New York: Free Press, 1969).

65. Burton Weisbrod, "Institutional Form and Organizational Behavior," in *Private Action and the Public Good*, ed. Walter Powell and Elisabeth Clemens, 69–84 (New Haven, Conn.: Yale University Press, 1998); Paul DiMaggio and Helmut Anheir, "The Sociology of Nonprofit Organizations and Sectors," *Annual Review of Sociology* 16 (1990): 137–59.

66. Sally Lubeck, *Sandbox Society: Early Education in Black and White America: A Comparative Ethnography* (Philadelphia, Pa.: Falmer Press, 1985), 74–78.

67. Peter D. Hart Associates, "Public Opinion Research on Pre-kindergarten: Summary of Findings, March 2004," in *Kids Can't Wait to Learn: Public Opinion/Communication Tools* (Washington, D.C.: The Trust for Early Education, 2004).

68. Peter D. Hart Associates, "Making the Case for Quality Pre-K: A Report of Findings from Opinion Research Conducted for the Trust for Early Education," in *Kids Can't Wait to Learn: Public Opinion/Communication Tools* (Washington, D.C.: The Trust for Early Education, 2004).

69. Hart Associates, *Kids Can't Wait to Learn*.

70. Marjie Lundstrom, "Preschool Becomes Universally Popular with Californians," *Sacramento Bee*, February 12, 2004.

71. Claus Offe, *Construction of the Welfare State* (Cambridge, Mass.: MIT Press, 1984).

72. Josh Kagan, "Empowerment and Education: Civil Rights, Expert-Advocates, and Parent Politics in Head Start, 1964–1980," *Teachers College Record* 104 (2002): 516–62.

73. Report on Preschool Programs, "Bush Signs Florida Pre-K Bill, Begins Implementation Plan" (January 19, 2005): 15.

74. Kimber Bogard and Ruby Takanishi, "PK-3: An Aligned and Coordinated Approach to Education for Children 3 to 8 Years Old," *Social Policy Report* 19 (July 2005): 1–23. The *Social Policy Report* is published by the Society for Research in Child Development.

75. Lowell Rose and Alec Gallup, *Gallup Poll of the Public Attitudes Toward the Public Schools* (Bloomington, Ind.: Phi Delta Kappa, 2006).

76. Michael Katz, *Improving Poor People: The Welfare State, the "Underclass," and Urban Schools as History* (Princeton: Princeton University Press, 1997).

77. John Boli and John Meyer, "The Ideology of Childhood and the State," in *Organizations and Environments: Ritual and Rationality*, ed. John Meyer and W. Richard Scott, 217–41 (Beverly Hills, Calif.: Sage, 1983).

78. Max Weber, *The Theory of Social and Economic Organization*, trans. Talcott Parsons (London: Collier Macmillan, 1942); Emile Durkheim, *Education and Sociology*, trans. Paul Fauconnet (New York: Free Press, 1956).

79. National Governors Association, *Building the Foundation for Bright Futures: Final Report of the National Governors Association Task Force* (Washington, D.C.: National Governors Association Center for Best Practices, 2005); Gov. Granholm cited in *Report on Preschool Programs* (February 2, 2005): 22.

CHAPTER 3

1. Pseudonyms are used for individuals and organizations.

2. Cultural models, sometimes called cognitive scripts, have descriptive, causal, and prescriptive elements that specify what's seen as normal and accepted, and what's right and good. These models are cultural in that they come to be tacitly accepted by many members of a group, defined by heritage, language, or racial characteristics. Roy G. D'Andrade and Claudia Strauss, eds., *Human Motives and Cultural Models* (Cambridge: Cambridge University Press, 1995); Clifford Geertz, *Local Knowledge: Further Essays in Interpretive Anthropology* (New York: Basic Books, 1983), 7–93.

3. Susan Holloway, Bruce Fuller, Marylee Rambaud, and Costanza Eggers-Piérola, *Through My Own Eyes: Single Mothers and the Cultures of Poverty* (Cambridge, Mass.: Harvard University Press, 1997); Bruce Fuller, Susan Holloway, Marylee Rambaud,

and Costanza Eggers- Piérola, "How Do Mothers Choose Child Care? Alternative Cultural Models in Poor Neighborhoods," *Sociology of Education* 69, no. 2 (April 1996): 8–104.

4. Douglas Besharov and Nanzanin Samari, "Child Care After Welfare Reform," in *The New World of Welfare*, ed. Rebecca Blank and Ron Haskins (Washington, D.C.: Brookings Institution, 2001), 461–81.

5. To assess the validity of these ethnographic data and our interpretations of them, Pai triangulated across multiple informants, observations, and interviews and continually presented findings to Fuller's research group for critical feedback. Tentative findings were discussed with preschool staff and PreKare managers. Thanks are due Bridget O'Brien for her help in this process.

CHAPTER 4

1. The enrollment rate was estimated at 74 percent of all four-year-olds by state officials, according to Sandy Garrett and Ramona Paul, "Implementing Quality Pre-Kindergarten with High Standards of Learning" (paper, National Association for the Education of Young Children, November 2004). Bob Harbison calculated that in 2004, 67 percent of five-year-olds entering kindergarten had attended preschool (interview, October 7, 2005).

2. Steven Dow, interview by telephone, March 4, 2005.

3. Joe Eddins, interview by telephone, February 16, 2005.

4. Phil Dessauer, Jr., "Tulsa Area Community Profile, 2005" (Tulsa: Community Service Council of Greater Tulsa, 2005).

5. Terri Duggan Schwartzbeck and Mary Kusler, "Declining Enrollments Impact Teaching in the Great Plains States," *Wingspread Journal* (2005): 27–31.

6. Oklahoma sociologist Robert Lee Maril details the problems of family poverty in *Waltzing with the Ghost of Tom Joad: Poverty, Myth, and Low-Wage Labor in Oklahoma* (Norman: University of Oklahoma Press, 2000).

7. Pete Churchwell, interview by author, January 27, 2005.

8. Bob Harbison, interview by telephone, March 3, 2005.

9. U.S. Census Bureau, "Tulsa: State and County Quick Facts (2006)." http://quickfacts.census.gov/qfd/states/40/4075000.html.

10. Cleta Mitchell, interview by author, January 24, 2005.

11. On May 13, 1998, the legislation approved amended Title 70 of the state education code to include four-year-olds enrolled in half- or full-day preschool classrooms, in § 70-1-114 and § 70-11-103.7 (quality requirements).

12. This number, provided by Bob Harbison, is about a thousand students less than the number provided by Ramona Paul for the 1997–98 school year.

13. The history of the wider child care field is recounted in Phil Dessauer, Jr., "Tulsa Community Conference on Early Childhood Development Partners, Special Report" (Tulsa: Community Service Council of Greater Tulsa, 2002).

14. Ken Neal, "La Fortune's Question, Plus," *Tulsa World*, February 20, 2000.

15. "Draft of the Executive Order" (Tulsa: February 28, 2000) (courtesy of the Community Services Council of Greater Tulsa).

16. Governor's Task Force on Early Childhood Education, *Final Report: Executive Summary* (Oklahoma City: Oklahoma Institute for Child Advocacy, 2001). These developments are reported in a brief by legislative staffer Kim Brown, "Senator Fisher— Talking Points," provided in a personal communication dated May 31, 2005.

17. Darcy Ann Olsen, *Blueprint for a Nanny State* (Oklahoma City: Oklahoma Council of Public Affairs, 2001).

18. Kelly O'Meara, "Medical Abuse of Children? Parents File Law Suit Against Head Start Program," *Insight on the News*, September 11, 2000. Available at www.find articles.com/p/articles/mi_m1571/is_34_16/ai_65133101 (accessed February 28, 2006).

19. The legislative history is summarized in Ginnie Graham, "Bills Seek Establishment of State Early Childhood Advisory Board," *Tulsa World*, March 16, 2001.

20. Garrett and Paul, "Implementing Quality Pre-Kindergarten with High Standards of Learning."

21. Tulsa Public Schools fiscal data are taken from Charles Stidham, "Tulsa Public Schools: Early Childhood Membership Funding" (Tulsa: Education Service Center, 2005).

22. Charles Stidham, interview by author, January 26, 2005.

23. Charles Stidham, in personal communication, April 14, 2005, cited a spending worksheet titled "Early Childhood Membership Funding" (Tulsa: Tulsa Public Schools, January 25, 2005). The state education department reported that $72.7 million was allocated statewide for UPK in the 2003–04 school year, equaling about $2,409 per child before adding the district's fixed costs.

24. Melanie Poulter, *Young Children in Tulsa County: Facts at Your Fingertips* (Tulsa: Community Service Council of Greater Tulsa, 2003).

25. Interview by author with Head Start directors at the Native American Coalition of Tulsa, January 28, 2005.

26. Bill LaFortune, "Welcome from the Mayor of Tulsa," in Phil Dessauer, Jr., *Special Report: Tulsa Community Conference on Early Childhood Development* (Tulsa: Community Service Council of Greater Tulsa, 2002), ii.

27. Tulsa Public Schools, "Language Arts Pacing Calendar: Kindergarten" (Tulsa, 2005). TPS's Pam Brooks reported that the pacing schedule has "a very appropriate developmental flow" and that she is trying to use it in ways that afford professional discretion. Personal communication, September 13, 2005.

28. Tulsa Public Schools, "Pre-kindergarten Growth Inventory" (Tulsa, revised July 2002). The "report of student progress" that goes to parents of preschool children is more balanced and includes fourteen social-behavior gauges of development ranging from "follows directions," "respects authority," and "follows district, school, and class procedures" to "works independently" and "selects task and completes work."

29. Carol Rowland, interview by author, January 29, 2005.

30. Pam Brooks, interview by author, November 4, 2005.

31. Administration for Children and Families, Head Start Bureau, "Information Memorandum: Description of the NRS Child Assessment" (Washington, D.C.: U.S. Department of Health and Human Services, June 26, 2003).

32. Since Project Head Start's inception the program has been under pressure to demonstrate results. See Chapter 6 for a review of recent findings. A historical overview appears in Vinovskis, *The Birth of Head Start.*

33. Helen Taylor and Head Start Bureau, *Using Child Outcomes in Program Self-Assessment* (Washington, D.C.: U.S. Department of Health and Human Services, August 10, 2000).

34. Roundtable discussion with Cindy Lance, Ana Bañuelos, Darlene Martinez, Lisa Moore, Debra Naifeh, and Mariela Ortiz, January 27, 2005.

35. Data provided in Even Start fact sheet, personal communication from Cindy Lance, June 2, 2005. For a history of Even Start, see Maris Vinovskis, *History and Educational Policymaking* (New Haven: Yale University Press, 1999).

36. Quoted in Graham, "Promising Partnerships."

37. Interview with William Gormley, Jr., January 25, 2005.

38. Quoted in Linda Jacobson, "Oklahoma Pre-k Program Found Effective," *Education Week* 19 (October 29, 2003). The paper is William Gormley, Jr., and Deborah Phillips, *The Effects of Universal Pre-k in Oklahoma: Research Highlights and Policy Implications"* (Washington, D.C.: Center for Research on Children in the United States, Georgetown University, 2003).

39. William Gormley, Jr., Ted Gayer, Deborah Phillips, and Brittany Dawson, "The Effects of Universal Pre-k on Cognitive Development," *Developmental Psychology* 41 (2005): 872–84.

40. Gormley, *The Effects of Universal Pre-k in Oklahoma.*

41. Gary T. Henry and Dana K. Rickman, "Effects of Peers on Early Education Outcomes," *Economics of Education Review* (forthcoming).

42. Personal communication with William Gormley, Jr., November 11, 2004.

43. Pseudonyms are used for the parents.

44. Judy Feary, interview by author, January 27, 2005.

45. Maria Carlota Palacios, interview by author, April 20, 2005.

46. Harriet Patterson, interview by author, January 29, 2005.

47. Fully 500 parents of four-year-olds and 786 parents of kindergartners petitioned TPS to leave their home area in order to enter another elementary school in the 2004–05 school year. Thanks to Gary Lytle and Linda Wade at TPS for running this tabulation. Personal communication from Linda Wade dated January 27, 2005.

48. Dixie Reppe, interview by author, November 5, 2004.

49. Harry Oosahwee, interview by author, January 28, 2005.

50. I arrived soon after the Cherokee Casino Resort had opened in Catoosa, just outside Tulsa. A ribbon-cutting ceremony featuring Principal Chief Chad Smith was

followed by "three days of music, giveaways, and special events featuring Ty England, former guitarist for Garth Brooks." On the weekends, the casino organized swimsuit competitions for men and women. See *Cherokee Phoenix and Indian Advocate*, "CNE Holds Grand Opening for Catoosa Casino Resort," The Cherokee Nation—Tahlequah, Oklahoma, http://virtuosity.cherokee.org/Phoenix/2005/ PhoenixPage. asp?ID=1311 (accessed February 28, 2006)

51. W. Richard Scott and John W. Meyer, "The Organization of Societal Sectors: Propositions and Early Evidence," in *The New Institutionalism in Organizational Analysis*, ed. Walter W. Powell and Paul J. DiMaggio, 108–42 (Chicago: University of Chicago Press, 1991).

52. E. M. Forster, *A Passage to India* (San Diego: Harcourt Brace, 1984), 178.

53. Mark Greenberg of the Center for Law and Social Policy in Washington, D.C., interview by author, January 25, 2005.

CHAPTER 5

1. Terri Robison, interview by author, December 14, 2004.

2. Neal Kaufman, interview by author, February 29, 2005.

3. UCLA Center for Health Policy Research, "Ask CHIS: The California Health Interview Survey" (Los Angeles: University of California, Los Angeles, 2004).

4. Yolie Flores Aguilar, interview by author, December 16, 2004.

5. Quoted in Michael Finnegan and Jessica Garrison, "Villaraigosa TV Ad Hits Hahn on Ethics Question," *Los Angeles Times*, May 3, 2005.

6. Carla Rivera, "Universal Preschool Provider Celebrates Funding the 100th Facility in Los Angeles," *Los Angeles Times*, October 7, 2005.

7. Quoted in Kevin Starr, *Americans and the California Dream, 1850–1915* (New York: Oxford University Press, 1973), 167.

8. Joan Didion, *Where I Was From* (New York: Random House, 2003), 16–17, 189.

9. Cited in William Deverell, *Whitewashed Adobe: The Rise of Los Angeles and the Remaking of Its Mexican Past* (Berkeley: University of California Press, 2004), 2–3, 13.

10. Deverell, *Whitewashed Adobe*, 27.

11. Census data for 2000 and 2001 reported in Robert Suro and Audrey Singer, "Latino Growth in Metropolitan America: Changing Patterns, New Locations" (Washington, D.C.: Brookings Institution, July 2002).

12. Suro and Singer, "Latino Growth in Metropolitan America," 15.

13. Just over 45 percent of all foreign-born residents of Los Angeles are from Mexico; they numbered 2.1 million in 2000. Central Americans form the next largest group at 15 percent, followed by Asians and Pacific Islanders at 21 percent. See Georges Sabagh and Mehdi Bozorgmehr, "From 'Give Me Your Poor' to 'Save Our State': New York and Los Angeles as Immigrant Cities and Regions," in *New York and Los Angeles: Politics, Society, and Culture*, ed. David Halle, 99–131 (Chicago: University of Chicago Press, 2003).

14. David Halle, ed., *New York and Los Angeles: Politics, Society, and Culture* (Chicago: University of Chicago Press, 2003).

15. The concept of spatial inequality is developed by Andrew Beveridge and Susan Weber, "Race and Class in the Developing New York and Los Angeles Metropolises," in *New York and Los Angeles: Politics, Society, and Culture*, ed. David Halle, 49–78 (Chicago: University of Chicago Press, 2003).

16. Children's Planning Council, "SPA Council Demographic Profiles," County of Los Angeles, http://www.lapublichealth.org/childpc/data/ddata.asp, (accessed February, 28, 2006).

17. Census data for 2000 as reported by Geoffrey Mohan and Ann Simmons, "Diversity Spoken in 39 Languages," *Los Angeles Times*, June 16, 2004, 1.

18. T. C. Boyle, *The Tortilla Curtain* (New York: Penguin Books, 1996), 12.

19. Edward Blakely and Mary Snyder, *Fortress America: Gated Communities in the United States* (Washington, D.C.: Brookings Institution, 1999).

20. The Lakewood episode is discussed in Kevin Starr, *Coast of Dreams: California on the Edge, 1990–2003* (New York: Knopf, 2004), 308–14.

21. Kristine Zentgraf, "Through Economic Restructuring, Recession, and Rebound: The Continuing Importance of Latina Immigrant Labor in the Los Angeles Economy," in *Asian and Latino Immigrants in a Restructuring Economy: The Metamorphosis of Southern California*, ed. Marta López-Garza and David Diaz, 46–68 (Stanford: Stanford University Press, 2001).

22. Current Population Survey data analyzed by Jennifer Cheng, "At Home and School: Racial and Ethnic Gaps in Educational Preparedness," *California Counts Population Trends and Profiles* 3, no. 2 (November 2001).

23. Bridges et al., "Preschool for California's Children."

24. Shannon McConville and Paul Ong, "The Trajectory of Poor Neighborhoods in Southern California: 1970-2000" (Washington, D.C.: Brookings Institution, 2003).

25. Children's Planning Council, "SPA Council Demographic Profiles."

26. Jacquelyn McCroskey, *Walking the Collaboration Talk: Ten Lessons Learned from the Los Angeles County Children's Planning Council* (Los Angeles: Los Angeles County Children's Planning Council, 2003).

27. "A History of Major Legislation Affecting Child Care and Preschool Funding," *On the Capitol Doorstep* (2003): 1.

28. Estimates are based on data provided by Child Development Division, "Child Care and Preschool Programs: Local Assistance, All Funds" (Sacramento: Department of Education, 2001). Linda Parfitt (Child Development Division), personal communication with author, November 2003. State methods of contracting with schools and CBOs are examined in Schumacher et al., "All Together Now."

29. Rosen, *The World Split Open*.

30. Lombardi, *Time to Care*, reviews parts of this history on p. 131. My interview with Patty Siegel, January 13, 2005, also helped me to understand the contemporary significance of these early developments.

31. For our report on creation of the Child Care and Development Block Grants, see Bruce Fuller and Susan Holloway, "When the State Innovates: Interests and Institutions Create the Preschool Sector," in *Research in Sociology of Education*, vol. 11, ed. Aaron Pallas, 1–42 (Oxford: Elsevier Publishing, 1996).

32. Carla Rivera, "Southern California Need for Preschools Is Acute, Study Says," *Los Angeles Times*, July 19, 2002, B3.

33. Sandraluz Lara-Cinisomo and Anne Pebley, "Los Angeles County Young Children's Literacy Experiences, Emotional Well-being and Skills Acquisition: Results from the Los Angeles Family and Neighborhood Study" (Santa Monica: RAND Corporation, 2003).

34. Elias Lopez and Patricia de Cos, "Preschool and Child Care Enrollment in California" (Sacramento: California Research Bureau, State Library, 2004). This estimate is close to the 49 percent enrollment rate for children age three to five (but not yet in kindergarten) found in a UCLA survey conducted for the state First 5 Commission. See Moira Inkelas, Ericka Tullis, Robin Flint, Janel Wright, Rosina Becerra, and Neal Halfon, *Public Opinion on Child Care and Early Education, California 2001* (Los Angeles: University of California, Center for Healthier Children, Families and Communities, 2002).

35. Karoly and Bigelow, *The Economics of Investing in Universal Preschool in California*.

36. David Halle, ed., *New York and Los Angeles: Politics, Society, and Culture* (Chicago: University of Chicago Press, 2003) 32.

37. California Department of Education, "Ready to Learn: Quality Preschools for California in the Twenty-first Century" (Sacramento: Child Development Division, 1998).

38. Quoted in Carol Brydolf, "Toddler Tech: Making the Case for Universal Preschool," *California Schools* (Winter 2004).

39. Quoted by Leslie Weiss, "Free Preschool for All? California Department of Education Task Force Calls for Quality Public Programs for All Three- and Four-Year-olds," *Children's Advocate* (May–June 1998).

40. California State Department of Education, *Pre-kindergarten Learning and Development Guidelines* (Sacramento: Child Development Division and Health and Education Communications Consultants, 2000). The quoted passages appear on pp. v, 13, 16, 19, and 20.

41. On the Capitol Doorstep, "Governor Responds to Child Care Questions and Other News" (e-mail bulletin, Sacramento, November 1, 2002).

42. A review of this effort to repeal Reiner's state Proposition 10 is in Magellan Health Services, "Prop. 10: These Cigarettes Are Good for Children," www.magellanassist.com/mem/library/default.asp?TopicId=268&CategoryId=0&ArticleId=46, accessed May 1, 2005.

43. Disclosure: our research center was asked to evaluate the commission's teacher development efforts. The evaluation reports appear on-line at pace.berkeley.edu.

44. A review of the task force report is in California First 5 Children and Families Commission, "Recommendations of the School Readiness Working Group for the New Master Plan for Education," *Building Blocks* 2, no. 1 (March 2002).

45. The figure of 78,366 four-year-olds not enrolled in preschool is from Karen Hill-Scott, "Universal Preschool: Master Plan" (Los Angeles: First 5 LA, 2004), 31. Assuming that the enrollment rate would top out at about 70 percent of all four-year-olds, Hill-Scott estimated an annual need of 32,397 additional preschool slots.

46. Quoted in Carla Rivera, "A Compromise on Preschool Plan: After Weeks of Debate County Officials Agree on the Makeup of a New Agency to Oversee $600 Million Program," *Los Angeles Times*, July 13, 2004, B3.

47. Interview of Don Knabe, with John Musella and Linda Tarnoff present, by author, March 2, 2005.

48. Summarized by Evelyn Larrubia and Carla Rivera, "Reiner Urges Preschool Access for All," *Los Angeles Times*, June 14, 2002, B3.

49. Quoted in Carla Rivera, "Universal Preschool a Daunting Task: Experts Say a Plan for a Countywide System Will Require Consensus-Building, Political Support," *Los Angeles Times*, September 16, 2002, B1.

50. Carla Rivera, "Veteran Educator to Head County's Preschool Effort," *Los Angeles Times*, November 15, 2002, B5.

51. Rob Reiner, "Presentation at the Universal Preschool Master Plan Advisory Committee" (Los Angeles, Our Lady of the Angels Cathedral, June 20, 2003).

52. For the basic contours and themes pressed by the subcommittee, see Hill-Scott, "Universal Preschool," 33–41.

53. Imelda Foley, interview by author, March 3, 2004.

54. Rivera, "Universal Preschool a Daunting Task," B1.

55. "Once Looked Upon as Child's Play, Preschool Education Is Now Serious Business," *California Educator* 5, no. 6 (March 2001).

56. Inkelas et al., *Public Opinion on Child Care and Early Education*.

57. Peter D. Hart Associates, "Is California Ready for School Readiness? A Statewide Survey of Attitudes Toward Early Education" (Sacramento: First 5 California, 2003), 8.

58. Raymond Buriel and Maria Hurtado-Ortiz, "Child Care Practices and Preferences of Native and Foreign-Born Latina Mothers and Euro-American Mothers," *Hispanic Journal of Behavioral Science* 22 (2000): 314–31.

59. Neal Halfon, Margaret Bridges, Jeanne Brooks-Gunn, Bruce Fuller, Alice Kuo, and Michael Regalado, "Mexican American Preschool Study" (unpublished manuscript, Los Angeles: University of California, Los Angeles, School of Medicine, 2005). Data analysis by Yueh-wen Chang.

60. Children's Planning Council, "Universal Preschool Initiative: Parent Survey Findings Report" (Los Angeles: Los Angeles County, 2003).

61. K. Malaske-Samu and A. Muranaka, *Child Care Counts: An Analysis of the Supply and Demand* (Los Angeles: County Chief Administrative Office, Child Care Planning Committee, 2000).

62. Children's Planning Council, "The Family Child Care Profession: Position Paper by SPA 8 Child Care Workgroup" (Los Angeles: Los Angeles County, 2003).

63. Michelle Cerecerez, interview by author, November 11 and December 10, 2004. Also see Jenya Cassidy, "Labor Movement Frontiers: Organizing the Child Care Workforce," *On the Move* (Fall 2003): 1–11. *On the Move* is the newsletter of the University of California Labor Center for Research and Education, Berkeley.

64. John Jackson, interview by author, September 26, 2003.

65. Karin Hill-Scott, "The Effects of Subsidized, Private, and Unregulated Child Care on Family Functioning," in *Continuity and Discontinuity of Experience in Child Care*, ed. Donald Peters and Susan Kontos, 147–67 (Norwood, N.J.: Ablex Publishing, 1987).

66. Quotes from Cooper and Hill-Scott come from a small meeting held on October 3, 2005 in downtown Los Angeles.

67. Patty Siegel, interview by author, January 13, 2005.

68. These data are detailed in Bruce Fuller, Alejandra Livas, and Margaret Bridges, "How to Expand and Improve Preschool in California: Ideals, Evidence, and Policy Options" (Working Paper 05-1, University of California and Policy Analysis for California Education, Berkeley, 2005).

69. Laurie Olsen, "Ready or Not? A California Tomorrow Think Piece on School Readiness and Immigrant Communities," *California Tomorrow* (Fall 2004): 9. Also, see Hedy Nai-Lin Chang, Amy Muckelroy, and Dora Pulido-Tobiassen, *Looking In, Looking Out: Redefining Child Care and Early Education for a Diverse Society* (monograph, Oakland: California Tomorrow, 1996).

70. Antonia Lopez, interview by author, June 2003.

71. Parent Voices, "Parent Principles on Universal Preschool" (San Francisco: Parent organization housed at the California Child Care Resource and Referral Network, 2003).

72. Children's Planning Council, "The Family Child Care Profession," 12.

73. The overall structure of the L.A. program was sketched in agenda materials distributed for Hill-Scott's September 19, 2003, meeting. The final report was approved and published by the First 5 LA commission in February 2004 (Culver City, Calif.: Hill-Scott & Company, 2004).

74. Quoted in Rivera, "A Compromise on Preschool Plan," B3.

75. Despite Hill-Scott's faith in the efficacy of preschooling, she also told me: "I stand firmly on the ideal of parent engagement as fundamental to early education . . . If the 'the program' alone were the solution, we would have ended inequality of educational outcomes a long time ago." Personal communication, November 4, 2005.

76. Karen Hill-Scott, "Invest in Better Learning Act, Sponsored by the CTA" (Los Angeles: Karen Hill-Scott & Company, October 27, 2003). Memo transmitted via the Web, October 29, 2003.

77. Rob Reiner, "Improving Classroom Education Act: Text of the Measure" (Sacramento: Office of the Attorney General, submitted November 14, 2003).

78. California Teachers Association, "Improving Classroom Education Act Introduced for November Ballot" (Sacramento: Press Relations Office, November 14, 2002).

79. Personal communication from Karen Hill-Scott, November 5, 2003.

80. Personal communication from Ben Austin, November 11, 2003.

81. Suzanne Pardington, "Preschool Plan Draws Criticism," *Contra Costa Times*, November 7, 2003.

82. Rob Reiner, "Presentation at the Universal Preschool Master Plan Advisory Committee," 8.

83. Antonia Lopez, "Meeting Notes, April 1, 2004" (Sacramento: National Council for La Raza, 2004).

84. Jennifer Coleman, "Anti-tax Groups Say School Initiative Would Hike Homeowners' Taxes," *North County Times*, April 7, 2004.

85. Karin Klein and editorial board, "Lessons Learned," *Los Angeles Times*, April 13, 2004, B8.

86. Letter from Lois Salisbury to grantees of the Packard Foundation, dated April 14, 2004.

87. Phil Yost, "Plan for Free Preschool Nears Ballot," *San Jose Mercury News*, November 18, 2005. www.mercurynews.com/mld/mercurynews/living/education, accessed November 19, 2006.

88. Speech quoted by Bruce Fuller, "Preschool Reform Measure Won't Close Learning Gaps for Poor," *San Jose Mercury News*, February 26, 2006, B7.

89. These quotations from state political figures are from Phil Yost, "Plan for Free Preschool Nears Ballot," *San Jose Mercury News*, November 18, 2005; Dana Hull, "Rob Reiner Pitches Preschool Plan to Leaders," *San Jose Mercury News*, December 14, 2005, B4; Seema Mehta, "Rural Preschool Provides a Preview of What May Be," *Los Angeles Times*, February 14, 2006.

90. Held October 3, 2005, at the Los Angeles County child care coordinator's office.

91. Mark Baldassare, *PPIC Statewide Survey: Special Survey on Education* (San Francisco: Public Policy Institute of California, 2006).

92. Dan Morain, "Reiner Takes Leave from Panel on Children," *Los Angeles Times*, February 25, 2006, www.latimes.com/news/local/la-me-reiner25feb, accessed February 25, 2006.

93. Dan Morain, "First 5 Panel Seeks Missing Funds," *Los Angeles Times*, April 14, 2006, www.latimes.com/news/local/la-me-preschool14April, accessed April 14, 2006.

94. Daniel Weintraub, "Tax-Financed Campaign to Change Minds on Preschool," *Sacramento Bee*, March 9, 2006, www.modbee.com/opinion/state/weintraub/story/14227897p, accessed March 12, 2006.

95. Quoted by Dan Morain, "Reiner Quits First 5 Panel," *Los Angeles Times*, March 30, 2005, www.latimes.com/news/local/la-me-30March, accessed March 30, 2005.

96. This analysis was conducted by Bruce Fuller and Alejandra Livas, *Proposition 82 — California's "Preschool for All" Initiative* (Berkeley and Stanford: Policy Analysis for California Education, 2006).

97. Los Angeles Times, "No on Proposition 82: Universal Preschool Is Too Expensive, Too Bureaucratic, and Could Harm K-12," *Los Angeles Times*, May 21, 2006, www.latimes.com/news/opinion/editorials/la-ed-preschool21may, accessed May 21, 2006.

98. Maryanne O'Sullivan, Say 'Yes' to Quality Preschool," *Tracy Press Enterprise*, June 5, 2006, www.tracypress.com/voice/2006-06-05-preschool.php, accessed July 7, 2006.

99. Nancy Strohl et al., *Preschool for All Initiative Concerns* (San Francisco: Child Care Law Center, 2005).

100. Schwarzenegger continued to push preschool expansion, even after Proposition 82 lost in the June 2006 election, and the legislature approved the governor's smaller-scale program. Legislative Analyst's Office, "Governor's Preschool Expansion." Sacramento, May 17, 2006.

101. Quoted by Carla Rivera, "Voters Widely Back Measure on Preschools," *Los Angeles Times*, March 13, 2006, B1.

102. Karin Klein, "Scary Preschool Utopia," *Los Angeles Times*, June 5, 2005, B8.

103. Bruce Fuller, Katie Gesicki, and Thea Sweo, *Community Voices: Preschool Directors Speak on Policy Options* (Berkeley and Stanford: Policy Analysis for California Education, 2006).

104. Daffodil Altan, "A Time-honored Alternative to Universal Preschool," *San Francisco Chronicle*, December 28, 2005, B7.

105. Evidence is reviewed in Bruce Fuller, Margaret Bridges, and Alejandra Livas, *How to Expand and Improve Preschool in California*, working paper 05-1 (Berkeley and Stanford: Policy Analysis for California Education 2005).

106. This episode was reported by the Associated Press's Juliet Williams, "Preschool Initiative Would Benefit Few, Study Finds," *Contra Costa Times*, April 5, 2005, A5.

107. Dan Morain, "Private Gifts Boost Races," *Los Angeles Times*, May 26, 2006, www.latimes.com/news/printedition/california/la-me-money26may, accessed June 10, 2006.

108. Mark DiCamillo and Mervin Field, "Voters Moving to the No Side on Prop. 82." San Francisco: The Field Poll, June 3, 2006.

109. Special thanks to Farnaz Calafi and Jill Darling Richardson at the *Los Angeles Times* for running tabulations from their exit poll data. Personal communication, June 8, 2006.

110. Los Angeles Universal Preschool, "Operating Guidelines for Child Care Centers, 2005–2006" (Los Angeles: LA-UP, First 5 Children and Families Commission, 2005).

111. Jürgen Habermas, "Three Normative Models of Democracy," in *Democracy and Difference: Contesting the Boundaries of the Political*, ed. Seyla Benhabib, 22–30 (Princeton: Princeton University Press, 1996).

CHAPTER 6

1. Tamar Lewin, "The Need to Invest in Young Children," *New York Times*, January 11, 2006. Sawhill and her colleagues argue that if the magnitude of benefits reported for the Perry Preschool could be realized through a national program (and if the conditions of the Perry control group of poor black families with no other child care options had remained unchanged over the past four decades), then the economic returns of the program would reach $988 billion. These analysts, funded in part by the Pew Charitable Trusts, "assume that the effect of the preschool initiative on educational attainment is the same for all children of all SES (socioeconomic status groups)." See Walter T. Dickens, Isabel Sawhill, and Jeffrey Tebbs, "The Effects of Investing in Early Education on Economic Growth" (draft manuscript, Washington, D.C., Brookings Institution, 2006).

2. Rusty Hammer, "Investing in 4 Year Olds," *Los Angeles Times*, August 17, 2005.

3. Cooper and Dukakis, *Kids Can't Wait to Learn*, 16.

4. Sue Urahn, interview by author, August 23, 2005.

5. The Perry Preschool is discussed in detail in John Berrueta-Clement, Lawrence Schweinhart, W. Steven Barnett, Ann Epstein, and David Weikart, *Changed Lives: The Effects of the Perry Preschool Program on Youths Through Age 19* (Ypsilanti, Mich.: High/Scope Press, 1984).

6. Berrueta-Clement et al., *Changed Lives*, 8.

7. Lawrence Schweinhart, Jeanne Montie, Zongping Xiang, W. Steven Barnett, Clive Belfield, and Milagros Nores, *Lifetime Effects: The High/Scope Perry Preschool Study Through Age 40* (Ypsilanti, Mich.: High/Scope Press, 2005).

8. Lawrence Schweinhart et al, *Lifetime Effects*, 47, 52, 56.

9. Frances Campbell and Craig Ramey, "Cognitive and School Outcomes for High-Risk African-American Students in Middle Adolescence," *American Educational Research Journal* 32 (1995): 743–72; Frances Campbell, Craig Ramey, Elizabeth Pungello, Joseph Sparling and S. Miller-Johnson, "Early Childhood Education: Young Adult Outcomes from the Abecedarian Project," *Applied Developmental Science* 6 (2002): 42–57.

10. W. Steven Barnett and Jason Hustedt, "Head Start's Lasting Benefits," *Infants and Young Children* 18 (2005): 16–24.

11. Lynn Karoly, Peter Greenwood, Susan Everingham, Jill Houbé, Rebecca Kilburn, Peter Rydell, Matthew Sanders, and James Chiesa, *Investing in Our Children: What We Know and Don't Know About the Costs and Benefits of Early Childhood Interventions* (Santa Monica, Calif.: RAND Corporation, 1998).

12. Schweinhart et al., *Lifetime Effects.*

13. California School Boards Association, "Annual Meeting Program Guide for Student Achievement Symposium on Preschool" (Sacramento, 2005).

14. The CPC program is detailed in Arthur Reynolds, "Effects of a Preschool Plus Follow-on Intervention for Children at Risk," *Developmental Psychology* 30 (1994): 787–804. RAND researchers compared the CPC model to a universal preschool model in the California context in Karoly and Bigelow, *The Economics of Investing in Universal Preschool in California.*

15. Interviews and visit to the Hansberry Child-Parent Center on September 9, 2005.

16. Arthur Reynolds at the University of California, Berkeley, March 3, 2006, and personal communication, March 14, 2006. Effects sizes that are linked to particular features of the Chicago child-parent centers are reported in a series of papers: see Arthur Reynolds, Judy Temple, Dylan Robertson, and Emily Mann, "Long-term Effects of an Early Childhood Intervention on Educational Achievement and Juvenile Arrest," *Journal of the American Medical Association* 285 (2001): 2339–49; Arthur Reynolds, Judy Temple, Dylan Robertson, and Emily Mann, "Age 21 Cost-Benefit Analysis of the Title I Chicago Child-Parent Centers," *Educational Evaluation and Policy Analysis* 24 (2002): 267–303; Melissa Clements, Arthur Reynolds, and Edmond Hickey, "Site-level Predictors of School and Social Competence in the Chicago Child-Parent Centers," *Early Childhood Research Quarterly* 19 (2004): 273–96.

17. For a detailed comparison of effect sizes for programs serving young children, see Duncan, "Modeling the Impacts of Child Care Quality on Children's Preschool Cognitive Development," 1454–75.

18. Westinghouse Learning Corporation and Ohio University, "The Impact of Head Start: An Evaluation of the Effects of Head Start on Children's Cognitive and Affective Development," report to the Office of Economic Opportunity (Athens, Ohio: Ohio University, 1969).

19. Ruth Hubbell McKey, Larry Condelli, and Harriet Ganson, "The Impact of Head Start on Children, Families and Communities, Final Report of the Head Start Evaluation, Synthesis and Utilization Project" (Washington, D.C.: U.S. Department of Health and Human Services, 1985).

20. The evaluation design and first-year findings appear in Westat et al., *Head Start Impact Study: First Year Findings* (Washington, D.C.: Office of Planning, Research and Evaluation, U.S. Department of Health and Human Services, 2005).

21. Westat et al., "Head Start FACES Study 2000: A Whole-Child Perspective on Program Performance, Fourth Progress Report" (Washington D.C.: U.S. Department of Heath and Human Services, 2003).

22. John Love et al., "The Effectiveness of Early Head Start for 3-year-old Children and Their Parents: Lessons for Policy and Programs," *Developmental Psychology,* 41 (2005): 885–901.

23. Special thanks to Janet Currie for improving our review of the Head Start evaluations. The initial results from the experimental design appear in Westat et al., *Head Start Impact Study: First Year Findings* (Washington, D.C.: Office of Planning, Research and Evaluation, U.S. Department of Health and Human Services, 2005).

24. Gary Henry, Laura Henderson, Bentley Ponder, Craig Gordon, Andrew Mashburn, and Dana Rickman, *Report of the Findings from the Early Childhood Study, 2001–2002* (Atlanta: Georgia State University, Andrew Young School of Policy Studies, 2003).

25. Gary Resnick et al., *Second Year Report on Early Childhood Education Programming in the 20 Abbott School Districts: Program Implementation and Children's School Readiness* (Trenton: New Jersey Departments of Human Services and Education, 2002).

26. W. Steven Barnett, Cynthia Lamy, and Kwanghee Jung, "The Effects of State Prekindergarten Programs on Young Children's School Readiness in Five States" (New Brunswick, N.J.: National Institute for Early Education Research, Rutgers University, 2005). Barnett argues that standardizing scores by age is unnecessary, since he believes these scales are not sufficiently sensitive to ages in months for specific subgroups. Gormley and Phillips, who also employed the regression-discontinuity technique in their Tulsa study, controlled on child age before estimating preschool effects.

27. Susanna Loeb, Bruce Fuller, Sharon Lynn Kagan, and Bidemi Carrol, "Child Care in Poor Communities: Early Learning Effects of Type, Quality, and Stability," *Child Development* 75 (2004): 47–65. To place these findings in the context of related studies, see Martha Zaslow, Kristin Moore, Jennifer Brooks, Pamela Morris, Kathryn Tout, Zakia Redd, and Carol Emig, "Experimental Studies of Welfare Reform and Children," *Future of Children* 12 (2002): 79–95; Pamela Morris, Ellen Scott, and Andrew London, "Effects on Children as Parents Transition from Welfare to Employment," in *Good Parents or Good Workers? How Policy Shapes Families' Daily Lives*, ed. Jill Berrick and Bruce Fuller, 87–116 (New York: Palgrave, 2005).

28. Janet Currie and Duncan Thomas, "Does Head Start Make a Difference?" *American Economic Review* 85 (1995): 241–64; Janet Currie and Duncan Thomas, "Does Head Start Help Hispanic Children?" *Journal of Public Economics* 74 (1999): 235–62; Eliana Garces, Duncan Thomas, and Janet Currie, "Longer-term Effects of Head Start," *American Economic Review* 92 (2002): 999–1012.

29. Janet Currie, "Early Childhood Education Programs," *Journal of Economic Perspectives* 15 (2001): 213–38; Janet Currie and Duncan Thomas, "School Quality and the Longer-term Effects of Head Start," *Journal of Human Resources* 35 (2000): 755–74.

30. Katherine Magnuson, Christopher Ruhm, and Jane Waldfogel, "Does Prekindergarten Improve School Preparation and Performance?" (Working Paper 10452, National Bureau of Economic Research, Cambridge, 2004).

31. Descriptive statistics reported in Duncan, "Modeling the Impacts of Child Care Quality on Children's Preschool Cognitive Development," 1463.

32. The proportion of time spent in a preschool center was derived from an ordinal count of the incidence of being enrolled a maximum of five times every four months between the child's 27th and 54th month. See Duncan, "Modeling the Impacts of Child Care Quality on Children's Preschool Cognitive Development."

33. Loeb et al., "How Much Is Too Much?" (forthcoming).

34. NICHD Early Child Care Research Network, "Early Child Care and Children's Development in the Primary Grades," *American Educational Research Journal* 42 (2005): 537–570. Russell Rumberger and Loan Tran, "Preschool Participation and the Cognitive and Social Development of Language Minority Children" (Santa Barbara: University of California Language Minority Research Institute, 2006).

35. Katherine Magnuson, Christopher J. Ruhm, and Jane Waldfogel, *Does Prekindergarten Improve School Preparation and Performance?*, Working Paper 10452 (Cambridge, Mass.: National Bureau of Economic Research, 2004).

36. David R. Francis, review of "Does Pre-kindergarten Improve School Preparation and Performance?" by Katherine Magnuson, posted by National Bureau of Economic Research, www.nber.org/digest/mar05/w10452.html (accessed March 10, 2006).

37. Belsky's original finding, drawing from the NICHD data, appears in NICHD Early Child Care Research Network, "Does Amount of Time Spent in Child Care Predict Socio-emotional Adjustment During the Transition to Kindergarten?" *Child Development* 74 (2003): 976–1005. The question was originally raised in Belsky and Laurence Steinberg, "The Effects of Day Care: A Critical Review," *Child Development* 49 (1978): 929–49; Magnuson, "Does Pre-kindergarten Improve School Preparation and Performance?"

38. This episode is summarized by Sandra Scarr, Deborah Phillips, and Kathleen McCartney, "Facts and Fantasies in Child Care," *Psychological Science* 1 (1990): 26–33.

39. For a review of this literature on child health outcomes, see Janet Currie, "Health Disparities and Gaps in School Readiness," *Future of Children* 15 (2005): 117–38.

40. Loeb et al., "How Much Is Too Much?" (forthcoming).

41. NICHD Early Child Care Research Network, "Does Amount of Time Spent in Child Care Predict Socio-emotional Adjustment?"

42. Arthur Reynolds, "One Year of Preschool or Two: Does It Matter?" *Early Childhood Research Quarterly* 10 (1995): 1–31.

43. Wen-jui Han, Jane Waldfogel, and Jeanne Brooks-Gunn, "The Effects of Early Maternal Employment on Later Cognitive and Behavioral Outcomes," *Journal of Family and Marriage* 63 (2001): 336–54. A portion of these findings were earlier foreshadowed in the analysis of Nazli Baydar and Jeanne Brooks-Gunn, "Effects of Maternal Employment and Child-care Arrangements on Preschoolers' Cognitive and Behavioral Outcomes: Evidence from the Children of the National Longitudinal Survey of Youth," *Developmental Psychology* 27 (1991): 932–45.

44. Jane Waldfogel, Wen-jui Han, and Jeanne Brooks-Gunn, "The Effects of Early Maternal Employment on Child Cognitive Development," *Demography* 39 (2002): 369–92.

45. Susan C. Crockenberg and Esther M. Leerkes, "Infant Temperament Moderates Associations Between Childcare Type and Quantity and Externalizing and Internalizing Behaviors at 2 Years," *Infant Behavior and Development* 28 (2005): 20–35.

46. Kathryn Tout, Michelle de Hann, Elizabeth K. Campbell, and Megan R. Gunnar, "Social Behavior Correlates of Cortisol Activity in Child Care: Gender Differences and Time-of-day Effects," *Child Development* 69 (1998): 1247–62.

47. Andrea C. Dettling, Megan R. Gunnar, and Bonny Donzella, "Cortisol Levels of Young Children in Full-day Childcare Centers: Relations with Age and Temperament," *Psychoneuroendocrinology* 24 (1999): 519–36.

48. Duncan, "Modeling the Impacts of Child Care Quality on Children's Preschool Cognitive Development."

49. David Blau, *The Child Care Problem: An Economic Analysis* (New York: Russell Sage Foundation, 2001).

50. Loeb et al., "Child Care in Poor Communities." The effects of discrete elements of quality may differentially shape children's cognitive versus social development. See, for example, Margaret Burchinal, Ellen Peisner-Feinberg, Donna Bryant, and Richard Clifford, "Children's Social and Cognitive Development and Child-care Quality: Testing for Differential Associations Related to Poverty, Gender, or Ethnicity," *Applied Developmental Science* 4 (2000): 149–65.

51. Martha J. Zaslow, "Variation in Child Care Quality and Its Implications for Children," *Journal of Social Issues* 47 (1991): 125–34.

52. NICHD Early Child Care Research Network, "Characteristics of Infant Child Care: Factors Contributing to Positive Caregiving," *Early Childhood Research Quarterly* 11 (1996): 266–306.

53. Alison Clarke-Stewart and Virginia Allhusen, *What We Know About Child Care* (Cambridge, Mass.: Harvard University Press, 2005), 108.

54. Margaret Burchinal, Joanne Roberts, Laura Nabors, and Donna Bryant, "Quality of Center Childcare and Infant and Language Development," *Child Development* 67 (1996): 606–20.

55. P. Blatchford, H. Goldstein, C. Martin, and W. Brown, "A Study of Class Size Effects in English School Reception Year Classes," *British Educational Research Journal* 28, no. 2 (2002).

56. For example, see Laurence Schweinhart and David Weikart, "The High/Scope Preschool Curriculum Study Through Age 23," *Early Childhood Research Quarterly* 12, no. 2 (1997): 117–43, for a description of their curricular philosophy and the methods used in the Perry Preschool.

57. Stipek et al., "Parents' Beliefs About Appropriate Education for Young Children."

58. Richard Marcon, "Moving up the Grades: Relationship Between Preschool Model and Later School Success," *Early Childhood Research and Practice* 4, no. 1 (2002).

59. Reviewed by David Yaden and his colleagues at the University of Southern California; see David Yaden, Robert Rueda, Tina Tsai, and Alberto Esquinca, "Issues in Early Childhood Education for English Learners," in *Contemporary Perspectives in Early Childhood Education*, ed. Bernard Spodek and Olivia Saracho, 215–42 (San Francisco: Jossey-Bass, 2004).

60. Grover Whitehurst, David Arnold, Jeffery Epstein, Andrea Angell, Meagan Smith, and Janet Fischel, "A Picture Book Reading Intervention in Day Care and Home for Children from Low-income Families, *Developmental Psychology* 30 (1994): 679–89.

61. Walter Gilliam and Edward Zigler, "A Critical Meta-analysis of Evaluations of State-funded Preschool from 1977 to 1998: Implications for Policy, Service Delivery, and Program Evaluation," *Early Childhood Research Quarterly* 15 (2000): 441–73; Marcy Whitebook et al., *Estimating the Size and Components of the U.S. Child Care Workforce and Caregiving Population* (Seattle: Human Services Policy Center, 2002).

62. W. Norton Grubb and Marvin Lazerson, "Child Care, Government Financing, and the Public Schools: Lessons from the California Children's Centers," *School Review* (November 1977): 22.

63. David Blau, "The Production of Quality in Child Care Centers: Another Look," *Applied Developmental Science, Special Issue: The Effects of Quality Care on Child Development* 4, no. 3 (2000).

64. This problem with the first generation of quality studies, circa 1970 through the mid-1990s, is discussed in Fuller et al., "How to Expand and Improve Preschool in California."

65. NICHD Early Child Care Research Network, "Characteristics and Quality of Child Care for Toddlers and Preschoolers," *Applied Developmental Psychology* 4 (2000): 116–35.

66. Sharon Ritchie and Carollee Howes, "Program Practices, Caregiver Stability, and Child–Caregiver Relationships," *Journal of Applied Developmental Psychology* 24 (2003): 497–516; NICHD Early Child Care Research Network, "Child-care Structure, Process and Outcome: Direct and Indirect Effects of Child-care Quality on Young Children's Development," *Psychological Science* 13 (2002).

67. Janet Currie and Matthew Neidel, "Getting Inside the Black Box of Head Start Quality: What Matters and What Doesn't?" *Economics of Education Review* (forthcoming).

68. Carollee Howes, Ellen Galinsky, and Susan Kontos, "Child Care Caregiver and Attachment," *Social Development* 7 (1998): 25–36; NICHD Early Child Care Research Network, "Nonmaternal Care and Family Factors in Early Development," *Journal of Applied Development Psychology* 22 (2001): 457–92.

69. Carollee Howes, Deborah Phillips, and Marcy Whitebook, "Thresholds of Quality: Implications for the Social Development of Children," *Child Development* 63 (1992): 449–60.

70. Blau, "The Production of Quality in Child Care Centers: Another Look"; Margaret Burchinal, Debbie Cryer, Richard Clifford and Carollee Howes, "Caregiver Training and Classroom Quality in Child Care Centers," *Applied Developmental Science* 6, no. 1 (2002); Carollee Howes, "Children's Experiences in Center-Based Child Care as a Function of Teacher Background," *Merrill-Palmer Quarterly* 43 (1997): 404–25; Howes et al., "Thresholds of Quality"; Lesley, Phillipsen, Margaret Burchinal, Carollee Howes, and Debby Cryer, "The Prediction of Process Quality from Structural Features of Child Care," *Early Childhood Research Quarterly* 12 (1997): 281–303.

71. Gary Henry, Bentley Ponder, Dana Rickman, Andrew Mashburn, Laura Henderson, and Craig Gordon, *An Evaluation of the Implementation of Georgia's Pre-K Program: Report of the Findings from the Georgia Early Childhood Study, 2002–2003* (Atlanta: Georgia State University, Andrew Young School of Policy Studies, 2004).

72. For example, see Margaret Burchinal et al., "Caregiver Training and Classroom Quality in Child Care Centers."

73. For example, Robert C. Pianta and Megan W. Stuhlman, "Teacher-Child Relationships and Children's Success in the First Years of School," *School Psychology Review* 33 (2004): 444–58.

74. Robert C. Pianta and the NICHD Study of Child Care and Youth Development, "Academic and Social Advantages for At-Risk Students Placed in High-Quality First Grade Classrooms," *Child Development* (forthcoming).

75. Loeb et al., "Child Care in Poor Communities."

76. Alison Wishard, Eva Marie Shivers, Carollee Howes, and Sharon Ritchie, "Child Care Program and Teacher Practices: Associations with Quality and Children's Experiences," *Early Childhood Research Quarterly* 18 (2003): 65–103.

77. Differences in teachers' attributes are reviewed in Fuller et al., "How to Expand and Improve Preschool in California."

78. Henry et al., *Report of the Findings from the Early Childhood Study, 2001–2002.*

79. Gary Henry and Craig Gordon, "Competition in the Sandbox: A Test of the Effects of Preschool Competition on Educational Outcomes," *Journal of Policy Analysis and Management* 25 (2006): 97–127.

80. Gary Resnick, A. Sorongon, D. Klayn, R. Hubbell-McKay, and J. DeWolfe," Second Year Report on Early Childhood Programming in the 30 Abbott School Districts," (Trenton: New Jersey Department of Human Services and Department of Education, 2002), 79. Erain Applewhite and Lesley Hirsch, *The Abbott Preschool Program: Fifth Year Report on Enrollment and Budget* (Newark, N.J.: Education Law Center, 2003).

81. Peggy Daly Pizzo and Elizabeth Edwards Tufankjian, "A Persistent Pattern of Progress: Parent Outcomes in Longitudinal Studies of Head Start Children and Families," in *The Head Start Debates*, ed. Edward Zigler and Sally Styfco, 193–214 (Baltimore, Md.: Brookes Publishing, 2004).

CHAPTER 7

1. Susan Chira, "Hispanic Families Use Alternatives to Day Care, Study Finds," *New York Times*, April 6, 1994, A19.

2. These findings appear in Fuller et al., "Family Selection of Child Care Centers."

3. Oscar Lewis, *La Vida: A Puerto Rican Family in the Culture of Poverty* (New York: Random House, 1965), xlv.

4. Lisbeth Schorr and Daniel Schorr, *Within Our Reach: Breaking the Cycle of Disadvantage* (New York: Anchor Press, 1988), 149.

5. William Julius Wilson, *The Truly Disadvantaged: The Inner City, the Under Class, and Public Policy* (Chicago: University of Chicago Press, 1987), 8.

6. Cooper and Dukakis, *Kids Can't Wait to Learn*, 16.

7. Antonia Lopez, quoted in Laurie Olsen, "Ready or Not? A California Tomorrow Think Piece on School Readiness and Immigrant Communities" (Oakland: California Tomorrow, 2004), 12.

8. Social anthropologist Adam Kuper offers an illuminating discussion of this post-Enlightenment debate in *Culture: An Anthropologist's Account* (Cambridge, Mass.: Harvard University Press, 1999), 47–53.

9. For a review of these perspectives on modern institutions and local community, see Charles Loomis, *Ferdinand Tönnies: Community and Society* (New York: Harper & Row, 1957).

10. Joe Zogby and Rebecca Witten, "Hispanic Perspectives" (Washington, D.C.: National Council for La Raza, 2004).

11. Data from the National Center for Educational Statistics are analyzed in Jennifer Hochschild and Nathan Scovronick, "Demography Change and Democratic Education," in *The Public Schools: Institutions of Democratic Society*, ed., Susan Fuhrman and Marvin Lazerson, 302–23 (New York: Oxford University Press, 2005).

12. Margaret Bridges, Bruce Fuller, Russell Rumberger, and Loan Tran, "Preschool for California's Children: Promising Benefits, Unequal Access" (Working Paper Series 05-1, Policy Analysis for California Education, Berkeley, 2004).

13. Historical data compiled by Jorge Durand, Edward Telles, and Jennifer Flashan, "The Demographic Foundations of the Latino Population," National Research Council (forthcoming).

14. U.S. Census Bureau, "Projections of the Resident Population by 5-Year Age Groups, Race, and Hispanic Origin with Special Age Categories" (Washington, D.C.: U.S. Census Bureau, Population Division, 2000).

15. Demographic statistics cited by Mireya Navarro, "For Younger Latinas, A Shift to Smaller Families," *Los Angeles Times*, December 5, 2004, A1.

16. Christopher Jepsen and Shelley de Alth, "English Learners in California Schools" (San Francisco: Public Policy Institute of California, 2005).

17. Census data reported by Ann Morse, "Language Access: Helping Non-English Speakers Navigate Health and Human Services" (Denver: National Conference of State Legislatures, 2003).

18. David Hayes-Bautista, *La Nueva California: Latinos in the Golden State* (Berkeley: University of California Press, 2004), 201.

19. National Center for Educational Statistics, "Language Spoken at Home," http://nces.ed.gov/pubs2003/Hispanics/Section11.asp (accessed March 13, 2006).

20. Donald Hernandez, "Demographic Change and the Life Circumstances of Immigrant Families," *Future of Children* 14 (2004): 17–36.

21. Jeffrey Passel, "The Rise of the Second Generation" (Washington, D.C.: Pew Hispanic Center, 2003).

22. Hayes-Bautista, *La Nueva California*, 65, 101.

23. Nancy Landale, R. S. Oropesa, and Cristina Bradatan, "Hispanic Families in the United States: Family Structure and Process in an Era of Family Change," in *Hispanics and the Future of America*, ed. Marta Tienda and Faith Mitchell, 138–78 (Washington, D.C.: National Research Council, 2006).

24. Hayes-Bautista, *La Nueva California*, xvi.

25. Landale et al., "Hispanic Families in the United States."

26. See findings from the Fragile Families Study, Center for Research on Child Well-being, "The Hispanic Paradox and Breastfeeding: Does Acculturation Matter?" (bulletin, Princeton University, Princeton, 2004).

27. Robert Bradley, Robert F. Corwyn, Harriett Pipes McAdoo and Cynthia García Coll, "The Home Environments of Children in the United States, Part I: Variations by Age, Ethnicity, and Poverty Status," *Child Development* 72, no. 6 (2001): 1844–67.

28. Hernandez, "Demographic Change and the Life Circumstances of Immigrant Families." National data on these positive social and health indicators are detailed in Marta Tienda and Faith Mitchell, eds., *Hispanics and the Future of America* (Washington, D.C.: National Academies Press, 2006).

29. John Ogbu, *Minority Education and Caste: The American System in Cross-cultural Perspective* (New York: Carnegie Foundation on Children, 1978).

30. Angela Valenzuela and Sanford Dornbusch, "Familism and Social Capital in the Academic Achievement of Mexican Origin and Anglo Adolescents," *Social Science Quarterly* 75, no. 1 (1994): 18–36.

31. Nancy Landale and R. S. Oropesa, "Migration, Social Support, and Perinatal Health: An Origin-Destination Analysis of Puerto Rican Women," *Journal of Health and Social Behavior* 42, no. 2 (2001): 166–83; Rubén Rumbaut and John Weeks, "Unraveling a Public Health Enigma: Why Do Immigrants Experience Superior Perinatal Health Outcomes?" *Research in the Sociology of Health Care* 13 (1996): 337–91.

32. Fuller et al., "How Do Mothers Choose Child Care?"; Xiaoyan Liang, Bruce Fuller, and Judith Singer, "Ethnic Differences in Child Care Selection: The Influence of Family Structure, Parental Practices, and Home Language," *Early Childhood Research Quarterly* 15 (2000): 357–384.

33. Amado M. Padilla and Rosemary Gonzalez, "Academic Performance of Immigrant and U.S.-Born Mexican Heritage Students: Effects of Schooling in Mexico

and Bilingual/English Language Instruction," *American Educational Research Journal* 38 (2001): 727–42.

34. Claude Goldenberg, Ronald Gallimore, Leslie Reese, and Helen Garnier, "Cause or Effect? A Longitudinal Study of Immigrant Latino Parents' Aspirations and Expectations, and Their Children's School Performance," *American Educational Research Journal* 38 (2001): 547–82.

35. Gary Resnick, A. Sorongon, D. Klayn, R. Hubbell-McKey, and J. DeWolfe, "Second Year Report on Early Childhood Programming in the 30 Abbott School Districts," (Trenton: New Jersey Department of Human Services and Department of Education, 2002).

36. Catherine Snow, M. Susan Burns, and Peg Griffin, *Presenting Reading Difficulties in Young Children* (Washington, D.C.: National Academies Press, 1998), 156.

37. Cited in Richard Shweder, Jacqueline Goodnow, Giyoo Hatano, Robert LeVine, Hazel Marcus, and Peggy Miller, "The Cultural Psychology of Development: One Mind, Many Mentalities," in *Handbook of Child Psychology*, 5th ed., vol. 1, ed. William Damon, 865–938 (New York: Wiley, 1998).

38. Findings reported to the technical advisory committee, National Task Force on Early Education for Hispanics, Arizona State University, December 16, 2005.

39. Greenfield and colleagues delineate three strands of work that emphasize the cultural context of development, (1) *cultural values*, where parents hold differing learning and developmental goals for their children; (2) the *ecocultural* frame emphasized in the present chapter; and (3) the *sociohistorical* frame, rooted in the work of Vygotsky, Cole, and Rogoff, which emphasizes how children's daily activities and requisite cognitive tools vary across ethnic groups and cultural settings. Patricia Greenfield, Heidi Keller, Andrew Fuligni, and Ashley Maynard, "Cultural Pathways Through Universal Development," *Annual Review of Psychology* 54 (2003): 461–90.

40. Grace Burkart, "Development of English Literacy in Spanish-speaking Children: Progress Report" (Washington, D.C.: Center for Applied Linguistics, 2003).

41. Barbara Rogoff, "Cognition as a Collaborative Process," in *Handbook of Child Psychology*, 5th ed., vol. 2, ed. William Damon, 680 (New York: Wiley, 1998).

42. Greta Fein and Allison Clarke-Stewart, *Day Care in Context* (New York: Wiley, 1973).

43. Deborah Johnson, Elizabeth Jaeger, Suzanne Randolph, Ana Mari Cauce, Janie Ward, and National Institute of Child Health and Human Development Early Child Care Research Network, "Studying the Effects of Early Child Care Experiences on the Development of Children of Color in the United States," *Child Development* 74 (2003): 1227–44.

44. Cynthia García Coll, Keith Crnic, Gontran Lamberty, Barbara Hanna Wasik, Renee Jenkins, Heidie Vásquez-García, and Harriet Pipes McAdoo, "An Integrative Model for the Study of Developmental Competencies in Minority Children," *Child Development* 67 (1996): 1891–1914.

45. Quoted in a 1960 paper by Beatrice and John Whiting; see Michael Cole, *Cultural Psychology: A Once and Future Discipline* (Cambridge, Mass.: Harvard University Press, 1996), 2.

46. Leslie Reese, "Morality and Identity in Mexican Immigrant Parents' Visions of the Future," *Journal of Ethnic and Migration Studies* 27 (2001): 455–72.

47. Nurit Sheinberg, "How Should I Raise My Child? Assessing the Parenting Beliefs and Practices of Latino and African American Mothers in the Context of a Parenting Intervention Program" (Ph.D. diss., Harvard University, Cambridge, 2003).

48. Written in 1930 by Vygotsky and quoted by James Wertsch, *Vygotsky and the Social Formation of Mind* (Cambridge, Mass.: Harvard University Press, 1985), 23.

49. Barbara Rogoff, "Cognition as a Collaborative Process," 682.

50. Wertsch, *Vygotsky and the Social Formation of Mind*, 35.

51. Sylvia Scribner and Michael Cole, *The Psychology of Literacy* (Cambridge: Harvard University Press, 1981), 9.

52. Michael Cole, in *Cultural Psychology*, discusses parallels between Vygotskian and Piagetian theories of child development.

53. Lave and Wenger, *Situated Learning*, 29.

54. See William Hanks's foreword to Lave and Wenger, *Situated Learning*, 14.

55. Robert Sternberg, "Culture and Intelligence," *American Psychologist* 59 (2004): 325–38.

56. Wertsch, *Vygotsky and the Social Formation of Mind*, 32–33.

57. Bureau of Labor Statistics, "Employment Status of Women by Presence and Age of Youngest Child, Marital Status, Race, and Hispanic or Latino Ethnicity, 2004" (Washington, D.C.: U.S. Department of Labor, Bureau of Labor Statistics, 2005).

58. For a review, see Andrea Hunter, "The Other Breadwinners: The Mobilization of Secondary Wage Earners in Early Twentieth Century Black Families," *History of the Family* 6 (2001): 69–94.

59. "Latinos in Education: Early Childhood, Elementary, Secondary, Undergraduate, and Graduate Levels," (Washington, D.C.: White House Initiative on Educational Excellence for Hispanic Americans, 1999).

60. For evidence on these factors, see Fuller et al., "State Formation of the Child Care Sector"; Margaret Bridges et al., "Preschool for California's Children."

61. M. Rebecca Kilburn and Barbara Wolfe, "Resources Devoted to Child Development by Families and Society," in *Child Rearing in America: Challenges Facing Parents and Young Children*, ed. Neal Halfon, Kathryn Taaffe McLearn, and Mark Schuster, 21–49 (New York: Cambridge University Press, 2002).

62. Judith Singer, Bruce Fuller, Margaret Keiley and Anne Wolf, "Early Child Care Selection: Variation by Geographic Location, Maternal Characteristics, and Family Structure" *Developmental Psychology* 34 (1998): 1129–44.

63. A. Ginario, L. Gutierrez, A. Cauce, and M. Acosta, "The Psychology of Latinas," in *Feminist Perspectives on the Psychology of Women*, ed. Cheryl Travis, 89–102 (Washington, D.C.: American Psychological Association, 1995).

64. Raymond Buriel and Maria Hurtado-Ortiz, "Child Care Practices and Preferences of Native and Foreign-born Latina Mothers and Euro-American Mothers," *Hispanic Journal of Behavioral Science* 22 (2000).

65. Peter Brandon, "The Child Care Arrangements of Preschool-Age Children in Immigrant Families in the United States," *International Migration* 42 (2004): 65–85.

66. Diane Hirshberg, Danny Shih-Cheng Huang, and Bruce Fuller, "Which Low-income Parents Select Child Care? Family Demand and Neighborhood Organizations," *Children and Youth Services Review* 27 (2005): 1119–48.

67. Liang et al., "Ethnic Differences in Child Care Selection," 357–84.

68. Head Start data analyzed by the Center for Law and Social Policy (2003), contained in personal communication, Katherine Hart, 2005. Enrollment data appear in Child, Youth and Family Services Branch, "Federal Fiscal Year 1999/2000 Child Care Annual Aggregate Report" (Sacramento: California State Department of Education, 2001).

69. Loeb et al., "How Much Is Too Much?" (forthcoming).

70. Qualitative data reported in Fuller et al., "How Do Mothers Choose Child Care?"

71. Karen Diamond, A. Reagan, and J. Bandyk, "Parents' Conceptions of Kindergarten Readiness: Relationships with Race, Ethnicity, and Development," *Journal of Educational Research* 94 (2000): 93–100.

72. Naomi Quinn and Dorothy Holland, "Culture and Cognition," in *Cultural Models in Language and Thought*, ed. Dorothy Holland and Naomi Quinn, 4 (Cambridge: Cambridge University Press, 1987).

73. Leslie Reese and Ronald Gallimore, "Immigrant Latinos' Cultural Model of Literacy Development: An Evolving Perspective on Home-school Discontinuities," *American Journal of Education* 108 (2000): 103–34.

74. Preschool supply analysis for Los Angeles County appears in Bruce Fuller and Danny Shih-chen Huang, *Targeting Investments for Universal Preschool: Which Families to Serve First? Who Will Respond?*, PACE Working Paper Series, no. 03-1 (Berkeley: Policy analysis for California Education [PACE] 2003).

75. Fuller et al., "State Formation of the Child Care Sector."

76. Fuller and Strath, "The Child Care and Preschool Workforce."

77. Kris Gutiérrez and Barbara Rogoff, "Cultural Ways of Learning: Individual Traits or Repertoires of Practice," *Educational Researcher* 32 (2003): 19–25.

78. Measures reviewed in NICHD Early Child Care Research Network, "Type of Child Care and Children's Development at 54 Months," *Early Childhood Research Quarterly* 19 (2004): 203–30; quote is from p. 209.

79. Michael Lamb, Kathleen Sternberg, Carl-Philip Hwang, and Anders Broberg, *Child Care in Context: Cross-cultural Perspectives* (Hillsdale, N.J.: Erlbaum, 1992).

80. P. M. Greenfield and L. Suzuki, "Culture and Human Development: Implications for Parenting, Education, Pediatrics and Mental Health," in *Handbook of Child Psychology*, 5th ed., vol. 4: *Child Psychology in Practice*, ed. I. E. Sigel and K. A. Renninger, 1089 (New York: Wiley, 1998).

81. For example, Ray Buriel, "Acculturation, Respect for Cultural Differences, and Biculturalism Among Three Generations of Mexican American and Euro American School Children," *Journal of Genetic Psychology* 154 (1993): 531–43; Cynthia García Coll, Elaine Meyer, and Lisa Brillon, "Ethnic and Minority Parenting," in *Handbook of Parenting*, vol. 3, ed. Marc H. Bornstein, 189–209 (New Jersey: Lawrence Erlbaum Associates, 1995).

82. Robin Harwood et al., "Culture and Class Influences on Anglo and Puerto Rican Mothers' Beliefs Regarding Long-term Socialization Goals and Child Behavior, *Child Development* 67 (1996): 2446–61.

83. Quoted by Olsen et al., "Ready or Not?"

84. Claude Goldenberg and Ronald Gallimore, "Immigrant Latino Parents' Values and Beliefs About Their Children's Education: Continuities and Discontinuities Across Cultures and Generations," *Advances in Motivation and Achievement* 9 (1995): 183–228, quotes on pp. 197–198.

85. García Coll et al., "Ethnic and Minority Parenting," 198.

86. Ross Parke and Raymond Buriel, "Socialization in the Family: Ethnic and Ecological Perspectives," in *Handbook of Child Psychology*, vol. 3, 469–89 (New York: Wiley, 1998).

87. T. Weisner, G. Ryan, L. Reese, K. Kroesan, and L. Bernheimer and Ronald Gallimore, "Behavior Sampling and Ethnography: Complementary Methods for Understanding Home-school Connections Among Latino Immigrant Families, *Field Methods* 13 (2001): 20–46.

88. Sheinberg, "How Should I Raise My Child?"

89. Ronald Gallimore and Leslie Reese, "Mexican Immigrants in Urban California: Forging Adaptations from Familiar and New Cultural Sources," in *Culture, Ethnicity, and Migration*, ed. Marie Claire Foblets and Ching Lin Pang, 245–64 (Leuven: Acco Publisher, 1999).

90. Goldenberg and Gallimore, "Immigrant Latino Parents' Values and Beliefs About Their Children's Education," 204.

91. See Lucinda Pease-Alvarez, "Moving Beyond Linear Trajectories of Language Shift and Bilingual Language Socialization," *Hispanic Journal of Behavioral Sciences* 24 (2002): 114–37; quote appears on p. 121. Leslie Reese, "Morality and Identity of Mexican Immigrant Parents' Visions of the Future," *Journal of Ethnic and Migration Studies* 27 (2001): 455–72.

92. On ecological theories of development applied to cross-cultural settings, see Sara Harkness, "Culture and Social Development," in *Blackwell Handbook of Child and Social Development*, ed. P. Smith and C. Hart, 60–78 (Oxford: Blackwell Publisher, 2002); John Berry, "Ecocultural Perspective on Human Psychological Development," in *Cross-cultural Perspectives in Human Development*, ed. T. Saraswathi, 51–69 (New Delhi: Sage Publications, 2003).

93. Inkelas et al., *Public Opinion on Child Care and Early Education, California 2001*.

94. Marlene Zepeda and Michael Espinosa, "Parental Knowledge of Children's Behavioral Capabilities: A Study of Low-income Parents," *Hispanic Journal of Behavioral Sciences* 10 (1988): 149–59.

95. Lisa López, "Adapting the Family as Educator Model for Young Latino Children" (draft manuscript, Harvard University, Department of Human Development, Cambridge, 2003), 25.

96. David Dickinson and Patton Tabors, eds., *Building Literacy with Language: Young Children Learning at Home and School* (Baltimore, Md.: Brookes Publisher, 2001).

97. Iliana Reyes, "Language Practices and Socialization in Early Bilingual Childhood" (paper presented at the American Educational Research Association meeting, San Diego, April 2004).

98. Leslie Reese, Helen Garnier, Ronald Gallimore, and Claude Goldenberg, "Longitudinal Analysis of the Antecedents of Emergent Spanish Literacy," *American Educational Research Journal* 37 (2000): 633–62.

99. Bradley et al., "The Home Environments of Children in the United States, Part I."

100. Leslie Reese, Silvia Balzano, Ronald Gallimore, and Claude Goldenberg, "The Concept of *Educación*: Latino Family Values and American Schooling," *International Journal of Educational Research* 23 (1995): 57–81.

101. For a review of the qualitative literature, see Carol Scheffner Hammer and Adele Miccio, "Home Literacy Experiences in Latino Families," in *Handbook of Family Literacy*, ed. Barbara Wasik, 305–28 (Mahwah, N.J.: Erlbaum, 2004).

102. Chaya Piotrkowski, Michael Botsko, and Eunice Matthews, "Parents' and Teachers' Beliefs About Children's School Readiness in a High-Need Community," *Early Childhood Research Quarterly* 15 (2001): 537–58.

103. López, "Adapting the Family as Educator Model for Young Latino Children," 29, 38.

104. Wishard et al., "Child Care Program and Teacher Practices."

105. Mary Ann Zehr, "Study Gives Advantage to Bilingual Education over Focus on English," *Education Week*, February 4, 2004, 12.

106. James Rodriguez, Rafael Díaz, David Duran, and Linda Espinoza, "The Impact of Bilingual Preschool Education on the Language Development of Spanish-speaking Children," *Early Childhood Research Quarterly* 10 (1995): 475–90.

107. Findings reviewed in Patton Tabors and Catherine Snow, "Young Bilingual Children and Early Literacy Development," in *Handbook of Early Literacy Research*, ed. Susan Neuman and David Dickinson, 159–78 (New York: Guilford Press, 2001).

108. Ann Eisenberg, "Maternal Teaching Talk Within Families of Mexican Descent: Influence of Task and Socioeconomic Status," *Hispanic Journal of Behavioral Sciences*, 24 (2002): 206–24.

109. Angela Willson-Quayle and Adam Winsler, "How Much Teacher Direction Is Best for Promoting Low-Income Latino Preschoolers' Learning, Motivation, and

Private Speech? A Controlled Experiment" (paper presented at the Head Start National Research Conference, Washington, D.C., June 2000).

110. Piaget quoted by Deborah Stipek, "Is Child-centered Early Childhood Education Really Better?" in *Advances in Early Education and Day Care*, vol. 5, ed. Stuart Reifel, 29–52 (Greenwich, Conn.: JAI Press, 1993).

111. Stipek et al., "Parents' Beliefs About Appropriate Education for Young Children."

112. Deborah Stipek, "Teaching Practices in Kindergarten and First Grade: Different Strokes for Different Folks," *Early Childhood Research Quarterly* 19 (2004): 548–68.

113. Stipek, "Is Child-centered Early Childhood Education Really Better?"

114. Greenfield and Suzuki, "Culture and Human Development."

115. Mari Riojas-Cortéz, "Preschoolers' Funds of Knowledge Displayed Through Sociodramatic Play Episodes in a Bilingual Classroom," *Early Childhood Education Journal* 29 (2001): 35–40.

116. Goldenberg and Gallimore, "Immigrant Latino Parents' Values and Beliefs About Their Children's Education."

117. Concha Delgado-Gaitán, "School Matters in the Mexican-American Home: Socializing Children to Education," *American Educational Research Journal* 29 (1992): 495–513.

118. Sociologists have studied the desire of groups to assimilate or to retain native social norms and parenting practices; see Alejandro Portes and Rubén Rambaut, *Legacies: The Story of the Immigrant Second Generation* (Berkeley: University of California Press, 2001).

CHAPTER 8

1. Rachel Donadio, "Betty Friedan's Enduring 'Mystique,'" *New York Times*, February 26, 2006, 23.

2. Data collected by the Families and Work Institute in New York is reviewed in Karen Kornbluh, "The Joy of Flex," *Washington Monthly*, December 2005.

3. Bianchi, "Maternal Employment and Time with Children." It's unclear whether this downward trend is caused by mothers concluding that the work-family balance is just untenable and they back out of jobs, or whether a softer labor market since 1995 discouraged employment among subgroups of women with young children.

4. R. W. Apple, Jr., "Basque Chefs, Sharing the Glory," *New York Times*, May 5, 2004.

5. William Vollmann's citation to Martin Heidegger, *Nietzsche: The Will to Power as Art*, vol. 1 (New York: Harper Row, 1979).

6. Sheila Kamerman, "An International Overview of Preschool Programs, *Phi Delta Kappan* (October 1989): 135–37.

7. Research and Policy Committee, Committee for Economic Development, *Preschool for All: Investing in a Productive and Just Society* (monograph report) (New York: Research and Policy Committee, Committee for Economic Development, 2002), 24.

8. Janet Gornick and Marcia Meyers, *Families that Work: Policies for Reconciling Parenthood and Employment* (New York: Russell Sage Foundation, 2003), 1.

9. Linda Haas, "Equal Parenthood and Social Policy: Lessons from a Study of Parental Leave in Sweden," in *Parental Leave and Child Care: Setting a Research and Policy Agenda*, ed. Janet Shibley Hyde and Marilyn Essex (Philadelphia, Pa.: Temple University Press, 1991), 375–405.

10. Reviewed in Siv Gustafsson, "Childcare and Types of Welfare States," in *Gendering Welfare States*, ed. Diane Sainsbury, 45–61 (London: Sage Publications, 1994).

11. Gornick and Meyers, *Families that Work*.

12. Families and Work Institute in New York is reviewed by Kornbluh in "The Joy of Flex."

13. Wen-jui Han and Jane Waldfogel, "Parental Leave: The Impact of Recent Legislation on Parents' Leave Taking," *Demography* 40 (2003): 191–200.

14. Jane Waldfogel, "Family and Medical Leave: Evidence from the 2000 Surveys," *Monthly Labor Review* 124 (2001): 17–23. For an overview of state family leave laws, see Jodi Grant, Taylor Hatcher, and Nirali Patel, *Expecting Better: A State-by-State Analysis of Parental Leave Programs* (Washington, D.C.: National Partnership for Women and Families, 2005).

15. James Bond, Ellen Galinsky, Michele Lord, Graham Staines, and Karen Brown, *Beyond the Parental Leave Debate: The Impact of Laws in Four States* (New York: Families and Work Institute, 1991).

16. Thomas MaCurdy, James Pearce, and Richard Kihlthau, "An Alternative to Layoffs: Work Sharing and Unemployment Insurance," Growth and Employment Policy Review series (San Francisco: Public Policy Institute of California, 2004).

17. Scott Adams and David Neumark, "A Decade of Living Wages: What Have We Learned?" *California Economic Policy* (July 1, 2005).

18. Office of Early Childhood Education, *Early Literacy Framework: Handbook for Early Childhood Classrooms* (Chicago: Chicago Public Schools, 2002).

19. Susan Neuman, seminar presentation at the Hechinger Institute session on early childhood education, Chicago, September 11, 2005, and personal communication with observation notes, September 15, 2005.

20. Rheta DeVries, Betty Zan, Carolyn Hildebrandt, Rebecca Edmiaston, and Christina Sales, *Developing Constructivist Early Childhood Curriculum* (New York: Teachers College Press, 2002).

21. Lowell Rose and Alec Gallup, "The 37th Annual Phi Delta Kappa/Gallup Poll of the Public's Attitudes Toward the Public Schools," *Phi Delta Kappan* 87 (September 2005).

22. Robert Wuthnow, *Saving America? Faith-based Services and the Future of Civil Society* (Princeton: Princeton University Press, 2004).

23. Gerald LeTendre, David Baker, Motoko Akiba, Brian Gosling, and Alex Wiseman, "Teachers' Work: Institutional Isomorphism and Cultural Variation," *Educational Researcher* 30 (2001): 3–15.

24. For reviews of political frameworks on this historical question, see Wuthnow, *Saving America?*; Bruce Fuller, *Inside Charter Schools: The Paradox of Radical Decentralization* (Cambridge, Mass.: Harvard University Press, 2000); Joseph Kahne, *Reframing Educational Policy: Democracy, Community, and the Individual* (New York: Teachers College Press, 1996); Jodi Dean, ed., *Cultural Studies and Political Theory* (Ithaca, N.Y.: Cornell University Press, 2000).

25. Beatty, *Who Speaks for America's Children*, 182.

26. Brian Stecher, George Bohrnstedt, Michael Kirst, Joan McRobbie, and Trish Williams, *Class-Size Reduction in California: A Story of Hope, Promise, and Unintended Consequences* (Santa Monica, Calif.: RAND Corp., 2003). For a review of this entitlement literature pertaining to policy reforms, see Stephen Ceci and Paul Papierno, "The Rhetoric and the Reality of Gap Closing: When the 'Have-nots' Gain but the 'Haves' Gain Even More," *American Psychologist* 60 (2005): 149–60.

27. Daria Hall, "Primary Progress, Secondary Challenge: A State-by-State Look at Student Achievement Patterns" (Washington, D.C.: The Education Trust, 2006).

28. Burton Beam, Jr., and John McFadden, *Employee Benefits*, 4th ed. (Dearborn, Mich.: Dearborn Financial Publishing, 1996).

29. Erin Kelly, "The Strange History of Employer-Sponsored Child Care: Interested Actors, Uncertainty, and Transformation of Organizational Fields," *American Journal of Sociology* 109 (2003): 606–49.

30. David Brooks, "Liberals, Conservatives and Aid," *International Herald Tribune*, June 27, 2005, 8.

31. Norton Grubb and Marvin Lazerson, *Broken Promises: How Americans Fail Their Children* (New York: Basic Books, 1982).

32. Richard Alba and Victor Nee, *Remaking the American Mainstream: Assimilation and Contemporary Immigration* (Cambridge, Mass.: Harvard University Press, 2003), 163.

33. For a critical review of Galston's argument, see Rob Reich, *Bridging Liberalism and Multiculturalism in American Education* (Chicago: University of Chicago Press, 2002), 51–55.

34. In other areas of education and social policy, a combination of policy instruments have been used to advance collateral public aims; see Lorraine McDonnell and Richard Elmore, "Getting the Job Done: Alternative Policy Instruments," *Educational Evaluation and Policy Analysis* 9 (1987): 133–52.

35. The perspective on sector formation comes from neoinstitutional theory in sociology and political science. For reviews, see W. Richard Scott and John W. Meyer,

"The Organization of Societal Sectors: Propositions and Early Evidence," in *The New Institutionalism in Organizational Analysis*, ed. Walter Powell and Paul DiMaggio, 108–42 (Chicago: University of Chicago Press, 1991).

36. Ellen Frede, interview by telephone, January 26, 2006.

37. Personal communication, phone interview, March 6, 2006.

38. For a comparison of local community action that bubbles up from the grass-roots versus action that is engineered from above, see Joel Handler, *Down from Bureaucracy: The Ambiguity of Privatization and Empowerment* (Princeton, N.J.: Princeton University Press, 1996).

THE RESEARCH TEAM, METHODS, AND MANY THANKS

1. Quoted in Colm Tóibín, *Homage to Barcelona* (London: Picador, 2001), 85.

Index

Habermas, Jürgen, 186
Hahn, James, 142
Halfon, Neal, 10
Hall, G. Stanley, 42
Hamburg, David, 52
Hammer, Mary, 160
Hammer, Rusty, 189–90
Hamre, Bridget, 165
Hanks, William, 244
Harbison, Bob, 105–6, 108–10, 112–14, 127, 134, 135
Harrington, Michael, 229
Hart, Peter D., 62, 63, 161
Harwood, Robin, 254, 255
Haskins, Ron, 208
Haycock, Kati, 66
Hayes-Bautista, David, 234
Head Start: benefits of, 199–201, 204–5; in California, 175; child development approach in, 120–21; comprehensive approach of, 59, 111, 201; curriculum requirements for, 66, 122–23; enrollments in, 15; funding for, 59; growth of, ix, x; and Latinos, 228; in Oklahoma, 107, 111, 117, 136; origins of, 27–28, 46–47, 59; quality of, 21–22, 24; staff diversity in, 165; teacher qualifications for, 171, 217; testing in, 66
Head Start Impact Study (HSIS), 199, 201
Heckman, James, 7
Hegel, G. W. F., 37
Heidegger, Martin, 276
Heinz, Teresa, 52
Helburn, Suzanne, 21
Helfon, Neal, 157
Henderson, Jane, 152, 160
Henry, Brad, 114–15
Henry, Gary, 127, 201, 219, 222–23
Herder, Johann Gottfried, 238
Hernandez, Don, 233, 238
Hernandez, Ray, 182, 184, 186, 187
Hertzberg, Robert, 158
Hess, Robert, 46, 57
High/Scope Foundation, 81, 166, 193
Hill-Scott, Karen, 10, 27, 149, 153–70, 174, 182, 184, 186, 322n75
Hirshberg, Diane, 251
Hochchild, Arlie, 55
Hochschild, Jennifer, v

Holland, Dorothy, 251
Holloway, Susan, 17, 153, 228, 248, 249
Holt, L. Emmett, 41
Hope Street Family Center, Los Angeles, California, 9, 164
Horn, Wade, 66, 123
Hornsby, Andre J., xiii
Howes, Carollee, 219, 221, 261–62
Huang, Danny, 251
Huezo, Cristina, 171
Human capital, students as, 7, 34
The Hurried Child (Elkind), 3
Hurtado-Ortiz, Maria, 162

I Am Your Child Campaign, 52
Ilg, Frances, 43
Individualism, 38, 93, 143, 253–54, 288
Inequality, in preschool services, 18–20, 23, 288
Infant schools, 2–3
Infant School Society of the City of Boston, 2
Inkelas, Moira, 258–59
Institutional liberals, 4–5, 33, 187, 295
Intelligence, environmental influence on, 46
Interaction, teacher-child, 220–21
Italiano-Thomas, Graciela, 168, 174, 182, 184

Jackson, John, 163
Jacobson, Linda, 150
James, William, 143
James S. McDonnell Foundation, 50
Johnson, Deborah, 240
Journal of the American Medical Association, 50

Kagan, Sharon Lynn, 20, 25, 155, 203, 291–92
Kaiser, George, 117, 131, 135, 288
Kamii, Constance, 38
Kant, Immanuel, 37
Karoly, Lynn, 152, 175, 195
Katz, Michael, 67
Kaufman, Neal, 139–40, 164, 167
Keating, Frank, 112–14, 135
Kendall-Whittier school, Tulsa, Oklahoma, 124
Kennedy, Edward, 20, 21, 22